"Lives of great men all remind us
We can make our lives sublime,
And departing, leave behind us
Footprints on the sands of time."

LONGFELLOW.

"Yet e'en these bones from insult to protect,
Some frail memorial still erected nigh,
With uncouth rhymes and shapeless sculptures decked,
Implores the passing tribute of a sigh."

GRAY.

NATIONAL WALLACE MONUMENT
ABBEY CRAIG, STIRLING.

MONUMENTS

AND

MONUMENTAL INSCRIPTIONS

IN

SCOTLAND.

BY THE

REV. CHARLES ROGERS, LL.D., F.S.A. SCOT.,

HISTORIOGRAPHER TO THE ROYAL HISTORICAL SOCIETY.

VOL. II.

A HERITAGE CLASSIC

LONDON:
PUBLISHED FOR THE GRAMPIAN CLUB.

1872.

A Facsimile Reprint
Published 1997 by

HERITAGE BOOKS, INC.
1540E Pointer Ridge Place
Bowie, Maryland 20716
1-800-398-7709

ISBN 0-7884-0685-X

PREFACE TO VOL. II.

IN completing the second volume of this work, the author closes a task which has upwards of eleven years occupied his attention. Reviewing his performance, he could have wished that his labours had been more fruitful, and that the work had presented the monumental records of every Scottish parish. As it is, the omissions are not very numerous ; while a necrological register has been produced ampler than any existing heretofore.

When the author entered upon his undertaking, he sought to awaken public attention to the degraded condition of country churchyards. As local reporters were generally reluctant to compromise parochial honour, he was led to abandon this part of his enterprise, not however before collecting some strange facts. Of these a few may be related. At New Machar, Aberdeenshire, the peasantry obtain their winter fuel by storing up portions of decayed coffins from the churchyard. During the summer of 1862 the parish schoolmaster of Ellon was obliged to cease teaching, owing to his schoolroom which adjoined the churchyard, being saturated

*

with the exhalations of mortality. In the churchyard of
Gamrie, overlooking the Moray Frith, bones, fragments
of coffins, and portions of gravestones are strewn about.
The parochial sextons of Lewis and North Uist perform interments within six inches of the surface, the
coffins after a heavy shower being frequently exposed.
The churchyard of Sandwich, in Orkney, is part of
an undrained marsh, and at interments coffins are
plunged into the water which fills every new-made
grave. These facts require no comment.

Additional to those to whom he formerly expressed
his obligations, the author cannot deny himself the satis-
faction of mentioning the considerable assistance he has
received from papers on the graveyards of the north
eastern counties prepared by Mr. Jervise. The author
learns with pleasure that Mr. Jervise contemplates a
separate publication. His work should have a place in
the library of every Scottish archæologist.

SNOWDOUN VILLA,
    LEWISHAM, KENT.
October, 1872.

CONTENTS.

CONTENTS.

X

CONTENTS.

MONUMENTS

AND

MONUMENTAL INSCRIPTIONS IN SCOTLAND.

BUTESHIRE.

PARISH OF CUMBRAY.

IN Milport churchyard, Isle of Cumbray, the gravestone of the
Rev. James Adam, minister of the parish, is inscribed thus :—

> " Fideles moralis et innuptus
> Sine natis, sine curis,
> Vixit, obit et surget.

> " Tho' here on a damp cold bed he lies,
> Without a friend to close his eyes ;
> Wrapt in his usual unsocial pride,
> Indifferent to all the world beside.

> " Sed quid sunt est vel erit
> Magnus dies declarabit."

Mr. Adam was some time a bookseller in Glasgow. He was
ordained minister of Cumbray in 1799, and died unmarried 25th
June, 1831, in his eighty-third year. Among other donations for
charitable purposes he bequeathed £1,100 to establish three
bursaries or exhibitions in connection with the University o
Glasgow.

In Milport Churchyard James Wood has engraved on his father's tombstone these lines :—

> " All you that walk among the tombs,
>   Above the silent clay,
> Consider how you've spent your time,
>   To fit you for this way.
> That mortal man returns to dust,
>   Experience lets us see,
> The high, the low, the rich, the poor,
>   Must lie as low as me."

John McHaffie has thus celebrated his departed wife :—

> " Farewell, my Helen dear ! thy heavenly mind,
> Happy in life, was yet in death resign'd.
> Upright, sincere, and in thy sphere of life,
> A kind and faithful daughter, sister, wife,
> In youth and hope cut down, thy tomb aloud
> Proclaims, ' Prepare thee for an early shroud.' "

In these lines James Forty commemorates his infant son :—

> " CHRIST'S VOICE IN THE CLOUDS.
>
> " Awake, you breathless little ones,
> And meet your Saviour when he comes;
> Though for a time you do sleep here,
> With Christ your Shepherd you'll appear,
> And follow him to Immanuel's land,
> With palms of victory in your hand.
> Oh ! glorious sight for to be seen,
> Those lovely babes following their King ! "

PARISH OF KILBRIDE.

Near the entrance of the churchyard is a horizontal slab, sculptured with a floral cross and two-handed sword. No history or tradition is associated with it. An adjacent stone representing the figure of a kilted Highlander, with a sword by his side, is believed to commemorate two petty landowners, Walter Fion and

Duncan Tait, who, through the misrepresentation of a worthless person named McNish, were led to engage in mortal combat. Both fell, and were buried in the same grave.

The Fullertons, of Kilmichael, inter in this churchyard. John Fullerton, who died in 1784, has these lines upon his tombstone:—

"This was the man who, free from toil and strife,
In his own ground did pass his peaceful life."

A monumental slab, bearing date 15th April, 1747, commemorates Nugent Kerr, "son to Robert Kerr, Director of His Majesty's Chancellary of Scotland." The family of Kerr is represented by the Marquis of Lothian.

PARISH OF KILMORIE.

At the clachan of Shisken, an old churchyard contains the grave of Saint Molio, "the bareheaded servant of Jesus." This saint originally resided at Lamlash; he subsequently removed to Shisken, and died here, as is alleged, at the age of 120. On the stone which covers his grave is sculptured a representation of the saint in the robes of a mitred abbot, with a pastoral staff by his side and a chalice in his hands.* It was a former custom that females after their confinement visited St. Molio's grave, and there in token of gratitude deposited a silver coin or some other offering.

PARISH OF ROTHESAY.

Within the burial enclosure which surrounds the parish church stands the choir of St. Mary's Cathedral. On the south side of the choir, under a low Gothic arch, is the recumbent figure of a knight

* McArthur's "Antiquities of Arran," p. 188. Glasgow, 1861. 8vo.

in armour extended on a tomb. From the coat of arms on the tomb it is certain that the deceased knight belonged to the Royal House. According to the most probable conjecture, the monument was reared by Robert II. in honour of his father, Walter the eighth High Steward, who married the daughter of Robert the Bruce. Walter the High Steward died at Bathgate in 1327 or 1328.*

In the north wall of the choir, under a canopy, is a female figure in low relief; also the figure of a child in a loose robe. The base of the monument is divided into eight compartments, which are occupied by an equal number of small figures. An effigy in the area of the choir, holding a sword and a bat-shaped shield, is supposed to belong to the early portion of the thirteenth century, when Angus, son of Somerled, Lord of Argyll, held the manor of Bute.†

The family mausoleum of the Marquis of Bute stands near the parish church on its north side. Here are interred James first Earl of Bute, who died in 1710, James, second earl, who died 28th January, 1723, and John, third earl, the celebrated statesman, who died 19th March, 1792. The last nobleman was born in 1713. He took part in the education of George III., and became His Majesty's Prime Minister in May, 1762. Owing to an unpopularity, which was in many respects unmerited, he retired from office in February, 1763 ; he thereafter devoted himself to literary and scientific studies. He was a patron of men of learning. Through his recommendation State pensions were bestowed on Dr. Samuel Johnson and John Home, the author of "Douglas." The architects George and Robert Adam were indebted to his patronage. He printed a work on British plants, in nine quarto volumes. He was president of many of the learned societies, Chancellor of Marischal College, Aberdeen, and a Trustee of the British Museum.

At the north-east corner of the churchyard a monumental cross

* For an elaborate and ingenious paper on this tomb, by J. C. Roger, see " Proceedings of Society of Antiquaries of Scotland," ii. 466—481.

† " Proceedings of Scot. Soc. of Antiquaries," ii., 475.

denotes the resting-place of Sir Daniel Keyte Sandford, D.C.L., Professor of Greek in the University of Glasgow, and M.P. for Paisley. This eminent individual was son of Bishop Sandford, of Edinburgh (Vol. I., 78), and was born in that city on the 3rd February, 1798. Having studied at Oxford, where he acquired distinction, he was in 1821 elected to the Greek chair in the University of Glasgow. In 1830 he received the honour of knighthood. In 1834 he was elected M.P. for Paisley; but owing to failing health, he soon retired from his parliamentary duties. He died at Glasgow, of fever, on the 4th February, 1838, at the age of forty. He composed an "Essay on the Rise and Progress of Literature," and other works.

Among the more notable persons commemorated in the churchyard are the Rev. Archibald McLea, D.D., minister of the parish, who died 12th April, 1824, aged eighty-seven; the Rev. Robert Craig, Minister of the Free Church, Rothesay, who died 26th May, 1860, aged sixty-eight; and Archibald M'Indoe and Dugald Munn, both provosts of the burgh.

On a tombstone bearing date 1828, Archibald Black, cooper thus celebrates his parents :—

> "Station obscure and moral worth
> Need no monumental fame;
> Duty alone this stone did rear,
> To mark the spot and bear the name."

William Stewart, shipmaster, who died in 1829, has on his gravestone these lines :—

> "Turn, Christian, turn, thy soul apply
> To truths divinely given,
> The bones that underneath do lie
> Shall live for hell or heaven."

In the retired churchyard of Ascog a mural tablet commemorates Montague Stanley, a short-lived and ingenious artist.

ARGYLESHIRE.

PARISH OF ARDCHATTAN.

IN the church and churchyard of Ardchattan Priory, founded in 1231, are several inscribed tombstones. One in the centre of the church contains, in Saxon characters, these words—

" Funallus Somherle Macdougalallus, Prior de Ardchattan MCCCCC."

At the south-east corner of the church a flat stone contains the following inscription :—

" Hic jacet venerandus et egregius vir Rodericus Alexander, Rector quondam Funnanni Insulæ, qui obiit anno dom.   "

Within the church at the east end of the northern wall a monument surmounting a stone coffin represents two dignified churchmen in monastic costume, a warrior in mail armour, and two weeping nuns, between, a human skeleton. The following inscription, in old Irish characters, occupies the sides and margin :—

" Hic jacent nati Somerledi Macdougall Duncanus et Dugallus, hujus monasterii successive priores, una cum eorundem patre, matre et fratre Alano, quorum Dugallus hujus monumenti fabricator, obiit anno Domini, MCCCCCII."

In the family burial-ground at Ardchattan, a monumental stone commemorates Patrick Campbell of Inverzeldies. It is thus inscribed :—

" Hic . jacet . Patricius Campbell . de . Inverzeldies . qui . obiit. veg . prim . die . Martis . anno . dom . 1678 . anno æt. 86."

" Vir probus hic situs est, cautus, providus, per honestus,
Judicio claro promptus et ingenio. In apothymatibus
Communis sermo fluebat
Facta suis dictis consona semper erant
Prole, parente, toro, rebus, virtute, senecta,
Justitia, et meritis, laude, beatus obiit."

Mr. Campbell's younger son, the Rev. Colin Campbell, was minister of the parish from 1667 till his death, 13th March, 1726. An eminent mathematician and astronomer, he conducted a correspondence in Latin with Sir Isaac Newton, who remarked of him to Dr Gregory, "Were he amongst us he would make children of us all." He was ancestor of the family of Barcaldine.

PARISH OF CAMPBELTON.

Within the church of Loland, now roofless, rest the remains of Elizabeth, wife of Archibald, first Duke of Argyll, and daughter of Sir Lionel Talmash of Helmington, Staffordshire. She died in May, 1735. Her eldest son was the celebrated John Duke of Argyll and Greenwich.

In the parish churchyard a tombstone commemorates Dr. John Smith, minister of the parish, who died 26th June, 1807, in the 60th year of his age, and thirty-second of his ministry. A distinguished Gaelic scholar, Dr. Smith, assisted in translating the Scriptures into that language. The published " Gaelic Antiquities," and various theological and other works.

The following metrical epitaphs are from Campbelton churchyard :—

" This little spot is all I've got,
And all that kings acquire,
My home's above, a gift of love,
O reader, there aspire.

" His God to him was good,
And gifts him did bestow ;
And he no chorle here prov'd
To neither high nor low.

" From stately palaces we remove
The narrow lodging of a grave to prove;
Leave the fair train and the light gilded room,
To lie alone, benighted in the tomb :
God only is immortal, man not so,
Life to be paid upon demand we owe."

In the old Gaelic church was interred Campbell " Captain of
Skipness." This valiant soldier was a powerful opponent of the
Marquis of Montrose, and was present at the battle of Philiphaugh.
He fell at the siege of the castle of Dunaverty. A stone which
covered his grave formerly bore these lines :—

" A Captain much renowned
Whose cause of fight was still Christ's right,
For which his soul is crowned.
So breifly then to know the man
This stone tells all the storie ;
On earth his race he ran with grace
In Heaven he reigns in glory."

PARISH OF COLONSAY.

Within the walls of the old church of St. Oran are several
ancient monuments, with the inscriptions obliterated. A marble
pillar is inscribed thus :—

" Hic jacet Malcolumbus Mac-Duffie de Collonsay."

The clan Macduff formerly possessed a portion of the islands
Colonsay and Oronsay.

PARISH OF CRAIGNISH.

In the valley of Barbreck, near Drimree, Olave, a Dane, and the
Scottish king engaged in single combat. Olave fell, and a tumulus
marks his grave. A grey stone denotes the spot where Ulric, a
Danish general, was slain.

PARISH OF DUNOON AND KILMUN.

In Dunoon churchyard are a number of ancient tombstones variously sculptured, but without inscriptions. The modern tombstone of a blacksmith bears these lines—

" By hammer and hand
All airts do stand."

At Kilmun is the family burying-place of the Duke of Argyle. Here were deposited the remains of Archibald, eighth Earl and first Marquis of Argyle, who was executed at Edinburgh, 27th May, 1661.

PARISH OF GLENORCHAY.

On a conical eminence in the vale of Glenorchay a monument celebrates Duncan Ban Macintyre, the eminent Gaelic poet. The monument is built of grey granite, and is constructed so as to resemble a Druidical temple. On a massive basement, twenty feet square, rest twelve square monoliths in circular form, and supported by a canopy. The entire height is forty feet. Macintyre was born on the farm of Drumliart in Glenorchay, on the 20th March, 1724. He died at Edinburgh in May, 1812, and his remains were consigned to the Greyfriars' churchyard (Vol. I., 43). His chief poem is *Bendourain, or the Otter Mount.*

PARISH OF INVERARY.

Within the burgh, at the end of the principal street, a stone cross bears, in Lombardic characters, the following inscription :—

" Hæc est crux nobilium virorum videlicet Dondcani M'Engyllichomghan Patrici filii ejus et Maelmore filii Patrici qui hanc crucem fieri faciebat."

The cross was brought from Iona.

Near the parish church a simple monument of chlorite commemorates seventeen gentlemen of the name of Campbell, who were executed by the government of James VII. during the three years which preceded the Revolution.

PARISH OF IONA.

The chapel of the nunnery—which alone remains of that religious establishment—contains forty-eight monumental stones, nearly all uninscribed. The oldest tombstone, so far as can be ascertained, bears date 1543; it is situated at the east end of the chapel, and is believed to commemorate the last prioress, the Princess Anne. On one portion of the surface is the figure of the prioress, an angel supporting her head on each side, surmounted by a mirror and comb. The other half (now broken off) exhibited the figure of the Virgin Mary, with head crowned and mitred—the child in her arms, and the sun and moon above her head. In Saxon characters there is the following inscription :—

"Hic jacet Domina Anna Donaldi Terliti, filia quondam Priorissa de Iona quo obiit anno m^0 d^0 xliii^0 ejus animam Altissimo commendamus. Sancta Maria, ora pro me."

In the chapel of the Nunnery, a mutilated stone is thus inscribed—

"Hic jacet Mariota filia Johannis Lauchlani Domini de."

The nunnery was founded not earlier than the twelfth century, monastic establishments for women forming no part of the religious system of Columba. In Romish times ladies of rank were buried in the Nunnery chapel.

According to tradition 360 stone crosses were erected as votive offerings in different parts of the island. Two only are entire. These are known as Maclean's and St. Martin's crosses. Maclean's Cross (situated midway between the monastery and the granary), is evidently the more ancient. It is supposed to suit the description of one which stood in the same locality in the time of Columba, as described by Adamnan. On both sides it is decorated with a profusion of carved work. On one side of the circle from which the arms project is a rude representation of the crucifixion. The figure on the cross is clothed in a long robe with loose sleeves, and girt round the waist with a belt. On one arm of the cross is sculptured the sacramental chalice, and a cruciform figure on the other. It consists of a single stone of trap rock, and stands eleven feet high, raised on a pedestal of granite.

St. Martin's Cross stands at a short distance to the south of the other. It is a solid column of mica schist, fourteen feet high, eighteen inches broad, and six inches thick. It is fixed in a massive pedestal of red granite. On its western front the cross represents on the upper part six lions with tails entwined. A lion or other quadruped occupies each arm of the cross. In the centre is a rude representation of the Virgin and child, with four cherubs. On the stem appear a priest administering the right of baptism, two musicians, one playing the harp and the other using a wind instrument, and a man erect shaking hands with another sitting on a stool. Besides other representations, there are at the base six granulated balls, entwined by twelve serpents.

Reilig Ourain, the burial-place of Oran, is the grand cemetery of the island. In this place of sepulture were interred, according to an early tradition, forty kings of Scotland, two Irish monarchs, a French king, and two Irish princes of the Norwegian race. The last kings who here found sepulchres were Duncan I., slain in 1034, and his assassin and successor the celebrated Macbeth. The Macdonalds, Lords of the Isles, also interred in Reilig Ourain. The graves are arranged in nine rows. Of these, the third from the entrance, is *the Ridge of Kings*. According to Dean Monro, who wrote in 1549, the Royal tombs were then covered by three small chapels of which portions of the foundations only remain.* From the recumbent tombstones every vestige of inscriptions has long been obliterated. An elegant monumental sculpture celebrates four priors of Iona. In old English characters it presents the following inscription :—

"Hic jacent quatuor priores de Y ex una natione, v. Johannes, Hugonius, Patricius, in decretis, olim Bacularius et alter Hugonius, qui obiit anno domini millesimo quingentesimo."†

In Oran's burial-place three sculptured stones commemorate McLean of Duart, McLean of Coll, and McLean of Loch Buy. The first is represented in armour, with a spear in his right hand, and a greyhound at his feet. McLean of Coll is in the act of drawing his sword, while on either side of his head is the figure of an angel, one armed with a sword. McLean of Loch Buy is buckling his sword. There is a tradition that he was a parricide, and that his headless body was wont to appear to those members of his House who were at the point of death. Dr. John Beton, one of the Betons in Pennycross in Mull, a family of eminent physicians, who died in 1567, is commemorated by a mural tablet, thus inscribed :—

"Ecce cadit jaculo victrici mortis iniquæ,
Qui toties alios solverat ipse malis.
Soli Deo gloria."‡

---

* These chapels covered the remains of the kings of Scotland and of Ireland and of the Norwegian princes respectively. Of the Scottish monarchs interred in Iona, sixteen were of the race of Alpin. Malcolm Canmore, who succeeded Macbeth, removed the burial-place of the kings to Dunfermline. According to the Annals of Ulster, Beatus Nial, King of Ireland, having abdicated his kingdom, died at Iona in 765 ; and B. Artgall McCatheld, King of Connaught, who likewise abdicated, died at Iona in 786. In his "Notitia Hyberniæ," Dr. Keating states that Cormac McAird, one of the kings of Ireland, was buried here. According to the Annals of Ulster, Amulabh or Aulay, son of Stirich, Prince of the Normen of Dublin, on his defeat at the Battle of Tarah, in 980, sought refuge in Iona, where he died.

† *Translation :*—Here lie four priors of Y (Iona), all of one clan, viz., John, Eugene, Patrick, formerly bachelor in degrees, and a second Eugene, who died in the year of our Lord 1500.

‡ *Translation :*—Behold! he who saved so many others from ills, himself falls by the conquering dart of wicked death. Glory to God alone.

The cemetery contains 159 tombstones, of which the greater number are broken and illegible. In 1833 the members of. the Iona Club made a search under the surface, and brought up several tombstones elegantly sculptured. Two bishops' tombs, in good preservation, are uninscribed. Some fragments of tombstones denote that numbers of the Macleods and Macdonalds had been interred in the ground.

The roofless chapel of St. Oran adjoins the cemetery. Sixty feet long and twenty-two feet broad within the walls, it is filled with monuments. A triple arch in the wall forms the canopy of a tomb, which, according to tradition, celebrates St. Oran. Near the arch, is the tomb of Macdonald, Lord of the Isles. On the upper·part is a galley with furled sails. The following inscription is en-graved in antique characters :—

" Hic jacet corpus Angusii, fili Domini Angusii, MacDomnill de Ila."

Angus, son of Sir Angus Macdonald, thus commemorated, was known by the name of *Angus Og*, or Young Angus. He was a friend of Robert the Bruce in the time of his greatest distress, and is the hero of Sir Walter Scott's "Lord of the.Isles." His genea-logy is presented in the notes to that poem.

An elaborately-decorated tomb in the centre of the chapel cele-brates McQuarrie, of Ulva. The chieftain is sculptured in full armour, but the inscription is nearly effaced. Adjoining is the tomb of McLean, of Grulin, adorned with various sculptures.

Under the triple arch lies the lower part of the Abbot Mac-kinnon's Cross. It is inscribed :—

" Haec est crux Lachlani Mac Fingone et ejus filii Johannis, Abbatis de Hy. Facta anno domini MCCCCLXXXIX."*

St. Mary's, or the Abbey Church of Iona, seems to have been completed in the twelfth century. On the' north side of the altar

---

* *Translation :—*This is the cross of Lachlan Mackinnon, and his son John, Abbot of Hy (Iona), made in the year of our Lord 1489.

is the tomb of the Abbot Mackinnon. Around the recumbent figure of the abbot is the following inscription :—

" Hic jacet Johannes Mac-Fingone, Abbas de Hy, que obiit anno domini millesimo quingentessimo, cujus animæ propitietur Deus altissimus. Amen."*

South of the chancel is the tomb of Abbot Kenneth Mackenzie, much defaced. In the centre of the chancel a large tombstone commemorates a Macleod of Macleod. Another tombstone in the chancel celebrates Maclean of Ross, in Mull. His head with bearded face rests upon a pillow, and a dog crouches at his feet; he is girded with a shield and claymore, and holds a spear in his right hand. From the other monumental sculptures in St. Mary's Church the inscriptions have disappeared.

PARISH OF KILLEAN.

In the parish church a handsome marble monument, erected by the heritors and kirksession, commemorates the generosity of Colonel Norman Macalister, of Clachaig, Governor and Commander-in-Chief of Prince of Wales' Island, East Indies, who bequeathed £1,000 to the parochial poor. Colonel Macalister was drowned in 1810, on his voyage to Britain.

PARISH OF LISMORE AND APPIN.

Near the church of Lismore a plain stone, with a two-handed sword engraved upon it, denotes the grave of Donald Stewart, known as *Domhnull nan ord*, Donald of the hammer. During his

* *Translation :*—Here lies John Mackinnon, Abbot of Iona, who died in the year of our Lord 1500, to whose soul may the most high God be merciful.

infancy his family, the Stewarts of Invernahyle, were cut off by
the Campbells of Dunstaffnage; but he escaped through the
fidelity of his nurse, who fled with him to Ardnamurchan, where
her husband, a blacksmith, resided. Informed of his descent when
he attained to manhood, he formed a party, and proceeding with
them to Dunstaffnage, slew *Carlein Uaine* and fifteen of his
retainers. Till his death he waged war against the Campbells.
Donald of the Hammer lived early in the seventeenth century.

PARISH OF SADDELL.

In the churchyard of the monastery are a number of ancient
monuments, variously sculptured, but uninscribed. A Lord of the
Isles is commemorated by the figure of a warrior, girt with a
two-handed sword. There is the tombstone of an abbot in his
pontifical robes and in the attitude of prayer. The inscription is
illegible. Mackay, a warrior to whom Robert the Bruce made a
grant of the lands of Ugadale, is commemorated by his figure on
a gravestone. In this churchyard rest the remains of Archibald
Campbell, of Carradale, who fell at the battle of Inverlochy, when
engaged with the forces of Montrose.

PARISH OF SOUTH KNAPDALE.

In the roofless chapel of Kilmory stands an interesting monument, known as the Macmillan Cross. The shaft is eight feet in
height, and the pedestal consists of several stones loosely put
together and resting on the ground. On the upper portion of one
side the cross presents a representation of the crucifixion. The
shaft is sculptured with a broadsword, enclosed in chain moulding.
On the opposite side the upper part is decorated with a series of

intertwisted lines, while the shaft represents the progress of a deer chase. On the base, in Saxon characters, are inscribed these words :—

" Haec crux Alexandri MacMulen."

The sept Mac Mullen formerly possessed lands in the district. In the churchyard of Kilmory are a number of flat gravestones sculptured with swords and shears, emblems common to ancient tombstones in the Western Highlands.

DUMBARTONSHIRE.

PARISH OF BONHILL.

A Tuscan column on the banks of the Leven commemorates Tobias Smollett, M.D., the historian and novelist. The inscription, prepared by the joint labours of Professor George Stuart, of Edinburgh, John Ramsay, of Ochtertyre, and Dr. Samuel Johnson, is as follows :—

" Siste, viator !
Si lepores ingeniique venam benignam,
Si morum callidissimum pictorem,
Unquam es miratus,
Immorare paululum memoriæ
TOBIÆ SMOLLET, M.D.
Viri virtutibus hisce
Quas in homine et cive
Et laudes et imiteris,
Haud mediocriter ornati :
Qui in literis variis versatus,
Postquam felicitate sibi propria,
Sese posteris commendaverat,
Morte acerba raptus,
Anno ætatis 51.
Eheu! quam procul a patria !
Prope Liburni portum in Italia,
Jacet sepultus.
Tali tantoque viro patrueli suo,
Cui in decursu lampada,
Se potuis tradidisse decuit,
Hanc Columnam.
Amoris, eheu! inane monumentum,
In ipsis Leviniæ ripis,
Quas versiculis sub exitu vitæ illustratas
Primis infans vagitibus personuit,
Ponendam curavit

c

Jacobus Smollet de Bonhill
Abi et reminiscere
Hoc quidem honore
Non modo defuncti memoriæ,
Verum etiam exemplo, prospectum esse;
Aliis enim, si modo digni sint
Idem erit virtutis præmium!"

Dr. Smollett was born in 1721, at Dalquhurn, in the parish of Cardross. He studied at the University of Glasgow, and obtained licence as a surgeon. Thrown on his own resources by the death of his grandfather, Sir James Smollett, who, owing to the early death of his father, attended to his education, he proceeded to London, in the hope of obtaining professional employment. In 1741 he was appointed surgeon on board a man-of-war, which joined the expedition to Carthagena. Quitting the naval service, and entering upon matrimony, he in 1746 returned to London. His first and most popular novel, "Roderick Random," appeared in 1748; it was followed in 1750 by "Peregrine Pickle." He attempted medical practice at Bath, but not succeeding, took up his residence at Chelsea. In 1753 he published "Count Fathom," which was followed in 1755 by his translation of "Don Quixote." His subsequent principal publications were "The Adventures of Sir Lancelot Greaves," "The Expedition of Humphrey Clinker," "Travels through France and Italy," and his "History of England." For some time he edited the *Critical Review*. He published several elegant poems, and "The Reprisal," a farce, which was performed in Drury Lane Theatre. Dr. Smollett died on the 21st October, 1774, at Monte Nuovo, near Leghorn, at the age of fifty-three. His monument was raised by his cousin, Mr. Smollett, of Bonhill.

PARISH OF DUMBARTON.

In the parish churchyard a handsome monument, in honour of William Scrogie, Bishop of Argyle, is inscribed thus :—

"D. Gulielmi Scrogii episcopi Lismorensis meritissimi, memoriæ sacratum.

> Stemmate de docto, dedit incunabula et artes,
>   Doctorum genitrix alma Abredona viro.
> Primitiis fruitur felix Rathvena laborum;
>   Hic radiosa micant ars pietasque diu.
> Hinc mitram meruisse datum; Lismora triumphis
>   Præsulis eloquii nobilitata sui.
> Omnibus officiis bene functus, inutile tempus
>   Sprevit et (hac lasso corpore) lætus obit.
> Spiritus, alta petens, comprendit jubila cœli;
>   Ossa, sub hoc tumulo (mox animanda) manent,
> Exuvias mortalitatis posuit 6 cal. Feb. anno Dom. 1678."

Bishop Scrogie was son of Dr. Alexander Scrogie, minister of Old Machar, Aberdeenshire. He was admitted minister of Rathven before 1650, and consecrated Bishop of Argyle in 1666.

A mortuary enclosure denotes the family burying-place of Mr. Robert Napier, of Shandon.

In the cemetery a monument, erected by working men, celebrates William Denny, shipbuilder; it bears these lines:—

> "Genius and worth sleep in this honoured grave :
>   Here the quick brain—the active fingers lie ;
> But his mind's offspring proudly breast the wave
>   On every sea where Britain's colours fly.

PARISH OF OLD KILPATRICK.

A monumental stone in the parish churchyard is, by a popular fiction, described as the tomb of St. Patrick, the apostle of Ireland. It presents the sculptured effigies of a knight in armour, and belongs to the fourteenth century.

At the old ruin of Dunglass Castle, near Bowling, an obelisk, reared by public subscription, commemorates Henry Bell, the first constructor of steamboats. This ingenious person was born at Torphichen, Linlithgowshire, on the 7th April, 1767. Originally apprenticed to a mason, he subsequently became a millwright and engineer. For some time he was employed in London, under the celebrated Rennie. In 1800 he submitted to Lord Melville his plans on steamboat propulsion, but the scheme was rejected by the Admiralty. In 1811 he had his small steamer, the *Comet*, constructed at Port Glasgow. It was launched in 1812, and, though only making some six miles an hour, it proved the pioneer of a system which has revolutionized navigation. Mr. Bell was unrewarded till a late period of his life, when he received an annuity of £100 from the Clyde Trustees. He died 14th November, 1830, aged sixty-three. His remains were interred in the churchyard of Row, and in the church of that parish a monumental statue has been erected to his memory.

PARISH OF KIRKINTILLOCH.

A granite obelisk in the Old Isle churchyard, reared by public subscription, celebrates David Gray, author of "The Luggie, and other Poems." This ingenious and short-lived poet was born on the 29th January, 1838, at Duntiblae, on the banks of the Luggie. His father, who was a hand-loom weaver, sent him to the University of Glasgow, with a view to the ministry. He early wrote verses, and contributed these and prose compositions to the local journals. In the hope of bettering his circumstances he in 1860 proceeded to London. Through the favour of Mr. Monckton Milnes he there procured literary employment, but his health broke down. He died of consumption at his father's house, Merkland, Kirkintilloch, on the 3rd December, 1861, aged twenty-four. His poems were published posthumously.

In the parish churchyard a tombstone commemorates a member of the old family of Gartshore, of that ilk. It is thus inscribed:—

"Memoriæ sacrum Joannis Gartshore de Gartshore. Obiit hæc vitæ die viginti Decembris, anno Domini MDCCCV. Ætatis LXV."

Tombstones commemorate John Gray, of Condarot, who died in 1741; James Gray, of Auchingiech, who died in 1733; and John Bankier, portioner, Kirkintilloch, who died in 1770.

PARISH OF LUSS.

In the parish churchyard are exhibited three ancient stone coffins, which are unassociated with any history or tradition.

The old chapel at Rossdhu constitutes the family burial-place of Sir James Colquhoun, Bart., of Luss.

The chapel contains a figure of Saint Kessog, the tutelary saint of the district. According to tradition this saint was buried in the chapel.

STIRLINGSHIRE.

PARISH OF AIRTH.

In the parish churchyard an ancient aisle constitutes the burial-place of the noble family of Elphinstone. Several of the Barons Elphinstone were here interred.

The churchyard also contains the family vault of the Earls of Dunmore. George, fifth Earl of Dunmore, who died 11th November, 1836, was buried here. By his widow, Susan, daughter of Archibald, ninth Duke of Hamilton, a monument was erected to his memory. It bears these lines :—

> " Oft to this spot will memory fondly turn,
> And love's pure flame still unextinguished burn
> Within her breast who here doth mourn his loss,
> But nails her sorrows to a Saviour's cross.
> O precious hope ! by faith to mortals given,
> That twining hearts, which have on earth been riven,
> May through that same dear Saviour's pleading love
> Again unite in realms of bliss above."

A monument commemorates Alexander Bruce, of Airth ; it is thus inscribed :—

" M. S. Alexandro Brussio, ex Roberti Brussii Scotorum regis filio natu secundo, progenito, baroni Airthensi. Primum in Belgio per annos XLII. Dein in Anglia pro tribuno regio. Viro cum strenvo tum pientissimo ; ætatis, anno LVI. vitaque simvl defvncto, A.D. XVII. kal. Oct. CIƆDCXLII. G. Lauderus affinis, M.P.

> Brussius hic sitvs est ; pietate an clarior armis,
> Incertum est ; certum regibus ortus avis.

Heer lyes a branche of Brusse's noble stem,
Airth's baron, whose high worth did svte that name.
Holland his courage, honovred Spain did feare
The Sweeds in Fvnen bought the trial deare.
At last his prince's service called him home,
To die on Thames his bank, and leave this tombe,
To bear his name unto posteritie,
And make all braue men loue his memorie."

The family of Airth were descended from Sir Robert Bruce, of Clackmannan, who married Janet, daughter of Alexander, fifth Lord Livingstone.

The Rev. John McGachan, who died minister of the parish in May, 1843, has celebrated his spouse (a daughter of John Ross, of Balgersho) in these lines :—

"One by one love's links are broken,
    One by one our friends depart,—
Voices that have kindly spoken,
    Heart that throbbed to kindred heart.

"Shed not for her the bitter tear,
    Nor give the heart to vain regret ;
'Tis but the casket that lies here,—
    The gem that filled it sparkles yet."

A tailor is thus commemorated :—

"Happie · is · he · who · dies
With · a · good · nane ·
Thowgh · volwnes · be · not ·
Written · of · his · fane."

PARISH OF ALVA.

In a vault of the parish church a tombstone is inscribed as follows :—

"Parenti optimo, Carolo Areskine, Car. Areskine de Alva, equitis, filio, qui, juventute, doctrina plurimum exculta; ætate provectior, in jure respondendo dicundoque feliciter versatus ; senectute serena placidus, summis in republica muneribus, ad LXXXIII, usque annum, gnaviter expletis. Vita honorifica satur, in sede tandem avita, ossa juxta paterna, heic lubens quiescit. Carolo quoque, fratri multum desiderato, familiæ suæ, patrioque, si fata tulissent, decori eximio ; Londini, in ædicula cœnobii Lincoln-ensis, sepulto, H.M.P.C. Jacobus Erskine. 1763."

Charles Erskine was third son of Sir Charles Erskine, Bart., of Alva, and his wife, Christian, daughter of Sir James Dundas, of Arniston. Born in 1680, he was in his thirtieth year appointed one of the four regents of the University of Edinburgh. He passed Advocate in 1711, and was elected M.P. for Dumfriesshire in 1722. He was Solicitor-General in 1725, and Lord Advocate in 1737. He was raised to the Bench, with the judicial title of Lord Tin-wald, in 1744, and appointed Lord Justice-Clerk in 1748. He died at Edinburgh on the 5th April, 1763. Other members of the Erskine family are buried in the vault.

In Alva Churchyard an elegant mausoleum constitutes the family burial-place of Johnstone of Alva.

PARISH OF CAMPSIE.

In 1810 a monument was reared in honour of John Bell, of Antermony, author of " Travels in Russia."

In the churchyard tombstones commemorate " James Kinkaid, of that ilk," who died in 1604 ; and " James Kinkaid, of that ilk," who died in 1606. The family of Kincaid is represented by the Hon. C. S. B. H. Kincaid Lennox, of Woodhead and Kincaid.

A martyr for the Covenant is celebrated thus :—

"William Buick, who suffered at Glasgow, June 14, 1633, for his adherence to the word of God and Scotland's covenanted work of reformation.

> Underneath this stone doth lie
> Dust sacrificed to tyranny ;

Yea, precious in Immanuel's sight,
Since martyred for His kingly right."

On the tombstone of a miller are these lines :—

" Eternity is
A wheel that turns,
A wheel that turned ever,
A wheel that turns,
And will leave turning never."

PARISH OF DRYMEN.

In the parish churchyard a tombstone celebrates the worth and ministerial fidelity of the Rev. Duncan Macfarlan, minister of the parish, who died 30th June, 1791, in the eighty-fourth year of his age, and forty-ninth of his ministry. His son, Duncan, who succeeded him in the cure, became Principal of Glasgow College (Vol. I., 479).

From a tombstone in the churchyard we have the following :—

" Here lie two sisters and a Brother,
Who pleasantly liv'd with each other;
For God anew did them create,
And in their death not separate.
Their dusty part does here remain
Till Christ, their Head, do come again
To call them hence to reunite
Their souls and bodies full complete,
That they His praises ay may sing
To Him as their immortal King,
Who hath redeem'd them by His blood,
And made them kings and priests to God.
O Lord, the sin of their fond Mother
Forgive through Christ, our elder Brother,
Who fondly wished they might not go,
But dwell with her still here below,
Until she pass through Jordan's deep,
There in Christ's arms to fall asleep;
Her soul to sing forth His praise
Through eternal ages, endless days."

PARISH OF FALKIRK.

A monumental statue of Arthur, Duke of Wellington, reared by public subscription, occupies a prominent position in the burgh. The parish churchyard contains several interesting memorial stones. A monument, consisting of three flat stones placed horizontally, and kept slightly apart by intervening supports, celebrates Sir John de Graham, second son of the knight of Dundaff, and the chief friend of the patriot Wallace, who fell at the battle of Falkirk, 22nd July, 1298. The original monument, a plain slab, was placed by Wallace himself; a second slab, with a renewed inscription, was afterwards added, while the uppermost stone, raising the monument to the height of three feet from the surface, was erected in 1772 by William Graham, of Airth. The uppermost stone contains the following inscription, believed to have been transcribed from the original slab, and composed by Wallace :—

" Mente manuque potens, et Vallæ fidus Achates,
Conditur hic Gramus, bello interfectus ab Anglis."

The following lines are engraved lengthways on the stone, two lines being along each of the side margins :—

" Here lys
Sir John the Grame, baith wight and wise,
Ane of the chiefs reskewit Scotland thrise ;
Ane better knight not to the world was lent,
Nor was gvde Grame of trvth and hardiment."

A few yards from the monument of Sir John de Graham a plain oblong block of sandstone denotes the grave of Sir John Stewart of Bonhill, brother of the Lord High Steward. It is inscribed :—

" Here lies a Scottish hero, Sir John Stewart, who was killed at the battle of Falkirk, 22nd July, 1298."

A massive tombstone, elegantly sculptured, commemorates Sir Robert Monro, Bart., of Fowlis, who was killed at the second battle of Falkirk, 17th January, 1746. This brave officer, whose virtues have been portrayed by Dr. Doddridge in his "Life of Colonel Gardiner," was twenty-seventh baron of the ancient house of Fowlis. He was engaged under the Duke of Marlborough in Flanders. Returning to Scotland in 1712, he, along with Lord Sutherland, aided in retarding the timely union of the forces of the Chevalier in 1715, and on the suppression of the rebellion of that year was appointed a commissioner on the forfeited estates. He then entered Parliament, but his military services being required abroad he proceeded to Flanders in 1740, and there greatly distinguished himself by his prudence and valour. At the battle of Fontenoy his skill and bravery were remarkably conspicuous. On his return he received the command of a regiment appointed to quell the insurrection under Prince Charles Edward, and his death at Falkirk was occasioned by the cowardly desertion of his troop. He fell by a musket-ball deliberately shot at him, when endeavouring to rally his men. His younger brother, whose name is recorded on the monument, also perished in the battle.

In the vestibule of the church, on each side of the entrance, supported on handsome tombs, are four stone figures, supposed to represent two of the old barons of Callander and their spouses. These figures lay in the south transept of the old parish church, and for many years were exposed to the weather, till April, 1852, when they were placed in the vestibule by the late Mr. William Forbes, of Callander. The family of Livingston, which produced successively the Lords Livingston and the Earls of Linlithgow and Callander, claim an Hungarian origin, and are said to have come to Scotland in the train of Margaret, queen of Malcolm Canmore. The several titles are now extinct, or in abeyance.

An antique fabric attached to the north-east corner of the church is a burial-place of the noble house of Dundas, represented by the Earl of Zetland.

A handsome monument in the vestibule of the church commemorates the Rev. John Brown Patterson, minister of the parish, and author of a "Prize Essay on the National Character of the

Athenians." This distinguished clergyman was son of Robert
Patterson, of Croft House, Alnwick, and was born on the 29th June,
1804. He much distinguished himself at the High School and
University of Edinburgh, and was licensed to preach 7th January,
1829. He was ordained minister of Falkirk 26th February, 1830,
and died of fever 29th June, 1835. His "Select Literary and
Religious Remains" were published in 1837, accompanied by a
Memoir.

In the churchyard a tombstone commemorates Richard Callender,
minister of the parish, who died 29th January, 1686. It is inscribed as follows :—

> "Stirpe sacerdotum prognatus utrinque, sacerdos
> Hic jacet innocuus, vir sine fraude sagax :
> Quotque dies mensis bissextus continet, annos
> Tot fuit huic divi credita cura gregis :
> Sex alibi, hic annos bis denos tresque peregit,
> Dum casto usque suas corde fovebat oves.
> Solis rite cyclo, quoad ævum, bis repetito,
> Nunquam, sat flendus, seu reverendus, obit."

Mr. Callender was eldest son of Alexander Callender, minister of
Denny. He was ordained minister of Cockburnspath in 1657, and
translated to Falkirk in 1663. He owned lands at Cockburnspath,
and married Alison, sister of Sir Roger Hogg, of Harcase, a Lord
of Session.

From gravestones in Falkirk Churchyard we have these lines :—

> " Death certain is ; but neither when nor where :
> Which teacheth us each day we should prepare."

> " Time was like thee
> I life possessed,
> And time will be
> When thou shalt rest."

> " All you that come my grave to see,
> As I am now so must you be ;
> Repent in time, make no delay—
> I in my prime was called away."

Within the enclosures of Callander House, an elegant mausoleum, erected by his widow, commemorates William Forbes, of
Callander, grandfather of the present proprietor. This enterprising
and prosperous gentleman was a native of Aberdeen, and for some
time engaged in trade in London. Having obtained the exclusive
privilege of coppering the vessels of the navy, he realized a large
fortune. He purchased the estates of Callander about the year
1786. He was an excellent landlord, and a zealous promoter of
husbandry. He died on the 21st June, 1815, and was succeeded
by his eldest son, who for some years represented the county in
Parliament.

PARISH OF KILLEARN.

Through the exertions of the Rev. James Graham, minister of
the parish, a monumental obelisk in memory of George Buchanan
was erected at Killearn in 1788. It is 103 feet in height, and was
built at the cost of £295, defrayed by subscription. Buchanan
was born at Moss, in Killearn parish, in February, 1506. Having
studied the classics in Paris, and philosophy at St. Andrews, he
imbibed the doctrines of Luther, and became a keen supporter of
the Reformation. His poem on the " Franciscan Friars " appeared
in 1538; he was in the following year subjected to imprisonment
by Cardinal Beaton, but effected his escape. He became Professor
of Latin at Bordeaux; he subsequently proceeded to Portugal,
where he officiated as a Professor in the University of Coimbra.
As an upholder of the Protestant doctrines he was thrown into the
dungeon of the Inquisition, where he remained eighteen months.
After some changes he returned to Scotland in 1560, when he
became classical tutor to Queen Mary. In 1566 he was appointed
Principal of St. Leonard's College, St. Andrews, and in the following
year was, though a layman, elected Moderator of the General
Assembly. In 1570 he was appointed preceptor to the young
king, and was nominated Director of the Chancery. Some time

afterwards he was chosen Lord Privy Seal, with a seat in Parliament. His great work, the "History of Scotland," occupied the
last twelve years of his life; it was completed within a month of
his decease. He died at Edinburgh on the 28th September, 1582,
at the age of seventy-six.

PARISH OF KILSYTH.

A modern tombstone is thus inscribed:—

"Beneath this stone are deposited the remains of Jean Cochrane,
Viscountess of Dundee, wife of the Honourable W. Livingston, of
Kilsyth, and of their infant son. Their deaths were caused by the
falling in of the roof, composed of turf, of a house in Holland.
Mr. Livingston was with difficulty extricated. The lady, her
child, and the nurse were killed. This occurred in the month of
October, MDCXCV. In MDCCXCV., the vault over which the
church at that time stood having been accidentally opened, the
bodies of Lady Dundee and her son, which had been embalmed
and sent from Holland, were found in a remarkable state of preservation. After being for some time exposed to view, the vault was
closed. This lady was the daughter of William, Lord Cochrane,
who predeceased his father, William, first Earl of Dundonald. She
married, first, John Graham, of Claverhouse, Viscount of Dundee,
who was killed at the battle of Killicrankie, MDCLXXXIX.; and
secondly, the Honourable William Livingston, who succeeded his
brother as third Viscount of Kilsyth in MDCCVI. Lord Kilsyth
married, secondly, a daughter of Macdougal, of Makerstoun, but
dying under attainder at Rome in MDCCXXXIII., without
surviving issue, this noble family became extinct. This stone
was erected by Sir Archibald Edmonston, of Duntreath, Bart.,
MDCCCL."

Jean Cochrane was of the family of Ochiltree. About a year
after the death of Viscount Dundee, her first husband, she became
wife of the Hon. William Livingston. In 1694 they proceeded,
with their infant child, to Rotterdam. The lady had married her
first husband in violent opposition to the Presbyterians, and,
according to Wodrow, had said that the day she heard a Presby-

terian minister preach she hoped the house would fall down and smother her. One afternoon she went to the Scotch Church, Rotterdam, to hear Mr. Robert Fleming, a Presbyterian minister, and the celebrated author of " The Fulfilling of Scripture." That evening Mr. and Mrs. Livingston went into a room where their child lay with its nurse, when the roof of the house fell in, and destroyed the entire party, with the exception of Mr. Livingston, who was rescued.

A tombstone formerly contained these lines :—

> " Beneath this stone here lies a man,
> Whose body was not full three span,
> A bon companion, day and night,
> Sir Thomas Henderson, of Haystoun, knight."

PARISH OF LARBERT.

In Larbert Churchyard a tombstone commemorates the Rev. Robert Bruce, of Kinnaird. This distinguished divine was born in 1554; he was second son of Alexander Bruce, of Airth, and was a collateral descendant of the famous King Robert. Having studied law, he had a judgeship secured for him by patent, but, much to the indignation of his relatives, he abandoned his legal prospects, and entered the Church. He became one of the ministers of Edinburgh, and in May, 1590, was chosen by James VI. to crown his queen, Anne of Denmark. In 1596 he resisted an attempt of the king to thrust episcopacy on the Church, and was obliged to seek refuge in England. He was permitted to return to Edinburgh in 1598, but having in 1600 refused to express his belief in the Gowrie Conspiracy he was prohibited from exercising his ministry. For some time he resided at Dieppe. He returned to Scotland in 1601, but did not thereafter hold any settled charge. For eight years subsequent to 1605 he was compelled to reside at Inverness ; he afterwards obtained permission to live at Kinnaird, but was in 1621 again banished to Inverness. On the death of James VI. he returned to Kinnaird; he preached every Sunday in Larbert church, for which no clergyman had been provided by the bishop. He died 13th August, 1631.

James Bruce, of Kinnaird, the celebrated traveller, sixth in descent from the Rev. Robert Bruce, rests in Larbert churchyard. His monument is thus inscribed :—

"In this tomb are deposited the remains of James Bruce, of Kinnaird, who died on the 27th of April, 1794, in the 64th year of his age. His life was spent in performing useful and splendid actions; he explored many distant regions; he discovered the fountains of the Nile; he traversed the deserts of Nubia. He was an affectionate husband, an indulgent parent, an ardent lover of his country. By the unanimous voice of mankind, his name is enrolled with those who were conspicuous for genius, for valour, and for virtue."

James Bruce was born at Kinnaird on the 14th December, 1730. He purposed to study for the Church, then followed legal pursuits, and afterwards became a wine merchant. Succeeding to Kinnaird, his patrimonial inheritance, he entered upon a course of adventure. For twelve years he was absent from Britain on foreign travel, and during the greater part of that period employed himself in striving to reach the source of the Nile. When he published his "Travels" he was accused of imposing on public credulity, but his statements have by subsequent travellers been fully verified. He keenly felt the charge of falsehood which was preferred against him, and to his daughter expressed a hope that she might be spared to witness his vindication. From the effects of a fall he expired on the 27th April, 1794, aged sixty-four.

In Larbert churchyard a tombstone, bearing date 1665, is thus inscribed :—

> " Here lyes interred within this urn
> The corpse of honest good John Burn,
> Who was the eight John of that name,
> That lived with love and died with fame.
> In changing tymes, saddest disaster,
> True to his king, lord, and master!

Kind to his kindred, neighbour, friend,
Who's good life had an happie end,
His soul to God he did bequeath,
His dust, to lye this stone beneath."

PARISH OF LOGIE.

On Abbey Craig, the most easterly of the three isolated crags which rise in the Vale of Stirling, stands the national monument to Wallace. The crag is 360 feet above the level of the Forth, and presents a precipitous front to the south-west. The monument, which rises on the highest point of the crag's front, represents (see vignette) a Scottish baronial tower of an early period. It is 220 feet in height, and at the base 36 feet square. The walls, 18 feet thick at the foundations, graduate to a thickness of 5˙ feet at the top of the structure. To the tower on the east side is attached the warder's lodge, a massive building of two stories. An open court-yard, entered by an arched gateway, with bold mouldings, separates the main building from the lodge. Above the gateway are the heraldic arms of the house of Wallace. Passing through the gateway into an arched passage, and turning to the left, a series of steps leads to an octagonal staircase which projects from the south-west angle of the tower, and runs up to a bartisan parapet at the top. Arrow-light apertures pierce the walls of the staircase, and imitation ropework, with moulded angles, bind the walls. On the ground-floor there is an elegant waiting-room, and three halls above. All the halls are arched with stone, and are each 24 feet square and 30 feet high ; they are intended for the reception of works of sculpture, ancient armour, and antiquarian relics. The bartisan parapet at the top of the staircase is 5 feet wide, and is protected by a wall 6 feet high and 18 inches thick. A few steps lead up to the bartisan platform, an open space 25 feet square paved with flags, and protected by a parapet consisting of large round balls. An imperial crown 50 feet in height, and built of

D

cube stone, forms the apex ; it is composed of eight arms stretching from the angles and sides, and converging in the centre, forming a series of flying buttresses, surmounted by crocketed pinnacles. The structure is composed of freestone. It was built from a design by Mr. J. T. Rochead, selected at a public competition.

A proposal for the erection of a monument to Wallace on Abbey Craig was made by the author of this work in a volume descriptive of Central Scotland, published in 1852.* No active measures were adopted till the spring of 1856, when Mr. C. R. Brown, a newspaper proprietor in Glasgow, communicated with the writer respecting a proposal to celebrate Wallace by a monument on Glasgow Green. In the course of a correspondence Mr. Brown approved of the Abbey Craig site as the more eligible, and several persons were called together at Glasgow, who requested the Provost of Stirling to convene a public meeting in that place to consider the proposal. At this meeting, which was attended by the leading inhabitants of Stirling, the writer "moved" that the monument should be built. To initiate proceedings a committee was appointed, with the writer as secretary. The duties of his office proved most irksome and arduous, for in addition to the ordinary difficulties of raising money for a public object, there had to be encountered and overcome the crude notions of one or more adherents of the enterprise. A national meeting was held in the King's Park, Stirling, on the 24th June, 1856, the late Earl of Elgin officiating as president. This most successful demonstration was followed by meetings in Edinburgh and Glasgow, and in other principal towns. Natives of Scotland held gatherings in the large towns of England, throughout the colonies, and in India. Money was collected at Constantinople, on the coast of Africa, and in the islands of the South Seas. The United States sent contributions. The foundation stone of the monument was, on the 24th of June, 1861, laid by the Duke of Athole as

* "A Week at Bridge of Allan." Edinburgh, 1852. 8vo. Pp. 39—41.

Grand Master Mason. By permission of the Commander-in-chief the Scottish Volunteers assisted in the proceedings, and a salute of artillery was discharged from Stirling Castle. About 80,000 persons assembled on the occasion. At a public banquet Sir Archibald Alison, Bart., and other speakers delivered orations appropriate to the event. On the 11th September, 1869, the monument was formally handed over to the Town Council of Stirling as its permanent custodiers. It was completed at the cost of £13,401 1s. 8d.

The position of the monument is peculiarly appropriate. Abbey Craig is geographically in the centre of Scotland. It overlooks the field of Stirling Bridge, where Wallace obtained his greatest victory. The scene around is picturesque and ennobling. A plain of every variety of landscape is guarded on the north and south by undulating hills and pastoral eminences ; and on the distant east and west is bounded by mountain ranges. In the far west the stupendous Grampians, crested by the lofty Ben Lomond, raise their majestic forms. Eastward the view terminates on the sloping hills of Clersh and Saline. Every point of the immediately surrounding scenery is replete with interest. Craigforth, on the west, stands forth in isolated majesty. North-west is " the lofty brow of ancient Keir," and Bridge of Allan, ensconced under the umbrageous shelter of wooded heights. To the north-east extend the masses of the undulating Ochils. Northward is Airthrey Castle, with its park and lake. Villages fringe the base of the Ochils far as the eye can reach. On a peninsula of the serpent-like Forth stands the hoary tower of Cambuskenneth, rejoicing in its seven centuries of age. Southward is Bannockburn, where Scottish freedom was won ; to the south-west, Stirling on its rock, surmounted by the towers of its ancient castle. The monument may be seen across a country extending from the Arrochar mountains on the west to the Lomond heights in the distant east.

Sir William Wallace was second of the three sons of Sir Malcolm Wallace, of Elderslie, in Renfrewshire. His mother was daughter of Sir Raynald Crawford, Sheriff of Ayr. Born about the year 1270, he was brought up under the care of his uncle, the priest of

Dunipace, who first inspired him with the love of liberty. He afterwards entered an ecclesiastical seminary at Dundee. While there studying he was insulted by a youth named Selby, son of the English governor : he slew him and fled. The country was under English rule, but some enterprising or desperate persons refused to submit to a foreign yoke. To these Wallace joined himself, and was acknowledged as their leader. He attacked and cut off English convoys and foraging parties, and when pursued found shelter in the forests. His successful exploits drew to his standard some valiant knights, who resolved under his leadership to attempt once more their country's liberation. The English governor at Lanark slew Wallace's wife, the heiress of Lamington; he avenged her death by slaying the murderer and destroying his garrison. He routed an English force at Biggar. He revenged the murder of his uncle, Sir Raynald Crawford, by burning the barracks of Ayr, which sheltered an English garrison. He expelled Bek, an English ecclesiastic, from the see of Glasgow, and scattered the forces of Ormsby, the English justiciary at Scone. Joined by numbers of the nobility and gentry, he proceeded to the north, and wrested a succession of strongholds from the invaders. He was storming the castle of Dundee, when he learned that an English army under the Earl of Surrey and Hugh Cressingham were marching towards Stirling. Raising the siege, he hastened to attack the invaders at the passage of the Forth. He encamped his followers on the north-eastern slope of the Abbey Craig, and from the spot where the monument now stands surveyed the movements of the enemy. When a portion of the army, under Cressingham, had crossed the Forth, he attacked them with such vigour that all were cut off or driven into the river. Those who, under Surrey, remained on the other side fled terror-stricken. The castles of Dundee and Dumbarton surrendered, and English domination was overthrown. The battle of Stirling Bridge was fought on the 11th of September, 1297. Wallace was appointed Guardian of Scotland: he proceeded to restore order in the state, and to develop the national resources. He enriched his followers by several incursions into England.

Hearing that Edward I. was hastening to Scotland with an army of 100,000, and 8,000 horsemen, he proceeded to render the country desert in his line of march. The Scottish and English armies met at Falkirk. Wallace's plan of operations was betrayed to the enemy by two Scottish nobles, and the troops under Comyn turned their banners and retired. Wallace was consequently defeated. Resigning the office of Guardian, he proceeded to France, where he remained five years. In 1303 he returned to Scotland, and engaged in a system of predatory warfare against the English. Edward I. offered a reward for his apprehension; and through the treachery of Sir John Monteith he was in August, 1305, captured at Robroyston, near Glasgow, and being laden with fetters was carried to London. He was arraigned for treason in Westminster Hall—a charge which he scornfully rebutted, since he owed no allegiance to a foreign prince. But his death was predetermined. He was executed at Smithfield with every circumstance of barbarity.

PARISH OF STIRLING.

A monumental statue of Sir William Wallace, by Ritchie, occupies a prominent position in King Street. It was reared in 1858, through subscriptions obtained by the writer, and a large donation from the late Mr. William Drummond, of Rochdale Lodge. The hero is represented in a contemplative attitude, with his two-handed sword girt to his back, the hilt projecting above his left shoulder.

In the *Valley* of Stirling Rock, the scene of ancient tournaments, three monumental statues celebrate John Knox, Andrew Melville, and Alexander Henderson, the distinguished reformers. The statue of Knox occupies a slightly elevated position,—he is represented in the attitude of preaching. John Knox was born at Gifford, Haddingtonshire, in 1505. He studied

at St. Salvator's College, St. Andrews, and was, under the age pre-
scribed by the canons, admitted to priest's orders. By perusing
the writings of the ancient fathers he was led to despise the
subtleties of the school theology, and through the preaching of
Wishart, the future martyr, and of Thomas Williams, a friar, he
began to discover the errors of the Romish faith. Embracing the
Protestant doctrines, he was subjected to persecution by Cardinal
Beaton, and afterwards by his successor, Archbishop Hamilton. In
1547 he obtained shelter in the castle of St. Andrews, with the
assassins of Cardinal Beaton, and here he was called to the ministry
of the Reformed Church. When the garrison of the castle was
forced to capitulate, Knox was taken prisoner ; he was detained on
board a French galley for nineteen months. Liberated in February,
1549, he proceeded to England, where he preached the reformed
doctrines at Berwick and Newcastle. In 1551 he was appointed
chaplain to Edward VI. Disapproving of the liturgy, he declined
the bishopric of Rochester, which was offered him. On the acces-
sion of Mary he removed to the Continent, and associated with
John Calvin at Geneva. He returned to Scotland in 1555, where
his preaching awakened the resentment of the Romish bishops, who
burned him in effigy. After a further residence at Geneva, he
proceeded to Scotland in 1559. Preaching at Perth against the
idolatry of the mass and image-worship, the excited populace
destroyed the churches and monasteries of that city. His preaching at St. Andrews and other places was attended with similar
results. In August, 1560, the reformed religion received the sanction of Parliament, and Romish worship was proscribed. Knox
became one of the ministers of Edinburgh, and in this capacity
opposed an attempt of Queen Mary to establish the mass at
Holyrood. On this account he was arraigned before a convention
of the nobility in December, 1563, the queen being present;
but he was honourably acquitted. He opposed the marriage of
the queen with Darnley, and becoming obnoxious at court, he
sometime withdrew from Edinburgh. In July, 1567, he preached
the coronation sermon of James VI. in the parish church of

Stirling; and in February, 1570, delivered the funeral discourse of the regent Murray. From the deadly attacks of his enemies he sought shelter at St. Andrews from May, 1571, to August, 1572. After an illness of some duration he died on the 24th November, 1572. He was the chief author of "The Confession of Faith and First Book of Discipline," and composed a "History of the Reformation," and other works.

A few yards from the statue of Knox, on the right, is that of Andrew Melville. Youngest son of Richard Melville, of Baldovy, Forfarshire, this eminent divine was born on the 1st August, 1545. Having distinguished himself as a classical scholar at the Universities of St. Andrews and Paris, he was, on the recommendation of Beza, appointed Professor of Humanity at Geneva. In 1574 he returned to Scotland, when he became Principal of Glasgow College, and minister of Govan. In 1580 he accepted the Principalship of St. Mary's College, St. Andrews, and assisted by his nephew, conducted service in the parish church. For some expressions used in the pulpit which were pronounced seditious by the Privy Council, he was in February, 1584, sentenced to imprisonment, but he effected his escape to England. On the disgrace of the Earl of Arran he returned to Scotland in November, 1585. In May, 1594, he was for the third time elected Moderator of the General Assembly. During the following year, when on a deputation to James VI., to remonstrate against the recall of the Popish lords, he in a moment of irritation touched the king's arm, and called him "God's silly vassal,"—a proceeding which James never forgave. In 1606 he invited Melville and other ministers to London, under the pretext that he wished to consult them about ecclesiastical affairs. At the famous conference at Hampton Court, Melville spoke with energy and his wonted boldness. Having denounced in a Latin epigram the service practised in the Chapel Royal, he was committed to the Tower, where he was imprisoned four years. In 1611 he was released on his accepting the appointment of Theological Professor in the Protestant University of Sedan. He died at Sedan in 1622, at the age of seventy-seven.

To the right of Knox is the monumental statue of Alexander Henderson (see Vol. I., p. 25). In another portion of the cemetery a monumental statue, raised by subscriptions obtained by the writer, celebrates James Guthrie, the Presbyterian martyr. This unbending upholder of Presbytery was a younger son of Guthrie of that ilk, in the county of Forfar. He studied at the University of St. Andrews, and became a regent in St. Leonard's College. In 1642 he was ordained minister of Lauder, from which parish he was in 1649 translated to the first charge of Stirling. As leader of the protesting party in the Church he rendered himself obnoxious to Charles II., who shortly after the Restoration caused him to be apprehended. He was arraigned before the Estates, and chiefly through the bitter hostility of the Earl of Middleton, whose excommunication by the Commission of the General Assembly he had published from the pulpit, he was condemned to suffer for high treason. He was hanged at the Cross of Edinburgh, 1st June, 1661, at the age of forty-nine. His head was placed on the port at the Nether-bow, where it remained for twenty-eight years. The statue presents an actual likeness of the martyr, being founded on an original portrait in possession of the magistrates. It was inaugurated in presence of the magistrates, clergy, and town council of Stirling, on the 26th November, 1857.

On the shoulder of the Ladies' Rock, and within the cemetery enclosure, a group of marble statuary, surmounted by a glass cupola, commemorates Margaret Wilson, one of the Wigton martyrs (Vol. I., pp. 349—356). The martyr is represented in the act of reading the Scriptures on the hill-side, with her younger and like-minded sister Agnes; a lamb rests quietly at their feet, and their guardian angel hovers near.

Not far from the Wilson monument, and on the margin of the Ladies' Rock, a monumental statue celebrates James Renwick, the last of the Scottish martyrs (Vol. I., p. 304). A statue in honour of the Rev. Ebenezer Erskine occupies the northern portion of the cemetery. It was erected in 1858 through the efforts of the writer, and was sculptured from a model founded on an original portrait.

Ebenezer Erskine was son of the Rev. Henry Areskine (Vol. I., p. 222), and was born at Dryburgh, Berwickshire, on the 22nd June, 1680. Having studied at the University of Edinburgh, he was licensed to preach in February, 1703, and in the same year was ordained minister of Portmoak. In 1731 he was translated to the third charge of Stirling. Having, as Moderator, opened the Synod held at Perth in October, 1732, with a discourse, in which he condemned several recent acts of the Church enforcing the law of patronage, he was pronounced censurable by the court. On an appeal to the General Assembly the judgment of the Synod was confirmed, and after various proceedings Erskine and three brethren who adhered to him were in 1734 loosed from their charges. They met in December at Gairney Bridge, near Kinross, and there constituted the Associate Presbytery, now represented by the United Presbyterian Church. Erskine ministered at Stirling, and frequently preached near the spot occupied by his statue, till a church for his accommodation was built. During the rebellion in 1746 he gallantly headed two companies of his congregation in defence of the town. He died 2nd June, 1754, aged seventy-four. He was twice married, and has had numerous descendants. Within the enclosure in front of the *Back Row Meeting-house*, near the spot of his interment, a handsome monument, in the form of a Greek temple, was in the year 1860 erected to his memory.

A pyramidical structure at the northern edge of the cemetery enclosure commemorates those who in Scotland suffered martyrdom in the cause of civil and religious liberty. It is inscribed with some Scriptural quotations, and adorned with sculptures and emblems. This structure, and the monumental statues of Knox, Melville, Henderson, and Renwick, and the elegant statuary group in honour of Margaret Wilson, were erected at the sole expense of the late Mr. William Drummond, of Rochdale Lodge, Stirling, who also largely contributed towards the statues of Wallace, Guthrie, and Ebenezer Erskine. This estimable individual has found a resting-place in the cemetery. His grave is denoted by a massive sarcophagus of Aberdeen granite. He was born at Bannockburn on the 14th February, 1793. His father, who bore the same Christian name, was a prosperous nurseryman in Stirling, and he, with several younger brothers, succeeded to the business. Having by a course of unflagging industry realized a competence, he devoted his latter years to the unostentatious exercise of benevolence. A descendant of the family which produced Margaret Wilson, the Wigton martyr and who bore the same Christian and family name, he educated her from childhood, and by a large gift secured her in permanent independence. Children of indigent but deserving neighbours, left orphans, were supported by his bounty. To every charitable institution he was a liberal contributor. An enlightened patriot, he rejoiced in celebrating those who had proved useful to their country. After a life, uneventful, save in performing kind and generous actions, he died at Stirling on the 25th November, 1868. He was unmarried, and bequeathed the bulk of his ample fortune to the Stirling enterprise for the dissemination of religious tracts.

Near the grave of William Drummond, a Gothic cross of Peterhead granite commemorates the officers, non-commissioned officers, and men of the 75th (Stirlingshire) Regiment, who were cut off during the period of the Indian Mutiny.

A handsome monument celebrates the Rev. Archibald Bennie, D.D., F.R.S.E. This eloquent divine was born at Glasgow on the 1st November, 1797. Having studied at the university of his native city he was licensed as a probationer in 1820. He was in 1823 elected assistant and successor to the minister of Albion Street Chapel-of-Ease, Glasgow, and in the following year was translated to the third charge, Stirling, from which he was promoted to the first charge in 1829. In 1826 he founded the Stirling School of Arts. In 1835 he was translated to Lady Yester's Church, Edinburgh, and was in 1841 appointed one of Her Majesty's Chaplains, and Dean of the Chapel Royal. He died suddenly at Dunoon on the 21st September, 1846. A volume of his discourses has been published, accompanied with a memoir.

In Bowie's aisle of the East Church a burial-vault was in 1632 acquired by Sir William Alexander, afterwards Earl of Stirling, and there the Earl was himself interred on the 12th April, 1640.* About 1632 Lady Alexander, afterwards Countess of Stirling, erected in the vault a mural tablet in memory of her parents. This tablet, which still exists in private keeping, is thus inscribed :—

" Hic jacet in spe resurrectionis Gulielmus Æreskinus equestris ordinis cum Joanna conjuge, illustri et communi Æreskinorum familia orta, singulari virtute femina, unica filia superstite quæ postera Gulielmo Alexandro Equiti egregio Jacobo regi a supplicibus libellis, Carolo regi ab Epistolis, proventusque regni annonis nupsit. Eam filiam amor ejus numerosa sobole auxit et hoc monumentum parentibus illustribus posuit."

Translation :—" Here lies, in hope of the resurrection, William Erskine, of the order of knights, along with his wife Joanna, a woman of singular virtue, of illustrious birth, and sprung from the main line of the Erskines, leaving behind them an only daughter, who was afterwards married to William Alexander, a distinguished knight, Master of Requests to King James, secretary and commissioner of exchequer to Charles. His love has blessed that daughter with a numerous offspring, and has reared this monument to her illustrious parents."

Sir William Erskine, who is thus commemorated, was a younger brother of the family of Erskine, of Balgonie, and a near relative of the Earl of Mar. He was Commendator of the Bishopric of Glasgow, and, as recipient of the teind, was styled Parson of Campsie. His only daughter, Janet Erskine, was married to William Alexander, of Menstry, about the year 1603. His son, Alexander, held some office about the court, and his grandson, Sir James Erskine, obtained lands in Ulster.†

The burial-vault of the Earl of Stirling is of some historical interest. From an early owner, known as Bowie's Aisle, it had become the property of Thomas Craigengelt, of that ilk, who on the 26th February, 1618, " resigned " it to the Governors of the Burgh

* Balfour's Historical Works, vol. ii., p. 427.
† Spottiswoode's Miscellany, vol. i., p. 104. note.

Hospital. On the 4th September, 1632, the Kirk Session confirmed to William, Viscount of Stirling, the disposition by the
Master of the Hospital (with consent of the Provost) "of their
Isle, situat on the south syde of their kirk, sometyme callit
Bowye's or Craigengelt's Iyle."* On the death of the Earl of
Stirling, Charles Alexander, his fourth son, succeeded to the
administration of his affairs, and as the Earl's estate was insuffi-
cient to meet his obligations, his property at Stirling, including the
burial-aisle, "was adjudged to the Masters of the Laigh Hospital."
By the hospital authorities the property was conveyed to Archibald, eighth Earl of Argyle. In May, 1764, it was exposed for
sale by John, fourth Duke of Argyle, when Bowie's Aisle was
acquired by James Wright, of Loss, and another. At the commencement of the century the East Church underwent extensive
repairs, when the Stirling family vault was closed, and the aisle
taken down. The agent for Mr. Wright of Loss, a solicitor in the
burgh, had meanwhile obtained from his client a right of interment
in the vault.† It was covered up, but the ingenious attorney
fixed on another portion of ground, adjoining the West Church,
which he enclosed as his family burial-place. The monumental
tablet commemorating Sir William Erskine was placed in the new
enclosure, and thereafter removed, before subscribing witnesses, to
the lawyer's own residence. The spot was now enclosed by a
railing, and when the Town Council, more than forty years afterwards, were repairing the structure of the church, the claimant's
daughter obtained an interdict against interference with a burial-
place thus peculiarly acquired. She is now dead, but she has
made provision in her settlement that her burial-place and its
deforming enclosure shall not be surrendered by those whom she
has elected to represent her.

In the interior of the West Church some marble tablets preserve
the names of founders of hospitals and other local charities,—viz.,
Robert Spittal, John Cowan, John Allan, Alexander Cunningham,

---

* Preface by Mr. David Laing to the Earl of Stirling's "Royal Letters," p. 106.
† Burgh Records of Stirling.

and John McGibbon. Spittal was tailor to the queen of James IV.; Cowan was a prosperous merchant. The revenues of Spittal's and Cowan's Hospitals are derived from lands, and are of considerable value.

A marble tablet commemorates Lieutenant-Colonel John Blackader. Son of a Scottish minister, an eminent sufferer in the cause of Presbyterianism (Vol. I., 207), he was born at Glencairn, Dumfriesshire, on the 14th September, 1664. In his twenty-fifth year he joined the 26th or Cameronian Regiment. During the Seven Years' War (1690—1697) in the Netherlands he was present in nearly every engagement. After some home service he joined the Confederate Army in Holland in 1703. He was severely wounded at the battle of Blenheim on the 2nd August, 1704. He received his commission as major in 1705. He was present at the battle of Ramillies in May, 1706, and took part in the battle of Oudinot in June, 1708. In the autumn of 1708 he distinguished himself at the siege of Lisle. During the campaign of 1709 he was in the covering army at the siege of Tournay, and was present at the battle of Malplaquet. At the close of the campaign he was promoted to the colonelcy of the 26th Regiment. After twenty-two years' active service he retired in 1711. For some years he resided at Edinburgh. During the Rebellion of 1715 he became honorary colonel of a body of Glasgow volunteers, and when the Duke of Argyle encountered the rebel army at Sheriffmuir, he guarded the bridge of Stirling. His patriotism was acknowledged by his being appointed Deputy Governor of Stirling Castle. He died on the 31st August, 1729. Colonel Blackader was distinguished for his religious devotedness.

In the West Church a marble tablet, erected by the magistrates, and adorned with some elegiac verses written by himself, commemorates the genius and learning of Dr. David Doig, Rector of the High School. This distinguished scholar was son of a small farmer in Forfarshire, and was born in that county on the 14th February, 1719. From extreme delicacy of eyesight he was, till the age of twelve, unable to read, but his progress was afterwards so rapid, that after being three years at the parish school he became a successful competitor for one of the foundation bursaries in St. Andrews University. He was in succession parochial schoolmaster of Monifieth, in Forfarshire, and of Kennoway and Falkland, in Fifeshire. In 1760 he was appointed Rector of Stirling School. He died on the 16th March, 1800, in his eighty-first year. Dr. Doig was the cherished friend of his learned contemporaries. Besides his familiarity with classical learning, he was conversant with oriental literature, and was an adept in the abstruse sciences. He composed "Two Letters on the Savage State," in answer to Lord Kames, and contributed the articles "Mystery," "Mythology," and "Philology," to the third edition of the "Encyclopædia Britannica."

A small chapel attached to the north wall of the High Church constitutes the family vault of Moir of Leckie. It contains the mortal remains of George Gleig, LL.D., Bishop of Brechin. This eminent prelate was born in the county of Forfar on the 12th May, 1753. He took orders in his twenty-first year. After various changes he was in 1808 consecrated coadjutor Bishop of Brechin; he was elected Primus in 1816. For many years he ministered to the Episcopal congregation at Stirling. He prepared a Supplement to the third edition of the "Encyclopædia Britannica," and published several other works. He died on the 9th March, 1840, in his eighty-seventh year. In the Episcopal church of Stirling a memorial tablet celebrates his virtues.

Lieutenant-General Samuel Graham, Deputy Governor of Stirling Castle, is by a memorial tablet commemorated in the West Church. He was born at Paisley on the 20th May, 1756. Having studied at the University of Edinburgh he chose the military profession, and joined the army as ensign in 1777. As captain in the 76th Regiment, lately raised, he took part in the American War under Earl Cornwallis from 1779 to 1784. He next served in the West Indies and in Holland; he was severely wounded and lost the use of his left eye at the action on the Helder. He joined as Lieutenant-Colonel the army of Sir Ralph Abercromby in the expedition to Egypt. In 1802 he was promoted to the full rank of colonel, appointed Lieutenant-Governor of Stirling Castle, and placed on the staff in North Britain as brigadier-general. About this period he married Jane, eldest daughter of James Ferrier Principal Clerk of Session—a lady celebrated by the poet Burns,* and whose sister, Miss Ferrier, was the accomplished novelist. For some years subsequent to 1808 General Graham commanded the garrison at Cork. He afterwards resided at Stirling Castle, devoting himself to his duties as governor of that fort. He died on the 25th January, 1831, and his remains were consigned to the burial-vault of Moir of Leckie.

Mural tablets in the West Church commemorate Major Alexander Munro, who died 31st October, 1814; John Burn, of Coldoch, who died 22nd June, 1814; and Edward Alexander, of Powis (father of Lieutenant-Colonel Sir James Edward Alexander, the distinguished traveller), who died in 1835. In the East Church a monument of chaste design commemorates Janet Roger, widow of the Rev. Thomas Davidson, minister of Dundee, who died in 1775, aged ninety-five.

On the interior walls of the East and West Churches, and in the adjacent churchyard, are memorial slabs and tombstones in honour of the following clergymen:—

The Rev. Thomas Randall, minister of the first charge; he was translated from Inchture in 1770, and died 21st July, 1780, in his seventieth year, and the forty-second of his ministry.

The Rev. John Russel, translated from Kilmarnock Chapel-of-Ease to the second charge of Stirling in 1800; died 23rd

---

* To the care of Mrs. Graham antiquaries are indebted for the preservation of the oak figures which adorned the ceiling of Stirling Palace. These figures were executed by John Drummond, of Auchterarder, Master of Works to James V., and "Andro Wood, carvour," one of his workmen (Lord Strathallan's "History of the House of Drummond"). The carvings were removed from the palace in 1777, and deposited in Stirling Jail, where some forty years afterwards they were discovered by Mrs. Graham, who had them cleaned and restored. Drawings of the figures, prepared by Mr. Blore, an ingenious draughtsman, have been engraved and published in a work entitled "Lacunar Stivilinense," Edinburgh, 1817, 4to. Several of the carvings have been suspended on the walls of the County Court-room.

February, 1817, in his seventy-seventh year, and the forty-third of his ministry. He is celebrated by the poet Burns.

The Rev. James Somerville, D.D., minister of the first charge, who died 23rd January, 1817, in his seventieth year, and forty-second of his ministry.

The Rev. John Macmillan, minister of the Cameronian Church, Stirling, and Professor of Theology in the Reformed Presbyterian Synod, who died 20th October, 1819, aged sixty-eight.

The Rev. Alexander Bruce, minister of the third charge, a native of Torphichen. He died by his own hand, 11th June, 1824, in the seventh year of his ministry.

The Rev. Alexander Small, D.D., minister of the second charge, who died 5th January, 1825, in the forty-fourth year of his age, and twentieth of his ministry.

The Rev. George Wright, D.D., minister of the first charge. He was translated from Markinch in 1817, and died 17th October, 1826, in his fiftieth year, and twenty-seventh of his ministry.

The Rev. John Wilson, D.D., minister of the first charge, author of a number of theological and other works. He was in 1844 translated from Irvine; he died 8th November, 1852, in his sixty-fifth year, and the forty-fourth of his ministry.

From tombstones in the churchyard we have these metrical inscriptions :—

> " John Adamson's here kept within,
>   Death's prisoner, for Adam's sin ;
>   But rests in hope that he shall be
>   Set by the Second Adam free."

> " Our life is but a winter day ;
>   Some only breakfast and away,
>   Others to dinner stay,
>   And are full fed.
>   The oldest man but sups
>   And goes to bed.
>   Large is his debt that lingers out the day,
>   He that goes soonest
>   Has the least to pay."

At a bend of the Forth, about one mile to the east of Stirling, is situated Cambuskenneth Abbey, one of the religious houses erected by David I. In 1864, when the ruins of the abbey were cleared out, the tomb of James III. and his queen, Margaret of Oldenburg, was discovered close by the high altar. The royal vault was surmounted with a slab of mountain limestone, about five feet square and seven inches thick. Beneath was a large coffin, of which the foot touched the enclosure of the altar, the head lying westward. Within the coffin was a skeleton, which on exposure to the air crumbled into dust. The lower jaw, remarkable for its large size, was entire, also the frontal part of the cranium, which exhibited a low and receding forehead. On the left of the male skeleton were the bones of a female, also those of a child. The two adult skeletons were held to be those of James III. and his queen, the position of their tomb verifying a uniform tradition as to the spot of their interment.

Queen Margaret of Oldenburg predeceased her husband. She was buried at Cambuskenneth on the 27th February, 1486-7. Two weeks after his slaughter at the battle of Sanchieburn, fought on the 11th June, 1488, James III. was interred at Cambuskenneth beside the remains of his queen.

The discovery of these royal remains having been intimated to the Queen, her Majesty commanded that the bones of her ancestors should be carefully re-interred, and that the place of sepulture should be denoted by a suitable monument. Accordingly, the remains were on the 23rd September, 1865, deposited in the recess of a sarcophagus, in presence of the magistrates of Stirling and others, and a massive altar tomb was thereafter erected at the spot, designed by Mr. Matheson of the Board of Works, Edinburgh. It is composed of beautiful freestone, about $4\frac{1}{2}$ feet in height, 8 feet long, and $4\frac{1}{2}$ feet broad at the base, and 3 feet at the top. On one side it is inscribed,—

" In this place, near to the high altar of the abbey of Cambuskenneth, were deposited the remains of James III., King of Scots, who died the 11th of June, 1488, and of his queen, the Princess Margaret of Denmark."

On the other side are these words,—

"This restoration of the tomb of her ancestors was executed by command of her Majesty Queen Victoria, A.D. 1865."

At one extremity of the memorial are the Scottish arms, with the motto, "Nemo me impune lacessit;" and at the other the Scottish arms impaled with those of Denmark, with representations of the thistle. The monument is enclosed by a railing.

PARISH OF ST. NINIANS.

Two upright stones, seventy yards apart, at Randolph Field, in the neighbourhood of St. Ninians' village, mark the scene of a gallant skirmish on the eve of the battle of Bannockburn, between Randolph, Earl of Murray, and Sir Robert Clifford, commanding a party of English troops. A tall flag-staff, erected by public subscription, denotes the Bore-stone, or portion of pierced trap rock, in which on the morning of the engagement the standard of King Robert the Bruce was planted. It rests on Caldam Hill, a gentle eminence near the old Kilsyth Road, and within half a mile of the hamlet of St. Ninians.

In St. Ninians' churchyard tombstones commemorate the Rev. James Logan, minister of the Relief Church, father of the late Alexander S. Logan, Sheriff of Forfarshire, who died 4th October, 1841; and George Harvey, father of Sir George Harvey, President of the Royal Scottish Academy, who died in 1835.

PARISH OF STRATHBLANE.

On the pavement of the parish church a monumental slab is thus inscribed:—

" Here lyes in the same grave with Mary, Countess of Angus, sister of King James I. of Scotland, from whom he is lineally descended, Archibald Edmonstone, Esq., of Duntreath, in this kingdom, and of Redhall, Ireland, who died in the year 1689, aged about 61 years."

Mary Stuart, daughter of Robert III., was thrice married. Her third husband was Sir William Edmonstone, of Duntreath, in whose burial-place she was interred. The grave was opened about thirty years ago, when the skull of the deceased princess was found entire. She was mother of James Kennedy, Bishop of St. Andrews, who in 1455 founded St. Salvator's College in that city, and of Patrick Graham, the first Archbishop of St. Andrews.

CLACKMANNANSHIRE.

PARISH OF ALLOA.

In the old church of Alloa the noble family of Mar formerly interred. A tombstone commemorates Charles Erskine, tenth Earl of Mar, and several of his sons ; it is thus inscribed :—

"P. M. Caroli Ereskin, comitis de Mar, parentis optimi, nati die xix. mensis Octob. anno MDCL. denati die xxiii. mensis April anno MDCLXXXIX. Ut et Georgii unius et alterius, Caroli item unius et alterius, et Francisci, fratrum impuberum ; Joannes hæres ex asse, itidem comes, patri pientissimo et germanis desideratissimis posuit, A. MDCCIX."

Charles, Earl of Mar, raised in 1679 the 21st Regiment of Foot or Royal Scots Fusiliers, of which he was appointed colonel.

A monument in the old church celebrated Margaret, daughter of Thomas, Earl of Kinnoul, and first wife of John, eleventh Earl of Mar. The inscription was as follows :—

" P. M. Margaritæ, Thomæ Hay, comitis de Kinnoul filiæ natæ die xxx. mensis Septemb. anno MDCLXXXVI. de natæ die xxv. mensis April anno MDCCVII. Et Joannis filioli trimestris, Joannes Ereskin, comes de Mar, conjugi bene de se meritæ et gnato dulcissimo posuit anno MDCCIX."

John, eleventh Earl of Mar, was Secretary of State for Scotland in 1706. He was mainly instrumental in the rising of 1715, and accordingly suffered attainder; he died at Aix-la-Chapelle in 1732.

A family mausoleum, erected in 1818, contains the remains of John Francis, fifteenth Earl of Mar, who died in 1866, and of

Walter Coningsby Erskine, twelfth Earl of Kellie, who died in 1872.

In the interior of St. John's Episcopal Church a monumental cross commemorates the late Earl of Mar; it is thus inscribed:—

"Sacred to the memory of John Francis Miller Erskine, ninth * Earl of Mar, and eleventh Earl of Kellie, who died on the 19th day of June, 1866, in the 71st year of his age. This tablet was erected by the founder of this church, Walter Coningsby Erskine, twelfth Earl of Kellie, &c., as a mark of esteem and affection for his cousin, whose remains rest in the neighbouring family vault."

Two other tablets in St. John's Church commemorate members of the Mar family; the inscriptions are as follow:—

"This tablet is erected by Lieut.-Col. W. C. Erskine, C.B., of H.M. Bengal Army, in memory of his beloved father, the Honble. H. D. Erskine (son of John Francis, 12th Earl of Mar), who died at Schaw Park on 30th December, 1846, aged 70 years. And of his beloved Mother, Mary Anne, wife of the above, who died at Wakefield on the 4th March, 1860, aged 78 years. Also in memory of his Brothers: John Francis, late of the Bengal Army, who died in Edinburgh 29th September, 1845, aged 36 years. Henry David, a Captain in the Royal Marines, who died at sea, 7th December, 1852, aged 37 years; Charles Thomas, in Holy Orders, who died at Wakefield, 5th November, 1861, aged 40 years."

"Sacred to the memory of Amelia Frances, who died at Sylbet, in India, on the 27th of October, 1838, aged 2 years and 4 months. Marion Elise, who died at Sylbet, in India, on the 24th of July, 1840, aged 1 year and 7 months. Francis Charles, who died at Landour, in India, on the 13th June, 1844, aged 1 year and 6 months. John Arthur Coningsby, who died at Schaw Park, 14th of January, 1849, aged 3 years. Henry David Muirson, who died at Schaw Park 14th of January, 1849, aged 18 months. Arthur Coningsby Delamain, who died at Inbulpore, in India, 6th of April,

---

* This is one of those errors in monumental inscriptions which are much to be deplored. In the tablet commemorative of his father, of which the legend is presented in the text, Colonel Walter Coningsby Erskine, afterwards twelfth Earl of Kellie, describes his grandfather, John Francis, as "twelfth Earl of Mar." In the present legend he describes his grandfather's descendant as "ninth earl." The discrepancy is entitled to remark, since it is one of those which have not unfrequently proved a stumblingblock to genealogists. The late Earl of Mar was fifteenth earl.

1854, aged 1 year and 10 months, children of Lieut.-Col. Walter
Coningsby Erskine, C.B., and of Elise his wife."

In St. John's Church a marble tablet, which formerly stood in
the east wall of the churchyard, commemorates John Alexander,
an eminent bishop of the Scottish Episcopal Church. He was son
of John Alexander, successively minister of Criech and Kildrummy,
and who was deposed for joining the Rebellion of 1715. Episcopal clergyman at Alloa, he was consecrated a bishop on the 9th
August, 1743, and was allotted the diocese of Dunkeld. He died
24th April, 1776, in his eighty-second year. He is commended by
Bishop Keith for his piety and benevolence. He bequeathed his
chapel at Alloa to his successors in office.

In Alloa parish church an elegant monument celebrates Major
Morison, of Greenfield. It is thus inscribed :—

"In memory of Major James Morison Foote Morison, of Greenfield, in this parish, and of her Majesty's Staff Corps, formerly of
the 29th Regiment Madras N. I., Nephew of the late Major-General
Sir William Morison, of Greenfield, K.C.B., and M.P. for this
county. He faithfully served his Country in the Army from 1842
until his death at Madras on 29th May, 1867. He shared the
danger and glory of several campaigns in India and China, while
the amiability and integrity of his private life endeared him to his
relatives and friends."

In the churchyard Robert Johnston is on his tombstone celebrated in these lines :—

"Before this Monument of stones
Lie honest Robert Johnston's bones ;
He lived devoutly, died in peace,
Prompt by religion and grace,
Endow'd a preacher for this place.
With consent of his wife to lie
Here by him when she falls to die,
At her expense this tomb was raised
For him whose worth she prized, and praised.

Obit R. J. Aug. 16, A.D. 1739."

Johnston was a merchant in the place ; he bequeathed some

property and the sum of £500 for the maintenance of an assistant minister in the parochial cure.

A monument celebrates the Rev. William Moncrieff, of the Associate Church; the inscription is as follows:—

"Beside this stone is reserved for the resurrection of the just, the earthly part of the Rev. William Moncrieff, minister of the Gospel, in the Associate Congregation at Alloa. Patris perdigni filius non degener. Likewise of Margaret Wilson, his spouse, who died in her 40th year, 18th Jany., 1778; and of Janet Watt, her mother, whom she survived nearly 17 years. Also of the eighth and tenth of their twelve children—three sons and nine daughters —Rachel and Matthew, who died within their first year, 1770 and 1772. He rested from his labours on 14th of August, 1786, in the 57th year of his life, the 37th year of his ministry, and 24th year of his being employed by the Associate Synod as their Professor of Divinity.

"He was an able, practical, and faithful preacher of the Gospel in its unadulterated purity and simplicity, *not with enticing words of man's wisdom*, and continued a zealous supporter of the Reformation testimony according to the genuine state of the Secession church, leaving his name in good remembrance among the true friends of that cause."

The following lengthy inscription commemorates the Rev. James Muckersie:—

"To the Memory of the Rev. James Muckersie, son of the Rev. John Muckersie, Minister at Kinkell, and grandson of the Rev. William Wilson, minister at Perth, one of the four brethren, the founders of the Secession Church. This Monument is erected by the first Associate Congregation of Alloa, of which he was pastor (ever beloved and revered) from his ordination, on the 21st February, 1788, till the 8th of March, 1827, in the 40th year of his ministry, and the 67th of his age, when he gently fell asleep in Jesus. He possessed mental excellences, seldom in the same degree combined:—a sound and vivid understanding, an elegant taste, a cheerful temper, and a sympathizing and benevolent heart, even from a child his delight was in the Holy Scriptures. The work of the ministry was his early choice. His literary and theological acquirements were ample and various. His pulpit discourses were characterized by a mild radiance of evangelical truth, by a winning sanctity of spirit and tendency, by a chaste sympathy of style, and by a grave and unhesitating utterance. He

discharged his other official duties, whether among his people at
large or among the afflicted, the destitute, the aged, and the young,
with calm diligence and affectionate wisdom. His habits were
domestic, and in his family he was equally benign. In his general
intercourse with society he maintained an easy but firm dignity;
and exerted for unpatronized and unknown talent, for unfortunate
rectitude, and for many a useful public institution, a general influence widely effective. In all the deliberative preparations for the
union of the two great bodies of Seceders he was conscientiously
co-operative : its happy consummation gladdened his heart; and
he never ceased to evince, as he had always done, a determined
but liberal zeal for the principles of the Secession Church, as the
most congenial to the spirit and conducive to the ends of the
Protestant Reformation."

In the churchyard the adherents of the West United Presbyterian Church have thus commemorated on a tablet two of their
late pastors and their families :—

"In Memory of the Rev. Thomas Waters, first Minister of the
Associate Burgher Congregation, who died on the 1st Aug., 1809,
in the 74th year of his age and 41st of his ministry, in the firm
belief and assured hope of that Gospel which he faithfully
preached.

"And the Rev. William Fraser, sometime of Crail, and afterwards for forty-three years the faithful Pastor of West U. P.
Congregation, who adorned throughout his life the doctrines which
he preached, and died in the esteem of his fellow-men on the 3rd
Septr., 1853, in the 74th year of his age and 51st of his ministry.

"And also of his children, Andrew, who died 12th Feby., 1812,
aged two months. John, who died 1st Feby., 1819, aged 9 years.
Magdalene, who died 31st Decr., 1837, aged 17 years."

The tombstone of the Rev. James Maxton, minister of the parish,
is thus inscribed :—

"The Rev. James Maxton, Minister of this parish, died 19th
March, 1828, in the 63rd year of his age and 25th of his Ministry.
Jean Bald, his wife, died 7th February, 1824, aged 38. Their
children, Jean, died 22nd March, 1852, aged 55. Fanny, died 11th
May, 1827, aged 28. Alexander, died at Montreal, 1839, aged 36."

A tombstone commemorates the Rev. Peter Brotherston, D.D.,

minister of the parish, who died on the 7th of July, 1862, in the eighty-third year of his age and the fifty-fourth of his ministry.

Alexander Bald, author of the "Corndealer's Assistant," who died 2nd September, 1823, in his seventy-ninth year, has on his gravestone these lines:—

> "With simple truth, it may indeed be said
> Here in the dust a worthy man is laid,
> Vice he abhorred, the Christian path he trod,
> Just in his actions, faithful to his God.
> Useful he lived, devoid of all offence,
> By nature sensible, well bred by sense,
> The Saviour's precepts were his rule and end,
> An upright servant, and a faithful friend."

Mr. Bald was father of Robert Bald, the distinguished mining engineer, who died 28th December, 1861, aged eighty-six, and of Alexander Bald, a respectable song-writer and patron of literary merit, who was born at Alloa 9th June, 1783, and died 21st October, 1859.

On the tombstone of James McIsack, bookseller, who died 15th May, 1834, aged sixty-six, are these lines :—

> "For all the books I've bound
> Here now with valley clods,
> In sheets I'm rotting under ground,
> Death makes as mighty odds !
>
> Waiting the final dawn
> Mine ashes here are laid;
> Life's labour's o'er, and I'm withdrawn,
> Here have I found my bed."

In the old burial-ground a schoolmaster is commemorated thus :—

> "To guide the thoughts of youth to pious lore,
> To guard from ill and show the path of right,
> Their minds with solid principle to store,
> He laboured much and laboured with delight.

"To earn vain wealth and honours he ne'er wrought,
Content if Heaven but gave his soul to live
For truth and peace he ever fondly sought,
Since these alone a lasting portion give."

Bailie Robert Forman's tombstone formerly bore these lines :—

"Stay, passenger, consider well
That thou ere long with me must dwell;
Since thou on earth hast but short stay,
Remember then to watch and pray,
To honour God with fear and dread,—
Learn thou this lesson from the dead."

A tombstone bearing date 1719 has the following legend :—

"The Law says doe, and ye shall live;
The Gospel sayes—ye most believe :
The Law is just indeed and good,
Yet it can give noe spiritual food,
Because believing comes in its room
To save poor sinners from its doom
By Christ the Son of God.
Sae hair I ly in sweet repose
Because when risen I'll rejoice
And theire in heaven sweetly sing
Praise to Jehovah King."

Within the old church of Tullibody are monuments commemorating several members of the noble house of Abercromby. A monument celebrates George Abercromby of Skeith and Tullibody; it was reared by his cousin and successor Alexander, second son of Sir Alexander Abercromby, first baronet of Birkenbog, and is thus inscribed :— '

"P. M. Georgii Abercrombie de Tulibodie, beneficentiæ et liberalitati assueti, injuriarum immemoris, beneficii memoris, cognatis benefici, amicis grati, vicinis chari; ob incorruptam mentem, inviolatam fidem, in justo proposito constantiam, veræ amicitiæ cultum, simulatæ odium et opportunam festivitatem, nemini secundi: ad extremum usque spiritum, vitam egit immaculatam, cœlebs vixit et obiit 26, die mensis Junii, anno Dom. 1699. Ætat 74. In cujus commemorationem, et benignitatis erga adoptivum meritissimam recordationem, sepulchrale, hoc monumentum extruxit Alexander Abercrombie. Nec curo me, ipse incertus quo periturus."

By the following inscription on a handsome cenotaph is commemorated General Sir Ralph Abercromby, the hero of Alexandria :—

"General Sir Ralph Abercromby, K.B., eldest son of the late George Abercromby, Esq., of Tullibody, and Mary Dundas, daughter of the late Ralph Dundas, Esq., of Manor, was mortally wounded in a battle, fought 21st March, 1801, with the French near Alexandria, in Egypt; and died the 28th of said month on board of a ship in the Bay of Aboukir; and interred at Malta, with Military Honours. Aged 66 years."

Ralph Abercromby was born in 1738, and entered the army as a cornet of dragoons in 1756. From 1774 to 1780 he represented the county of Kinross in Parliament. He was afterwards professionally engaged in Flanders and Holland; he served under the Duke of York in the campaigns of 1794 and 1795. He was in 1795 appointed commander-in-chief of the troops employed against the French in the West Indies; his successes in this expedition were signally brilliant. Having held the successive offices of Governor of the Isle of Wight and Commander-in-Chief in Ireland and Scotland, he became first commander of the expedition for restoring the Prince of Orange as Stadtholder. He afterwards distinguished himself at the landing at Aboukir on the 8th March, 1801, and on the 21st of the same month gained the great battle of Alexandria. From the effects of a musket wound received in action he expired a few days thereafter. To his memory a monument was reared in St. Paul's Cathedral, and his widow was created a baroness.

The Baroness Abercromby, relict of Sir Ralph Abercromby, is interred in the church of Tullibody. Her monument is thus inscribed :—

"Mary Ann, daughter of John Menzies, Esq., of Fern Tower, Baroness Abercromby, Widow of General Sir Ralph Abercromby, was born the 4th day of April, 1747, and died 11th February,

1821; possessed of every gentle virtue that adorns the female character, she fulfilled in an exemplary manner as a Wife, a Mother, and a Friend, every duty of this life; while in its vicissitudes her faith and piety never ceased to anticipate a better."

Memorial tablets commemorate George, Baron Abercromby, and his amiable baroness. The inscriptions are as follow:—

"Sacred to the Memory of Montague, Baroness Abercromby, born 30th April, 1772, died 10th March, 1837. After a long and severe illness, when returning strength seemed to hold out the promise of future health, she was unexpectedly removed from the midst of her family and friends. Those who knew her require no monument to keep her in their affectionate remembrance, but when they like her shall have been gathered to their rest, this tablet may then serve to remind her descendants that born to high station she formed the centre round which the affections of her family clung, while she was the channel through which comfort and happiness were diffused over the wide circle of all around her. Her remains were committed to the tomb amidst the heartfelt tears of those who had known her and loved her in life, and in the humble hope of her resurrection to an eternal reward through the merits of her Redeemer."

" Here, by the side of his beloved partner in life, repose the mortal remains of George, Baron Abercromby, Lord Lieutenant of the county of Stirling. He was the eldest son of General Sir Ralph Abercromby, and Mary Ann Menzies, and was born on the 14th October, 1770. For many years he represented his native county of Clackmannan in Parliament. While he abstained from mingling in the strife of party, he quietly but earnestly advanced the true interests of his country ; in the promotion of which he bore his part, and lived to see accomplished many most important legislative measures. Residing on his property, he justly earned for himself the title of an upright magistrate, a kind landlord, and a generous friend. To the oppressed he was ever open, and his sound judgment always at their service ; and the unfeigned tears of the poor bore testimony to his never-failing but unostentatious charity. Beloved by his children, esteemed by all who had the good fortune to know him, and in full reliance on the merits and mercies of his Redeemer, he closed his mortal career on the 18th February, 1843, bequeathing to those who follow him a bright example of spotless integrity, unwearied benevolence, and unaffected piety."

George Ralph, Baron Abercromby, son of the preceding, is cele-brated thus :—

"In Memory of George Ralph, 2nd Baron Abercromby, Lieu-tenant-Colonel in the Army and Lord Lieutenant of the County of Clackmannan. He was born on the 30th of May, 1800, and after enduring for several years the calamity of the loss of sight with great patience and cheerful resignation to the will of God, was suddenly removed by death on the 25th of June, 1852. 'Watch therefore, for ye know not what hour your Lord cometh ; but the end of all things is at hand ; be ye therefore sober, and watch unto prayer.' "

In Tullibody churchyard an exposed sarcophagus is known as the *Maiden's Stone.* According to tradition, Peter Beaton, priest of Tullibody, about the year 1449 became enamoured of Martha, only child of Wishart, laird of Myreton. In the hope that her lover would renounce his priestly vows, the lady reciprocated his affec-tion. He proved insincere. Lured by the prospect of ecclesiastical advancement, he forsook the maiden, who died of blighted affection. As her dying request, she entreated her father to enclose her remains in a sarcophagus, to be placed at the door by which her unworthy lover entered the church to perform his priestly offices. The position has not been changed.

PARISH OF CLACKMANNAN.

The parish church contains the remains of many members of the illustrious House of Bruce.* Within the church a monument commemorates Robert Bruce, of Kennet, one of the Senators of the College of Justice, who died 8th April, 1785, aged sixty-six; also his son, Alexander Bruce, of Kennet, who died 12th July, 1808. In the churchyard a monument celebrates the late Robert Bruce, of Kennet ; it is inscribed thus :—

* Lothian's "Alloa and its Environs," p. 60.

"Robert Bruce, Esq., born at Kennet, 8th December, 1785. In 1813 he entered the army, and served in the Grenadier Guards in the Peninsula and at Waterloo. Beloved and lamented he died at Kennet, 13th August, 1864."

Mr. Bruce was son of Alexander Bruce of Kennet, and grandson of Robert Bruce of Kennet, Lord of Session. From 1820 to 1824 he was Member of Parliament for the county of Clackmannan; he was afterwards Convener of the County, and having an aptitude for business he obtained many other public offices. Some years before his death he was a claimant for the Burleigh Peerage, as heir of line through his great-grandmother. In 1868 the House of Peers affirmed the claim to his son, Alexander Hugh Bruce, who on the reversal of the attainder the year following assumed the title of Baron Burleigh.

In Clackmannan churchyard a monument, erected by William Wylie, farmer, commemorates his children. His second son, James, a physician, settled in Russia, and became medical attendant to the Emperor Nicholas. He received the honour of knighthood, and amassed a large fortune. Sir James Wylie died at St. Petersburg in February, 1854, aged eighty-six.

Tombstones commemorate the Rev. Robert Moodie, D.D., minister of the parish, who died 30th April, 1832; the Rev David Lindsay, who died 21st October, 1834; and the Rev. Peter Balfour, minister of the parish, who died 18th March, 1862, in his sixty-eighth year, and thirty-fourth of his ministry.

PARISH OF DOLLAR.

In a sequestered spot by the bank of the Devon is the burial-place of the family of Tait, formerly of Harviestoun. On a handsome monument the late Crawfurd Tait is thus celebrated:—

"Crawfurd Tait, Esq. of Harviestoun, died May, 1832, aged 67. His taste adorned this lovely valley, in the bosom of which he lies. His genius, in advance of the age in which he lived, originated in a great measure the improvement of the district, and pointed the way to much throughout the country destined to be accomplished by a future generation. His children, thankful for Abraham's gift, a Tomb, and the promise of a Redeemer, here record his name in humble hope that, though the place which knew him shall know him no more, he has, through Christ, found a home 'not made with hands, eternal in the heavens.' "

The poet Burns was entertained by Mr. Tait at Harviestoun; he composed, in memorial of his visit, his songs commencing " How pleasant the banks of the clear winding Devon," and " Sweetest maid on Devon's banks." Mr. Tait's youngest son, Dr. Archibald Campbell Tait, born 22nd December, 1811, was on the 4th February, 1869, enthroned as Archbishop of Canterbury.

Colonel Tait, third son of Crawfurd Tait, of Harviestoun, is on his monument commemorated in these lines :—

"To the Memory of Colonel Thomas F. Tait, C.B., and A.D.C. to the Queen, third son of Crawfurd Tait, Esq., of Harviestoun. He served in India with much distinction, commanding the Third Bengal Irregular Cavalry (Tait's Horse) in the campaigns of Affghanistan, the Sutlej, and the Punjaub. He died on 16th March, 1859, surrounded by his brothers and sisters in the house of his youngest brother, the Bishop of London, and is buried at Fulham.

Loving Brother,
Faithful Friend,
Gallant Soldier,
Rest in Christ."

To the credit of this amiable and excellent family we present an inscription from another monument, celebrating two of their domestics :—

" Sacred to the Memory of Betty Morton and Mary Russell, who lived as faithful nurses and servants in the family of Crawfurd Tait, Esq., of Harviestoun, the former for 30, the latter for 50 years.

" Not with eyeservice as menpleasers, but as the servants of Christ,—

" They cherished our childhood,
They comforted our youth."

"They directed our thoughts to that heavenly country, where, through our Redeemer's love, we hope to meet them again.

"Erected by the family,—1856."

In Dollar churchyard a monumental tablet commemorates the Rev. John Gray, of Teasses, minister of the parish, who died 16th February, 1745, in his sixty-fifth year and forty-fifth of his ministry. For many years Mr. Gray acted as a private banker, much to the convenience of his neighbours and his own prosperity. There are tombstones commemorating the Rev. John Watson, minister of the parish, who died 16th December, 1815, and his successor, the Rev. Andrew Mylne, D.D., who died 27th October, 1856, in his eighty-first year, and forty-first of his ministry. Dr. Mylne was author of several educational works.

FIFESHIRE.

PARISH OF ABBOTSHALL.

IN the parish churchyard is the family burial-place of Sir Andrew Ramsay of Abbotshall. This notable person was son of the Rev. Andrew Ramsay, successively minister of Arbuthnot, and of Greyfriars, and the Old Church, Edinburgh, and Principal of the university of that city. Engaging in mercantile concerns in the capital, he was in 1654 elected Provost of Edinburgh, and held that civic office for many years. In 1667 he obtained authority from Charles II. to assume the designation of Lord Provost, with precedence similar to that enjoyed by the Lord Mayor of London. He was sworn of the Privy Council and admitted an ordinary lord of session on the 23rd November, 1671. Dreading impeachment for malversation as a magistrate, he retired from the office of Lord Provost, and from his judgeship in November, 1673. He afterwards resided on his estate of Abbotshall, where he died, 17th January, 1688.

In the parish church an elegant monument celebrates Robert Ferguson, of Raith, Lord Lieutenant of Fifeshire. This amiable and accomplished gentleman was born in 1767. He passed advocate in 1791, and afterwards engaged in Continental travel. Detained in France by the Government of the Revolution, he became an associate of the celebrated Baron Cuvier, and was elected a member of the Institute. In 1806 he was chosen M.P. for Fifeshire. After the passing of the Reform Bill he was returned to Parliament for the Kirkcaldy burghs. In 1837 he was appointed

Lord Lieutenant of Fifeshire. He died at London, 3rd December, 1840.

In the grounds of Raith, in an elevated and picturesque spot, an altar-tomb commemorates the late Colonel Robert Munro Ferguson, of Raith, son of General Sir Ronald Ferguson, G.C.B., of Raith. This estimable gentleman was born in 1802. Entering the army, he became Lieutenant-Colonel Commandant of the 79th Regiment. Succeeding to the estate of Raith in 1841, he was elected M.P. for the Kirkcaldy burghs, which he continued to represent till 1862. Colonel Ferguson died at Raith on the 27th November, 1868.

PARISH OF ABDIE.

In the parish churchyard Alexander and John Bethune, two ingenious brothers in humble life, are interred in the same grave. These remarkable persons were born in the condition of agricultural labourers. The elder brother was only a few months at school; the younger was entirely self-taught. Amidst the toils incident to a life of manual labour, they contrived to surmount the disadvantages of their humble lot; they procured books, and obtained an acquaintance with general literature. Alexander published "Tales and Sketches of the Scottish Peasantry;" John composed admirable verses, which were published posthumously. To a native delicacy of constitution both the brothers early succumbed. John died in 1839, at twenty-seven; Alexander in 1843, at thirty-nine. On a plain tombstone, erected at the brothers' grave, are inscribed these lines :—

> " This is a place of fear, the firmest eye
> Hath quailed to see its shadowy dreaminess;
> But Christian hope and heavenly prospects high,
> And earthly cares and nature's weariness,
> Have made the timid pilgrim cease to fear,
> And long to end his peaceful journey here."

PARISH OF ABERCROMBIE.

Attached to the ruin of the old parish church of Abercrombie is the ancient burial-place of the House of Abercrombie of that ilk. Built in the western gable of the church an old tombstone bears, in raised letters, these words :—

"Here lyes ane honourable man, Thomas Abercrombie, of that ilk, quha deceased in the yeir ——."

In the centre of the tombstone is engraved the family shield, representing three boars' heads, the armorial insignia of the house. Thomas Abercrombie died about the year 1520. He was ancestor of the Abercrombies, baronets of Birkenbog, and of the Lords Abercromby and Dunfermline.

Disused as a place of worship since 1646, when the parishes of Abercrombie and St. Monance were conjoined, the area of the church forms the burial-place of the Anstruthers, baronets of Balcaskie, and of the parochial incumbents. On the south wall of the church, a monument commemorates Sir Philip Anstruther, second baronet of Balcaskie, who died in 1763. He was succeeded in the baronetcy and estates by Robert, his eldest son, who also is interred and commemorated in the church. He died 2nd August, 1818. The eldest son of this baronet, Brigadier-General Robert Anstruther was the companion-in-arms of Sir John Moore. He commanded the rearguard of the army at Corunna. From the fatigue endured in the battle he died on the 14th January, and was interred in the north-east bastion of the citadel of Corunna. Sir John Moore was by his express desire buried by his side. In the east gable of Abercrombie church a handsome monument celebrates his valour and patriotism.

Sir Ralph Abercrombie Anstruther, fourth baronet, elder son.of General Anstruther, is celebrated by a monument on the north wall of the church. Born on the 12th March, 1804, he entered the army and became a captain in the Grenadier Guards. Succeeding his grandfather in 1818, he thereafter devoted himself to the improvement of his estates. For many years he was Convener of the County. On the 20th December, 1859, he was chosen Rector of the University of St. Andrews, being the first layman who ever held that office. After a period of failing health, he died on the 18th August, 1863.

Sir Ralph married, in 1831, Mary Jane, eldest daughter of Major-General Sir Henry Torrens, K.C.B. In Abercrombie church a small marble monument commemorates Sarah, wife of Sir Henry, and daughter of Colonel Robert Paton, of Kinaldy, sometime Governor of St. Helena.

A mural tablet commemorates the Rev. Robert Swan, minister of the parish, who died 16th November, 1849, in the seventy-seventh year of his age, and forty-sixth of his ministry.

In the churchyard a massive tombstone, of Aberdeen granite, commemorates the family of Cooper, who for 350 years rented the farm of Stenton, in this parish. From a branch of this family, which removed to England, the poet Cowper is believed to have been descended.

A handsome obelisk celebrates John Rodger, of St. Monance, one of the representatives of the Roxburghshire family of Roger, which early settled in Fifeshire.

By a Latin inscription an old tombstone commemorates Robert Nicol, physician, in Cupar, who died in 1579, aged seventy-two years. On an altar-stone is inscribed the name of Alexander Ireland, "who deceased in the fear of God, 1639, aged 52 years."

The churchyard of St. Monance surrounds the church of that name, a fine Gothic structure, reared in 1366 by David II., in honour of St. Monan,* and which was restored in 1827 under the superintendence of Sir Walter Scott. In the church were buried the Barons of Newark, including the celebrated General David

---

* Monamus or Monan was Archdeacon of St. Andrews. With Adrian, Bishop of St. Andrews, and many others, he was slain by the Danes in the Monastery of the Isle of Mary, about the year 874 (Breviary of Aberdeen).

Leslie. In the north transept a handsome marble cenotaph commemorates Lieutenant Henry Anstruther, who fell at the battle of the Alma on the 20th September, 1854. Younger son of Sir Ralph A. Anstruther, Bart., he was born on the 4th June, 1836. In his sixteenth year he entered the army as ensign of the 23rd Royal Welsh Fusiliers, and from his soldierly qualities afforded excellent promise of professional eminence. He died in his eighteenth year. His monument bears that it was reared by residents on his father's estates, " as a tribute to his simple faith, affectionate heart, and undaunted courage, and as a token of their deep sorrow for his early but glorious death."

In St. Monance churchyard rest the remains of Thomas Mathers, fisherman, an ingenious poet. With a limited education, and amidst a career of severest toil, Mathers contrived to cherish the lyric Muse. He published a volume entitled "Musings in Verse," which contains much respectable poetry. He died on the 25th September, 1851, aged fifty-seven. From tombstones in St. Monance churchyard we have the following quaint inscriptions. Of Mrs. Barron, of Barron Hall, her survivor remarks,—

> " Her excellence indeed to all
> Was so brilliant and rare,
> That very few in social life
> Could once with her compare."

On the tombstone of one who died young are these lines :—

> " My dear relations, pray again,
> Obey the Lord, and follow me ;
> Prepare for death, make no delay,
> You see God soon took me away."

PARISH OF ABERDOUR.

Near the west end of the parish church is the ancient burial-vault of the Earls of Morton. The vault, which is in a state of entire disrepair, has strewn on its surface the remains of eight leaden coffins. One of these is inscribed with the name of James, fifteenth Earl of Morton, who died 13th October, 1768. This noble representative of the House of Douglas was devoted to scientific pursuits, and founded the Philosophical Society of Edinburgh. He was elected President of the Royal Society, and was a Trustee of the British Museum.

In the side wall of the church a tablet commemorates the Rev· Robert Blair, minister of St. Andrews, who died at Meikle Couston, in this parish, on the 27th August, 1666. This distinguished divine was born at Irvine, Ayrshire, in 1593. He studied at the University of Glasgow, and was appointed a regent of that college in his twenty-second year. He afterwards ministered to a Presbyterian congregation at Bangor, in Ireland. Intending to emigrate to New England with some other ministers, he proceeded on shipboard, but was driven back by a storm. Returning to Scotland he sometime ministered at Ayr; he was afterwards settled by the General Assembly at St. Andrews. In 1640 he accompanied the Scottish army into England, and assisted in negotiating the peace at Ripon. In 1645 he went to Newcastle to reason with Charles I., and on the death of Alexander Henderson was appointed his Majesty's chaplain. After the Restoration he suffered from the tyranny of Archbishop Sharpe, by whom he was prohibited from preaching within twenty miles of St. Andrews. His latter years were spent in the neighbourhood of Aberdour (Vol. I., 40, 200).

In Aberdour churchyard, Robert Moyes, who died in 1725, is celebrated thus :—

> " Here lyes interr'd below this ston
> A man of vertus rare,
> Of justice, probity, and truth,—
> Few with him could compare.
> Yea, virtues all in him combin'd
> Each one outweigh'd y other,
> Y^t in y^t place where he did live
> You'd scarce find such another,
> Yet death y^t strikes a^t all alike
> Has vanquished him at last,
> The body to ye dust has sent,
> His soul's to glory past."

The monastery of Inchcolm, situated on the island of this name in the Firth of Forth, belongs to this parish. It was founded by Alexander I. in 1123, and dedicated to St. Columba. The heart of Richard of Inverkeithing, Chamberlain of Scotland, who died in 1272, was deposited in the choir. For a course of centuries the ecclesiastics of Dunkeld buried at Inchcolm. All the monuments have disappeared.

PARISH OF ANSTRUTHER-EASTER.

In the parish church a monument commemorates Rear-Admiral William Black, a native of the place, who died in 1846. He bequeathed £14,000 to the Kirk Session for charitable purposes. His younger brother, Captain James Black, a distinguished naval officer, who died in 1835, is celebrated by a monument in the churchyard. Within the church a mural tablet, inscribed with initial letters, commemorates the Rev. John Dyks, minister of Kilrenny, who died 9th September, 1634. Mr. Dyks was an accomplished theologian, and a sufferer in the cause of Presbytery.

Near the east side of the church a marble tablet commemorates John Chalmers, merchant, father of the celebrated Dr. Thomas Chalmers, and the members of his family. It is thus inscribed :—

" Erected in 1827 by their sorrowing grandchildren,
To the Memory of
John Chalmers,
Late Merchant in Anstruther,
Who died 26th July, 1818, in the 78th year of his age.
And of his spouse,
Elizabeth Hall,
Who died 14th February, 1827, in the 77th year of her age.
' Blessed are the dead that die in the Lord.'
Within this burial-place are also interred the remains of five of
their children, viz. :

John, who died in infancy in 1785.
George, who died in 1806, aged 29.
Barbara, who died in 1808, aged 33.
Lucy, who died in 1810, aged 37.
Isabella, who died in 1824, aged 43.
And also the remains of James Chalmers, Merchant in Anstruther,
Father of John and son of the Rev. James Chalmers, Minister of the Gospel in Elie ; he died in 1788, aged 74.
Barbara Anderson,
The spouse of James Chalmers, and mother of John ;
She died in 1793, aged 85.
Christian Chalmers,
The sister of James; she died in 1793, aged 85.
Thomas Ballardie,
Late Master in the Navy, who died in 1809, aged 77.
And his spouse Elizabeth Chalmers, sister of John ;
She died in 1792, aged 50.
Jean Chalmers,
Sister of John ; she died 15th August, 1827, aged 75.

Restored in 1867 by the grandchildren of John Chalmers.
His other children not buried here, being then all dead, viz. :
William, lost in the ' Queen,' at Rio Janeiro, in 1800, aged 22.
David, died at sea, in 1811, aged 27.
Alexander, Surgeon at Kirkcaldy, died 1829, aged 35.
James, died at London, in 1839, aged 67.
Thomas, D.D., D.C.L., died at Edinburgh, in 1847, aged 67.
Helen, widow of the Rev. John McClellan, Kelton,
Died at Edinburgh, 1854, aged 67.
Patrick, died at Wishaw, in 1854, aged 64.
Jane, wife of John Morton, died in Gloucestershire, in 1864, aged 76.
Charles, died at Merchiston, Edinburgh, 1864, aged 72."

In the churchyard, reared by public subscription, a monument commemorates William Tennant, LL.D., author of "Anster Fair," and Professor of Oriental Languages in the University of St. Andrews. It is inscribed thus :—

"H. S. E.

"Gulielmus Tennant, LL.D., in Coll. Beatæ Mariæ ad fanum Andreæ L.L. orient Prof. vir magnis animi dotibus insignis doctrina multiplici et exquisita ornatus, benignitate et comitate amabilis poeta, disertus, dulcis, facetus.

" Natus in hoc oppido honesta stirpe et in Coll. S. Salv. et Divi Leon, apud Andreapolit optimis disciplinis institutus ann. xv in schola Dollariensi Litt. Humanior atque Orient. feliciter docuit deinde in almæ matris sinum revocatus ibi annos fere xiv officio cumulate satisfecit tandem senio infirmaque valetudine confectus magno suorum et bonorum omnium desiderio supremum obiit diem Dollariae id Octobrib. A.D. MDCCCXLVIII et hic loci xiv proxim kal. Nov. inter cineres avorum conditus est. Vixit annos LXIV menses v. dies. x."

Dr. Tennant was son of a small trader in Anstruther, where he was born on the 16th May, 1784. Being malformed in both his limbs, his parents sought to qualify him as a teacher. After studying at the University of St. Andrews for two sessions, he became clerk to his brother, a corn-factor, in Anstruther, while he devoted his leisure hours to self-culture. In 1813 he was elected schoolmaster of Dunino, near St. Andrews, and three years afterwards obtained the more lucrative office of parish teacher at Lasswade, near Edinburgh. In 1819 he was elected Classical Master of Dollar Academy, and in 1834 was promoted to the Professorship of Oriental Languages in St. Mary's College, St. Andrews. He died at Devongrove, near Dollar, on the 15th October, 1848. His poem "Anster Fair" appeared in 1812. He published a " Synopsis of Syriac and Chaldaic Grammar," and other works.

PARISH OF ANSTRUTHER-WESTER.

A portion of a sarcophagus resting against the wall of the parish church is said to have belonged to St. Adrian, and to have been brought thither from the Isle of May. This islet is situated at the mouth of the Firth of Forth, about six miles distant from the Fifeshire coast. It contains a ruinous monastery, dedicated to St. Adrian. Reared by David I., it was designated " The

Priory of St. Ethernan, or St. Colman." It contains the remaining portion of St. Adrian's coffin. Adrian was Bishop of St. Andrews in the latter half of the ninth century. During an incursion of the Danes he took refuge, with some ecclesiastics and a large number of the Christian population, in the ancient monastery of this island, which, however, proved no respected sanctuary, for all were massacred.

In the churchyard of Anstruther-wester an old tombstone, which has recently disappeared, bore the name of Friar Haldane, who ministered in the parish about the middle of the fifteenth century.

At the east end of the church a tombstone denotes the resting-place of John Fairfull, minister of the parish, who died in 1626, aged eighty. He was father of Andrew Fairfowl, Bishop of Glasgow (Vol. I., 114).

A tombstone marks the grave of Erskine Conolly, an ingenious and short-lived poet. Born at Crail on the 12th June, 1796, he was at an early age apprenticed to a bookseller in Anstruther. After some changes he engaged in legal pursuits, and practised as a solicitor in Edinburgh. He died on the 7th January, 1843. He composed "Mary Macneil," and other songs.

An altar tombstone commemorates William Thomson, a magistrate of the burgh, who died in 1797; he bequeathed £650 to the parochial funds, of which the greater portion was to be employed in founding a bursary in connection with the University of St. Andrews.

PARISH OF AUCHTERMUCHTY.

The gravestone of David Ferry, schoolmaster, who died 1st June, 1726, aged 62, is inscribed thus :—

" Here doth a good man's aged ashes dwell,
    Who conquer'd death by faith before he fell ;

He's fond to flit into a proper sphere,
Who traffics long with heaven and lives by prayer.
In all the learning of the schools deep skill'd,
Poor students found him generous and kind,
On his love-feasts they very often dined ;
He fed at once their body and their mind.
No miser many of his goods did share,
Food to the needy gave, and clothed the bare,
Grace and good nature thro' his actions ran,
By heaven approv'd, and loved of every man,
Reader, receive instruction from this stone,
And imitate his virtues when he's gone."

On his tombstone Andrew Richardson, farmer, is thus com
memorated :—

"Beneath this burial-stone a tenant lys,
Nam'd Andrew Richardson, in Ridie Leys,
Who died in May,
The seventeenth day, 1736.
A husbandman he was, who ploughed with art,
In hope he sow'd, and thereof did partake,
With skill the produce of the earth improv'd,
And to his wife and children, whom he lov'd,
With judgment he bequeathed his honest gain,
When death to him appear'd, and to remain
No more on earth did give the last command,
Which neither king nor peasant can withstand,
In which he acquiesc'd and bow'd his head,
Submissive to the Divine will and died.
Belov'd by all, by his dear wife lamented,
Who on her proper charge this stone erected,
His name to transmit to posterity
With this MEMENTO, 'Thou and I must die.'"

PARISH OF BALMERINO.

The Abbey of Balmerino was founded in 1227 by Queen
Ermengarde, daughter of Richard de Beaumont, and second wife
of William the Lion. She died on the 11th February, 1233, and

near the high altar of Balmerino Abbey her remains were honourably entombed. The spot is unmarked.

Within the aisle of the old church are the sepulchral enclosures of the old families of Morrison of Naughton, and Scrimgeour-Wedderburn of Birkhill. A branch of the family of Stark also inter in the aisle.

In the parish churchyard a tombstone bears, in raised letters, the following inscription:—"Her layes ane faithful sestre Isabel Ramsay, spovs to Alexandr Mathev of Kirktovn of Balmerinoh, quha depertit the 8 day of Octobre, anno 1596, of age 61." The stone bears the arms of Matthew impaled with those of Ramsay.

A tombstone belonging to the sixteenth century is thus inscribed:—" Heir lyis ane honest man and faithful callit George Ramsay Burges and Brother Gild of Dundie and portioner of Boddumcraig, quha depairtit yis present lyfe 15 of December, and of his age 90."

Tombstones commemorate Margaret Henderson, wife of James Knox, in Peasehil, who died in February, 1673; Christian Glen, portioner of Cultra and Bottomcraig, and spouse of John Wan, in St. Fort, who died in 1687, aged 67; and John Wyllie, parish schoolmaster, who died 17th December, 1705.

A granite monument celebrates Robert Donaldson, of Rosebank, Aberdeenshire, founder of the Donaldson Fund for religious and educational purposes in the counties of Fife and Aberdeen. Mr. Donaldson was born in the adjacent parish of Kilmany, and died at Rosebank, 17th April, 1829, in his eightieth year.

From tombstones in Balmerino churchyard we have the following metrical epitaphs—the latter being a variation from Pope :—

> " O father, mother, and brother dear,
> Weep not for us, though sleeping here,
> For in one time we think to rise,
> And strive to gain the glorious prize."

> " Whoe'er thou art, O mortal man, draw near,
> Here lies the friend most loved, the spouse most dear,

Who ne'er knew joy that friendship might divide,
Or gave her husband grief but when she died.
How vain is reason ! eloquence how weak !
The husband feels beyond what he can speak !
Oh, let thy once-loved friend inscribe thy stone,
And with his children's sorrows mix his own."

PARISH OF BURNTISLAND.

In the parish churchyard are numerous mottoes illustrative of
the brevity and uncertainty of life. The following are specimens :—

"Read here as you pass by,
Look on this grave wherein I lie ;
From cares and sorrow I'm set free,
Mourn for yourselves, but not for me."

"No mortal man
Can reach the peaceful sleepers here,
While angels watch their soft repose."

"How soon this life is past and gone,
And death comes softly stealing on !
Then let us choose that narrow way
Which leads no traveller's foot astray."

PARISH OF CARNBEE.

In the churchyard a tombstone commemorates Robert Gillespie
Smyth, of Gibliston ; major in the County Militia, and a Deputy
Lieutenant. Son of Dr. James Gillespie, Principal of St. Mary's
College, St. Andrews, he was born in that city on the 4th February,
1777. He assumed the name of Smyth on his marriage with the
heiress of Gibliston. He died at Gibliston on the 11th November,
1855. Mr. Smyth was esteemed for his beneficence.

PARISH OF CARNOCK.

In the parish churchyard a monument celebrates the Rev. John Row, minister of the parish, and author of a History of the Church of Scotland. It contains in raised letters the following epitaph :—

"Hic jacet M. Jo. Row, pastor hujus Ecclesiæ Fidelissimus : vixit acerrimus veritatis et fœderis Scoticani assertor : Hierarchias Pseudo-episcopalis et Romanorum rituum cordicitus osor : in frequenti symmistarum apostasia cubi instar constantissimus. Duxit Griselidem Fergussonam, cum qua annis 51 conjunctissime vixit. Huic Ecclesiæ annis 54 præfuit. Obiit Iunii 26, anno Dom. 1646, ætatis 78. Obiit et illa Januarii 30, 1659."

Mr. Row was third son of John Row, minister of Perth, a celebrated reformer, who first introduced into Scotland the study of Hebrew literature. He was born in January, 1568. After teaching in different places, he was ordained minister of Aberdour in 1592. In July, 1606, he signed the Protest to Parliament against the introduction of Episcopacy. He was summoned before the Court of High Commission in 1619, and confined to his parish. He was a member of the celebrated General Assembly of 1638. He died in 1646, in the seventy-eighth year of his age, and fifty-fourth of his ministry. His "History of the Kirk of Scotland from 1558 to 1637" has been published by the Wodrow Society.

On Mr. Row's monument are commemorated Margaret Gibbon, his grandchild, and her husband, Adam Stobie, of West Luscar. Mr. Stobie, who died in 1711, was a zealous Covenanter, and harboured many ministers and others who were persecuted by the Government of Charles II. He was some time imprisoned in the Bass, and was condemned to transportation beyond seas, but the vessel in which he sailed landed on the coast of England, and he was permitted to escape.

PARISH OF CERES.

In the family mausoleum rest the remains of John, twentieth Earl of Crawford, who is appropriately commemorated. This eminent military commander was eldest son of John, nineteenth Earl of Crawford, and was born on the 4th October, 1702. He entered the army in 1726, but subsequently held several offices at Court, and sat in the House of Lords as a representative peer. Desirous of military distinction, he served in the army of the Emperor of Germany, then at war with France; he distinguished himself at the battle of Claussen, in October, 1735. He next volunteered into the Russian service, joining the army of Field-Marshal Munich in his expedition against the Turks. In a sanguinary battle, fought on the 26th July, 1738, with the Turks and Tartars, he accompanied the Cossacks, and greatly distinguished himself by his dexterity. At the battle of Krotzka, near Belgrade, he was severely wounded in the left thigh. Returning to England he found himself advanced to the colonelcy of the Grenadier Guards. At the battle of Dettingen, fought on the 16th of July, 1743, he commanded the brigade of the Life Guards, acting with his usual skill and intrepidity. He distinguished himself at the battle of Fontenoy, in April, 1746, conducting the retreat in admirable order. During the Scottish Rebellion of 1745 he commanded the corps of 6,000 Hessians. He afterwards rejoined the army in the Netherlands, and evinced his accustomed valour at the battle of Roucoux, in October, 1746. After some other important services, he died at London on the 23rd December, 1749.

PARISH OF COLLESSIE.

In the parish churchyard a mortuary enclosure contains the remains of Sir James Melville, of Hallhill, the great diplomatist and statesman. On one of the walls is the following inscription :—

" Ye loadin' pilgrims passing langs this way,
    Paus on your fall, and your offences past,
For your frail flesh, first formit of the clay,
    In dust mon be dissolvit at the last.
Repent, amend, on Christ the burden cast,
Of your sad sinnes who can your savls refresh,
Syne raise from grave to gloir your grislie flesh.

" Defyle not Christ's kirk with your carion,
    A solemn sait for God's service prepar'd,
For praier, preaching, and communion,
    Your byrial should be in the kirk yard.
On your uprising set your great regard,
When savll and body joynes with joy to ring,
In heaven, for ay, with Christ our Head and King."

Third son of the proprietor of Raith, Fifeshire, Sir James Melville, was born about the year 1535. He was page of honour to Queen Mary, when she was Consort of the Dauphin, and some time served under the Constable of France. He was afterwards employed by the Elector Palatine in negotiating with the German princes. In 1564 he returned to Scotland, when he was nominated a Privy Councillor. In two embassies to the English Court he announced to Queen Elizabeth the proposed marriage of his royal mistress with Lord Darnley, and the birth of James VI. He opposed Queen Mary's marriage with Bothwell, but subsequently gave his acquiescence and was present at the ceremony. By James VI. Melville was employed in various responsible offices. He died 1st November, 1607. His " Memoirs," written for the use of his son, have been published.

PARISH OF CRAIL.

Within the parish church is preserved an ancient Runic cross. On its right side are a portion of a horse, a wild boar, the legs of a man, a second horse, and a ram. On the left side are presented a figure seated in a chair with the head of a bird, a portion of a horse and part of a dog.

In the north-west corner of the churchyard is an elegant monument, belonging to the old House of Lumsdaine, of Airdrie. With the date 1598 is this inscription :—

"Prima decus thalamos et opes mihi contulit ætas
Proxima et immeritis aucta periatis malis
Vivere cum decore vixi, quod defuit ævi
Mortalis, nobis vita beata dedit."

An undated mural monument, of simple form, in the west wall of the churchyard celebrates John Douglas in these lines :—

"Of doughty Douglas, kind he came,
And so he did well prove ;
He livèd always in good fame,
And died with all men's love."

A son of General Scott, of Balcomie, who died young, is interred in the church.

In the churchyard a handsome monument commemorates Robert Inglis, of Kirkmay, who died 6th January, 1834, aged sixty-one. A native of the parish, Mr. Inglis realized a fortune in India : he was distinguished for his beneficence.

From a plain gravestone we have the following :—

"Here lies a woman who was virtuous inclined,
She was not in the least to any vice inclined ;
Though to her praise but little is set forth,
Blame ye my pen, but magnify her worth."

PARISH OF CREICH.

A tombstone discovered in the parish church, under the pavement, represents a man clad in mail, and a lady in an embroidered robe. On two shields are emblazoned the arms of the families of Barclay and Douglas. On the bevelled edge of the stone is the following inscription:—

"Hic jacet David Barclay de . . . us de . . . qui obiit die mensis . . . anno diy. M^mo CCCC.
"Hic jacet Helena de Douglas uxor predicity qui obiit XXIX die mensis Januarii anno di°. M° CCCCXXI."

In the churchyard rest the remains of David Cook, of Carphin and Luthrie, who died 8th June, 1865. Mr. Cook was a native of Auchterderran; as an engineer in Glasgow he attained a large fortune. His latter years were spent in the quiet exercise of benevolence.

PARISH OF CULTS.

On Walton Hill is the modern mausoleum of the noble House of Crawford. It is of Greek architecture, and was raised by James, the fifth earl.

In the parish church, a monument sculptured by Chantrey commemorates the Rev. David Wilkie, minister of the parish; it was erected by his son, Sir David Wilkie, the eminent painter. Mr. Wilkie was born on the farm of Ratho-byres, near Edinburgh, in 1738. Licensed to preach in May, 1770, he was ordained minister of Cults in April, 1774. He died 30th November, 1812, in his seven-fourth year, and the thirty-ninth of his ministry.

A tombstone in the churchyard is thus inscribed:—

"Here lies, retired from mortal strife,
A man who lived a happy life,—
A happy life—and sober too,
A thing that all men ought to do."

PARISH OF CUPAR.

In the parish burial-ground a monument, supposed to have been executed in Holland, celebrates the Rev. William Scott, minister of

the first charge, and an eminent upholder of Presbyterianism.
Son of Robert Scott, in Mylnedene, and "eighty-third" in descent
from the ancient family of Balwearie, Mr. Scott took his degree at
the University of St. Andrews, in November, 1586. He was ordained minister of Kennoway in 1593, and was translated to Cupar
in 1604. One of the eight ministers summoned to London in 1606,
he was permitted to return to his parish in 1607, where he continued
keenly to oppose episcopal tendencies. He was a member of the
General Assembly of 1618, and opposed the five articles then
agreed to. He died on the 20th May, 1642. At his own cost he
built the spire of the parish church, and he bequeathed funds for
the education of poor children. His monument is inscribed
thus :—

" Scotis resuscitatis, Anglis excitatis, renovato fœdere reparata
religione, prostrata hierarchia, restituto presbyterio, succenturian-
tibus illustrissimis e prima nobilitate et ministerio bene meritis in
ecclesiam, nunquam satis memorandis, confirmante Cæsare Bri-
tannico, adstipulantibus regni ordinibus, obiit placidissime in
Domino unus, qui nobis cunctando restituit rem, Gulielmus Scotus,
ecclesiæ Cuprensis pastor, ex illustri et antiquissima familia Scoto-
Balviriana 849, anno æræ Christi MDCXLII. A.D. cal. Junii 13."

A tombstone denotes the burial-place of the Rev. James
Wedderburn, senior, and his son who bore the same Christian
name. Both father and son were ministers of Moonzie. Their
tombstone bears the following epitaph :—

" Sepulchrum Magistri Jacobi Wedderburni, viri pietate eximia
et præclaris dotibus aucti ; ecclesiæ Munsiæ fidelissimi pastoris :
qui obiit 23 die Julii, A.D. MDCLXXXVII. ætatis suæ 52. Cum
patre, jacet optimæ spei filius Gulielmus Wedderburn ; qui obiit
paulo ante patrem nono die Julii MDCLXXXVII.

" Hic, cum prole, parens una requiescit in urna,
  Marmore dignus erat genitor : lunaris ocelli
  Lux, solis radiis lustrata et lucida stella :
  Et proles tanto fuit haud indigna parente,
  Hic febre in fluvio periit. Proh ! tristia fata
  Attingunt unum, quæ sunt contraria, finem,
  Unda ignis cœlo ponunt, cum prole parentem."

In the churchyard a tombstone formerly bore these lines :—

"Davidis hic corpus Forrethi dormitur altum;
Mens, evecta polum, Christo duce, pace potitur :
Aucupis in terris celebrata est fama superstes.
Post undena suæ vitæ bene lustra peractæ
Gloriam in excelsis, nunc cum jove fando triumphat."

David Forret was a cadet of the family of Forret of that ilk. To the family belonged Thomas Forret, vicar of Dollar, an early upholder of the reformed doctrines, and who, at the instance of Archbishop Beaton, was burned at Edinburgh on the 28th February, 1538.

A monument commemorative of James Bethune, M.D., of Nether Tarbet, was thus inscribed :—

"Monumentum pii et generosi D.D. Jacobi Bethune, medicinæ doctoris, Tarbet inferioris domini ; qui obiit 4 cal. Januarii, 1680. Ætatis anno 77.

"Hippocrates alter fuit hic heros, medicinæ
Artibus et musis semper amicus erat;
Belgis ac Italis, Gallis simul atque Britannis
Nota fuit virtus ingeniique vigor.
Ille, forisque domi clarus, cecidit, remanente
Jucunda prole et hic situs ipse jacet,
Pulvis es et ad pulverem redibis,
Qui legis hæc, hospes, mortis tu sæpe memento,
Beati morientes in Domino."

In the old churchyard a tombstone commemorates three sufferers for the Covenant. It is inscribed thus :—

"Here lie interred the heads of Laur Hay : and Andrew Pitulloch, who suffered martyrdom at Edinburgh, July 13th, 1681, for adhering to the word of God, and Scotland's covenanted work of reformation ; and also one of the hands of David Hackston, of Rathillet, who was most cruelly martyred at Edinburgh, July 30th, 1680.

' Our persecutors filled with rage,
Their brutish fury to assuage,
Took heads and hands of martyrs off,
That they might be the people's scoff.

They Hackston's body cut asunder,
And set it up a world's wonder
In several places; to proclaim
These monsters' glory and their shame."

David Hackston, or Haxton, was proprietor of Rathillet, in the parish of Kilmany. A zealous upholder of the Covenant, he was present at the assassination of Archbishop Sharpe, in May, 1679; he afterwards fought along with the Covenanters at the battle of Drumclog, and at Bothwell Bridge. A reward being offered for his apprehension, he was taken prisoner at Airsmoss, on the 22nd July, 1680. Carried to Edinburgh, he was subjected to trial, and being pronounced guilty was put to death with many circumstances of barbarity. The martyrs' monument was renewed in 1792.

Within the parish church, on the western wall, is a full-length statue commemorative of Sir John Arnot, of Fernie, who fell in the last Crusade. In the same wall a marble tablet celebrates the worth and ministerial fidelity of the Rev. George Campbell, D.D., minister of the parish. Dr. Campbell was son of the schoolmaster of St. Andrews, and grandson of a farmer in the parish of Cameron. Having studied at the University of St. Andrews, he obtained licence in December, 1770; in 1773 he was admitted assistant and successor in the second charge of Cupar; he was translated to the first charge in October, 1791. He died 25th November, 1824, in his seventy-eighth year, and the fifty-second of his ministry. His second son, John, joined the English bar, and was appointed Lord High Chancellor, and raised to the peerage as Baron Campbell of St. Andrews.

A gravestone marks the sepulchre of David Dickson, of Westhall, an eminent agriculturist. Mr. Dickson was largely employed as a valuator and arbiter. He died at Westhall, on the 5th January, 1859, aged seventy-five.

Near the railway bridge is a monumental statue of the late David Maitland Makgill Crichton of Rankeilour, erected by subscription. This patriotic gentleman was descended from the noble family of Lauderdale, and represented the old house of Makgill of Rankeilour; he was also heir of line of Viscount Frendraught. Son of Colonel Maitland of Rankeilour, he was born in March, 1801. He passed Advocate in 1822, but soon afterwards succeeding to the family estate, he occupied himself with rural affairs. During the Voluntary controversy he became a strenuous advocate of the Established Church, holding Church Defence meetings in different districts. In the Non-intrusion controversy he actively supported the views of the majority; and after the Disruption vigorously upheld the claims of the Free Church. He died in 1851.

In St. James's Church a monumental brass, fixed in a tablet of black marble, commemorates Lieutenant Spens, of the 42nd Regiment, son of Nathaniel Spens, of Craigsanquhar; he died at Cherat, in India, 22nd June, 1867.

On the gravestone of William Rymour, maltman, are these lines :—

> "Through Christ I'm not inferior
> To William the Conqueror."

John Crombie's monument is inscribed thus :—

> "Here rests his body, whose soul above
> Knows nothing else but joy and love;
> By death he is not hurt, although cut down;
> Life comes by death, and by his faith a crown:
> His spouse and children might lament and cry,
> Did hope not list, and wipe all tears away.

PARISH OF DALGETY.

In the old churchyard a mortuary enclosure, now built up, is the burial-place of the old Earls of Dunfermline. This noble House, now extinct, originated in the person of Alexander Seton, an eminent lawyer, third son of George, sixth Lord Seton, and brother of Robert, first Earl of Winton. Born about the year 1555, Alexander Seton studied at Rome in the College of

Jesuits, with a view to the Church; but the establishment of the reformed religion led him to adopt legal pursuits. By James VI. he was in 1583 appointed an extraordinary lord of session; he became a lord ordinary in February 1587, and was elected president of the court in May, 1593. He was one of the Octavians, or eight commissioners of the Treasury, in 1596. For nine successive years he was elected Provost of Edinburgh. · In March, 1597-8, he was, by letters under the great seal, constituted a lord of Parliament, by the title of Lord Fyvie; soon afterwards he was appointed preceptor to Prince Charles. In 1606 he was raised to the office of Lord High Chancellor, and created Earl of Dunfermline. In 1609 he was sworn a member of the English Privy Council. He was commissioner to the parliament held at Edinburgh in June, 1610, when the Act of 1592 establishing Presbyterianism was rescinded. He died at Pinkie, near Musselburgh, on the 16th June, 1622, aged sixty-seven.

Charles, son of the preceding, was second Earl of Dunfermline. A zealous adherent of the Covenant, he negotiated on the part of the Scots encamped at Dunse, the pacification with Charles I. in June, 1639. In August, 1640, he commanded a regiment in the Scots army, which, under General Leslie, crossed the Tweed and occupied the city of Dunham. In October following he was one of the Scottish Commissioners for the treaty of Ripon. From Charles I., in June, 1641, he received a long lease of the abbey of Dunfermline; he was afterwards sworn a Privy Councillor. He supported the engagement in 1648; and after the King's execution went to the Continent to wait on Charles II., whom he accompanied to Scotland in 1650. At the Restoration he obtained various offices and honours. He died in January, 1673.

The third earl died young. James, the fourth and last earl, commanded a troop of horse, under Viscount Dundee, at the battle of Killiecrankie in 1689; in the following year he was outlawed and forfeited. He died in exile in 1694. The estates reverted to the Crown.

These rhymes are from tombstones in the old churchyard :—

" A Christian true,
     To man a friend.
  A loving husband,
     Father kind."

" Here is the dust of innocence, whose breath
  Was caught by early not untimely death ;
  Hence he did go, just as he did begin
  Pain to know before he knew to sin."

" Through faith he lived, through faith he died,
  Through faith the forerunner espied ;
  With patience ran the Christian race,
  And gained the crown, the prize of grace."

PARISH OF DUNFERMLINE.

Malcolm III., surnamed Canmore, and Margaret his sainted queen, had their chief residence at Dunfermline. In the vicinity Malcolm founded, about the year 1075, the church of the Holy Trinity, which was elegantly constructed in Norman architecture. He resolved that it should supersede Iona as a place of royal sepulchre.

Holy Trinity Church had two altars—the high altar and the altar of the holy cross. Before the high altar were deposited the remains of Malcolm, the founder. He fell at the siege of Alnwick Castle, on the 13th November, 1093. His remains were at first consigned to the monastery at Tynemouth, but were about the year 1115 conveyed to Dunfermline by his son Alexander I.

Queen Margaret survived her husband only a few days. Tidings of his death, and of the mortal wound of Edward, her eldest son, overcame and prostrated her. She died in the castle of Edinburgh, and her remains were brought to Dunfermline, and there reverently deposited in Holy Trinity Church, before the altar of the holy cross. Edward, her eldest son, fell by a mortal wound in the forest of Jedwood, during the flight of the Scottish army ; his body was conveyed to Dunfermline, and laid in a sarcophagus* beside the remains of his mother. There too were sepulchred his brother Elthelred in 1094, and his brother Edmund in 1105.

Before the high altar of Holy Trinity Church were deposited the remains of Edgar, fourth son of Malcolm Canmore, who died in 1107 ; Alexander I, who died in 1124; and David I., who died in 1153. These successively occupied the throne. Here also were placed, in 1165, the remains of Malcolm IV., surnamed the Maiden.

In 1250 Alexander III. erected, in pointed Gothic, the new abbey church, close by the east end of the church of the Holy Trinity, which became the vestibule of the new structure. On the completion of the choir or Lady aisle, Queen Margaret being canonized, her remains were transferred from the outer church to the aisle, where a tomb was prepared for their reception. In the *translation*, as it was called, there was a procession, consisting of the king and ecclesiastics of highest rank, the latter bearing on their shoulders the bones of the saint collected in a silver casket. The tomb was now built up and completed. Save the plinth stones, the structure has disappeared. On the upper plinth stone are eight circular hollows, on which rested the shafts which supported the shrine. Here pilgrims from all lands met and did homage. The tomb was destroyed at the Reformation ; it is now in the open air, not having been included within the walls of the modern church.

In the church of 1250 (partly demolished at the Reformation, and entirely so in 1818, to suit the erection of the present church) were interred, near the high altar, the remains of Alexander III. (1285), and of Margaret, his queen, who predeceased him in 1274.

---

* In 1849 two stone coffins were discovered at the east end of Holy Trinity Church, a little to the west of the high altar. One of these contained a leathern shroud ; it is supposed to have enveloped the body of Prince Edward, and to have been used in transporting it from the forest of Jedwood to the place of sepulture. The other coffin had probably contained the remains of Ethelred, a younger brother of Edward, who, like himself, did not come to the throne.

Immediately in front of the high altar were sepulchred, in 1329, the remains of King Robert the Bruce. He died at Cardross, Dumbartonshire, on the 7th June, 1329. He was only fifty-five, and many of his plans were unfulfilled. Of these the most important was his vow that on the restoration of national order he would proceed to Palestine, and there give help against the infidel. To indicate his sincerity, he on his death-bed requested his friend, Sir James Douglas, to carry his heart to Jerusalem, and there deposit it in the Church of the Holy Sepulchre. Sir James sought to fulfil the dying wishes of his royal master. He set out on his journey with a suitable retinue, bearing round his neck, by a silver chain, the Bruce's heart, enclosed in a casket. In his journey through Spain he was led to assist King Alphonso against the Saracens, and fell in battle mortally wounded. The casket was secured, and brought to Scotland by Sir William Keith, and was laid in the abbey of Melrose (Vol. I., 250). The body of King Robert was deposited at Dunfermline in the sepulchre of the kings.

According to Fordun, King Robert's remains were laid in a tomb in the centre of the choir, and from the Chamberlain's Rolls it would appear that a monument, executed in France, was reared upon the spot. Traces of the monument had long disappeared when, in 1818, operations were proceeded with for the construction of the present church on the site of the ancient edifice, dedicated to the Holy Trinity. On the 17th February the workmen came upon a vault which was opened in presence of the authorities. The vault was seven and a half feet long, twenty-eight and a half inches broad, and eighteen inches deep, and was constructed of polished sandstone. On the removal of two large flat stones which covered it, an inner vault was discovered, seven feet long, and about twenty-two inches in breadth. In this lay a body encased in lead, and surrounded with detached portions of fine linen, interwoven with gold. At the breast, knees, and toes the leaden shroud was much decayed. The skeleton was nearly entire. There were some vestiges of an oak coffin; several nails used in its construction lay at the bottom of the tomb. The re-interment of the remains took place on the 5th November, 1819, in presence of two Barons of Exchequer, Sir Henry Jardine, the Queen's Remembrancer, Dr. Gregory the celebrated physician, Dr. Monro the anatomist, and the magistrates, clergy, and principal citizens. Indubitable evidence was now obtained that the remains were those of King Robert, for the breast-bone was found to have been sawn asunder, in order to the removal of the heart according to the monarch's last wish.

The king's skull was entire. A cast was taken, and phrenological ingenuity proceeded to determine the mental and moral qualities of the monarch. Mr. George Combe made the following report :— " The individual would possess great activity, courage, and determination, modified by prudence and cautiousness. He would be acute in perceiving what was presented to his mind, and decided in determining on his course of action. But his view would not be extensive. He would not see far before him what was to be the remote consequences of his present doings. He would not be naturally amiable ; but he would know how to please others when his interests required him to do so. He would be steady in his attachments, although he would not always use his friends well. He would be disposed to religion ; but his small portion of reflection and benevolence would give it a tendency to run into superstitious observances. He would be fonder of power than of money."

A measurement of the skeleton indicated that the king had stood about five feet ten inches, or perhaps a little taller. The formation of the lower jaw, which was strong and deep, indicated uncommon strength in its possessor. The upper jaw bore marks of a fracture. The entire remains were carefully collected, and placed in a leaden coffin, which was filled with melted pitch, as the best preventive of decay. On the coffin being deposited in the vault it was enclosed in a wall of brick, and carefully arched over. The present pulpit covers the tomb. On a vacant space in front it was proposed to erect a sarcophagus, and an elegant Latin inscription was composed for it by Dr. Gregory. The intention has not been realized. The square tower, which rises to the height of a hundred feet immediately over the tomb, supplies in some measure the want of any other memorial. On its summit are exhibited in open hewn work the words KING ROBERT THE BRUCE, one of the words being introduced in each of the four sides of the balustrade. Near the tomb of King Robert were deposited the remains of his second queen, Elizabeth, daughter of Aylmer de Burgh, Earl of Ulster, and mother of David II., who died in 1274; also two of his daughters, Christina and Matildas. Near the same spot were interred, in 1403, Annabella, queen of Robert III.

These notable persons were entombed within the Abbey Church: —Malcolm, Earl of Fife; Andrew, Bishop of Caithness; Thomas Randolph, Earl of Murray, in 1332; Robert, Duke of Albany, Regent of Scotland, who died 3rd September, 1420; and Andrew Forman, Archbishop of St. Andrews, who died in 1521. Robert Henryson, schoolmaster of Dunfermline, author of "Fables" and other poems, died some time before 1508, and was interred in the Abbey Church.

On the north wall of the church a monument celebrates Robert Pitcairn, commendator of the abbey, and Secretary of State. It is inscribed thus:—

"D. Roberto Pitcarnio, abbati Fermiloduni, archidecano St. Andreæ legato regio, ejusque majestati a secretis.

> Hic sitvs heros modica Robertvs in vrna
> Pictarnus, patriæ spes colvmenque suæ;
> Qvem virtvs, gravitas generoso pectore digna,
> Ornant, et cum vera pietate fides:
> Post varios vitæ flvctvs, jam mole relicta
> Corporis, elysivm pergit in vmbra nemus.
> Obiit anno 1584, 18 Octob. Ætatis 64."

The panegyric is excessive. Pitcairn's public policy was vacillating, and his private conduct was a scandal to the church and to society.*

---

* In front of his residence in Maygate, Dunfermline, Pitcairn inscribed the following couplet as a caution to his censurers:—

> "Sen' vord is thral, and thocht is fre,
> Keip veil thy tonge, I counsel the."

On the north wall of the church a monument commemorates a son of Abbot George Dury, and a modern tablet celebrates the abbot and some of his descendants. Abbot Dury was son of John Dury, of Dury, Fifeshire, and was born in 1496. Under his uncle, Archbishop Beaton, he in 1530 assumed the functions of abbot and commendator of Dunfermline, and on the death of that prelate in 1539 was promoted to the office by James V. In 1541 he was appointed an extraordinary Lord of Session. He was Keeper of the Privy Seal in 1554. He died in 1561, and was canonized by the Church of Rome, probably from his zeal in the suppression of heresy. He aided in condemning Patrick Hamilton and Walter Mill, the Protestant martyrs, and subscribed the sentence of death passed in 1540 on Sir John Borthwick. He had two illegitimate children; his descendants became proprietors of Craigluscar, in Dunfermline parish.

The monument of William Schaw, Master of Works to James VI., formerly rested against the north wall of the church. About the beginning of the century it was placed in the lower part of the steeple. It is thus inscribed :—

"Integerrimo amico Gulielmo Schaw,
Vive inter superos, æternumque optime vive ;
Hæc tibi vita labor, mors fuit alta quies,
Alexander Setonius, D.D.

"D. O. M.

" Humilis hæc lapidum structura tegit virum excellenti peritia, probitate eximia, singulari vitæ integritate, summis virtutibus ornatum, Gulielmum Schaw, regiis operibus præfectum, sacris ceremoniis præpositum, reginæ quæstorem. Extremum is diem obiit, 18 Aprilis 1602.

"Mortales inter, vixit annos quinquaginta duos ; Gallias multaque alia regna, excolendi animi studio, peragravit : nulla liberali disciplina non imbutus ; architecturæ peritissimus, principibus imprimis viris, egregiis animi dotibus commendatus ; laboribus et negotiis non indefessus modo et insuperabilis, sed assidue strenuus et integer ; nulli bono non carissimus cui notus ; ad officia et demerendos hominum animos natus ; nunc inter superos, æternum vivit.

"Anna regina, ne virtus, æterna commendatione digna, membrorum mortalitate tabesceret, optimi integerrimique viri memoriæ, monumentum poni mandavit."

On the east wall of the north porch a handsome marble monument commemorates Adam Rolland, of Gask. It has the following legend :—

"M. S. Adami Rolland de Gask, viri non uno nomine celebrandi uptote non paucis virtutibus ornati ob pietatem erga Deum amorem in patriam, benevolentiam in genus humanum amabilis; ob vitæ integritatem, morum comitatem, affectuum temperantiam, spectabilis; quisvos paterno, probos quosvis fraterno omnes benigno animo amplexus; in publicis privatisque officiis prudens, fidus, diligens ; mente et manu munificus, futurorum providus, fortunæ semper securus : Ita volente D. O. M. XII. calend. August MDCCLXIII., ætat. LVII. animam creatori, exuvias terræ, reddidit; triste sui desiderium, amicis relinquens."

On the interior walls of the church monuments commemorate William Hunt, of Pittencrieff, merchant, who died in 1788, and Major David Wilson, for many years Provost of the burgh, who died in 1822.

In the vault of the Wardlaw family are entombed the remains of Elizabeth Lady Wardlaw, authoress of the fine ballad of " Hardyknute," second daughter of Sir Charles Halket, second baronet of Pitferrane. She was born in April, 1677. She married, in June, 1696, Sir Henry Wardlaw, of Pitreavie, and died in 1727.

Under the south transept of the church is the burial-vault of the noble family of Elgin. A handsome monument to the memory of Charles, fifth Earl of Elgin, bears the following inscription composed by Dr. Hugh Blair :—

" Sacred to the memory of Charles, Earl of Elgin and Kincardine, who died the 14th of May, 1771, aged thirty-nine years. By the goodness of his heart and the virtues of his life he adorned the high rank which he possessed. In his manners amiable and gentle; in his affections warm and glowing; in his temper modest, candid, and cheerful ; in his conduct manly and truly honourable ; in his characters of husband, father, friend, and master, as far as human imperfections admit, unblemished. Pious without superstition, charitable without ostentation; while he lived, the blessing of those who were ready to perish came upon him. Now their tears embalm his memory! Reader, beholding here laid in the dust the remains which once so much virtue animated, think of the vanity of life, look forward to its end, and prepare as he did for eternity."

The last member of the house of Elgin consigned to the Dunfermline funeral vault was Colonel the Honourable Robert Bruce, who long held the responsible offices of Equerry and Private Secretary to H.R.H. the Prince of Wales.

Interred in the Abbey Church, but without any existing memorial, are the remains of the Rev. David Fergusson, first minister of the parish after the Reformation. This distinguished clergyman was bred a glover at Dundee, and never attended a university; he was, however, an expert classical scholar and an accomplished theologian. His pulpit talents were of the first order. He was on two occasions Moderator of the General Assembly. At Dunfermline he ministered from 1560 till his death, 23rd August, 1598 ; he died Father of the Church. He was of peaceful dispositions, and abounded in humour. A collection of "Proverbs," published at Edinburgh in 1641, has been attributed to him. Short compositions or "Tracts," from his pen, were printed in 1860 for the Bannatyne Club. He commenced a History of the Church, which was continued by his son-in-law, Mr. John Row, minister of Carnock (see supra). Among his descendants were the Right Hon. William Adam, Lord Brougham, and John Clerk, of Eldin.

Also interred in the Abbey Church without memorial stone is the Rev. Thomas Gillespie, founder of the Relief Church. This accomplished and excellent man was born at Duddingstone, near Edinburgh, in 1708. He obtained licence to preach from a body of English Dissenters, under the moderatorship of Dr. Doddridge, and in 1741 was admitted minister of Carnock. Disobeying the orders of the General Assembly with most of his brethren in settling an unacceptable precentor in the parish of Inverkeithing, he was deposed from the ministry, 23rd May, 1752. After preaching four months in the open air, a meeting-place was built for him at Dunfermline. Being joined by two other ministers Mr. Gillespie founded the Relief Synod, 23rd of October, 1761. He died 19th January, 1774.

In front of the United Presbyterian Church, Queen Anne Street, a monumental statue (reared in 1849) commemorates the Rev. Ralph Erskine, one of the founders of the Secession Church. Third son of the Rev. Henry Areskine (Vol. I., 222) Ralph Erskine was born at Monilaws, Northumberland, on the 15th March, 1685. Licensed to preach in 1709, he was admitted to the second charge, Dunfermline, in 1711, and promoted to the first charge in 1716. In the controversy with the General Assembly, which led to the secession, of which an account is presented in the sketch of his brother Ebenezer (see *supra*), he adhered to the protests of the four brethren. In 1737 he joined the Seceders, and was formally deposed by the Assembly. For two years thereafter he continued to minister in the parish church, but in 1739 a large meeting-place on the site of the present Queen Anne Street Church was erected for his use. He continued his ministerial labours at Dunfermline till his death, which took place on the 6th November, 1752. His theological writings have been published in two folio volumes, and his sacred poems, especially his " Gospel Sonnets," have been frequently reprinted. Mr. Erskine's remains were interred in the parish churchyard, and a tombstone was erected at his grave.

In the churchyard a granite monument, raised by his congregation, commemorates the Rev. James Mackenzie, minister of the Free Abbey Church. . From tombstones in the churchyard we have the following quaint inscriptions :—

" Here lyes the corps of Andrew Robertson, present Deacon Convener of Weavers, in this burgh, who died 13th July, 1745."

" Time cuts down all,
        Both great and small."

" Readers, see how death all downpulls,
    And nought remains but shanks and skulls;
    For the greatest champion ere drew breath,
    Was always conquered by death."

PARISH OF DUNINO.

In the parish churchyard a monumental cross commemorates Lord William Robert Keith Douglas of Dunino, who died in 1859. It is thus inscribed :—

" Beneath this cross are interred the mortal remains of Lord William Robert Keith Douglas, youngest son of Sir William Douglas, Bart., of Kilhead, Dumfriesshire, and brother of Charles, Marquis of Queensberry. He was born March 6th, 1783, and died December 5th, 1859."

A second inscription on the monument is as follows :—

" Here lies the mortal remains of Elizabeth, widow of Lord William Douglas, and daughter of Walter Irvine, Esq., of Dunino. She was born on the 25th November, 1798 ; and died 25th April, 1864."

On the same monument are also commemorated Charles Irvine Douglas, eldest son of Lord William Douglas, and Elizabeth Irvine, born 29th September, 1822, died August 23, 1825 ; and of William Douglas Irvine, second son of the above, born` 12th April, 1824 ; died 24th August, 1867.

A second monumental cross denotes the burying-ground of another parochial landowner. It is inscribed, " The burying-place of Hugh Cleghorn, Esq., of Stravithie ; and of Rachel Makgill, his wife, and of their family." Mr. Cleghorn was some time Professor of Civil History in the University of St. Andrews, and was afterwards employed in Government service abroad. His grandson, Dr. Hugh Cleghorn, formerly Professor of Botany at Madras, is author of a work on "The Plants of India."

A handsome monumental enclosure forms the burial-place of the family of Purvis of Kinaldy. A tablet commemorates Alexander Purvis of Kinaldy, who died 28th April, 1844, aged seventy-eight.

In the churchyard are interred the remains of the Rev. James Roger, minister of the parish, who died 23rd November, 1849, in the eighty-third year of his age, and forty-fourth of his ministry. His only son is author of this work.

A tombstone commemorates the Rev. John Burns, for thirteen years minister of the parish, who died 18th November, 1863, aged forty-seven; Alexander Farmer, tenant, Balmouth, who died 18th April, 1866, aged seventy-eight; and William Gray, tenant, Cornceres, who died 1st October, 1839, aged sixty-six.

The following lines are from the tombstone of Alison Trotter, a gardener's daughter, who died 2nd April, 1815, aged seventeen :—

" In this green bed sleeps the dear dust
    Of her was once so blooming ;
Stranger, thine earthly form too must
    Lie in a grave consuming.

" Friend for the dead who heav'st a sigh,
    Know Ally Trotter's yonder,
Where saints in heaven raise the glad cry
    Of gratitude and wonder.

" This is a bounding, dashing wave,
    On which in life we hover,
Few days at most these storms to brave,
    And all our griefs are over."

PARISH OF DYSART.

On the gravestone of a professed Atheist his family have raised a tombstone, inscribed with these lines :—

"Foe to no sect, he took a private road,
And oft exclaimed; ' Oh, what is nature's God ? '
Of scoffs and scorn he had great share
When in this world as you now are ;
But now his body turns to gas,
As this your world will do at last."

PARISH OF FALKLAND.

At Falkland an elegant monument, erected by public subscription, commemorates the late Onesiphorus Tyndal Bruce of Falkland, Convener of the county. A native of Bristol, Mr. Tyndal married Miss Bruce in 1828, when he assumed the name of Bruce, and established his residence on the Falkland estates. He was much beloved for his urbanity. He died on the 19th March, 1855. His monument includes his statue in bronze, executed by Mr. Steell.

In the churchyard a monument commemorates Emilia Geddes, the subject of a scarce and curious old tract; she was born at Falkland about the year 1665.

PARISH OF FERRY-PORT-ON-CRAIG.

In the churchyard of this parish are many quaint poetical inscriptions. James Martin, a child who died in 1803, is thus commemorated :—

Like a rose in bloom,
He forth did come,
The blossom soon was gone,
And now he's laid
In death's cold bed,
Where all of us must come."

Nathaniel Young's epitaph is as follows :—

" Ye parents dear,
Refrain your tear ;
Though here in dust I lie,
When God doth please,
He will me raise
To meet Him in the sky."

Alexander Duncan, who died in 1839, is celebrated thus :—

" See here a man laid low,
That lived a pious life,
Respected and esteem'd
For counsel and advice,
His soul, we trust, has fled
To yonder regions high ;
To praise redeeming love
To all eternity."

From other tombstones we have these pious sentiments :—

" How frail is man !
Life's but a span,
Youth's bloom doth soon decay ;
Since Adam's fall,
Both great and small
Is swept by death away."

" Lo, what is life ? 'tis like a flower
That blossoms and is gone ;
We see it flower for an hour,
With all its beauty on.
But death comes like a wintry day,
And cuts the pretty flower away."

" Stop, mortal man, as you pass by
This gravestone under which I ly ;
Read and remember what I tell,
That in the cold grave you must dwell,
For worms to be your company,
Till the last trumpet set you free ;
For neither coffin nor the grave,
Can your immortal soul receive.
Seek mansions new, while here you may,
Before you leave this house of clay."

PARISH OF FLISK.

The castle of Ballinbreich in this parish was long a principal residence of the Earls of Rothes. Within the old parish church lies entombed Andrew Leslie, fourth Earl of Rothes, a promoter of the Reformation. Succeeding his father in 1558, he joined the lords of the congregation in the year following, when they were threatened by the troops of the Queen Regent. On the marriage of Queen Mary with Lord Darnley, in July, 1765, he was with other malcontent lords forced to take refuge in England. By the Queen he was afterwards pardoned; he joined the association on her behalf, and fought for her at Langside. He was one of the jury at the mock trial of the Earl of Bothwell, and in 1581 sat on the jury which condemned the Earl of Morton. He died in 1621.

PARISH OF KILCONQUHAR.

In the parish church an elegant marble tablet commemorates Alexander Small, D.D., minister of the parish, who died 27th November, 1812, in his eightieth year, and the forty-sixth of his ministry.

Within the area of the old church is the family burial-place of Thomson of Charlton. At the same spot is a mortuary enclosure belonging to Sir John Lindsay Bethune, Bart., of Kilconquhar. A marble cenotaph commemorates the late Major-General Sir Henry Bethune, who was born 12th April, 1789, and died in Persia, 19th February, 1851. He assisted the Persians in the war with Russia, and gained extraordinary favour with the Persian king, who was governed by his counsels.

A tombstone, presenting the effigy of a knight in armour, is supposed to celebrate John Burnard, laird of Ardross, who received his death-wound while fighting with David II. in the attack on the fortress of Liddel in 1326.

To the north of the old church is a tomb belonging to the Gourlays, of Kincraig, an old Fifeshire family ; it presents a marble tablet in memory of William Gourlay, who died in 1827.

A stately monument in the centre of the churchyard celebrates James Carstairs Bruce, of Balcrystie, who died 10th March, 1835 ; also his widow, Eliza Cecilia, fourth daughter of James, seventh Lord Rollo, who died 6th April, 1861.

The family tomb of Lumsdaine, of Lathallan, records the names of several recent owners of that property, who all died young.

On the southern slope of the churchyard an obelisk of polished granite denotes the grave of a benevolent gentlewoman, a native of the parish. It is thus inscribed :—" In memory of Elizabeth Duncan, of Edengrove, a native of the parish of Kilconquhar, who died 24th August, 1867, aged eighty-five years ; the kind, unostentatious, and benevolent founder of the Duncan Institute, in the county town; and the munificent friend of many religious, charitable, and literary institutions." On an adjacent tombstone are recorded the names of Miss Duncan's parents and other relatives.

In the churchyard tombstones commemorate Bethune J. Walker Morrison, of Falfield and Pitkerrie, who died 13th March, 1868 ; Rear-Admiral Duddingstone, of Earlsferry ; William Ferrie, D.D., minister of the parish, and Professor of Civil History at St. Andrews, who died 7th June, 1850 ; and James Maclaren, parochial schoolmaster, who died in 1854, aged sixty-seven.

PARISH OF KILMANY.

On a tombstone in the parish churchyard a widow laments her deceased husband thus:—

" In what soft language shall my thoughts get free,
My dearest Cairnie, when I talk of thee ?
Ye Muses, Graces, all ye gentle train
Of weeping loves, assist the pensive strain.

But why should I implore your moving art ?
'Tis but to write the dictates of my heart;
And all that knew his real worth will join
Their friendly sighs and pious tears with mine.
His soul was formed to act each glorious part
Of life unstained with vanity or art;
No thought within his generous breast had birth,
But what he might have owned to heaven and earth;
Practised by him, each virtue grew more bright,
And shone with more than its own native light;
Whatever noble warmth could recommend—
The just, the active, and the constant friend,
Was all his own. But oh ! a dearer name
And softer tyes mine endless sorrows claim;
Left now alone, comfortless and forlorn,
The lover I, and tender husband mourn :
As thou alone hast taught my heart to prove
The highest raptures of a virtuous love,
That sacred passion I to thee confine,
My spotless faith shall be for ever thine."

PARISH OF KILRENNY.

At the east end of the parish church a roofless enclosure
denotes the burial-place of Cardinal David Beaton. The enclosure
is twenty feet wide and eight feet high; it fronts the east, and is
adorned with pillars having decorated capitals. In the interior,
the centre of the east wall presents the armorial escutcheon of the
House of Beaton, or Bethune. After the assassination of the
cardinal in the castle of St. Andrews, on the 29th May, 1546,
his body was exhibited to the citizens on the wall : it was afterwards deposited with salt in the castle dungeon. From the
dungeon it was removed by the cardinal's kinsman, John Bethune,
of Kilrenny and Silverdykes, and deposited in this structure.
The erection was recently repaired by Admiral Bethune, of Balfour,
the representative of the House.

At the north-west corner of the churchyard a magnificent

mausoleum in Roman architecture denotes the burial-place of the celebrated Major-General John Scott, of Balcomie, who died in December, 1775. It was erected by his eldest daughter, the Duchess of Portland, and is uninscribed. General Scott was second son of David Scott, of Scotstarvet and Thirdpart, an advocate at the Scottish bar, and M.P. for Fifeshire; and whose father, who bore the same Christian name, was grandson of Sir John Scot, of Scotstarvet, Director of the Chancery, and author of a curious work, entitled "The Staggering State of Scottish Statesmen."

Near the entrance of the churchyard is the handsome tomb of the Lumsdaines of Innergellie, erected in 1823. Sir James Lumsdaine, founder of the Innergellie family, was colonel in the army of Gustavus Adolphus of Sweden.

A tombstone with the date 1597, and the initials A. S., lies at the east door of the parish church. It is supposed to have marked the grave of the father of John Strong, who in 1609 was owner of Rennyhill; that estate he acquired from John Bethune, relative of the cardinal. The Strongs held important estates in the eastern district of Fifeshire, but their lands have long been alienated.

Near the church at the north-east corner is the tomb of Johnstone of Pitkerrie, formerly of Rennyhill, a family belonging to the town of Anstruther, and which about the middle of last century attained considerable opulence. Mr. Andrew Johnstone, the present proprietor of Pitkerrie, was some time M.P. for the St. Andrews burghs.

Tombstones commemorate three parochial incumbents, the Rev. William Beat, author of a volume of "Sermons," who died 21st December, 1797, in his eighty-seventh year, and fifty-second of his ministry; Rev. Joseph Duncan, who died 28th May, 1818; and the Rev. James Brown, who died 16th August, 1834, in his forty-sixth year, and sixteenth of his ministry. To the last a mural tablet of white marble has been reared by his friends and parishioners.

PARISH OF KINGHORN.

The tombstone of James Betson, of Kilrie, is thus inscribed :—

" Hic est sepultus Jacobus Betson de Kilrie ; qui obiit 29 Maii, 1647, ætatis 76.

" Tu quies tranquilla piis ; te cernere, finis."

William Betson, of South Glasmount, is commemorated thus :—

" Hic jacet Gulielmus Betson de Souther-Glasmont, cum Anna Smith, sponsa; quorum ille diem obiit 22 Augusti, 1682, illa autem obiit 31 Januarii, 1676, ætatis suæ 49. Mors ultima linea rerum 1687.

" Conditur hoc tumulo generosi cultor honesti,
Virtute, ingenio, prole bonisque potens."

Robert Glen, Treasurer of the City of Edinburgh, has the following epitaph :—

" Hic jacet prius et honorabilis vir M. Robertus Glen de Enchky, qui obiit 4 Maii, 1597. Olim balivus et thesaurarius Edinburgi."

On the tombstone of Archibald Angus are these words :—

" Spe vivevs, dissolvi cupiens, stationem quærens, portum inveni 1598. Ar. Angus."

From the tombstone of William Knox, of Common, who died 1st October, 1677, we have these lines :—

" Of terror's king the trophies here you see ;
Frail man ! his days like to a shadow flee,
Or like the path of eagle's wing on high,
That leaves no traces on the distant sky ;
Fair as these flowers that fleeting fade away,
So does this life expand, then droop, decay !
But future springs shall renovate the tomb,
And we, in gardens of th' Eternal, bloom."

PARISH OF KINGSBARNS.

In the church a marble tablet is thus inscribed :—

" In memory of Sir Charles Erskine, Bart., of Cambo, who died in March, 1796, aged sixty years ; of David Erskine, his brother, who died 5th August, 1793 ; and Miss Penelope Erskine, who died 8th November, 1838, aged sixty years."

Sir Charles was sixth baronet of Cambo ; his only son, Sir Charles, the seventh baronet, became eighth Earl of Kellie ; he died unmarried in October, 1799, aged thirty-five. He was succeeded by his father's younger brother, Thomas Erskine, who became ninth Earl, and who, acquiring wealth by trade in Sweden, restored the dilapidated fortunes of his House.

In the north-east corner of the churchyard, enclosed by an iron railing, is the burial-place of the old family of Monypenny of Pitmilly. A memoral tablet celebrates the late David Monypenny, Lord Pitmilly. It is thus inscribed :—

" Sacred to the memory of David Monypenny, Esq., of Pitmilly ; for many years one of the Senators of the College of Justice, who died at Pitmilly on the 24th December, 1850, in the eighty-second year of his age, and was here interred. Also to the memory of his second wife, Maria Sophia Abercrombie, daughter of Sir George Abercrombie, of Birkenbog, Bart., who died at Pitmilly on the 15th June, 1846, aged sixty-three, and was here interred."

Another monumental tablet commemorates Lord Pitmilly's brother and successor in the estate. It is inscribed thus :—

" Sacred to the memory of William Tankerville Monypenny, Esq., of Pitmilly, who died at Pitmilly on the 10th January, 1869, in the eighty-sixth year of his age, and was here interred."

A mortuary enclosure, with a decorated tomb bearing date 1638, forms the burial-place of the family of Corstorphine of Kingsbarns Several members of the family are commemorated on marble tablets. Within the enclosure, Captain Thomas Gray, son of Captain Charles Gray, author of " Lays and Lyrics," is celebrated thus :—

"Sacred to the memory of Thomas Carstairs Gray, Captain Royal Marine Light Infantry, of the Naval Brigade of H.M.S. *Shannon;* born at Kingsbarns, 1st February, 1820; died at Gyub, 8th May, 1858."

An altar tombstone marks the grave of the Rev. Robert Arnot, D.D., minister of the parish, and Professor of Divinity in St. Mary's College, St. Andrews, who died 2nd July, 1808, aged sixty-four.

In the burial-place of his family, a plain tombstone commemorates the Rev. Andrew George Carstairs, D.D., minister of Anstruther-wester, who died 11th October, 1838, in his fifty-ninth year, and thirty-fourth of his ministry. Dr. Carstairs composed "The Scottish Communion Service," Edinburgh, 1829, 12mo.

A monumental obelisk, reared by subscription, celebrates Alexander Latto, for forty-five years schoolmaster of the parish; he was born 1st June, 1786, and died 1st October, 1864.

PARISH OF KIRKCALDY.

In the parish churchyard a monument to James Wemyss, of Bogie, is inscribed thus:—

> "Boggius hic, octo vitæ post lustra Iacobus
> In tumulo Vemius, præcoce morte jacet;
> Filius in patrios at sic quæsivit in annos,
> Ut rogitet patris addere fata suos.
>   Obiit 1 Februarii 1631."

Henry Montgomery, *alias* Miller, who died 15th February, 1596, has on his gravestone these lines:—

> "Quæ terrena mei pars est sub marmore dormit;
> Quæ pars cœlestis cœlica regna colit:
> Corpus humo surget redivivum spiritus illud
> Intrabit, vita sic sine fine fruar."

Henry Boswell, chief magistrate, who died in 1681, is thus celebrated:—

"Henrici corpus Bosuelli conditur infra,
Vir genio magnus, clarus in arte sua;
Prætor erat decies, semel et præfectus in urbe,
Tempore quo toto jus sine labe fuit:
Vixerat innocuus, Christi decessit amator
Et nunc cum Christo cœlica regna calit."

On the monument of Provost John Williamson, who died in 1657, are these lines:—

"Navita præclarus positus jacet hic Ioannes
Williamsonus, splendidus ingenio;
Urbis quindecies prætor; legatus et omni
Conventu in magno non sine laude, fuit;
Vir pietate clarus, nulli virtute secundus
Nunc, cum cœlicolis, quod patefecit, habet."

Matthew Anderson, a captain in the merchant service, and Provost of the burgh, who died in 1694, is commemorated thus:—

"Navita præclarus, probitate verendus et annis,
Moribus eximius et pietatis amans;
Strenuus assertor recti; virtutibus amplis
Ornatus, cana conspicuusque fide:
Consulis officio qui functus in urbe frequenter,
Partibus a regiis strenuus usque stetit.
Sed cadit heu! tandem longo consumptus ab ævo
Grande decus patriæ, summus et urbis honos."

The monument of Robert Whyte, of Pouran, and his wife, Janet Tennant, is thus inscribed:—

"Hic jacet Robertus Whyte, a Pouran, apud suos inter primos conspicuus; sæpius prætura, bis urbis patriæ præfectura nobilitatus; qui, primos urbis honores adeptus, adeo sine fastu fastigium id cum fructu temperavit, ut præesse posset, prodesse velle videretur. Obiit anno 1667, ætatis 68. Hic etiam conjugis amantissimæ, Janetæ Tennant, reponuntur cineres. Obiit anno 1670, ætatis 62."

These lines adorn the tombstone of David Barclay, of Tough, who died 12th July, 1688, aged forty-one:—

"Non vigor ingenii, non cultæ gratia linguæ,
　Non honor aut virtus clara, nec alma fides,
Non gazæ ingentes, nec firmo in pectore vires,
　Nec pietas mortis sistere tela potest.
Mors sua sceptra tenet, toti communia mundo
　Omnibus obscuras injicit illa manus."

The Rev. James Symson, minister of the parish, who died 3rd January, 1665, in his eighty-fifth year, and the fifty-fourth of his ministry, has on his monument these lines :—

" Ille ingens vates, fama super æthera notus,
　Symsonus, Domini sedulo pavit oves ;
Quinquaginta annos, pugnanda fortiter idem
　Nusquam de recto tramite flexit iter.
Presbyter hic prudens, doctor pius æquus, acutus.
　Regi fidus erat, propositique tenax."

By a Latin inscription is commemorated the Rev. Kenneth Logie, minister of the parish, who died 29th November, 1669. In his epitaph he is thus described :—

" Genio erat ille mitis, gravitate reverendus, pietate et integritate cordis clarus, laborum patiens et viscerum plenus, vita et voce docebat facienda et faciendo."

A tombstone commemorates "John Melvill, of Raith, father and son, who departed this life in the Christian faith; viz., the father 13th January, 1603, the son 17th January, 1626."

A handsome tombstone celebrates Robert Philp, manufacturer, who died in 1828, bequeathing £74,000 for educating and clothing 400 children. Under his benevolent trust three schools have been established.

A monument denotes the grave of George Anderson, of Luscar, sometime provost of the burgh. Born at Kirkcaldy in 1787, he entered the civil department of the navy in 1804. After a period of active service he left the navy on half-pay in 1814, and for some years conducted business in Liverpool. In 1822 he became managing partner, at Havre de Grace, of the mercantile house of

Dennistoun and Co. In 1834 he settled in Kirkcaldy as agent of the Union Bank. To the best interests of the place he energetically devoted himself, and was twice elected chief magistrate. In 1850 he purchased the estate of Luscar, in the parish of Carnock, on which he resided several years. He latterly removed to Ferrybank, near Cupar, where he died on the 31st August, 1863. His eldest son, Mr. George Anderson, is one of the parliamentary representatives of the city of Glasgow.

Among other notable persons commemorated in Kirkcaldy churchyard are Alexander Law, bailie, who died 9th May, 1642, aged ninety; David Hutcheon, died 28th November, 1615, leaving a bequest to the parochial charities; John Bruce, merchant, who died 15th March, 1667; and Captain John Tennant, who died 8th February, 1667.

These rhymes are from different tombstones :—

> " James Baxter, wright, his wyfe here lyes!
> Grave Janet Wallace, meeke and wyse ;
> James Baxter, wryght, here laid besyde hys wyfe,
> Ye ninth of March departed from this lyfe.
> He made their coffins baith now laid in clay ;
> Oh mortal man, for James and Janet pray."

> " Below this stone doth David Baxter lie,
> Prais'd in his life for wit and honesty.
> A godly man, and well belov'd was he
> By persons all of high and low degree ;
> His worth and merit we cannot decide,
> In peace he liv'd, in Christ he did confide."

> " Twice twenty years old Anna Berrill lies
> Here buried ; a matron grave and wise ;
> Religious, modest, virt'ous, just, and kind ;
> To all in straits a present help and friend ;
> A tender mother and a loving wife ;
> Who in sixth birth departed this frail life.
> Now she is gone, yet shall her name remain ;
> The grave her bones, the heaven her soul contain."

> " Of Coblehaugh, here Robert Chapman lies,
> A theam for mourning to all readers' eyes ;

When baillie of this burgh, straight, good, and just,
He was a credite to his place of trust;
Chief of his name, most loyal, virt'ous, kind,
Of a religious, humble, faithful mind;
Obliged all, and gain'd all men's love;
The trade of merchandizing did improve;
Did live a quiet life, in peace did die;
Whose soul 'mongst saints enjoys eternity."

PARISH OF LARGO.

The old churchyard, now disused, contains two vaults belonging respectively to the families of Wood and Durham. Sir Andrew Wood, of Largo, the famous admiral, was originally a trader at Leith. His genius in naval warfare recommended him to James III., who made him a knight, and granted him and his heir the lands and village of Largo. His exploits at sea form part of the national history. Retiring from his duties as a naval commander, he settled on his estate. From his mansion at Largo to the neighbourhood of the parish church he constructed a canal, that he might sail every Sunday to his place of worship. At an advanced age he died about 1540, and his remains were deposited in the family aisle of the parish church. His tomb is still pointed out.

In the Durham vault several members of that house have been entombed.

On the estate of Lundin three upright stones of irregular form—the highest reaching sixteen feet above the surface—are supposed to celebrate some Danish chiefs who here fell in battle.

PARISH OF LESLIE.

In the family mausoleum were interred, in 1681, the remains of that dissolute royal favourite, John Duke of Rothes. Born in

1630, he succeeded his father in his eleventh year as sixth Earl of Rothes. He carried the Sword of State when Charles II. was crowned at Scone, on the 1st January, 1651. Taken prisoner at the battle of Worcester, he was three years confined in the Tower. At the Restoration he was appointed President of the Council, and was afterwards advanced to other dignities. Through the influence of the Duke of York he was, in 1680, created Duke of Rothes and Marquis of Ballinbreich. He died at Holyrood House on the 27th July, 1681. Extremely ignorant, Rothes was chiefly remarkable for the extent of his licentiousness, and his efforts for the overthrow of Presbyterianism.

In the parish churchyard a servant of the Rothes family is thus quaintly portrayed :—

> " John Brown's dust lies here below,
>   Once served a noble Earl ;
> At his command he ne'er said no
>   Had it been on his peril.
> His days and years they were spun out
>   Like to a thread most fine,
> At last a period came about
>   Snapt it at ninety-nine.
> 'Twas on the seventeenth day of May,
>   In the year forty-six,
> This honest man was called away
>   To Heaven we hope did fix."

When tutor at Leslie House the Rev. Ebenezer Erskine composed these lines, which are inscribed on a tombstone :—

> " Here lies within this earthen ark
>   An Archer grave and wise,
> Faith was his arrow, Christ the mark,
>   And glory was the prize.
> His bow is now a harp, his song
>   Doth Halleluiahs 'dite,
> His consort Walker went along
>   To walk with Christ in white.

In quaintness the following is unique :—

> " Here lies the dust of Charles Brown,
> Some time a wright in London town,
> When coming home parents to see,
> And of his years being twenty-three,
> Of a decay with a bad host
> He died upon the Yorkshire coast
> The 10th of August 1752
> We hope his soul in Heaven rests now."

PARISH OF LEUCHARS.

Within the chancel, or ancient part of the parish church, a tombstone is thus inscribed :—

" Hoc tegitvr lapide corpvs probi viri ROBERTI CARNEGY de Kynnard, militis, Senatorii Ordinis, qvi obiit in Castro de Lvthers, qvinto die mensis Ianvarii anno Dni 156-, et ætatis svæ anno. . . ."

Sir Robert Carnegy, of Kinnaird, was son of John de Carnegy, who was killed at Flodden; he and his ancestors were cupbearers to the kings of Scotland. In July, 1547, Sir Robert was nominated an ordinary lord of session, and in the following year was sent to England to treat for the ransom of the Earl of Huntly, Chancellor of Scotland, taken at the battle of Pinkie. On his return he was knighted, and he was afterwards employed in various matters of diplomacy. When the Reformation movement commenced he supported the Queen Regent; he subsequently joined the Congregation. He died 5th January, 1566. Sir David Carnegy, his second son, was, by his second marriage, father of the first Earl of Southesk.

In the chancel a tombstone commemorates Sir William Bruce, of Earlshall, who died 28th January, 1584; it is inscribed thus :—

" Hic iacet vir probvs ac omni memoria dignvs Dns GVLLIELMVS

1

BRVCEVS de Erlishal, miles, qvi obiit 28 die mensis Ianvarii anno Dni 1584, annoqve svæ ætatis 98.   Mors omnivm et finis.

> " Heir lyis of al piete ane lantern brycht,
> Schir VILLZAM BRVCE. Erlshal knycht."

Sir Alexander Bruce, of the House of Clachmannan, acquired the property of Earlshall about the end of the fifteenth century; he married a daughter of Sir David Stewart, of Rosyth, and became father of Sir William, commemorated on the tombstone.

In the chancel the second wife of Bruce of Earlshall, son of Sir William, is celebrated on a tombstone, sculptured with the representation of a lady, and on the margin thus inscribed :—

" D. AGNES LYNDESAY, Lady of William Brvce of Erlshall, vho in hir life was charitable to the poore, and profitable to that hovse, dyed 1635, of her age sixty-eight, and waiteth in hope.—D. A. L."

A marble tablet in the chancel commemorates the Rev. Thomas Kettle, minister of the parish, who died 14th November, 1808, in his sixty-eighth year, and the thirty-fifth of his ministry; also his son, Alexander Kettle, W.S., Edinburgh, who died in 1841, bequeathing £500 for behoof of the parochial poor.

In the churchyard a tombstone marks the resting-place of Mrs. Cochrane Stewart, daughter of Sir John Stewart, Bart., of Allanbank, who died 9th April, 1807, aged eighty-one.

PARISH OF MONIMAIL.

On the Mount, a considerable eminence in this parish, a massive column one hundred feet in height, is one of the several monuments raised in honour of John, fourth Earl of Hopetoun.   (Vol. I., 9; 179.)

In the parish churchyard is the family burial-place of the Earls of Leven and Melville.   By a monument is commemorated Leslie Melville Lord Balgonie, who died in 1857.   Born on the 10th November, 1831, Lord Balgonie entered the army in 1850 as an officer of the Grenadier Guards. With his regiment he continued in active service during the whole of the Crimean war, when he contracted the seeds of a complaint to which he succumbed at the age of twenty-six.

Monimail churchyard contains the burial-place of the family of Makgill Crichton, of Rankeilour. (See *supra*, p. 85.)

PARISH OF NEWBURGH.

Surrounded with trees at a short distance to the westward of Newburgh village is the cross of Mugdrum. The name is a corruption of Magridin, the saint in whose honour it was reared. The cross is firmly mortised in a block of sandstone, five feet long, three feet six inches broad, and two feet thick. The shaft is about eleven feet in height, and the transverse part has long since disappeared. The shaft is sculptured with the representation of a boar hunt.

About a mile south of Mugdrum cross stood the celebrated cross of Macduff. The basement stone only remains, the shaft which it supported having been destroyed by a party of Reformers in 1559. By iron staples were attached to the cross, at its basement, nine rings, any of which on being grasped by a member of the clan Macduff who had offended against the law exempted the offender from punishment. This privilege was conferred by Malcolm Canmore on the thane Macduff and his descendants. It was claimed in the seventeenth century by Spence of Wormiston, for killing an individual named Kinninmouth. Macduff's Cross is the subject of a poem by Sir Walter Scott.

In Lindores Abbey (a religious house founded in 1178 by David, Earl of Huntingdon, and now in ruins) several stone coffins were recently exhumed. Two small stone coffins in front of the high altar contained the bodies of two children of the

founder. A large sarcophagus contained, it is believed, the remains
of David, Duke of Rothesay, eldest son of Robert III., who died
at Falkland Palace on the 27th March, 1402. Another sarcophagus is associated with James ninth Earl of Douglas, who spent
his last years in the abbey, and there died on the 15th April, 1438.

PARISH OF PITTENWEEM.

An altar tombstone, now built into the south wall of the parish
church, celebrates, in a long Latin epitaph, the Rev. George Hamilton, proprietor of Cairnes, a zealous upholder of Presbyterianism.
Ordained minister of Newburn in 1628, he was, in August, 1637,
served with letters of horning charging him to purchase and read
the Service-book. In 1638 he was one of the ministers named for
tendering a complaint to the General Assembly against the thirteen
bishops. In 1649 he was translated to Pittenweem. In 1653 he
suffered imprisonment in Edinburgh for eight days for praying for
Charles II.; and after the Restoration he was deprived for rejecting
Episcopacy. He was allowed to minister to his people till his
death, which took place on the 8th April, 1677, in his 76th year
and the 49th of his ministry. He married Euphemia Douglas, who
died 28th January, 1673.

An elegant monument celebrates the Right Rev. David Low,
D.D., LL.D., Bishop of Moray, Ross and Argyll. Born at Brechin
in November, 1768, he took orders in 1787, and in 1790 was settled
as Episcopal pastor in Pittenweem. He was consecrated bishop in
1819, but continued to minister to his congregation. He died at
Pittenweem on the 26th January, 1855, in his 87th year and the
66th of his ministry.

In the north wall of the church a marble tablet has been erected
by Robert Henderson, merchant in Glasgow, in memory of his
parents and other members of his family. It is thus inscribed :—

" Erected by Robert Henderson, merchant in Glasgow, in memory of his parents, George Henderson and Janet Tod, who died at Pittenweem; the former on 13th May, 1824, aged 48 years; the latter on 4th July, 1832, aged 61 years. Also, of his sisters and brothers who died—Janet, at Pittenweem, 9th Nov., 1815, aged 8 years; Patrick, at Glasgow, 21st July, 1841, aged 33 years; George, at Glasgow, 24th Dec., 1852, aged 50 years; Thomas, at Leghorn, 11th Oct., 1854, aged 52 years; John, at Pittenweem, 27th Nov., 1854, aged 50 years."

By his son, David Wilson, of Inchyre, a monument has been erected in memory of his father, the Rev. David Wilson, minister of the Relief congregation, Pittenweem, who died 20th January, 1813.*

Tombstones commemorate James Horsburgh, of Firth, who died in 1856, aged 81; Thomas Martin, writer, Edinburgh, who died in 1826; Dr. James Nairne, minister of the parish, who died 15th July, 1819, in his 69th year and 44th of his ministry; and the Rev. John Cooper, who died 26th March, 1854, in his 53rd year and the 22nd of his ministry.

PARISH OF ST. ANDREWS.

In the chapel of St. Salvator's College (now styled the College Church) are several mural and other monuments. Of these the most ancient and interesting is that in celebration of Bishop Kennedy, founder of the college. This elegant structure was constructed by the prelate, whom it commemorates, shortly before his decease. Reared in Gothic architecture it is rich in finely clustered columns, elegantly sculptured canopies, and studded pendants. On the top is a representation of the Saviour surrounded by his angels. A tablet of brass containing an inscription was affixed to the lower part of the structure, but it has long since disappeared. Under the

* One of his sons, the Right Rev. William Scott Wilson, LL.D., is Bishop of Glasgow and Galloway.

central arch are two lines of a Latin inscription almost effaced. The Rev. C. J. Lyon, the ingenious historian of St. Andrews, has thus rendered* the second line and a portion of the first:

" Magister
Hicce finit fanum qui largis intulit ortum."

According to Lindsay of Pitscottie,† the monument was reared at the expense of £10,000 sterling, a sum equal to that expended in the erection of the college. To account for this heavy expenditure it has been conjectured that the various niches had been filled with silver images. In the interior of the tomb were found, in 1683, six highly decorated maces. Of these three were presented to the Universities of Aberdeen, Glasgow, and Edinburgh, and the other three were retained—two being deposited in St. Mary's College, and one in the College of St. Salvator. The mace retained by St. Salvator's College is the most ornate, and it is composed of solid silver, while the others are plated. It is four feet long and weighs nearly twenty pounds. Three labels are attached, which bear these inscriptions :—" Jacobus Kennedy, illustris Sancti Andreæ Antistes, ac fundator collegii St. Salvatoris cui me donavit, me fecit fieri Parisiis. An. Dom. MIIIILXI." " John Mair gooldsmythe and verlotte of chamer til the Lord Dauphin has made this masse in the towne of Paris in the year of our Lord 1461." " Dr. Alex. Skene, collegii St. Salvatoris nostri praepositus, me temporis injuria læsum et mutilatum, publicis dicti collegii sumptibus reparandum curavit ann. 1685."

During the popular outbreak at the Reformation, Bishop Kennedy's tomb was deprived of its ornaments; it suffered additional injury about a century ago, when the original roof of the chapel was taken down. In 1842 the interior of the tomb underwent examination. Under the large slab of black marble in its recess was found a shallow irregular space filled with stones and rubbish.

* History of St. Andrews, by the Rev. C. J. Lyon, Edinb., 1843, II. 195.
† Lindsay of Pitscottie, folio p. 68.

Immediately beneath was discovered a strong arch, supporting the entire weight of the monument, under which was a quantity of loose earth. Scattered among the earth were fragments of bones, the leg and arm bones being entire, also the skull. These were partially covered with cerecloth, thus bearing marks of embalmment. Portions of a wooden coffin were also discovered. On the earth being removed from under the arch there appeared a large square cell eight feet long, three and a half feet broad, and five feet in height, with a cross cut in marble at the east and west ends. Fragments of painted tiles strewn among the earth had evidently been used in forming a floor. The cell had doubtless contained the bishop's remains, the head resting against the western cross. The bones were collected in a box and placed in the cell, which was carefully built up. Examined phrenologically the bishop's skull was pronounced to evince firmness, conscientiousness, and veneration, with very ordinary intellectual power.

Bishop James Kennedy was younger son of James Kennedy of Dunure, by his wife the Countess of Angus, daughter of Robert III., and was born about the year 1405. By his uncle, James I., he was, in 1437, appointed to the see of Dunkeld; three years afterwards he was advanced to the diocese of St. Andrews. In 1444 he became Lord High Chancellor, an office which he held only a few weeks. He was entrusted with the education of James III., and acted as one of the lords of the regency during that Prince's minority. Under Papal sanction he founded St. Salvator's College in 1455, dedicating it to the honour of God, of the Saviour, and of the Virgin Mary. He also built a magnificent "barge" called the St. Salvator, which he used in foreign trade; it remained the property of the see till 1472, when it was wrecked on the coast of Bamborough. Bishop Kennedy died 10th May, 1466.

In the vestibule of St. Salvator's Chapel, inserted in the pavement, is the tombstone of Dr. Hugh Spens, provost of the college from 1505 to 1534. In the centre is a figure of the provost in his academic robes, with a representation of his family shield, while along the margin is the following inscription in raised letters :—

" Hic requiescit ——endus et egregius vir magister noster Hugo Spens, theologus eximius in utroque jure —— qui hunc locum variis ditavit muneribus obiit ann. dom. 1534 et 21 die Julii." Provost Spens's monument seems to have been removed to its present position from the vicinity of the high altar, where, as provost of his college, he would certainly be entombed.

In the south wall of the vestibule a marble tablet commemorates Dr. Alexander Pitcairn, Principal of St. Mary's College from 1693 to 1698. In the north wall of the church an elegantly sculptured cenotaph commemorates William Dalgleish Playfair, lieutenant in the Indian army, eldest son of the late Lieutenant-Colonel Sir Hugh Lyon Playfair, Provost of St. Andrews. An inscription bears that he fell " on the 16th February, 1846, in the memorable battle of Sobraon, while gallantly leading his company in the attack made by Sir Robert Dick's division on the right of the Sikh entrenchments."

St. Leonard's College, founded in 1512 by Prior John Hepburn, contains in its roofless chapel several ancient monuments. On the north wall a monument, richly decorated, which presents no trace of an inscription, is supposed to commemorate the founder. Prior Hepburn died in 1522.

On the wall of the chapel a monument in Greek architecture, fifteen feet in height, commemorates Robert Stewart, Earl of March, brother of the Regent Lennox. Bishop elect of Caithness before the Reformation, he joined the Reformers, and thus secured the temporalities of his see ; he also obtained from his brother the office of Commendator of the Priory of St. Andrews, which included St. Leonard's College. On the upper portion of his tomb a small tablet bears these words :—" R. S. obiit anno 86 Agu 29 ætatis suæ 63." On the architrave are these hexameters :—

" In portu fluctusque omnes classemque relinquo
Me spectans mundumque omnem fascesque relinque." *

* The troubles to which the inscription refers, were doubtless, the forfeiture which he endured for having joined his brother, the Earl of Lennox, against the Earl of Arran's government.

Another mural monument in St. Leonard's chapel celebrates Robert Wilkie, principal of the college from 1579 to 1611, and founder of six bursaries in connection with it. The inscription proceeds thus:—

"Clariss. viri D. Rob. Vilichii academiæ Rectoris, qui huic gymnasio ann. XXI. summa cum laude præfuit. Aream ab occidente ædibus clausit; ab oriente auxit; testamento 4200 mercas pauperibus alendis legavit. Ob. ann. ætat 63 ann. dom. 1611, men. Jun. 26 — Ditavi, excolui, ornavi, auxique, lyceum, doctrina, fama, sedibus, ac opibus; testis doctrinæ est, academia Scotianæ stant sedes. Opibus nutrio 6 inopes."

In the floor of St. Leonard's Chapel are several memorial stones. One at the north-east corner celebrates James Wilkie, Principal of the College, and predecessor and uncle of Principal Robert Wilkie. He died in 1590, aged 78. He was one of those held by the General Assembly of 1560 to be qualified both for "ministering and teaching."

On the pavement a tombstone bearing the device of a ram on a heraldic shield, commemorates John Wynram, Sub-prior of St. Andrews. This ecclesiastic accommodated himself to the prevailing sentiments of his period. He assisted at the trial and condemnation of Wishart and Mill, and in 1560 joined the Reformers, by whom he was appointed Superintendent of Fife. He was one of the committee who framed the Confession of Faith and the Books of Discipline. He died in 1582, aged 90.

A flat tombstone, presenting a robed figure, commemorates, in a half-effaced Latin inscription, Emanuel Young, a canon of the Priory, who died in 1544.

In the west end of the chapel a pavement tombstone commemorates, by a Latin epitaph, John Archibald and Margaret his wife. Archibald founded an altarage in 1525, and deposited £200 in the hands of Gavin Logie, Regent of the College, as an endowment for performing an annual obit for his soul.*

A memorial stone, celebrating William Ruglyn, a canon and

---

* Logie was suspected of favouring the new opinions, and during the persecution of Archbishop James Beaton effected his escape to the Continent.

"master of works, who died 8th April, 1502," has been, for greater safety, placed in St. Leonard's Chapel; it was a few years since found in a private garden.

In Trinity or Town Church, a magnificent memorial structure on the east wall of the great aisle commemorates Archbishop James Sharp. This noted prelate was son of the Sheriff Clerk of Banff-shire, and was born in the castle of Banff on the 4th May, 1618. Having studied at Marischal College, Aberdeen, and visited the Universities of Oxford and Cambridge, he became a Regent in St. Leonard's College, St. Andrews. In January, 1648, he was ordained minister of Crail. Joining the Resolution party in the Church, he was seized by order of Cromwell, and for some months detained a prisoner in London. In 1657 he waited on the Protector, with other ministers, to obtain his authority for holding a General Assembly, but failed in his mission. After the ascendancy of General Monk, in 1660, he was appointed by the leading Presbyterians to wait on him, in order to obtain the sanction of Charles II. to the proposed settlement of the Presbyterian Church. He returned to Scotland bearer of a royal letter, in which his Majesty expressed a resolution to preserve the government of the Church as "settled by law." But the restoration of Episcopacy had been resolved upon, and Sharp was privy to the resolution. During his absence he was offered one of the city churches of Edinburgh, and on his declinature he was elected Professor of Divinity at St. Andrews. He was also appointed his Majesty's chaplain for Scotland, with a salary of £200 per annum. On the overthrow of Presbytery by Parliament in August, 1661, Sharp proceeded to London, when he was appointed Archbishop of St. Andrews, and, with three others, was, on the 15th December, consecrated at Westminster. He became a vigorous opponent of Presbyterianism, and an oppressor of his former friends. His tyranny became odious. An attempt to assassinate him was made in the High Street of Edinburgh in July, 1668, but failed. On Saturday, the 3rd May, 1679, while travelling with his eldest daughter from Edinburgh to St. Andrews, his carriage was intercepted on Magus Muir, within three miles of the latter city, by nine zealous Presbyterians, goaded to madness by the oppression of the times. They struck down the coachman, and stopped the horses; then, calling on the Archbishop to come forth, they adjured him to prepare for death. His entreaties for mercy were unheeded, and he was slain pierced with many wounds. Thirteen days after his slaughter his remains were deposited with great pomp in the aisle of the parish church, and a sculptor in Holland was commissioned by his son, Sir William Sharp, of Strathtyrum, to construct a splendid mausoleum over his remains.

The monument, which in 1849 underwent a thorough repair, is a triumph of sepulchral art. Composed of white and black marble, the upper part presents a representation of the archbishop supporting the church. Below are two angels, with wings extended, supporting the shield, mitre, and crosiers. In the centre of the monument the archbishop is kneeling, while an angel is exchanging the crown for the mitre,—*pro mitra coronam*, which became the motto of his House. Beneath is an elegant urn containing the inscription, under which is a bas-relief representation of the murder. In the background of the picture are the assassins in pursuit of the carriage, which is drawn by six horses. In the foreground the primate is on his knees, surrounded by his assassins; Haxton, of Rathillet, lingering aside on horseback, and the archbishop's daughter detained by two of the conspirators, while in an imploring attitude she begs her father's life. The inscription is as follows :—

"D. O. M.
Sacratissimi antistitis, prudentissimi senatoris, sanctissimi
martyris
cineres pretiosissimos,
Sublime hoc tegit mausoleum.
Hic namque jacet
Quod sub sole reliquum est reverendissimi in Christo patris,
D.D. Jacobi Sharp, Sti. Andreæ archiepiscopi, totius
Scotiæ primatis, &c. ;
Quem
Philosophiæ et theologiæ professorem, academia ;

Presbyterum, doctorem, præsulem, ecclesia ;
Tum ecclesiastici, tum civilis statis ministrum primarium,
Scotia ;
Serenissimi Caroli Secundi monarchicique imperii
restitutionis suasorem
Britannia ;
Episcopalis ordinis in Scotia instauratorem, Christianus
orbis ;
Pietatis exemplum ; pacis angelum ; sapientiæ oraculum ;
gravitatis imaginem ; boni et fideles subditi ;
Impietatis, perduellionis, et schismatis hostem accerimum ;
Dei, regis, et gregis inimici viderunt, agnoverunt,
admirabantur.
Quemq.
Talis et tantus cum esset, novem conjurati parricidæ, fanatico
furore perciti, in metropoliticæ suæ civitatis vicinio, lucente
meridiano sole, charissima filia primogenita et
domesticis famulis vulneratis, lachrymantibus,
reclamantibus, in genua, ut pro ipsis etiam
oraret, prolapsum, quam plurimis
vulneribus confossum sclopetis
gladiis, pugionibus, horren-
dum in modum truci-
darunt, 3 die Maii
1679, ætatis
suæ 61."

During the course of the recent repairs it was resolved to make
an examination of the monument's interior. An entrance was
effected by the removal of several large flat stones in front of the
structure.. A square vault seven feet long, four feet broad, and
three and a half in height, was found to contain, scattered among
rubbish, eight coffin handles and a few remains of a coffin. There
were no human remains. It is to be feared that these had been
removed and scattered, when in 1725 "certain ryotous and dis-
orderlie persons" broke into the church by night and defaced the
monument, carrying away a portion of the marble.*

At Magus Muir, within an enclosure, near the village of Strath-
kinnes, and known as the Bishop's Wood, a plain tombstone

---

* Records of Town Council of St. Andrews, September 1275.

commemorates Andrew Guillan, one of the archbishop's assassins, who was executed at Edinburgh on the 20th July, 1683. It is inscribed thus :—

> "A faithful martyr here doth lye,
> A witness against perjury ;
> Who cruelly was put to death,
> To gratify proud prelates' wrath ;
> They cut his hands ere he was dead,
> And after that struck off his head.
> To Magus Muir then did him bring,
> His body on a pole did hing.
> His blood under the altar cries
> For vengeance on Christ's enemies."

Guillan was a hand-loom weaver in the village of Balmerino. After his execution his head was fixed up at Cupar, and his body hung in chains at Magus Muir. By his friends his body was taken down and buried in the Long-cross of Clermont, near Magus Muir.*

Haxton of Rathillet, another of the archbishop's nine assassins, was made prisoner at the skirmish at Airs-Moss in 1680, and was tried and executed at Edinburgh.

A few hundred yards to the westward of Guillan's tombstone, in an open field, is the grave of four covenanters who were taken prisoners at the battle of Bothwell Bridge in June, 1679, and who by sentence of the Justiciary Court were executed at Magus Muir on the 18th November following. A tombstone raised to their memory in 1726, by the Cameronians of Dumfriesshire, but which long since has disappeared, was thus inscribed :—

"Here lie Thomas Brown, James Wood, Andrew Sword, John Waddel, and John Clyde, who suffered martyrdom on Magus Muir for their adherence to the word of God and Scotland's covenanted work of Reformation, November 25th, 1689.

> 'Cause we at Bothwell did appear,
> Perjurious oaths refused to swear ;
> 'Cause we Christ's cause would not condemn,
> We were sentenced to death by men,
> Who rag'd against us in such fury,

* " Cloud of Witnesses."

> Our dead bodies they did not bury;
> But up on poles did hing us high,
> Triumphs of Babel's victory.
> Our lives we fear'd not to the death,
> But constant prov'd to the last breath."

At the west end of the Scores Walk, at the top of the declivity leading towards the Links, and overlooking St. Andrews Bay, an obelisk, forty-five feet in height, is known as the *Martyrs' Monument*. It was reared in 1842 by public subscription, to commemorate John Resby, Paul Craw, Patrick Hamilton, Henry Forrest, and George Wishart, who suffered by fire at St. Andrews for upholding the principles of the Reformation.

The parish churchyard surrounds the ruins of the cathedral.* At the foot of the great altar are three projecting stone coffins, supposed to be those of Archbishop William Shevez, James Stewart, and James Beaton. Shevez recommended himself to James III. by his skill in astrology, and was appointed Archbishop of St. Andrews in 1478. He established a library in connection with the University. The Archbishopric of Glasgow was constituted during his primacy, but in entire opposition to his will. He died in 1496, and was interred before the high altar of the cathedral, a monument of brass being placed over his remains. Archbishop James Stewart was second son of James III., by his Queen, Margaret of Denmark. He was appointed to the archbishopric as successor to Shevez in his twenty-first year, and was about the same time created Duke of Ross and Marquis of Ormond. He died in his twenty-eighth year.

Son of the proprietor of Balfour, in Fife, Archbishop James Beaton was successively Bishop of Galloway and Archbishop of Glasgow; he also held office as Lord High Chancellor. In 1523

---

* St. Andrews Cathedral was founded in 1159 by Arnold, nineteenth bishop of the see, and was completed by Bishop Lamberton, in 1318. After standing 240 years, it was demolished in June, 1559, by the citizens, after a sermon by Knox. When entire it had five towers, and a great central steeple. Three of the towers remain, with the south wall of the nave, and that on the west side of the south transept.

he was elevated to the primacy as Archbishop of St. Andrews. He endured four months' imprisonment in 1524 for uniting himself to the party against Arran and the queen-mother, who desired that James V. should be declared of age in his twelfth year. On his restoration to favour he was appointed one of the Privy Council for educating the youthful sovereign and administering the national affairs. At much personal inconvenience he enabled the young king to rescue himself from the control of the Douglases. He erected at his own expense a considerable part of St. Mary's College, St. Andrews, now used as a theological seminary. He died in 1539.

Within the area of the cathedral, on the floor of the south transept, are several tombstones, three of which have the inscriptions legible. The oldest is inscribed thus :—

"Hic jacet sepultus dompnus [dominus] Robertus Cathnic canonicus istius loci qui obiit anno dom MCCCLXXX."

A second tombstone has this legend :—

"Hic jacet Jacobus Elioly, canonicus metropolitane ecclesie Sancti Andree, qui obiit XVIII. die Novemb. ann. dom. MDXIII."

On the four corner compartments are these words:—" Fratres-obsecro-orate-pro me."

The third tombstone is inscribed as follows :—

"Hic jacet Ro-Graie, quondam vitriarius ac plumbarius hu almi templi, qui obiit primo Maii, ann. dom. MDIV."

At the corners of the stone are four shields, the first containing the letters I.H.S. [Iesus hominum Salvator] ; the second a lion rampant within an ingrailed border, being the arms of the House of Gray ; the third and fourth shields exhibit two arrows lying crossways.

Among the monuments of the seventeenth century one of the most interesting is a plain tombstone commemorating the cele-

brated Mr. Samuel Rutherford (vol. i., 326). The stone is inscribed
thus :—

"What tongue, what pen, or skill of men,
Can famous Rutherford commend,
His Learning justly raised his fame,
True godliness adorn'd his name.
He did converse with things above
Acquainted with Emmanuel's love.
Most orthodox he was and sound,
And many errors did confound.
For Zion's King and Zion's cause
And Scotland's covenanted laws
Most constantly he did contend
Until his time was at an end.
Thus he won to the full position
Of that which he had seen in vision."

A tombstone, now removed, commemorated Catherine Carstairs,
wife of Mr. James Wood, an eminent divine, and who was associated with Mr. Samuel Rutherford in maintaining the authority
and independence of the Scottish Church. The tombstone was
inscribed as follows :—

" Hic, beatæ resurrectionis spei plenæ, requiescunt, redemptoris
præstolantes adventum, exuviæ lectissimæ fœminæ Catharina
Carstairs, Jacobi Sylvii quondam conjugis charissimæ ; quæ vitam
terrenam, a prima ætate, modestia, sobrietate, industria, pietate,
aliisque virtutibus christianis, citra fucum ornatissimam ; tandem
morbi pertinacis torminibus confecta, insignemque de hoste salutis
humanæ, in gravissimo certamine, victoriam, Domini virtute, ingenti
solatio spectantium, adepta, cum cœlesti commutavit 9 Septembris,
anno 1658. Ætatis suæ 38. 18 conjugii, in quo xi liberos,
5 filios, 6 filias enixa, ter insuper abortum passu, pie et religiose
obiit. Anagrammate vero, casta, rara christiana."

Descended from the old and renowned family of the name,
James Wood was son of a merchant in St. Andrews. Having
acquired distinction at St. Andrews University, he was appointed
a regent in St. Salvator's College. In 1640 he was ordained
minister of Dunino. To the Greyfriars' Church, Aberdeen, and
Professorship of Divinity in Marischal College of that city he was
elected in 1644, but in the following year he was inducted as

Professor of Divinity in St. Mary's College, St. Andrews. From his early training he had some Episcopal leanings, but he was led, through the conversation of the celebrated Mr. Alexander Henderson, to cordially embrace the Presbyterian doctrines.* He took part with the Resolution party, which temporarily estranged him from Rutherford, who was principal of his college. On the recommendation of Mr. James Sharp, the future archbishop, he was in 1657 appointed Principal of St. Salvator's College.† When Episcopacy was established at the Restoration, Sharp used every effort to induce Mr. Wood to renounce his opinions, but without success. He caused him to be summoned before the Council in July, 1663, and on his appearing he was deprived of his principalship and ordered to confine himself within the city of Edinburgh. He was afterwards permitted to return to St. Andrews to visit his father, who had fallen sick. He was now seized with illness, and was some time confined to his chamber. By the primate he was frequently visited, and report was assiduously given forth that in the prospect of death he had expressed himself as indifferent about forms of church government, and was content to submit such matters to magisterial authority. Informed of the rumour, Mr. Wood subscribed a declaration, affirming his belief that " Presbyterian government was the ordinance of God ; " that " he never had the least change of thought concerning the necessity of it ; " and that were he to live, he " would account it his glory to seal this word of his testimony with his blood." His declaration was subscribed on the 2nd of March, 1664, and on the 15th day of the same month he breathed his last.‡

One of the witnesses to Mr. Wood's declaration was his brother-in-law, Mr. John Carstairs, minister of the Cathedral Church, Glasgow. This eminent person was eldest son of James Carstairs, merchant and magistrate in St. Andrews, and was descended from

* Correspondence of the Rev. Robert Wodrow, III., 34.
† Baillie's Letters and Journal, III., 216, 376.
‡ Wodrow's History, I., 404. Glasg., 1828.

the old family of Carstairs, of Newgrange, Fifeshire. Having obtained licence, he was ordained minister of Cathcart in June, 1647. While attending the army at the battle of Dunbar, in September, 1650, he was severely wounded, stripped, and left among the dead. He became minister of the Cathedral Church, Glasgow, in 1655. Summoned before the court of High Commission for witnessing the signature of Mr. Wood to his declaration, he retired to Ireland, and afterwards sought refuge in Holland. He was subsequently permitted to reside in Edinburgh, where he suffered from protracted sickness. He attended the Earl of Argyll before his execution in June, 1685, and was invited to administer death-bed consolation to the Lord Chancellor Rothes. In devotional fervour he excelled all his contemporaries. He died on the 5th February, 1686, in his sixty-fourth year, and thirty-ninth of his ministry. His eldest son, William, was the distinguished principal. His father, *Bailie* James Carstairs, died at St. Andrews, 29th September, 1671. On his tombstone were inscribed these lines :—

> " Reader, who on this stone doth cast thine eye,
> Do not forget the blessed memory
> Of Bailie James Carstairs; to whom God did impart
> A candid mind, without a double heart,
> To virtue, grace, and honesty inclin'd;
> To all his friends most singularly kind;
> He wisely did, with all men, follow peace ;
> At length expyr'd, full both of years and grace."

The following Latin verses commemorate John Carstairs, a youth of eighteen years, son of a Bailie James Carstairs, merchant in St. Andrews, who died 11th January, 1653 :—

> " Nate, patris matrisque amor, et spes una senectæ,
> Quamdiu vita fuit, nunc dolor et lachrymæ,
> Accipe quæ mœsti tibi solvunt justa parentes,
> Funere, naturæ vertitur ordo, tuo.

> " Charæ pater luctum, mater charissima planctum
> Siste ; piis placidam mors dat in astra viam.
> Ante diem morior ; nulla hinc dispendia ; non tam
> Mors nocet ante diem, quam beat ante diem."

A tombstone, long since removed, bearing the name of William Wood and his wife Catherine Balfour, who both died in 1622, severally aged twenty-seven, probably celebrated the grandfather and grandmother of the future Principal of St. Salvator's College. According to Monteith, the inscription was as follows :—

"Memoriæ sacrum. Hic jacet spectatæ pietatis, probitatis et fidei, illustris civis, Gulielmus Wood; cum fœmina lectissima, conjuge dilectissima Christiana Balfour, qui simul morbo et morte correpti diem obierunt, ejusdem consortes tumuli, ut participes thalami. Hic obiit anno 1612, ætatis 27. Hæc obiit anno 1612, ætatis 27, dies 14.

David Balfour, sometime one of the Royal Scottish Guard in France, and latterly Provost of St. Andrews, is on his tombstone thus commemorated :—

"Hic jacet honorabilis vir David Balfour, quondam regi Galliæ ab excubiis corporis; civitatis sancti Andreæ præfectus : qui obiit Andreapoli, 16 Februarii 1625, D.B.

"Victima pro Batavis, Germanus morte litavit;
Sæve tamen sua est hostia cæsa manu :
Ipse redux, ramum referens pacalis olivæ,
Ad tumulum statui hunc arma virumque meum."

On his monument, David Falconer, bailie, was celebrated thus :—

"Hic jacet David Falconer, ex sat honesta familia oriundus, qui honestam matronam Jonetam Jack in hac civitate duxit, ex qua octo liberos habuit; sub præfecto, urbis magistratum, summa cum laude gessit; et ingenium, candorem, urbanitatem, aliasque virtutes ubique monstravit : quæ ei natalium honestatem et erectam satis indolem redolebant. Decessit autem ætatis 47, anno Dom. 1668, 27 Aprilis."

From the burial-place of the family of Trail we have these epitaphs :—

"Memoriæ sacrum Helenæ Myrtonæ, optimæ matronæ, D. Andreæ Trallii, tribuni militum, viri optimi, primum conjugis ; dein D. Roberti Danestoni equitis, consiliarii conservatoris, quæ obiit 13 Feb., 1608. Neonon Mathildæ Melvinæ, Jacobi Trallii conjugis lectissimæ et piissimæ fœminæ, mœrens posuit. Obiit 23 Novembris, 1608."

" Hic jacet honorabilis mulier Helena Traill, uxor Petri Arnot de Balcormo, quæ obiit 25 Februarii, 1607. Job xix. 25 ; 1 Cor. xv. 55.

Hugh Scrymgeour, of Balrymont, who died in 1646, is on his tombstone commemorated thus :—

" Exuviæ egregii et generosi viri, Hugonis Scrimgeri a Balraymont ; quem prudentia, constantia aliæque virtutes præclarum ; dictorum, factorum et amicitiæ fides inviolata, percharum reddidere ; hoc marmore teguntur. Obiit æræ christianæ 1646, Feb. 7, Ætatis 53. Memento mori."

James Sword, Provost of the city, who died 6th February, 1657, aged sixty-four, has on his monument these lines :—

" Gloria municipum quondam, nunc alta gravedo,
Laus olim, jam mœror, hac in lychnite quiescit ;
Cujus vita fuit pietatis normula veræ,
Urbem Andreanam diuturna pace gubernans ;
Fidus in officio, cunctis et jura ministrans ;
Non, propriis inhians ; in publica commoda pronus ;
Mens invicta malis ; nimis haud elata secundis ;
Vixerat in Christo : in Christo sua vota suprema,
       Mors ultima linea rerum."

John Echline, of Pittadrow, twelve years Regent of Philosophy in St. Leonard's College, is thus celebrated :—

" D. O. M. S. Hic situs est vir doctissimus, Magister Joannes Echline, a Pittadrow ; qui bonas literas et philosophiam in collegio Leonardino, annos 12 cum singulari eruditionis et ingenii laude, docuit : pie et placide obiit 7 Novembris, 1603. Ætatis 52.

"Hujus habet pietas venturæ et præmia vitæ ;
Dulce mihi Christo vivere : dulce mori
Immatura nimis ne quis mea fata queratur,
Nunc vitam hanc, vita perpete, penso brevem."

Mr. John Sword, eldest son of Provost James Sword, who died in 1654, aged thirty-two, has these lines on his monument :—

" Insignis juvenis, charitum ditatus abunde
Magnificis donis, hac requiescit humo ;
Namque in eo probitas præluxit, pallade juncta,
Cunctaque quæ juvenem nobilitare solent.

Spiritus in cœlis, corpus tellure quiescit;
Nobis virtutes ut paradigma forent:
Reliquit famam mundo, nomenque poetis,
Dulcia dum Christo cantica dulce canit."

Likewise celebrated in Latin verse are John Wilson, commissary clerk at St. Andrews, who died in 1666, and his wife Janet Robertson, who died in the following year. Their epitaph proceeds thus:—

"Hunc vitæ integritas, hunc mens et acerrima, virtus
Omnigena certant condecorare virum;
Hic odit scriba et bifrontis bivia Jani;
Conscribens, cur sic secla futura beeut,
Hac itur ad superos; hac dum pulvisculus urna
Dormit in exili, mens petit astra poli.
Fœmina, præclaris fata avibus, ecce marito
Est consors tumuli, quæ fuit ante tori."

A monument formerly commemorated Mr. William Preston, son of Sir John Preston, baronet of Airdrie, who died 27th March, 1657, aged 26. It was inscribed as follows:—

"Hic conditus est generosus præstans et perdoctus juvenis, magister Gulielmus Preston; filius clarissimi viri domi Joannis Preston equitis ac baronis de Airdry; philosophiam in gymnasio Leonardino, per triennium totum professus, ingenio, industria, moribusque probatis, omnium. Suffragia meruit; hinc præmatura morte abreptus intacta fama obiit 6 Cal. Aprilis (Martii 27), anno Dom. 1657. Ætatis 26. Dignum laude virum musa vetat mori. Vive memor lethi; fugit hora."

A plain tombstone commemorates the Rev. William Wilkie, D.D., author of the *Epigoniad*, a poem written in the manner of the "Iliad." Dr. Wilkie was born in the parish of Dalmeny, Linlithgowshire, on the 5th October, 1721, and having studied theology and obtained licence, was settled minister of Ratho 17th May, 1753. In November, 1759, he became Professor of Natural Philosophy at St. Andrews. He died 10th October, 1772. An ingenious philosopher and expert agriculturist, Dr. Wilkie was held in esteem by his contemporaries. As a poet he enjoyed considerable celebrity. Afflicted by a perpetual chill, which he sought to overcome by profuse clothing, his habits were eccentric. To his influence the Rev. David Wilkie, his father's cousin, was indebted for the living of Cults; the son of that gentleman was Sir David Wilkie, the distinguished artist.

By an ordinary gravestone is marked the resting-place of Dr. George Hill, Principal of St. Mary's College, an accomplished theologian and ecclesiastical leader. He was born at St. Andrews in June, 1750, his father being one of the ministers of the city. In his twenty-second year he was appointed assistant and successor to the Professor of Greek in the United College. In 1780 he received the additional office of minister of the second parochial charge. In 1787 he was preferred to the Professorship of Theology in St. Mary's College, and in other three years was advanced to the Principalship. In 1808 he was appointed to the office of minister of the first charge. He died 19th December, 1819, in his seventieth year, and the forty-second of his ministry. Dr. Hill held all the honours which could be obtained by a clergyman of the Scottish Church. He was one of the King's Chaplains, Dean of the Order of the Thistle, and Dean of the Chapel Royal. He was leader of the General Assembly, and an extensive dispenser of Crown patronage. As a preacher he enjoyed an unrivalled popularity. His lectures in divinity, published posthumously, have been frequently reprinted.

A handsome mural monument, with an appropriate epitaph, celebrates the learning and virtues of Professor Adam Ferguson. Born in 1724, at Logierait, Perthshire, of which parish his father was minister, he was early enrolled a student of St. Andrews University. He prosecuted his theological studies at Edinburgh, where he enjoyed the intercourse of William Robertson, Hugh Blair, John Home, Alexander Carlyle, and other distinguished contemporaries. Licensed as a preacher, he obtained the chaplaincy of the 42nd Regiment, an appointment, which he held for thirteen years. In 1757 he became tutor in the family of the Earl of Bute, and in other two years was appointed Professor of Natural Philosophy in the University of Edinburgh. This chair he ex-

changed for that of Moral Philosophy in 1764, which he resigned
in favour of the celebrated Dugald Stewart in 1785. He afterwards
resided in Peeblesshire, and latterly at St. Andrews. He died at
St. Andrews on the 22nd February, 1816, at the age of ninety-two.
His best known works are his "History of the Roman Republic,"
and his "Principles of Moral and Political Science."

Another distinguished nonagenarian is in the cathedral churchyard celebrated by an appropriate tombstone. Dr. John Hunter,
Professor of Humanity in the United College, died at St. Andrews
on the 18th January, 1837, aged ninety-one. Of humble parentage, he
was born in the parish of Closeburn, Dumfriesshire, in September,
1746. Educated at the Free School of Wallacehall in his native
parish, he afterwards became a student at the University of Edinburgh. Attracting the notice of Lord Monboddo, he became his
private secretary. On his lordship's recommendation he was
appointed in 1775 to his professorial chair. After discharging his
duties as Latin professor upwards of sixty years with remarkable
acceptance, he was appointed Principal of the United College.
He died in the following year. His editions of the Latin classics
are much valued.

Dr. Thomas Gillespie, successor of Dr. John Hunter in the
Humanity Chair, has a plain tombstone erected at his grave
Born at Closeburn in February, 1778, he was educated at Wallace-
hall, and in 1802 entered the University of Edinburgh. Having
obtained licence he was in 1813 appointed to the church living at
Cults through the influence of Dr. John Hunter, whose daughter
he had married. In 1828 he became Dr. Hunter's assistant in the
Humanity Chair, and eight years afterwards succeeded to the full
emoluments of the office on his constituent's elevation to the
Principalship. He died at Dunino, near St. Andrews, on the 11th
September, 1844, aged sixty-seven. Dr. Gillespie excelled as a con-
versationalist, and was an accomplished scholar. He composed
respectable verses. Articles from his pen in *Constable's* and
Blackwood's Magazines abound in genuine humour.

Within the ancient chapel of St. Regulus, a mural tablet commemorates Professor George Cook, D.D., who is there interred. This eminent ecclesiastical leader was born at St. Andrews, in March, 1773. Having completed his theological studies and obtained licence, he was in his twenty-second year ordained minister of Laurencekirk. In 1828 he succeeded Dr. Thomas Chalmers as Professor of Moral Philosophy and Political Economy in the United College. He died at St. Andrews, on the 13th May, 1843. He was Dean of the Order of the Thistle, and one of her Majesty's chaplains. His principal works are his " History of the Reformation," and a " History of the Church of Scotland." He succeeded his relative, Principal Hill, as leader of the moderate section of the Church.

Dr. John Reid, the eminent physiologist, rests in the cathedral churchyard. Born at Bathgate, 9th April, 1809, he was educated at the University of Edinburgh. Having attained his medical degree, he in 1833 became a partner in the Edinburgh Anatomical School. In 1836 he accepted the physiological lectureship in the Edinburgh extra-Academical School. In 1838 he was appointed Pathologist to the Edinburgh Infirmary, and in 1841 was preferred to the chair of Anatomy at St. Andrews. Attacked by the terrible malady of cancer in the tongue, in November, 1847, he underwent several operations without lasting benefit : he died at St. Andrews on the 30th July, 1849. During his last illness he prepared for the press his " Physiological, Anatomical, and Pathological Researches," a work which was published posthumously.

A tombstone marks the grave of Professor William Spalding, of the United College. This accomplished individual was born at Aberdeen, in 1808. Having studied at the University of Edinburgh, he passed advocate, and was afterwards elected Professor of Rhetoric in the University of Edinburgh. In 1845 he was preferred to the chair of Logic and Rhetoric at St. Andrews. To his professorial duties, till enfeebled by illness, he indefatigably devoted himself. He died at St. Andrews, on the 16th November, 1859, aged fifty-two. He published a work on Italy, and a compendious " History of English Literature."

A handsome monument marks the grave of Lieutenant-Colonel

Sir Hugh Lyon Playfair, LL.D., provost of the city; it was reared during his lifetime at his own expense. Son of James Playfair, D.D., Principal of the United College, he was born on the 17th November, 1786. Obtaining a cadetship in the Indian army, he proceeded to Calcutta in 1805. There as an artillery officer he greatly distinguished himself, chiefly by his powers of arrangement and administration. As superintendent of the great military road between Calcutta and Benares, 440 miles in length, he obtained for his services the highest commendation of his superiors. In 1827 he was promoted to the rank of major. He retired from active service in 1834, and established his residence at St. Andrews. In 1842 he was elected provost, when he commenced those reforms in the city which are associated with his name. His services were honourably acknowledged. The university conferred upon him the degree of Doctor of Laws; his portrait, painted at the expense of the citizens, was placed in the Town Hall. The corporation presented him with a piece of plate, and he was knighted by the Queen. Full of age and honours, Sir Hugh died at St. Andrews, on the 23rd January, 1861, aged seventy-five.

In the cathedral churchyard repose the remains of James Frederick Ferrier, Professor of Moral Philosophy in the United College. His grave is denoted by a tombstone; he is likewise commemorated in St. Cuthbert's churchyard, Edinburgh (Vol. I., 70).

A suitable monument denotes the resting-place of John Robertson, D.D., minister of the Cathedral Church, Glasgow. This excellent man and accomplished scholar was born at Perth on the 9th April, 1824. Having distinguished himself at the Grammar School, he entered the University of St. Andrews, and after a brilliant career was licensed to preach in February, 1848. Before the close of that year he was, on the invitation of the people, ordained to the pastoral charge of the united parishes of Mains and Strathmartin, in the county of Forfar. Declining several offers of preferment, he accepted in 1858 the office of minister of the Cathedral Church, Glasgow. Here his services were as acceptable as they were faithful and laborious. But his health proved unequal to his exertions. After an illness of some duration, he died at St. Andrews on the 9th January, 1865. For some years preceding his death he held office as Vice-Chancellor of the University of Glasgow. His discourses have been published posthumously, accompanied with a memoir.

A tombstone commemorates the Rev. John Park, D.D., minister of the parish. This accomplished clergyman was born at Greenock about the year 1805. After ministering for eleven years as pastor of Rodney Street Presbyterian Church, Liverpool, he was in 1843 translated to the parish of Glencairn, Dumfriesshire. To the first charge of St. Andrews he was preferred in 1854. He died suddenly on the 8th April, 1865. An elegant and powerful preacher, Dr. Park was also distinguished for his powers as a musician. Several of his musical compositions have been pronounced equal to those of the great masters. The song, "Where Gadie rins," is from his pen.

A suitable memorial stone marks the grave of John Cook, D.D., Professor of Ecclesiastical History in St. Mary's College. Son of John Cook, D.D., Professor of Divinity in the University of St. Andrews, he was born in 1807, and having obtained licence, was in 1828 ordained minister of Laurencekirk. He was translated to St. Leonard's in 1845, and in 1860 was appointed to the chair of Church History. In 1859 he was elected Moderator of the General Assembly, and in 1863 was appointed a Dean of the Chapel Royal. He died 17th April, 1869, in his sixty-second year, and the fortieth of his ministry. Expert in the concerns of business, Dr. Cook held the convenership of many important committees of the General Assembly.

Within the chapel of St. Regulus rest the remains of Robert Chambers, LL.D., author and publisher. This gifted and amiable gentleman was born at Peebles on the 10th July, 1802. Thrown in early youth on his own resources, he commenced business at Edinburgh as a dealer in old books; he afterwards joined his elder brother William as a bookseller and printer. When William started *Chambers's Edinburgh Journal* in 1832, he became the principal contributor, and the success of the two brothers was henceforth secure and constant. Dr. Chambers spent his latter years at St. Andrews, where he died on the 17th March, 1871. His principal works are "The Traditions of Edinburgh," "The Picture of Scotland," "Histories of the Rebellions," "Lives of Eminent Scotsmen," "Popular Rhymes of Scotland," "Ancient Sea Margins of Scotland," "The Domestic Annals of Scotland," and "The Book of Days."

PARISH OF SCOONIE.

In the parish churchyard is a mortuary enclosure belonging to the family of Anderson of Montrave. A mural tablet commemorates the late Major Alexander Anderson of Montrave, who died 24th June, 1855, aged sixty-one. For several years Major Anderson was engaged in active military service in India. Succeeding to his patrimonial estates in 1818, he returned home, and continued thereafter to devote himself to his duties as a landowner.

An obelisk of polished granite celebrates Alexander Boswell, proprietor of the Hawkslaw Works, Leven. This enterprising individual (a cadet of the old house of Boswell of Blackader) was born at Leven in 1805. In early life he became a clerk in the Kirkland Works; he subsequently was appointed manager of the spinning establishment at Prinlaws, and latterly he opened the Hawkslaw Works on his own account. He died 18th January, 1867, aged sixty-two.

A mural monument commemorates Colonel Thomas Gibson, of the 83rd Regiment, who died in 1838, aged eighty-four. He was youngest son of the second last proprietor of Durie of his name. The founder of this branch of the family of Gibson was Sir Alexander Gibson, President of the Court of Session, author of the "Decisions" known as *Durie's Practicks.*

Tombstones commemorate Henry Balfour, of Levenbank, son of

a manufacturer in Dundee, and father of the senior partner of the firm of Balfour, Williamson, and Co., Liverpool, who died 6th July, 1854; Thomas F. Ballingal, architect, who died 13th November, 1866, aged forty-five; and Robert Nairn, farmer, Burnhill, who died in 1858, aged sixty-three.

The following ministers of the parish are by admiring friends and grateful parishioners appropriately commemorated :—The Rev. David Swan, D.D., ordained 10th May, 1764; died 22nd October, 1812, aged seventy-seven. The Rev. George Brewster, D.D. (brother of Sir David Brewster), ordained 26th August, 1812; died 20th June, 1855, aged seventy-two; and the Rev. James Blackwood, born 19th August, 1830; ordained 1860; died 16th May, 1866.

PARISH OF STRATHMIGLO.

From tombstones in the parish churchyard, we have the following metrical inscriptions :—

" Passenger, be to Thyself so kind
    As on this stone to cast thine eyes and mind,
    And think on death while life is lent to you,
    For Thou art commanded so to do."

" The precious soul possesseth heaven above,
    Which was the hope and wishes of its love;
    Now free from storms of sinful time,
    In heavenly mansions thou doth shine."

" Death from his stroke none are exeemed ;
    This mournful tomb doth grace,
    The names of such who were esteemed
    Among the faithful race."

PARISH OF TORRYBURN.

The following quaint epitaphs are from the parish churchyard :—

" In this churchyard lies Eppie Coutts,
    Either here or hereabouts ;
    But whaur it is nane can tell
    Till Eppie rise and tell hersel.' "

" At anchor now, in death's dark road,
        Rides honest Captain Hill,
    Who served his king and feared his God,
        With upright heart and will.

" In social life sincere and just,
        To vice of no kind given,
    So that his better part, we trust,
        Hath made the port of heaven."

" Here lieth one below this stone
        Who loved to gather gear ;
    Yet all his life did want a wife
        Of him to take the care :
He won his meat, both ear and late,
        Betwixt *Cleish* and *Craigflour*,
    And craved this stone might lie upon
        Him at his latter hour."

KINROSS-SHIRE.

PARISH OF KINROSS.

In the old churchyard on the north bank of Lochleven, a tomb-stone with a suitable inscription commemorates James Rankine, younger, of Coldun, who died in 1722. There is a tradition that the mason who engraved the legend was in the habit of boasting of his skill, when a comrade pointing out that he had sculptured the word "Coldoch " for " Coldun," he was so overcome with shame that he forthwith committed self-slaughter.

In the old churchyard Mary Craig Dalzel is celebrated thus :—

> " Her's were the active mind, the grateful heart,
>   And hand stretched out affliction to relieve ;
> 'Twas her's to eat that truly Christian fruit
>   Which feels more bless'd to give than to receive."

PARISH OF PORTMOAK.

Of this parish the Rev. Ebenezer Erskine was many years in-cumbent, before his translation to Stirling (see *supra*, p. 40). In the churchyard a flat tombstone commemorates his first wife, Mrs. Alison Turpie, and several of their children. The inscription is as follows :—

" Here lyes the valuabell dust of Alison Turpie, spouse to Mr. Ebenezer Ereskin, minister of the gospel in Portmoak, who de-parted to glory, after she had born ten children, four of which lye here interred with her. She died August the 31, 1720, aged 39

years.   Henrie Ereskin, born August the 6, 1705 ; depairted June,
1713.   Alexander, born July the 20, 1708 ; depairted June the 20,
1713.   Ralph, born Januarie the 17, 1712; died April, 1713 ;
Isabel, born July the 21, 1716 ; died Decem. 7, 1770.

> "The law brought forth her precepts ten,
>   And then dissolved in grace ;
> This saint ten children bore, and then
>   In glory took her place.

"Awake and sing, ye that dwell in dust, for the dew is as the
dew of herbs, and the earth shall cast out her dead."

In the churchyard a handsome monument, reared in 1812, celebrates Michael Bruce, the ingenious and short-lived poet.   It is
thus inscribed :—

"To the memory of Michael Bruce, who was born at Kinnesswood
in 1746, and died while a student, in the 21st year of his age.
Meek and gentle in spirit, sincere and unpretending in his Christian
deportment, refined in intellect and elevated in character, he was
greatly beloved by his friends, and won the esteem of all; while
his genius, whose fire neither poverty nor sickness could quench,
produced those odes, unrivalled in simplicity and pathos, which
have shed an undying lustre on his name.

> "Early, bright, transient, chaste as morning dew,
>   He sparkled and exhaled, and went to heaven."

Bruce was born on the 27th March, 1746.   Though in humble
circumstances, his parents determined to educate him for the
ministry.   During four years he prosecuted his classical studies at
the University of Edinburgh.   He subsequently entered on the
study of theology, and employed himself in tuition as a means of
support.   Under incessant mental toil, a constitution naturally
feeble began to decline.   He died of a lingering consumption, 6th
July, 1767, aged twenty-one.   At college he had as his companion
Mr. John Logan, a person of considerable genius, and who afterwards becoming minister of Leith, acquired reputation as a
preacher.   Subsequent to Bruce's death Logan visited his parents,
and offered to publish their son's poems for their pecuniary benefit.
He was accordingly intrusted with the whole of the MSS., including

an unpublished book of hymns, which the parents designated their son's "Gospel Sonnets." Of the latter, several were familiar to the neighbours, who had derived their knowledge of the compositions from the deceased poet himself. After a considerable delay, Logan published a small volume, entitled "Poems on Several Occasions, by Michael Bruce," accompanied by a laudatory preface commemorative of the writer. The scantiness of the compositions, and the absence of the "Gospel Sonnets," disquieted the parents. Asked by the father of the deceased poet to return the MS. book of hymns, Logan stated that it was lost. Logan was afterwards associated with other clerical brethren in preparing a collection of Scripture Paraphrases for the use of the Scottish Church. He became the most conspicuous member of the committee by contributing a number of compositions, which were readily included in the collection. But Michael Bruce's father recognised them as his son's "Gospel Sonnets"—and such, with a few verbal alterations, they undoubtedly were. The best esteemed of Bruce's lyrical compositions is his "Ode to the Cuckoo."

PERTHSHIRE.

PARISH OF ABERDALGIE.

Within the old parish church a monument of black marble, with a statue in full armour, formerly commemorated Sir William Olifaunt, or Oliphant, Lord of Aberdalgie, a valorous adherent of King Robert the Bruce. The monument was thus inscribed :—

"Hic jacet dominus Willielmus Oliphant, dominus de Aberdalgy, qui obiit quinto die mensis Februarii, anno 1329."*

Sir William Oliphant was one of the *magnates Scotiæ*, who subscribed the famous letter to the Pope in 1320, asserting the independence of the kingdom. From King Robert he received grants of land in the counties of Edinburgh and Perth. His son, Sir Walter Oliphant, his successor in the lordship of Aberdalgie, received in marriage Elizabeth, a younger daughter of King Robert. The representative of the House was by James II. constituted a Lord of Parliament. In 1839 James Blair Oliphant, of Gask and Ardblair, served himself heir male of Francis, tenth Lord Oliphant, and of William Oliphant, of Newton, the younger brother of Laurence, third Lord Oliphant. Mr. Blair Oliphant is now represented by his nephew, Thomas Laurence Kington Oliphant, of Gask, who has succeeded to the family estates as heir of line. The gravestone of Sir William Oliphant rests in the churchyard ; the three crescents, the arms of his House, are traceable on it.

* Douglas's Peerage, p. 526.

L

PARISH OF ABERFOYLE.

At the east end of the church a gravestone is thus inscribed :—
" Robertus Kirk, A.M. Linguæ Hiberniæ lumen."
The Rev. Robert Kirk was seventh son of Mr. James Kirk,
minister of Aberfoyle. Having studied at the Universities of
Edinburgh and St. Andrews, he was, in 1664, ordained minister
of Balquhidder. From this parish, in 1685, he was translated to
Aberfoyle. An eminent Celtic scholar, he prepared a Gaelic
version of the Psalms, and superintended the republication of the
Irish Bible, adding a brief Gaelic vocabulary. He also produced a
remarkable work on " Fairy Superstition and the Second Sight,"
which was reprinted at Edinburgh in 1815. He died 14th May,
1692, aged about fifty-one, and in the twenty-eighth year of his
ministry.

PARISH OF AUCHTERARDER.

A handsome mausoleum in Aberuthven churchyard constitutes the burial-place of the ducal house of Montrose. Within
the vault are deposited the remains of James, second Marquis of
Montrose, son of " the great Marquis," and styled *the Good*, on
account of his amiable qualities ; he died in 1669. The vault also
contains the remains of James, third Duke of Montrose, who died
30th December, 1836. This nobleman was Lord Justice-General
of Scotland, Lord Lieutenant of Stirlingshire, and Chancellor of the
University of Glasgow.

In Aberuthven churchyard Robert Carrick, of Kilders, who
died in 1775, is celebrated in these lines :—

> " In him
> Beauty, merit, noble virtue shined,
> Of manners, gentle, easy, gen'rous, kind ;
> Upright, a friend to truth, of soul sincere,

In action faithful, and in honour clear;
True to his word, his goodness unconfined,
Warm in his friendships,—friend to human kind :
His feeling heart with welling pity glowed,
His willing hand as liberally bestowed;
And his short life did a true pattern give
How husbands, parents, neighbours, friends, should live,
Honoured by all, approved and loved so well,
Though dying young, like fruit that's ripe he fell.
To him so mourned in death, so loved in life,
The grieving parent and the weeping wife
With tears inscribes this monument of stone
That holds his ashes and awaits her own."

From tombstones erected by parents in memory of their children at Aberuthven we have the following inscriptions :—

" Weep not for me, be now content;
I was not yours, but only lent;
Dry up your tears,—and weep no more,
I am not lost, but gone before."

" To this sad shrine, whoe'er thou art, draw near,
And mingle with maternal woe a tear,
For her whose worth, whose charms effulgent shone,
Equalled by few, nor e'er eclipsed by one.
Her quickness darted with superior ray,
Uncommon wisdom for her short-lived day ;
Though few in years, too few, alas ! she told,
She seemed in all things but in beauty old.
Ah, cruel death ! who early thus unstrung
The strength of one so lovely and so young.
These charms are faded, and their worth is flown,
Love, beauty, goodness, mourn your darling gone."

PARISH OF BALQUHIDDER.

In the parish churchyard is an old burial-place of Clan Alpin where are four tiers of graves parallel to each other, three of which had been included within the chancel of the church in its original form; the tiers are denoted by a number of oblong blocks of gravestones, for the most part without inscription or emblem. In the third range from the church, the centre stone of the tier denotes the resting-place of the celebrated Rob Roy Macgregor. It is six feet in length by fourteen inches in breadth and depth, and has its surface adorned with antique and interesting emblems. In the centre are represented a man and a broadsword ; on the upper part are a number of dogs, and in the lower portion several crosses of a peculiar form. It seems of older origin than Roy's period, and had probably served another purpose before it was placed upon his grave. Adjoining this stone, on the north, an altar tombstone commemorates Rob Roy's eldest son, who died a year before his father. It bears the shield of the clan, with the following inscriptions, one on its upper and the other in its lower division. This stone is erected by Lieutenant Gregorson, 1770. "Here lies the corpse of Colonel Macgregor, who died in the year 1735, aged 31 years."

Rob Roy Macgregor, called Roy, or red, from the colour of his hair, was second son of Donald Macgregor of Glengyle, a colonel in the king's service, and his wife, a daughter of Campbell of Glenfalloch; he was born about the year 1670, at Inverlochlarig, in Balquhidder. For a period he lived at Craig Royston, near the eastern border of Loch Lomond, on an estate presented to him by a relative, adding to his finances by receiving imposts from the neighbouring gentry for protecting their herds from Highland banditti. Attempting business as a cattle dealer, he involved himself in embarrassments, and the Duke of Montrose, who was a principal creditor, pursued him with all the stern appliances of the law. He proceeded to Glen Dochart, where he obtained the protection of the Duke of Argyll and the Earl of Breadalbane, hereditary enemies of the Grahams. Incited by his wife, a daughter of Macgregor of Conan, he seized the cattle and even the rents of the Duke of Montrose, and penetrating into the Lowlands, plundered the herds of all who refused by subsidy to secure his friendship. This lawless violence awakened the attention of the authorities, and a reward of £1,000 was offered for his apprehension. Though often in the greatest danger, he escaped capture, and died in his own house about the year 1736, at a somewhat advanced age. He was benevolent to his followers, by whom he was sincerely lamented.

Near the south-west corner of Balquhidder church a flat grave-stone commemorates Isabel Campbell, daughter of Sir Colin Campbell, of Mochester, and first wife of the Rev. Robert Kirk, minister of this parish, and afterwards of Aberfoyle. There is the following inscription :

"Isabel Campbell,
Spouse to Robert Kirk, minister,
Died Dec. 25, 1680.
She had two sons,
Colin and William.
Her age 25.

Stones weep though eyes are dry—
Choicest flowers soonest die ;
Their sun oft sets at noon
Whose fruit is ripe in June.

Then tears of joy be thine,
Since earth must soon resign
To God what is divine.
Nasci est ægrotare
Vivere est sæpe mori,
Et mori est vivere.
Love and live."

PARISH OF BLACKFORD.

In the churchyard are interred and suitably commemorated Archibald and Sir William Moncreiff, Bart., successively ministers of Blackford. The former died in August, 1649 ; the latter, 9th December, 1767. In 1744 William Moncreiff succeeded to the family baronetcy on the death of Sir Hugh Moncreiff of Tipper-mallo. He was great-great-grandson of Archibald Moncreiff, minister of Abernethy, second son of William Moncreiff of that Ilk, who died in 1634, and whose elder brother John was on the 22nd April, 1626, created a baronet of Nova Scotia. The eldest son of Sir William Moncreiff, was Sir Henry Moncreiff Wellwood, Bart., successively minister of Blackford and of St. Cuthbert's, Edinburgh, who died 9th August, 1827. The eldest son of this gentleman became a Lord of Session; also his grandson (Vol. I. 132).

In the secluded churchyard of Gleneagles, is the old burial-place of the family of Haldane; it now belongs to the Earl of Camperdown. Within the old chapel of Tullibardine, the Dukes of Athole formerly interred; the chapel is now the burial-place of Viscount Strathallan.

PARISH OF BLAIR-ATHOLE.

Within the old parish church in the vault of the ducal house of Athole were deposited the remains of John Graham of Claverhouse, Viscount Dundee, who fell at the battle of Killicrankie, 27th July, 1689. An erect stone on the field of battle marks the spot where he received his death-wound. Eldest son of Sir William Graham of Claverhouse, and his wife Lady Jean Carnegie, fourth daughter of John, first Earl of Northesk, he was educated at the University of St. Andrews. In 1672 he became a Cornet in the Guards of the Prince of Orange. Returning to Scotland in 1677, he received from Charles II. the command of a regiment of horse raised against the Covenanters. In May 1679, he captured several Covenanters who were proceeding to Loudonhill, Ayrshire, to celebrate the Holy Communion. In a few days afterwards he was encountered by the congregation of the Covenant at Drumclog, where he and his dragoons were signally defeated. In June was fought the battle of Bothwell Bridge, so disastrous to the Covenanters. On this occasion Graham commanded the cavalry under the Duke of Monmouth: after the victory he evinced that cruelty towards the vanquished which led to his being thereafter known as " the bloody *Clavers.*' In 1682, he was appointed Sheriff of Wigtown, in which office he proved himself so expert in suppressing freedom of worship, that he was constituted Captain of the Royal Regiment of horse, and sworn of the Privy Council. By James II. he was in 1688 created Viscount Dundee, and raised to the military rank of Major-General. He was in London when the king's affairs became desperate, and made offer to raise an army to resist the approach of the Prince of Orange. James felt that it was too late, and Graham, with a troop of sixty horse, returned to Scotland. In the following year he raised an army in support of the exiled monarch. General Mackay was sent to resist him, and the two armies met at the Pass of Killicrankie on the 17th June, 1689. After a severe conflict Mackay was defeated with serious loss ; but wounded by a musket ball Graham fell in the moment of victory. He expired the following day.

Beside the remains of Viscount Dundee rest those of George, sixth Duke of Athole, who died 16th January, 1864, aged 50. He is commemorated by a mural monument in the aisle of the old church. The monument, which is executed by Mr. John Steell, is nine feet in height and five feet in breadth ; it has as a principal figure the trunk of a stricken oak ; and at the point where it is broken through, a branch of ivy which entwined it droops towards the ground. On one side of the tree a vigorous offshoot remains in full blossom, and upon it hangs the plaid, or mantle of the deceased. At the other side of the tree is a figure of one of the Duke's retainers—a stalwart volunteer, leaning on the top of his reversed rifle, lamenting his chief.

PARISH OF CALLANDER.

At Little Leny, the burial-place of the Buchanans of Leny and Cambusmore, a gravestone denotes the resting-place of Dugald

Buchanan, the eminent Gaelic poet. This remarkable person was son of a farmer at Balquhidder, and was there born in 1716. At first he engaged in trade, but subsequently he became schoolmaster and catechist at Kinloch-Rannoch ; he aided in translating the New Testament into the Gaelic language. Buchanan died on the 2nd June, 1768. His "Hymns" have been frequently printed. As a writer of Gaelic poetry he holds a foremost place.

PARISH OF COLLACE.

In the parish churchyard an altar tombstone commemorates John Mather, a native of Brechin, who while conveying contraband liquor from thence to Perth was in a scuffle shot by a party of soldiers. This took place at Collace in 1740. Two of the soldiers were tried for murder, found guilty, and sentenced to be hanged. They obtained a royal pardon, much to the dissatisfaction of the citizens of Edinburgh, who had resolved to wreak vengeance upon them in the manner in which the mob had previously dealt with Captain Porteous. The soldiers were liberated at midnight. Mather's tombstone is thus inscribed :—

> "Stay passenger, as you go ;
> Think on him who now lys lo.
> As you now walk, so once did I,
> Remember, friend, all men must die ;
> And then God's awful throne attend.
> O speedily your life amend,
> Now whilst you health and strength enjoy,
> Your time if wise you'll weel employ."

PARISH OF COMRIE.

On Dunmore Hill a handsome obelisk, seventy-two feet in height was, as an inscription bears, reared by his friends in Perthshire in honour of Henry Dundas, first Viscount Melville (Vol. I.,

9, 14, 172). The obelisk is composed of granite, and was reared at the cost of £1400.

PARISH OF COUPAR-ANGUS.

The parish churchyard includes the site of the abbey, founded by Malcolm IV. in 1164. An arched doorway flanked with buttresses, is the only remaining portion of the structure.

A monumental slab, preserved in the parish manse, is thus inscribed :—

" Hic . iaet . dns . Archibald' . M'Vi . olim prpos . de . Kilmvn."

The person commemorated is supposed to be Archibald Macvicar Provost of the Collegiate Church of Kilmun, Argyleshire, from 1529 to 1548.

There was formerly in the churchyard a monumental fragment inscribed—

" . . . . . Willhelmvs . de . Montefixio. . . . . . "

This had doubtless commemorated a member of the old Norman House of Montfichet, or Muschet. Richard de Montfichet received a charter of the lands of Cargill and Kincardine from William the Lion: The Muschets were benefactors of the abbey of Cupar. About the middle of the fourteenth century one of the three co-heiresses of the house married Sir John Drummond, a progenitor of the Earls of Perth. With other children, Sir John and Lady Drummond had a daughter Annabella, who became queen of Robert III. and mother of James I.

On another monumental fragment were the words Gilbertvs de Hay. The family of Hay of Errol, large benefactors to the abbey, are interred within its precincts. Here were interred in 1333 Gilbert Hay, who died at Aberdeen ; and in 1466 Gilbert Hay, son and heir of William de Hay of Errol. Most probably the latter was celebrated on the fragment. The Earls of Errol

were interred in Coupar-Angus Abbey at a period subsequent to the
Reformation. Andrew, seventh Earl of Errol, who died on the
8th October, 1585, was here buried.*

In the vestibule of the church, on a marble tablet, Dr. Robert
Robertson, Physician to the Royal Hospital, Greenwich, thus
commemorates his mother and sister :—

"In memoriam parentis amantissimæ et percaræ quæ A.D. 1771,
obiit 68 annos nata, filius Rob^{tus} Robertson, M.D., F.R.S., F.A.S.L.,
Nosocomij Reg. Grenovic Medicus ; *Itemque*, in memoriam ANNÆ
sororis suæ, hoc marmor ponendum curavit."

Dr. Robertson was a surgeon in the Royal Navy, and was
appointed physician to Greenwich Hospital in 1790. Among
other professional works, he was author of "Voyages to the Coast
of Africa and the West Indies " (Lond., 1779, 4to.) and "Diseases
incident to Seamen " (1807, 4 vols., 8vo.). He died 30th September,
1829.

A mural monument, erected by the parishioners, celebrates the
Rev. John Halkett, minister of the parish, who died 21st April,
1828, in the fifty-first year of his age and twenty-first of his
ministry. Samuel Halkett, late Keeper of the Advocates Library,
Edinburgh, was a nephew of this gentleman (Vol. I., 128).

In the churchyard a monument to the memory of Thomas Bell,
comedian, is thus inscribed :—

"Sacred to the memory of Mr. THOMAS BELL, Comedian, late of
the Theatre Royal, Edinburgh, a respectable performer, an agree-
able companion, and an honest man. While on the *stage* of life
he encountered some of the rudest shocks of adversity, and felt the
chill gripe of penury in many a checkered *scene;* but, possessed of
a happy equanimity of temper, a social disposition, and a well-
informed mind, the arrows of misfortune fell powerless. On the
31st of August, 1815, the *curtain* of fate dropt on the *drama* of
his existence, and he *retired* from the *theatre* of this world, to the
sorrow and regret of all who had the pleasure of his acquaintance.—
Erected by the Dundee Eccentric X Society, in testimony of their
esteem and respect for Mr. BELL, an honorary member."

* "Coppy of the Tabill quhilk ves at Cowper of al the Erles of Erroll, quhilk ver
buryd in the abbey kirk their."—*Miscellany of the Spalding Club*, vol. ii., p. 347.

PARISH OF CRIEFF.

In the parish church a marble bust celebrates James Drummond, fifth Laird of Milnab, a cadet of the noble House of Perth. He was forty years steward-depute of Strathearn. His monument is thus inscribed:—

" Juridici, millo sæcli data crimine pessum,
Obruta quin senio, busta verenda vides.
Hunc juvenem amplexæ illusæ charitesque, senectæ
Sed fuerat gravitas consiliumque decus.
Quantus adest heros ! Viridi ipse pavesco juventâ,
Ut cineres tanti ceperat urna viri !

" Obiit anno M.DC.LXIV. Kal. Decembris xvii. ætatis suæ, lxxxiii."

PARISH OF DRON.

In the parish churchyard a tombstone marks the grave of John Welwood, an eminent preacher of the Covenanters. Second son of Mr. James Welwood, minister of Tundergarth, Dumfriesshire, he was born about the year 1649. With the usual course of study he obtained licence as a probationer. Not seeking any settled charge, he held an itinerant ministry in the southern and midland counties. Several predictions are associated with his name ; among others, one foretelling that Archbishop Sharp would suffer a violent death. His discourses were pervaded with a rich devotional fervour. He died of consumption, at Perth, in 1679, and was by a party of his followers secretly interred in Dron churchyard. His father was deprived in 1662. He is believed to be represented by the families of Welwood, and the Maxwells of the Grove, Munches, and Glenlee.

PARISH OF DUNBLANE.

Dunblane Cathedral was one of the religious houses reared by David I. ; it was founded in 1140, and remained entire till the Reformation. Since that period the choir has been used as the parish church. A portion of the nave forms the burial-ground of Stirling of Keir, an ancient house, now represented by Sir William Stirling Maxwell, Bart., of Keir and Pollok.

Under one of the windows of the nave is a recumbent figure of Michael Ochiltree, bishop of the see in the middle of the fifteenth century, who, according to Spotswood, richly adorned the church fabric. In the vestry of the choir a flat block of gritstone presents full-sized figures of Malise, eighth Earl of Strathearn, and his countess ; it was discovered in the choir surmounting a leaden coffin, inscribed with the date 1271. In an arch under a window of the choir a recumbent figure represents Finlay Dermock, bishop of the see in the beginning of the fifteenth century, who built the first bridge across the Allan at Dunblane.

Three blue marble slabs, now used as pavement, two being situated at the entrance and the other in the vestibule of the choir, lay together in the centre of the choir prior to 1817, when the church underwent repair. These slabs protected the remains of three daughters of John, first Lord Drummond — Margaret, Euphemia, and Sybella, who were there interred. The history of the eldest daughter, with the tragical fate of the other two, forms an historical episode. All the three, of whom the second, Euphemia, was married to the Lord Fleming, died in Drummond Castle, their father's house, some time in 1502, from the effects of poison. The eldest, Margaret, on whose account the two other sisters experienced an untimely end, was an early favourite of James IV., who had formed her acquaintance when she acted as one of the maidens of his deceased mother. On the demise of his father and his own elevation to the throne James secretly espoused the fair object of his early attachment, and undertook that the nuptials should be publicly celebrated, on obtaining a dispensation from the Pope, on account of their relationship being within the prohibited degrees. A daughter was born in 1495 of the private marriage, who was educated in the castles of Stirling and Edinburgh with the care pertaining to her rank as a legitimate princess. The father of Margaret Drummond was of an ancient and distinguished race; he was president of the Secret Council; and his family, through the Queen Annabella Drummond, was already connected with the throne, so that the full completion of the nuptials would not have been degrading to the monarch.

But the majority of the nobility determined that the young king should wed a daughter of England, and as the monarch persisted in his fidelity to his betrothed bride, it was resolved that she and her sisters should perish. Through the treachery of an attendant who administered poison in their morning meal, the three ladies were cut off. The king, who suspected the plot, was for a period inconsolable; he pensioned two priests to celebrate mass for the soul of his deceased spouse, and, removing their little daughter Margaret from Drummond Castle, tended her as his lawful child, and afterwards gave her in marriage to John, Lord Gordon, the eldest son of the Earl of Huntly. In 1503 he married Margaret Tudor, daughter of Henry VII., a connection which a century afterwards led to the union of the kingdoms. The remains of the unfortunate sisters were deposited in Dunblane Cathedral by permission of their uncle, Dean Sir William Drummond.

In the vestibule of the choir a mural monument is thus inscribed :—

" This stone, sacred to the memory of James Finlayson, one of the Ministers and Professors of Logic in the University of Edinburgh, is erected by his friends as a memorial of their admiration and attachment. He was born at Nether Cambuskenie 15th February, 1758, and died at Edinburgh, 28th Jan., 1808."

Dr. Finlayson is commemorated at Edinburgh (Vol. I., 54). Son of a small farmer, he was enabled to procure a university education by acting as a private tutor. Licensed to preach in 1785, he was, in the following year appointed Professor of Logic in the University

of Edinburgh, and was soon after admitted to the church living of
Borthwick, which he held in conjunction with his chair. In 1790
he was translated to Lady Yester's, Edinburgh; he subsequently
became colleague of Dr. Blair in the High Church. In 1802 he
was chosen Moderator of the General Assembly. He died suddenly in his fiftieth year. Dr. Finlayson was a leader in the
General Assembly; a volume of his discourses was published
posthumously.

A monument commemorates John Stirling, of Kippendavie, who
died at Kippenross 17th June, 1816, aged seventy-five, and Patrick
Stirling, his eldest son, who died at Hastings 30th March, 1816,
aged thirty-three.

In the churchyard a tombstone, reared by the congregation,
celebrates the piety and ministerial fidelity of the Rev. Robert
Stirling, minister of the parish, who died 17th October, 1817, in
the fifty-second year of his age and twenty-seventh of his ministry.

From tombstones in the parish churchyard we have the following metrical inscriptions:—

"The wise, the just, the pious, and the brave
Live in their deaths and flourish from the grave.
Grain hid in earth repays the peasant's care,
And evening suns but set to rise more fair."

" O be not proud, for soon you'll be
A heap of dust as well as me ;
Make Christ your stay and God adore,
And you shall live for evermore."

" Nature feels when grief assails,
Nature falls when death prevails;
Religion lifts our thoughts on high,
The Saviour teaches how to die.
Friends must part, may mourn, may weep,
But nature's onward course must sweep.
We live to die, but die to live,
And hopes to meet in heaven above."

In the old churchyard of Kilbride a modern erection constitutes
the new family burial place of Sir James Campbell, Bart., of Aber-
ruchill and Kilbride (Vol. I., 118).

PARISH OF DUNKELD.

The area of the ancient cathedral forms the parochial burying-ground. In the vestibule of its choir is the monument of Alexander Stewart, Earl of Buchan, third son of Robert II., better known as *the Wolf of Badenoch*. His figure is exhibited in a recumbent position, clad in armour, with a lion at his feet. Round the margin is the following inscription :—

" Hic jacet Alexander Senescalus, filius Roberti Regis Scotorum et Elizabeth More, Dominus de Buchan et Dns. de *Badenoch, qui obit vigessimo quarto die Julii.*"

The words in italics are cut in a different kind of stone, and are comparatively modern ; the restorer had mistaken the date, since Alexander Stewart died on the 20th February, 1394. He received his *sobriquet* of " the Wolf " from the lawless acts with which his name is associated. For some predatory outrage he was excommunicated by the Bishop of Moray ; he proceeded to retaliate by ravaging the bishop's diocese, and burning the town of Elgin with its hospital and magnificent cathedral. To atone for his sacrilege he was ordained by the Church, and compelled by his royal father to appear barefoot and in sackcloth at the door of the Blackfriars' monastery at Perth, and afterwards at its high altar, and there to make promise of restitution. Having died free of ecclesiastical censure, his remains were honourably deposited in the cathedral church, to which he had proved a benefactor. The monument originally stood in the choir ; it was removed to the vestibule at the Reformation.

In the south aisle of the cathedral is the monument of Bishop Cardney, lying in the recess of the wall under a crotcheted canopy. The bishop is represented in his pontifical robes, wearing a mitre. That portion of the inscription which remains legible is as follows :—

" Hic jacet Dns. Robertus de Cardony Eppis Dunkeldenni qui .   .   —   .   .   .   .   ad incarnationem Dne M.CCCC.XX. "

Shortly before his death Bishop Cardney built and dedicated a chapel to St. Ninian. There his monument was originally placed, but it was removed to the cathedral subsequent to 1464. A decapitated statue of Bishop Sinclair stands in the eastern aisle. He held office from 1312 till his death, 27th June, 1337. On account of his valour and patriotism he was styled by King Robert the Bruce " his own bishop," but it is painful to reflect that on the king's death he forsook allegiance to his dynasty. In 1332 he assisted at the coronation of Edward Baliol, and in the following year subscribed the instrument by which the Scottish Parliament, held at Edinburgh, surrendered to the English monarch the national independence. He built the choir of the cathedral, and there raised for himself a marble monument, with his statue in alabaster. The monument was probably removed at the Reformation.

The Ducal House of Athole inter in the vault of the chapterhouse. Over the vault a monument commemorates John, Marquis of Athole, who died 7th May, 1703. It is thus inscribed :—

" Hic subter in hypogæo, in spem beatæ resurrectionis, conduntur cineres illustris herois, Joannis, marchionis Atholiæ, comitis Tullbardini, vicecomitis de Balquhider, D. Murray, Balvenie et Gask, Domini regalitatis Atholiæ balivi, hereditarii dominii de Dunkeld, senescalli hereditarii de Fife et Huntingtour, Stuartorum Atholiæ, et Muraviorum Tillibardini comitum hæredis ; qui, utroque parente, Joanne Atholio et Joanna filia D. de Glenurchy, nondum decennis, orbatus, a rege Carolo II. reduce, ob gnaviter, adversus rebelles, dum adhuc juvenis XVIII. circiter annorum, navatam operam, summamque exinde in bello et pace constantiam et fidem, multis muneribus accumulatus est : quippe erat justiciarius generalis supremæ curiæ in civilibus, extra ordinem senator, cohortis prætoriæ equestris præfectis, parliamenti interdum præses, sigilli privati custos, ab ærario, saccario et a conciliis, vicecomes Perthensis, locum tenens comitatus Argatheliæ et Tarbat, et denique, a rege Jacobo VII. nobilissimi ordinis Andreani eques factus est. Obiit 7 die Maii, 1703."

John, Earl and afterwards Marquis of Athole, raised, in 1653, for the service of Charles II., two thousand men, an act which on the Restoration was acknowledged by his being sworn of the Privy

Council and constituted master of the king's household. His other rewards are recorded in his epitaph.

In the chapterhouse a marble statue celebrates John, fourth Duke of Athole, who died 29th September, 1830. He was the last representative of this ducal House who held sovereign authority in the Isle of Man; he disposed of his privileges to the British Crown for the sum of £409,000. The monument, which was erected by his duchess, represents the Duke in his parliamentary robes.

George, sixth Duke of Athole, Grand Master Mason of Scotland, who died 16th January, 1864 (see *supra*, p. 151), is commemorated by a memorial fountain in the centre of the market-place. On a square basement, having on each side a stone basin, rest four massive columns of Peterhead granite, with an appropriate vase occupying the centre. In the tympanum of the main arches are introduced the ducal coronet and crest of the Athole family. The upper portion of the fabric is of octagonal shape, the lower part being formed into an arcade, with polished Peterhead columns at the angles. The structure, which is forty feet in height, terminates in a floriated cross.

In the choir, a monument commemorates Lieutenant-Colonel William Cleland, of the Cameronian Regiment. Upon it are inscribed these lines :—

> " Grace, learning, valour, centered in one,
> Adorned that dust lies here below this stone ;
> Because on earth his equals were but few
> His soul took wing, and early heavenward flew ;
> That he might shun earth's follies, stains, and care,
> And with his mates sing hallelujahs there."

Colonel Cleland was born about the year 1661 ; he supported the Covenanters at Drumclog, and held at Bothwell Bridge the rank of captain. For a period he found refuge in Holland; he returned to Scotland in 1685. After the Revolution he was appointed Lieutenant-Colonel in the Cameronian Regiment, under the command of the Earl of Angus. On the 21st August, 1689, he fell at the head of his corps, while defending the churchyard of Dunkeld against a body of Highlanders, the remains of the army of Lord Dundee, who a month before had triumphed at Killicrankie. A writer of humorous poetry, Cleland's compositions were published in 1697, in one volume duodecimo. His son William Cleland composed the Prefatory Letters to the "Dunciad;" he was the original of "Will Honeycomb," in the *Spectator*. He died in 1741. His son John Cleland, who died in 1789, was author of several novels, which enjoyed a temporary popularity.

In the vestibule of the choir a marble cenotaph commemorates Sir Robert Dick, of Tullymett, who fell at the head of his division at the battle of Sobraon, in India, 10th February, 1846.

Recently a magnificent monument has been reared in the cathedral by the officers and men of the 42nd Regiment in memory of departed members of that corps. Executed by Mr. Steell, the monument displays as its chief feature a panel of white marble richly sculptured. An officer of the regiment is represented on the battlefield in quest of a missing comrade; having found his friend's lifeless body, he stands with uncovered head, paying silent homage to departed valour. On the left, beneath a shattered gun-carriage, lies the body of a young ensign, his hand still grasping the flag he had stoutly defended, and his face wearing a peaceful expression, as befitted a man who had died at his post. A slab underneath the sculpture bears the following inscription :—

"In memory of the officers, non-commissioned officers, and private soldiers of the 42nd Royal Highlanders—the Black Watch—who fell in war from the creation of the regiment to the close of the Indian Mutiny, 1859. The ten Independent Companies of the Freacadan Dubh, or Black Watch, were formed into a regiment on the 25th October, 1739, and the first muster took place in May, 1740, in a field between Taybridge and Aberfeldy.

> Here 'mong the hills that nursed each hardy Gael
> Our votive marble tells the soldier's tale ;
> Art's magic power each perished friend recalls,
> And heroes haunt these old cathedral walls.

"Erected by the Officers of the Corps, 1872."

On each side of the inscription are recorded the names of the fields in which the regiment gained honours. These are Fontenoy, Flanders, Ticonderoga, Martinique, Guadaloupe, Havannah, Egypt, Corunna, Fuentes D'Onor, Pyrenees, Nivelle, Nive, Orthes, Toulouse, the Peninsula, Waterloo, Alma, Sebastopol, and Lucknow.

In the vestibule an elegant marble monument commemorates the ministerial zeal of the Rev. John Robb, minister of the parish, who in his fortieth year and the third of his ministry was drowned on board the Forfarshire steamer, when she was lost on Big Harker Rock, Fern Islands, 7th September, 1838.

PARISH OF ERROL.

In the parish churchyard a small monument is sculptured with various emblems; it contains on a scroll the Creed in Latin, and a translation in the same language of Rev. ii. 10.

In the churchyard wall, sculptured in white sandstone, is the figure of a warrior in chain armour, in the attitude of devotion.

Within a sarcophagus are entombed the remains of the Rev. William Bell, minister of the parish. After ministering in the parishes of Auchtertool and Dron, he was translated to Errol in 1651; he died 11th December, 1665, in his sixty-first year, and the thirtieth of his ministry. He bequeathed seven acres of land at Dron for maintaining a student of theology at St. Mary's College, St. Andrews. On his sarcophagus are engraved these lines :—

" Here ceast and silent lie sweet sounding Bell,
Who unto sleeping souls rung many a knell;
Death crackt this Bell, yet doth his pleasant chiming
Remain with those who are their lamps a-trimming.
In spite of death, his word some praise still sounds
In Christ's church, and in heaven his joy abounds."

PARISH OF FORGANDENNY.

In the churchyard, on the south side of the church, a martyr's tombstone is inscribed thus:—

"Here lys Andrew Brodie, wright in Forgandenny, who at the break of a meeting, October, 1678, was shot by a party of Highlandmen commanded by Ballechan at a cave's mouth flying thither for his life, and that for his adherence to the word of God and Scotland's covenanted work of Reformation."

According to Wodrow, a conventicle was held at the hill of Caltenachar, now called Culteuchar, one of the Ochils, when a company of Highlanders came suddenly upon them, and at once discharged their firelocks among the unarmed worshippers. Andrew Brodie alone fell; he left a widow and four children.

PARISH OF FOWLIS-WESTER.

In the centre of the parish hamlet stands an ancient Runic cross. On one side are figures of men on horseback, in pursuit of a wolf, which seems to be holding in its jaws a human head. On the same side six men, in grotesque costume, are following an animal supposed to be led to sacrifice. The figures on the opposite side are defaced, but it bears the marks of having had a chain attached to it, by which criminals were fastened as in a species of pillory.

PARISH OF GASK.

In a modern chapel, built for Episcopal service, upon the site of the old parish church, rest the remains of Carolina Oliphant, Baroness Nairne. This highly gifted and accomplished gentlewoman was born on the 16th July, 1766, in "the auld house" of Gask, which she has celebrated in one of her songs. By her father, Laurence Oliphant, of Gask, a famous Jacobite, she was named Carolina, in honour of Prince Charles Edward. On account of her personal beauty she was known in early life as "the Flower of Strathearn." In her fortieth year she married her maternal cousin, Major Nairne, who subsequently, on the reversal of the family attainder, became Lord Nairne. After the death of Robert Burns, a number of Scottish songs, not included in his works, but of equal merit with his own, floated into circulation. These were generally attributed to the Ayrshire bard, and editors began to include them in new editions of his works. "I'm wearin' awa, John," the last word being altered to Jean, in supposed allusion to Jean Armour, was early claimed for the deceased poet. The real author remained silent to the last. Averse to any kind of publicity, she was altogether unwilling that it should ever become known that she had composed verses. Yet from her pen proceeded such compositions as "The Land o' the Leal," "Caller Herrin'," "The Laird o' Cockpen," "He's ower the hills that I loe weel," "The Lass o' Gowrie," "Wha'll be king but Charlie?" "The Hundred Pipers," "Will ye no come back again?" and many other popular lyrics. After a life attended with some severe trials, which she bore with Christian fortitude, Lady Nairne died at Gask on the 26th October, 1845, aged seventy-nine. Her poetical compositions, accompanied by a memoir, have been collected and published by the author of this work.* In the little chapel which contains her dust, a small plate, inscribed with her name, denotes her resting-place. Within the chapel and near her grave was deposited in December, 1847, the body of James Oliphant, of Gask, the eighteenth in unbroken male descent from William Oliphant, upon whom Robert the Bruce bestowed the family estates †

---

* "Life and Songs of Baroness Nairne." London. 12mo.

† "Jacobite Lairds of Gask." By T. L. Kington Oliphant, Esq. Printed for the Grampian Club.

PARISH OF KILMADOCK.

A mural tablet in the tower of the parish church bears that it was erected by the heritors of the parish in honour of Francis, ninth Earl of Moray. His lordship died 12th January, 1848.

PARISH OF KINCARDINE-IN-MENTEITH.

In the parish churchyard, over the entrance of a burial-place at the east end of the site of the old church, a shield of arms, consisting of two chevrons, gules, on a field ermine, with a pigeon for crest, and the motto, "I thank my God," denotes the ancient resting-place of the Muschets of Kincarne, or Kincardine. Above the shield is the date 1686, and below it this inscription,—" Sepultura antiquissimæ Mushetorum familiæ a Gulielmo de Montefixo qui hic floruit circa annum M.C.C.C. progenitæ."

The Muschets, originally called Montfichett and De Montefixo, were a distinguished Norman house, and were descended from the Earls of Montfort, who were Dukes of Bretagne. The Duchess of John de Montfort was daughter to the Earl of Flanders, and her daughter Anne was married first to Charles VIII. and afterwards to Louis XII., Kings of France. Having established a settlement in England at the Conquest, the representatives of the house latterly acquired lands in Roxburghshire. Branches of the family afterwards settled in Perthshire. Richard de Montfichet received from William the Lion the lands of Cargill and Kincardine (see *supra*, p. 153). Richard Muschet, of Cargill, swore fealty to Edward I. Sir William de Montefixo was Justiciary of Scotland in 1332. He inhabited a castle in the immediate vicinity of Kincardine churchyard, the foundations of which were removed within a modern period. Dying without male issue, the eldest of his three daughters married Sir John Drummond, and brought the three estates of Cargill, Kincardine, and Stobhall into that family. Other branches of the House of Muschet owned the estates of Burnbank, Culgirth, Miln of Torr, Miln of Goodie, Cuthill, &c., all in the Vale of Menteith. In the orchard of Burnbank, near the spot where the mansion-house stood, is a tombstone thus inscribed:—

" Here lyes the corpes of Margaret Drummond, third daughter of the Laird [of Invermay] and [spouse to] Sir George Muschet of Burnbanke : her age 26. Departed this life in the visitation, with her three children at Burnbanke, the 10 of August 1647."

The estates of the Muschets of Perthshire have long been alienated; the male representative of the house is John S. Muschet, M.D., of Birkhill, Stirlingshire.

In the parish church a monument with an inscription in elegant Latin commemorates George Drummond, of Blair-Drummond, who in 1684 acquired part of the ancient barony of Kincardine from the Earl of Perth. Monumental tablets also commemorate several of his descendants.

In the churchyard a monument marks the resting-place of Henry Home, Lord Kames. This distinguished judge and metaphysical writer was son of George Home, of Kames, Berwickshire, and was born in 1696. He passed advocate in 1724, and after a brilliant career at the bar was raised to the bench in February, 1752. In 1763 he was appointed a Lord of Justiciary. During a career of remarkable industry he produced many valuable professional works. His " Elements of Criticism," and " Sketches of the History of Man," the latter containing some curious disquisitions regarding the gradation of the race, are his best known works. A sound lawyer and a zealous agriculturist, Lord Kames was, notwithstanding some personal eccentricities, much esteemed by his contemporaries. By his marriage in 1741 with Agatha Drummond, he became possessed in 1766 of the estates of Blair-Drummond. He died 27th December, 1782. Mrs. Home Drummond died in June, 1795 ; her remains are interred beside those of her husband. In the church Lord Kames and his Lady are commemorated on a monument, bearing an inscription composed by the celebrated Dr. Hugh Blair.

In the church memorial tablets celebrate George Home Drummond, of Blair-Drummond, only son of Lord Kames, who died 28th October, 1819 ; and Henry Home Drummond, for many years M.P. for Perthshire ; born 28th July, 1783 ; died 12th September, 1867.

Within the church a monument, with a Latin inscription written by himself, commemorates John Ramsay, of Ochtertyre, a learned country gentleman and early patron of Robert Burns. Experiencing amusement in the composition of Latin verse, he had classical inscriptions placed on erections and tablets in various parts of his demesne. With the poet Burns he maintained a friendly correspondence. He died in March, 1814, and his remains were consigned to the family burial-place in the old parish church. He left MSS. on various subjects connected with Scottish history, but these have not been published by his executors.

PARISH OF KINFAUNS.

In the parish church, in a vault under the aisle, is the burial-place of the old family of Charteris, of Kinfauns. About a century ago there was found in the vault a head-piece or kind of helmet, made of several folds of linen, painted over with broad stripes of blue and white. This is supposed to have formed part of the fictitious armour which had enclosed the remains of Sir Thomas de Longueville. Of this individual the history is associated with that of Wallace. According to the narrative Longueville was connected with an ancient family in France, but having at the court of Philip le Bel killed a nobleman in the king's presence he was subjected to exile. He became a pirate, and was known as the Red Rover, from the colour of his flags. On his voyage to France in 1301 or 1302 he was encountered by Wallace, who took him prisoner, and afterwards successfully interceded on his behalf with the French king, who not only gave him a free pardon, but granted him knighthood. Longueville attached himself to his benefactor, and became a sharer of his exploits. On Wallace's betrayal and execution he retired to Lochmaben, but when Bruce began to assert his right to the crown, he heartily joined his standard. In January, 1313, he aided King Robert at the taking of Perth. In reward of his services the King granted him lands in the vicinity, and he assumed the name of Charteris on marrying the heiress of Kinfauns. The two-handed sword of Sir Thomas de Longueville is preserved in Kinfauns Castle; it is five feet nine inches long, two and a half inches broad at the hilt, and of a proportionate thickness.

PARISH OF KINNAIRD.

In the parish churchyard a lengthened eulogy on a departed family is summed up by the intimation that they all " paid twenty shillings in the pound." These metrical inscriptions are from different tombstones:—

> " The bloom of innocence
> Was blighted when half blown ;
> The child that feared to give offence,
> Down to the grave is gone."

> " Stop, friend, thy hand thy soul to save,
> And hear the dead—hear from the grave.
> Thou springs from dust and dwells in clay—
> Thy soul must flit and haste away.

> Noe faith, nor no—beneath the ground.

> Wouldst thou be saved when death alarms,
> Then die with Jesus in thy arms."

" Here rests the mortal part of one
Who held in virtue's path the van;
In friendship warm, to flatt'ry cold;
In years a youth, in wisdom old;
A pious teacher, well approved,
By parent, guardian, pupil loved."

PARISH OF KINNOULL.

In the centre of the churchyard, an aisle which was attached to the old parish church, now removed, was an early burial-place of the House of Kinnoull. Within the aisle is the splendid monument of Sir George Hay, first Earl of Kinnoull, and Lord High Chancellor. In a recess behind four columns, enriched with a variety of ornaments and surmounted by a canopy, embellished with escutcheons, is the statue of the Earl in his robes. Above are two seraphs in the act of flying. Sir George Hay, first Lord of Kinnoull, was second son of Peter Hay, of Megginch. Born in 1572, he was educated at the Scots College of Douay with his uncle Edmund, well known as Father Hay. In 1596 he was introduced to Court by his relative, Sir James Hay, of Kingask, and was appointed a Gentleman of the Bedchamber. After holding a succession of offices, he was, in 1622, elevated to the chancellorship. He was created Earl of Kinnoull in 1633. He died at London, on the 16th December, 1634, and his remains were brought to Scotland and interred at the spot surmounted by his monument.

On Murray's Hall Hill, one of the Sidlaws, an obelisk commemorates General Sir Thomas Graham, afterwards Lord Lynedoch. This distinguished individual was born at Balgowan, Perthshire, in 1750. Having sustained the loss of a devoted wife, to whom he was tenderly attached, he abandoned the life of a country gentleman and joined the army at the ripe age of forty-three. He served as aide-de-camp to Lord Mulgrave at the landing at Toulon, and received his lordship's thanks for his gallant and able services. In 1794 he raised the first battalion of the 90th Regiment, of which he was appointed colonel commandant. In connection with the garrison of Mantua, in 1796, he distinguished himself by an act of intrepidity; and after a two years' siege, took Malta from the French in 1800. In 1809 he served in Spain under Sir John Moore, and was present at the battle of Corunna. Appointed a lieutenant-general, he returned to Spain in 1811; in February of that year he gained the battle of Barossa. He won fresh honours at the battle of Vittoria, fought on the 21st June, 1813. After some distinguished services in Holland, he was, in May, 1814, raised to the peerage by the title of Lord Lynedoch. He died at London on the 18th December, 1843, at the advanced age of ninety-three.

In the churchyard tombstones commemorate James Paton, of Glenalmond, died 1830; James Thomas, of Cotton, died 12th March, 1855; William Dickson, of Bellwood, died 1835; and George Seton, of Potterhill, died 5th February, 1842.

Andrew Sharp, cobbler, musician, and drawing-master, is celebrated in these lines :—

> " Halt for a moment, passenger, and read :—
> Here Andrew dozes in his daisied bed ;
> Silent his flute, and torn off the key,
> His pencils scattered, and the Muse set free."

From different tombstones we have the following : —

> " Death comes to mortals often by surprise,
> Death even to genius a respite denies ;
> Reader, reflect, uncertain is the hour,—
> Prepare to meet thy God while in thy power."

> " I like a rose did appear ;
> My blossom soon was gone ;
> And now I'm laid in silent grave,
> Where all of you must come."

> " This last memorial fond affection rears
> To one whose simple manners still endears—
> A man so humble, little known to fame,
> That seldom heard his voice or name;
> Meek, innoffensive, and of morals pure,
> Few faults or foibles could his life obscure."

> " Mourn not, dear friends, for my decease,
> I hope with Christ I have made peace;
> Life is uncertain, death is sure,
> Sin gave the wound, but Christ the cure.
> A loving wife and tender mother proved,
> And died lamented, as she lived beloved."

PARISH OF LECROPT.

Within the grounds of Keir House, the seat of Sir William Stirling Maxwell, Bart., is situated the old parish churchyard. The site of the old parish church is denoted by a tall Gothic cross and an elegantly sculptured sundial. In the churchyard two elegant memorial crosses commemorate Hannah and Elizabeth Stirling, daughters of Archibald Stirling, Esq., of Keir, and sisters of Sir William Stirling Maxwell, Bart. Elizabeth Stirling was born 24th August, 1822, and died 12th September, 1845; Hannah Ann Stirling was born at Kenmure, 17th August, 1816, and died at Carlsbad, 18th July, 1843. By her brother she is celebrated in these lines :—

> " Sister, these woods have seen ten summers fade
> Since thy dear dust in yonder church was laid ;
> A few more winters, and this heart, the shrine
> Of thy fair memory, shall be cold like thine.
> Yet may some stranger, lingering in these ways,
> Bestow a tear on grief of other days.
> For if he too have wept o'er grace and youth,
> Goodness and wisdom, faith and love and truth,
> Untinged with worldly guile or selfish stain,
> And ne'er hath looked upon the like again,
> Then imaged in his sorrow he may see
> All that I loved and lost and mourn in thee."

PARISH OF LITTLE DUNKELD.

In the parish church a marble tablet commemorates Neil Gow, the celebrated composer and violinist, whose remains are interred in the churchyard. Gow died in the hamlet of Inver, of which he was a native, on the 1st March, 1807, aged eighty. Retained by the Athole family as their musician, he lived amidst his native solitudes. As a player of reels and strathspeys he was unsurpassed. About one hundred tunes which he composed have been preserved and published.

PARISH OF MEIGLE.

In the park of Belmont, a tumulus called Belliduff is associated with the tradition that here Macduff slew Macbeth, while a whinstone nodule of twenty tons weight, about a mile distant, is known as Macbeth's Stone. According to history Macbeth was slain at Lumphanan, in Kincardineshire.

In the parish churchyard are several ancient sepulchral stones, variously sculptured. One represents a huge serpent fastened to a bull's mouth, another two wild beasts tearing a human body, and a third a body attached to chariot wheels. A tradition, evidently fabulous, associates these sculptures with Vanora, the supposed queen of King Arthur, in the sixth century, who on account of her infidelity was, by her husband's order, torn to pieces by wild beasts.

In the north aisle of the church, Robert Cranston, Bishop of Dunkeld, is thus commemorated :—

· " Heir lyeth the body of ane honest and discreet gentleman, Robert Cranston, descended of the family of Cranston, who after several yeirs travelling and serving in the warrs in Germanie and Poland returned to his native countrie, and having for some yiers faithfully served Lord Bishope of Dunkele, died at Meigle, May, 1685, and of his age 47."

Tombstones in Meigle churchyard present these metrical inscriptions :—

> " Under this stone here lys ane vertous one,
> Ane friend to all, ane enemie to none;
> If literature had polished what nature did bestow,
> So short ane epitaph justice wald not alow."

> " O happy sovl, Thy after labours . .
> To heauins Eternal mansions . .
> T' enjoy the pleasures of eternal rest
> With triumph mongst angels be blest.
> Happy who, after so uncertain chance,
> Can safly to the heauen of heauens advance."

> " While old grey heads escape the rage
>   Of cruel death, sometime
> Young ones, alas ! may quit the stage,
>   Ev'n in their very prime.
> Oh, death, how fierce thy fiery blows,
>   No forester like thee ;
> Cuts down the cedar while it grows,
>   And spares the withered tree."

> " In her who under this stone
>   Many bráve virtues shone ;
> For every day it was her care
>   To help each needy one.
> And thus we trust her soul at rest,
>   Doth now remain above ;
> With the triumphant pious ones,
>   Who their Redeemer love."

> " Here is interr'd, believe you may,
>   This monument that views,
> The kindest neighbour ever was,
>   Friend, father, and a spouse.
> Beloved, and loving, still averse
>   To every sordid art ;
> Without deceit he plainly spoke
>   The language of his heart.

Untainted was his character,
The paths of peace he trode,
For which we hope he glorious shines
In heaven now with God."

PARISH OF METHVEN.

A spot enclosed by a railing on the banks of the river Almond denotes the burial-place of Bessy Bell and Mary Gray, celebrated in national song. Miss Bell was daughter of the laird of Kinvaid; and Miss Gray was daughter of the laird of Lednock. The terrible plague of 1645 having broken out, the two ladies retired to a rush-thatched cot, at Burn Braes, a romantic spot on the Lednock estate. There they lived for some time, when a lover of one or both visited them occasionally, and brought them provisions. Unhappily he also brought the epidemic, of which both the damsels sickened and died. Their remains were deposited in the same grave. The original ballad commemorating the tragedy has these lines :—

"They wadna lie in Methven kirkyard,
Amang their gentle kin ;
But they wa'd lie on Dronach Haugh,
To beak fornent the sun."

PARISH OF MONIVAIRD.

On the hill of *Tom-a-chastel* a handsome obelisk of granite, eighty-two feet in height, was erected in 1831, in honour of Sir David Baird, the hero of Seringapatam. This distinguished commander was born at Edinburgh, on the 6th December, 1757. Entering the army as ensign in the 2nd Foot, he joined his regiment at Gibraltar in 1773. Returning to Britain in 1776, he was two years thereafter appointed Captain of the Grenadiers in the 73rd Regiment, then raised by Lord Macleod. Proceeding to India in 1790, Captain Baird bore a distinguished part in the battle of Perimbancum, when after a protracted and desperate encounter between the troops of Hyder Ali and a portion of the British Indian army, commanded by Colonel Baillie, the latter experienced defeat. With other officers, Captain Baird was detained a prisoner three years and a half in the fortress of Seringapatam, each being allowed for provisions a sum equal to sixpence per. day. On the cessation of hostilities, in March, 1784, he was released, when he rejoined his regiment at Madras. The number of the regiment was changed to the 71st, and Captain Baird was, in 1790, appointed its lieutenant-colonel. After some other important services he was, in 1798, appointed major-general. On the 4th May, 1799, he commanded the storming party at the assault of Seringapatam, when Tippoo Saib was slain, and the British obtained possession of the place. In 1804 General Baird received the honour of knight-hood, and the military Companionship of the Bath. In 1806 he wrested Cape Colony from the Dutch ; in 1807 he took part in the siege of Copenhagen, and in 1803 commanded the first division at Corunna, and succeeded to the first command on the death of Sir John Moore. He was created a baronet, and for the fourth time received the thanks of Parliament. In 1820 he was appointed commander of the forces in Ireland, and in 1828 he became Governor of Fort George. He died on the 18th August, 1829. Sir David married, in August, 1810, Miss Campbell Preston, of Ferntower, Perthshire, who survived him.

On the site of the old parish church stands the mausoleum of the ancient House of Murray of Ochtertyre. The church was, in 1511, the scene of a terrible tragedy connected with a feud between the Murrays and the Drummonds, the particulars of which are related by Sir Walter Scott, in his introduction to " The Legend of Montrose."

PARISH OF MONZIE.

In the Small Glen, the upper portion of the vale of Glenalmond, a large stone, eight feet in height, and nearly cubical in form, is traditionally reported to mark the grave of Ossian, the great Caledonian bard. It is known as *Clach Ossian*, or Ossian's stone. When General Wade was constructing the military road through the Glen in 1746, some of his men removed *Clach Ossian* from its ancient bed. They found beneath it a small sepulchral chamber 2 feet long, 1½ feet broad, and 2 feet deep, containing bones and some pieces of coin. The bones were re-interred. In allusion to the burial-place of the Caledonian bard, the poet Wordsworth has these lines :—

> " In this still place, remote from men
> Sleeps Ossian, in the Narrow Glen;
> In this still place, where murmurs on,
> But one meek streamlet, only one :
> He sang of battles, and the breath
> Of stormy war, and violent death,
> And should, methinks, when all was past.
> Have rightfully been laid at last,
> Where rocks were rudely heaped and rent
> As by a spirit turbulent;
> Where sights were rough and sounds were wild,
> And everything unreconciled,
> In some complaining dim retreat,
> For fear and melancholy meet;
> But this is calm, there cannot be
> A more entire tranquillity.
> Does then the bard sleep here indeed ?
> Or is it but a groundless creed ?
> What matters it ?   I blame them not
> Whose fancy in this lonely spot
> Was moved; and in such way expressed
> Their notion of its perfect rest.
> A convent even, or hermit's cell,
> Would break the silence of this dell ;
> It is not quiet, it is not ease,
> But something deeper far than these

The separation that is here
Is of the grave; and of austere
Yet happy feelings of the dead;
And, therefore, was it rightly said
That Ossian, last of all his race,
Lies buried in this lonely place."

PARISH OF MUCKHART.

In the churchyard, a tombstone is thus inscribed : "Jacobus Paton de Middle Ballilisk quondam episcopus de Dunkeld, qui obiit 20 Julii 1596." Paton was appointed minister of Muckhart in 1567, and in 1572 was promoted to the Bishopric of Dunkeld, through the influence of Archibald Earl of Argyle. He was accused before the Church Courts of obtaining his bishopric by simony, of not residing in his diocese, and of neglecting his episcopate. Latterly he resigned his see, and resided on his estate.

PARISH OF PERTH. .

At the foot of High Street is an elegant monumental statue of Sir Walter Scott, supported on a suitable pedestal. The illustrious author is represented in a standing attitude with his favourite greyhound at his feet.

An elegant structure, used as a Library and Museum, commemorates a late chief magistrate, Lord Provost Marshall.

At the south-east corner of the North Inch is the Perthshire monument of the late Prince Consort. Elegantly sculptured by Brodie, the statue presents a correct representation of the deceased

Prince. He is uncovered, and the mild character of his features is admirably portrayed. Over a court costume, well adapted to the pose and proportions of the figure the Prince wears a military cloak, and is decorated with the star and collar of the Garter. His left hand rests gracefully on the belt of his dress, while in his right hand he holds the design of the Crystal Palace, which he seems in the act of explaining. The monument, which is supported on an appropriate pedestal, was reared at the cost of £560; it was inaugurated on the 30th August, 1864, in presence of Her Majesty the Queen, who in token of her royal approbation knighted the Lord Provost of the city.

At the west end of the town stood the Charter House or Carthusian Monastery, founded by James I. and his Queen, in 1429. Here were interred James I. and his Queen, and Margaret Tudor Queen of James IV. James I. was slain in the Blackfriars Monastery of Perth on the 20th February, 1437, by Sir Robert Graham and other conspirators. An accomplished prince, and educated at the English court, he exercised a beneficial influence on the rude manners of his subjects. He was the originator of Scottish music, and a considerable poet. He married the lady Jane Beaufort, daughter of the Duke of Somerset, of the blood-royal of England. Her remains were laid beside those of her husband.

Queen Margaret Tudor, who also rests in the Carthusian Monastery, was daughter of Henry VII. Surviving her first husband, James IV., she afterwards espoused Archibald Douglas, Earl of Angus, whom she divorced; she latterly married Henry Stewart, second son of Lord Ochiltree, who was created Lord Methven. She died 25th October, 1521.

The Dominican Monastery stood in the north part of the city; it was founded by Alexander II. in 1231. Herein were entombed the remains of Elizabeth Mure, first Queen of Robert II. Daughter of Sir Adam Mure, of Rowallan, she was celebrated for her personal charms and amiable qualities. The reality of her marriage with the king was long a matter of doubt, but it was conclusively determined in the affirmative by the discovery in

1789 of the Pope's dispensation for the solemnization of the union.

St. John's church was formerly surrounded with a graveyard. Here, James Earl of Gowrie, was interred in 1588. Under the north transept of the church a burial vault belonged to the family of Mercer of Aldie.

In 1580 the grounds of the Franciscan Monastery were granted to the citizens as a place of sepulture. These grounds now form the parochial churchyard. In the churchyard wall a memorial tablet thus commemorates Robert Mylne, master mason to James VI. It is inscribed as follows:—

" Near this spot lies John Mylne, master mason to James VI., who about two centuries ago, rebuilt the ancient Bridge over the Tay, opposite the High Street, which a dreadful inundation swept away, xiv. October MDCXXI."

" Robert Mylne, Architect, erected this stone to restore and perpetuate the memory of his ancestors,

MDLXXIV."

A flat stone in front of the tablet is inscribed thus :—

" This stone entombs the dust of famous *Mill*,
Renowned chiefly in his time for skill
In architecture; his learned art did lay
The spacious arches of the Bridge of *Tay*,
Which as demolished by a mighty spate,
So was his fabric by the course of fate.
Six *lustres* since, and more his progenie,
Succeeding to that art their sire outvy,
And this assign'd, his worth deserved one
Of jet or marble, not of common stone.
Seven foot of ground, clay floor, clay wall,
Serve both for chamber and for hall
To Master *Mill*, whose squrbuile* brain
Could ten Escurialls well containe,
Whill he breath'd life, yet in his sonne
And sonn's sonne, he lives two for one,
Who to advance *Mill's* art and fame,
Make stocks and stones speak out his name."

* Ingenious.

From the reign of James III. till that of Charles II. the office of Royal Master Mason was hereditary in the family of Mylne. The son and successor of John Mylne here commemorated was M.P. for the city of Edinburgh. He and one of his descendants, the last who held the hereditary office of Master Mason to the king, were interred in Greyfriars churchyard, Edinburgh (Vol. I. 27, 28). Robert Mylne, described on the tablet as having caused it to be erected to the memory of his ancestors was the most celebrated architect of his House. Born at Edinburgh on the 4th January, 1734, he studied architecture at Rome and other continental schools. Having fixed his residence in London, his design for the erection of the bridge at Blackfriars on the Thames was selected at a public competition, and he was entrusted with the erection of the work. He was afterwards appointed surveyor of St. Paul's Cathedral, and Clerk of Works to Greenwich Hospital. He died on the 5th May, 1811.

A tombstone, with inscription effaced, commemorates Mrs. Catherine Buchanan, wife (as is supposed) of Henry Adamson, author of the "Muses' Threnodie," a poem, containing an account of the Gowrie conspiracy, a description of Perth, &c. Adamson was son of James Adamson, Lord Provost of Perth in 1610, and brother of Principal Adamson of the University of Edinburgh. He died in 1639. According to some accounts he was unmarried.

A plain tombstone commemorates the Rev. William Wilson, one of the founders of the Secession Church, who died in 1741, aged fifty-one. With a short Latin inscription, it contains these verses :—

"More brave than David's mighty men,
    This champion fought it fair
In truth's defence, both by the pen,
    The pulpit and the chair.

"He stood with his associates true
    To Scotland's solemn oath,
And taught to render homage due
    To God and Cæsar both.

> " Earth raging, from his sacred post
> 　　Debarr'd the worthy sage ;
> Heaven frowning, sent a furious host
> 　　To avenge the sacrilege.

> " Mourn, your Elijah's gone,
> 　　And wafted to the skies ;
> Mourn till his fiery car bring down
> 　　A soul of equal size."

Mr. Wilson was son of Gilbert Wilson, proprietor of a small estate near East Kilbride, which he forfeited for his attachment to the Presbyterian cause ; he went to Holland, and returning at the Revolution, was appointed Comptroller of Customs at Greenock. His son was born at Glasgow, 19th November, 1690, and was named after William III. Having studied at the University of Glasgow and obtained license, he was ordained minister of the West Church, Perth, in November, 1716. He associated with the supporters of the "Marrow of Modern Divinity," and was one of the three ministers who joined Mr. Ebenezer Erskine (*see supra*, p. 41), for which they suffered deposition by the General Assembly. Mr. Wilson's adherents erected a meeting-house for his use, and the Associate Presbytery appointed him their Professor of Divinity. He died 8th October, 1741. The English verses on his tombstone were composed by the Rev. Ralph Erskine of Dunfermline, who likewise inscribed these lines on the tombstone of Colin Brown, Chief Magistrate of Perth, who died 17th October, 1744, aged seventy-one :—

> " Friend, do not, careless on thy road,
> 　　O'erlook this humble shrine ;
> For if thou art a friend of God,
> 　　Here lyes a friend of thine.

> " His closet was a Bethel sweet,
> 　　His house a house of prayer,
> In homely strains at Jesus' feet
> 　　He wrestled daily there.

" He to the city was a guide,
And to the church a fence,
Nor could within the camp abide
When truth was banished thence.

" His life and death did both express
What strength of grace was given,
His life a lamp of holiness.
His death a dawn of heaven."

In the churchyard, tombstones commemorate Rev. Robert Kay, minister of the West Church, died 15th October, 1819; John Young, of Bellwood, died 6th June, 1819; Rev. Henry Sangster, minister of Humbie, died 5th April, 1820; Rev. Adam Peebles, minister of the English Episcopal church, Perth, died 18th December, 1804; Rev. Samuel George Kennedy, minister of the West Church, died 30th December, 1835; Dr. Alexander Robertson, Deputy Inspector of Army Hospitals, died 1st September, 1830; Major-General Sir John Ross, K.C.B., died 21st April, 1835; Major-General William Farquhar, died 11th May, 1839; Rev. Alexander Pringle, D.D., died 12th May, 1839; Rev. Forest Frew, Minister of the first Relief Church, Perth, died 6th February, 1842; Rev. John Findlay, D.D., Minister of St. Pauls, died 4th April, 1846; Adam Anderson, LL.D., Professor of Natural Philosophy in the University of St. Andrews, died 4th December, 1846; Andrew Heiton, architect, died 8th August, 1858; Sir John Bisset, K.C.B., Commissary-General, died 3rd April, 1854; Rev. Andrew Gray, Minister of the Free West Church, Perth, died 15th March, 1861; and Rev. William A. Thomson, Minister of the Middle Church, Perth, died 17th March, 1863.

Perth parochial churchyard exhibits a due proportion of metrical epitaphs; one of the oldest tombstones is thus inscribed:

" Here lyes ane worthie man, John Conqueror, who died a Bailie of Perth, the first day of September, 1653.

"O'er death a conqueror he now lyes whose soule,
Freed from this dust, triumphes above the pole.
One less than twyce twelve children by one wife
He had, of which to everlasting life
Twyce ten he sent before him, and behynd
He left but three to propagate his kynd.
He ran ten lustres out, when rigid fate,
Robbed him of life, Perth of a Magistrate.

"This trophee, Margaret Jack, his spouse, did raise
O'er her dear husband, to her lasting praise;
Through his respectful care, his memory
Shall be deryved of posterity."

On the tombstone of John Gow, hammerman, is this couplet :—

"Till God has wrought us to his will,
The hammer we must suffer still."

On the tombstone of John R. Gow, teacher, who died in 1857,
are these lines :—

"Reader, one moment
Stop and think,
That I am in eternity
And you are on the brink."

John Knox has thus inscribed a tombstone in memory of his
wife :—

"Though greedy worms devour my skin,
And gnaw my wasting flesh,
Yet God shall build my bones again,
And clothe them all afresh."

From the tombstone of David Taylor, mason, who died 21st
September, 1816, we have the following :—

"On this stone tablet gently tread,
It marks of human dust the bed,
Of dust once sensible to pain,
Dust that once lived shall live again:

Remember as thou steppest upon
Life ceased : such dust thou'lt be anon.
Then as thou would'st thine own to rest,
Now lightly let this dust be press'd."

James Galloway, a shipwrecked mariner, who died in 1852, is commemorated thus :—

"Who go to ships and in
Great waters trading be,
Within the deep those men God's works
And his great wonders see ;
For He commands, and forth in haste
The stormy tempest flies,
Which makes the sea with rolling waves
Aloft to swell and rise."

Robert Clark has thus inscribed his wife's tombstone :—

"Lo, where the silent marble weeps,
A friend, a wife, a mother sleeps,
A heart within whose sacred cell
The peaceful virtues loved to dwell."

On the tombstone of James Hunter, surgeon, who died in 1774, are these lines :—

"Short was the space allotted him to run—
Just entered on the lists he gained the crown ;
His prayer scarce ended ere his praise begun."

The Rev. Donald Fraser thus celebrates his wife, Ann Dalgarnie, who died 2nd March, 1822, aged thirty :—

"She had a grace which stole upon the heart,
Smiling as childhood, and as void of art ;
A look that spoke the friendly feeling breast ;
A voice to soothe the troubled soul to rest ;
A temper gentle as the vernal breeze,
Which ever pleased without a thought to please ;
Virtues that time and change and sorrow brave,
Unfading charms which triumph o'er the grave ;
Yet shall her mouldering form more lovely rise,
For brighter beauties dawn in other skies.
A form celestial the pure soul enshrines,
And virtue in its native lustre shines."

Within the new cemetery, memorial stones denote the graves of Donald Sinclair Maclagan, of Glenquiech, died 5th July, 1858 ; John Marshall, of Rosemount, died 23rd July, 1862 ; Flora, wife of General Sir Alexander Lindsay, K.C.B., died 25th July, 1863, and Isabella Menzies, wife of Sir John Ross, died 18th March, 1867.

On the gravestone of his wife and children, Robert Duncan has inscribed these lines :—

> " Their names are graven on this stone,
>   Their bones are in the clay,
> And very soon we will be gone,
>   And lying low as they."

In memory of his children, Peter Anderson has engraved the following :—

> " Farewell thou vase of splendour,
>   I need thy light no more,
> No brilliance dost thou render
>   The world to which I soar.

> " Nor sun nor moonbeam brightens
>   Those regions with a ray ;
> But God himself enlightens
>   Their one eternal day.

> " Farewell each dearest union
>   That blest my earthly hours,
> We yet shall hold communion
>   In amaranthine bowers.

> " The love that seems forsaken
>   When friends in death depart,
> In heaven again shall waken,
>   And repossess the heart.

> " The harps of heav'n steal o'er me,
>   I see the jasper wall,
> Jesus who pass'd before me,
>   And God the Judge of all."

> " So sung the parting spirit,
>   While round flow'd many a tear,
> Then spread her wings t' inherit
>   The throne in yonder sphere."

Within the interior of the East Church, a monumental tablet, representing two figures, is supposed to have been erected in commemoration of the three Earls of Gowrie:—

A marble monument, in the East Church, is thus inscribed :—

" In memory of their comrades who fell during the Crimean War, 1854—55, and as a tribute to their gallantry, this monument is erected by the officers of Her Majesty's 90th Light Infantry, Perthshire Volunteers, A.D. 1857."

In the cathedral of the episcopal church rest the remains of the Right Reverend Patrick Torry, D.D., Bishop of St. Andrews, Dunkeld and Dunblane, and who is also commemorated by a monument. This eminent divine was born in the parish of King Edward, Aberdeenshire, on the 27th December, 1763. After a respectable education at various country schools, Mr. Torry was, in 1782, admitted to deacon's orders by Bishop Kilgour, of Aberdeen. For seven years he conducted episcopal service at Arradoul, Banffshire ; he subsequently became assistant to Bishop Kilgour, in the episcopal church at Peterhead. There he laboured for the long period of sixty years. In 1808 he was consecrated bishop. After a long episcopate, marked by affectionate faithfulness and sterling efficiency, he was called to his rest on the 3rd October, 1852, in his 89th year."

In the Sheriff Court Room, marble tablets commemorate Patrick Murray, sheriff-clerk of Perthshire, who died 5th September, 1731, and James Paton, of Glenalmond, Sheriff-clerk of Perthshire, who died in 1850.

PARISH OF PORT OF MENTEITH.

On the island of Inchmachome, in the Lake of Menteith, are the remains of a famous Priory, founded in 1238 by Walter Comyn, Earl of Menteith. Near the centre of the choir, a recumbent monument, contains two figures, supposed to represent

Walter Stewart, Earl of Menteith, son-in-law of the founder, and his countess. In the choir another monument of inferior workmanship celebrates Sir John de Drummond, son-in-law of the preceding earl.

Surmounting part of the church and dormitory a mausoleum, consisting of a vault and apartment above it, was constructed to receive the remains of Lord Kilpont, son of William, eighth Earl of Menteith, who was killed by James Stewart, of Ardvoirlich, in Montrose's camp, at Collace, in 1644. The event of Lord Kilpont's death is embodied with fictitious colouring by Sir Walter Scott, in the " Legend of Montrose." In the introduction to that romance there is an interesting narrative respecting the unhappy author of the assassination, and the circumstances connected with it. The estate of Kilpont, or Kilpunt, is situated near the river Almond in Linlithgowshire.

PARISH OF REDGORTON.

On the banks of the Tay, about two miles above the mouth of the Almond, two upright stones denote the scene of the famous battle of Luncarty, fought between Kenneth III., and an invading army of Danes. The battle took place about the year 990. The Danes had landed at the mouth of the Esk, and after destroying the town and castle of Montrose, had marched towards Perth, and in their progress laid waste the country. They were on the field of Luncarty attacked by the royal forces, who would have sustained defeat but for the timely intervention of Hay, a farmer, and his two sons. These persons, armed with some ploughing utensils, encouraged their worsted countrymen, and so renewed the conflict with the invaders. The result was a complete victory over the Danes, whose king was slain at the spot denoted by the larger memorial stone. Hay was invited to Court, and obtained a large grant of land in the vicinity, which is still in the possession of his descendants. He is held as a progenitor by the Marquess of Tweeddale and the Earls of Kinnoull and Erroll.

PARISH OF ST. MADOES.

After the battle of Luncarty, Farmer Hay had from his sovereign the choice of a portion of territory equal to a hound's race or a falcon's flight. Having chosen the latter, the bird being let loose pursued her flight for many miles, and at length lighted on a stone in this parish, which in memorial of the occurrence is named the Hawk's Stone.

A Runic cross in the churchyard is thus described in the new Statistical Account:

"The St. Madoes stone is about seven feet in length, and in width about three at bottom, and two and a half at top. Its thickness is eight inches. It is composed of grey sandstone, similar to that which is found at Murray's Hall, full six miles off. On the one side the sculpture is divided into five compartments, right under each other and nearly equal in size. Each of the uppermost three is occupied by the figure of a man on horseback, the horse and rider being of the most grotesque form and unseemly proportions. The bridle, reins, bit, rings, and buckles, are minutely, though rudely cut, and are in perfect preservation. The rider wears a cloak or mantle, somewhat like the short waterproof cloaks of our time, but with a flat crowned head-piece, which leaves only a small portion of the face to be seen. In the fourth compartment is a serpent shaped figure, with fretted ornaments, and something like a double-headed broken sceptre, both of which ornaments are to be found on most stones of the same class. Still lower down is the figure of a goat, a good deal defaced, and adjoining this, various sculptures almost obliterated. This side of the stone, though minutely carved, does not seem to have been squared or dressed beforehand. It bears no tool marks, and has several warts, as if just newly taken from the quarry. The side opposite is by far the richer and more beautiful. Its lines are as clear as if just from the hands of the artist. The principal figure is that of a cross, the upright portion of which occupies the whole length of the stones. The shaft and transept are beautifully enriched with very complicated tracery ; both round the point where they cross are wreathed with a carved circle or halo. On each side of the shaft of the cross beneath its transept is a monstrous lizard-like figure, apparently in the agonies of death, from being crushed through at the loins by a savage-looking creature, with a head like a wolf, body like a dog, and thick curled tail. The two compartments adjoining the top of the cross are occupied by nondescripts, with monstrous and diminutive bodies, apparently gnawing their own backs. On the top, equally visible from both sides of the stone, are lizard figures *couchant* facing each other."

PARISH OF SCONE.

An upright pillar, thirteen feet high, slightly ornamented at the top and standing on a pedestal, denotes the site of the old village or "royal city" of Scone. There certain members of the court had official residences. In the foundations of the ancient monastery and in the churchyard many stone coffins have been dug up, but generally without inscription or emblem.

In the aisle of the old church a magnificent monument commemorates Viscount Stormont, Lord Scone. Executed in marble and alabaster, it bears a figure of his Lordship in armour, supported by two other figures, supposed to represent the Marquis of Tullibardine and the Earl Marischal. Lord Stormont, so created in 1621, was formerly styled Sir David Murray of Gospertie, Lord Scone. Second son of Sir Andrew Murray, of Arngask and Balvaird, he was early attached to the court of James VI. who in 1598 appointed him comptroller of the royal revenues. He accompanied the king to Perth on the 5th August, 1600, when the Gowrie conspiracy was enacted, and afterwards obtained the barony of Ruthven, and other lands which had belonged to the Earl of Gowrie. In 1603 he accompanied James to London, and was afterwards appointed a commissioner for the projected union of the kingdoms. As High Commissioner to the General Assembly, he sought to gratify the royal wishes by introducing episcopal innovations and crushing freedom of debate. At a Synod held at Perth in April, 1607, he insulted the Moderator during prayer, and afterwards locked the doors of the building against the admission of the members. For his zeal in obtruding on the church the four articles adopted at Perth in 1618, and other services, he was raised to the Peerage. He died without issue, 27th August, 1631.

PARISH OF TIBBERMUIR.

In the parish churchyard were interred upwards of three hundred Covenanters who fell at the battle of Tibbermuir on the 1st September, 1644. The Covenanters, who numbered about 6,000 horse and foot, were attacked by Montrose, and decisively routed.

Within the church, a tombstone presents, in raised letters, the following inscription :—

"This memorial erectet be Sir Iames Mvrrey of Tibbermvir, Knicht, anno Dom. 1631, wharin lyis the bodyis of ISBELL RVTHVEN, his grandmother, Captane DAVID and ROSINA MVRRAYIS, two of hir brither . . IOHNE FENTONE, sone to Rosina. Item, IOHN MVRRAY, father to Sir IAMES and HELEN SCRIMGEOR his last spovs, and MERIORIE COLVIL, first spovs to Sir Iames, and GEILS and PATRIK MVRRAYIS, tvo of hir bearnis to him, and ELISBET and IOHNE MVRRAYIS with his . . . ."

The Murrays of Tibbermuir were descended from Alexander, 5th son of Sir David Murray, of Gask, who died in 1446,—an ancestor of the Ducal House of Athole.

PARISH OF TULLIALLAN.

In the churchyard a tomb belongs to the old family of Blackadder, who for five generations were owners of the castle and lands of Tulliallan.

The old church at Overtown constitutes the burial-place of Admiral George Keith Elphinstone, afterwards Viscount Keith. This distinguished naval commander was fourth son of Charles, tenth Lord Elphinstone, and was born in 1747. In his sixteenth year he entered the navy as midshipman, under Captain Jervis, afterwards Earl St. Vincent. Devoting himself to his profession he speedily rose in the service. During the war on the American coast he honourably acquitted himself, and when Europe was the theatre of war from 1793 till the battle of Waterloo he gained a series of splendid victories. In 1815, as commander of the Channel Fleet he had the honour to prevent the escape of Napoleon. He was created Viscount Keith in 1814. On the close of the war he retired from active service; he successively represented in Parliament the counties of Dumbarton and Stirling. He died 10th March, 1823.

PARISH OF WEEM.

At the east end of the old church a monument of curious and varied sculpture commemorates by a latin inscription Sir Alexander Menzies, of Castle Menzies, and his wife Marjory, daughter of Sir John Campbell, of Glenorchy. Sir Alexander was created a Baronet of Nova Scotia, 2nd September, 1665.

FORFARSHIRE.

PARISH OF ABERLEMNO.

In the parish churchyard a sculptured stone presents on one side a cross, surrounded with floral decorations ; on the other are figures of men on horseback, engaged in warfare. A few hundred yards to the north of the church, a stone eight feet in height bears on one side a richly carved cross, with two female figures in the act of weeping ; while on the other side are figures of men, some on horseback, others on foot, intermingled with dogs. These stones are believed to commemorate the defeat of a party of Danes by Malcolm II. in the year 1012. In honour of his victory Malcolm founded a monastery at Brechin, which he dedicated to the Virgin.

In the old chapel of Auldbar, and also in the interior of the parish church, tablets of brass and marble celebrate certain members of the House of Chalmers. In Aberlemno church William Chalmers of Auldbar, and his wife, are commemorated thus :—

"Hic conduntur reliquiæ Gulielmi Chalmers de Aldbar, qui vixit annos 65, ob. 7 Id. Jul. 1765 ; et Cæciliæ Elphinston conjugis adamatæ quæ vixit annos 58, ob. Non. Mart. 1761. Sacrum memoriæ parentum bene merentum hoc marmor filius posuit."

Mr. Chalmers belonged to the family of Hazelhead, Aberdeenshire. Obtaining a fortune as a trader in Spain, he purchased the estate of Auldbar in 1753. He was succeeded by his son Patrick, who became sheriff of the county. In Aberlemno church he is on a monumental tablet, thus celebrated :—

"Patrick Chalmers, Esq., of Auldbar, advocate, died on the 15th February, 1824, aged 87.

Virtuous and learned, polished and refined,
Of pleasing manners and enlightened mind ;
Beloved in life, lamented in his end,
Here sleeps the sire, the grandsire, and the friend."

In Auldbar chapel, two monumental brasses have these inscriptions :—

"In memory of Patrick Chalmers, Esquire, of Aldbar, for many years a merchant in London. He was born at Aldbar, A.D. 1777, and died there on the 8th day of December, 1826. Also of Frances Inglis, his wife, who died at Aldbar on the 10th day of February, 1848, in the 70th year of her age."

"Outside the walls of this chapel are interred the mortal remains of Patrick Chalmers, Esquire, of Aldbar, late Captain in H.M.'s 3rd Dragoon Guards, sometime Member of Parliament for the Montrose District of Burghs, Author of the Sculptured Monuments of Angus. He re-edified this chapel in the year 1853. Died at Rome, on June the 23rd, 1854."

Patrick Chalmers died in his fifty-second year. An intelligent and accomplished antiquary, he edited the chartularies of Arbroath and Brechin, which he presented to the Bannatyne Club. His work on the sculptured stones of Forfarshire is much valued.

From tombstones in Aberlemno churchyard we have these rhymes :—

"In hopes in peace his Lord to meet,
    Here lies interred in dust,
One in his temper ever kind,
    In all his dealings just.
Kind to the poor, the widow's friend,
    He always did remain,
Till heaven's great Lord by His decree
    Recalled his life again."

"Here lies the man, who peace did still pursue,
And to each one did render what was due ;
With meek submission he resign'd his breath
To God, the sovereign Lord of life and death.
Here different ages do promiscuous lie ;
The old man must, the young may die."

> " Man's life on earth, even from the womb,
> Is full of troubles to his tomb ;
> He enters in with cries and fears,
> And passeth thro' with cares and tears.
> He goeth out with sighs and groans,
> And in the earth doth lodge his bones ;
> A Lodging place beyond the grave
> To rest, and Hallelujah sing
> Eternally to Heaven's King."

The gravestone of John Nicol, weaver, who died in 1728, is inscribed thus :—

> " Tho' this fine Art with skilful hand
> Brings Foreign Riches to our Land ;
> Adorns our Rich and shields our Poor,
> From cold our bodies doth secure :
> Yet neither Art nor Skill e'er can
> Exempt us from the lot of man."

On a tombstone belonging to the family of Spence, who resided in the parish for nearly four centuries, are these lines :—

> " Here lye an honest old race
> Who in Balgavies land had a place
> Of residence, as may be seen,
> Full years three hundred and eighteen."

PARISH OF AIRLIE.

In the churchyard a coffin-slab commemorates a member of the family of Roger.* On the sides are sculptured a sword and hunting-horn, while the top represents an ornamental cross, in the shaft of which are engraved in Roman characters the following legend :—

" Lyis . heir—Roger . and . Yofan . Rolok . qva . died . in . Ridie . 1640."

* See " The Scottish Branch of the Norman House of Roger," Edin-burgh, 1872, p. 20.

These rhymes are from different gravestones in Airlie churchyard :—

    " We of this child had great content,
      For to get learning of his God and Christ was his intent,
    Tho' soon cut off the stage of time,
    We dare not to reflect that we so soon did part,
    For it was his latter will
    That he God's counsel should fulfil."

      " While nature shrinks to be dissolved,
        Relentless death strikes hard ;
      Nor blooming youth, nor parents' tears,
        Procure the least regard.
      The lovely child fond parents boast,
        Sunk in a sea of grief ;
      Hard fate—fret we 'gainst heaven ? No,
        Submission gives relief. "

      " This worthy pair, both free of fraud,
        Made Truth their constant aim ;
      You might depended on their word,
        For still it was the same.
      They loved to live with all around
        In unity and peace ;
      And with a spotless character
        They finished their race."

    " Sure death may kill, but cannot give surprise
    To those whose views are fix'd beyond the skies ;
    He with his spear that vital spring untied,
    And sore my spouse did sicken till she died.
    With winged flight her soul did speed away
    E'en to the regions of immortal day ;
    Her husband, children, left to weep and moan—
    The best of wives, the kindest mother gone."

PARISH OF ARBIRLOT.

At the parochial manse is preserved a sepulchral stone which
was discovered in the foundation of the old parish church. It is

5½ feet in height and 2¾ feet in breadth, and is sculptured with two crosses, two open books, and a small circle. The old church was dedicated to Saint Ninian.

PARISH OF ARBROATH.

The parochial churchyard includes the area and precincts of the ancient abbey. This magnificent structure was founded by William the Lion in 1178, and dedicated to the memory of Thomas à Becket. It was planted with monks of the Benedictine order, and the abbot was privileged to exercise episcopal functions, and to sit in Parliament as a spiritual peer. The fabric was dilapidated at the Reformation, when the lands and other endowments belonging to the institution were converted into a temporal lordship.

Prior to his death William the Lion selected the abbey as his place of sepulture, and therein he was buried before the high altar on the 4th December, 1214, in presence of his successor and a vast assemblage of the nobles. After the neglect of centuries, a party of workmen who were cleaning the area of the church discovered on the 20th March, 1811, the tomb of the founder. The stone coffin contained a portion of the monarch's bones. These represented a man of goodly stature. The coffin-lid is of madrepore, a dark spotted marble; it bears the effigies of the king, in a robe simply draped,—the waist girt with a narrow belt to which is attached a purse. The head is gone; and the feet rest on the figure of a lion. Small figures surround the king, and are in the act of arranging his dress.

Within the abbey a monument with an inscription round the sides represents the full-length figure of a monk, but his name is effaced.

In the chancel is preserved the front of a mural tombstone, which was found near the high altar. Divided into four compartments, each contains a figure carved in bold relief. In the first an angel with outstretched wings holds a shield, placed upon a crozier. A figure in the second division holds a pitcher and the brush for sprinkling holy water. The third figure holds the paten, and the fourth displays an open book. As the shield presents the bearings of his house, the monument has been described as that of Walter Paniter, or Panter, who was abbot of the institution for many years prior to 1443, when he resigned office.

On modern tombstones in Arbroath churchyard we have the following metrical inscriptions :—

" George and Helen are dead and gone,
    And we their parents mourn full sore ;
But when we leave this sinful world
    We will be sorrowful no more."

" Jean and Agnes are gone to a world of love,
    Where sorrow are known no more ;
They have gone to inherit a land of bliss
    On Canaan's happy shore."

" By him whose conquests through the world are known
I to my mean original am thrown;
My dust lies here, my better part's above,
So I, not death, the conqueror prove."

" How bless'd are they, the Word proclaims,
    That are in Jesus dead !
Sweet is the savour of their name,
    And soft their silent bed.
Far from this world's toil and strife,
    And ever with the Lord,
The sufferings of this mortal life
    End in a rich reward."

" Now slain by death, who spareth none,
And his full bow—under this stone,
Take heed and read, and thou shalt see,
As I am now, so shalt thou be—

Rotting in dark and silent dust,
Prepare for death, for die thou must;
Life is uncertain—death is sure;
Sin is the wound, Christ is the cure."

" Go, blessed spirits, mount where cherubs sing
Sublime hosannahs to the Saviour King;
Go soon triumphant from earth's drear domain,
The seat of sin, of misery, and of pain.
The stars will light you on the way
To realms of glory and eternal day;
Then let your eyes behold the bright abode
Prepared for you by an indulgent God."

PARISH OF AUCHTERHOUSE.

In an aisle attached to the parish church rest the remains of
the members of the noble families of Airlie, Buchan, and Strathmore.
In the churchyard a tombstone is thus inscribed :—

" Heir lyes ane godly and vertous man Iames Christie of Bal-
buchlie, who departed ye 20 of Decem : 1651, and his age 97 :—
Dulce fuit, quondam mihi vivere ; non quia vixi;
Sed quoniam, ut vivam, tunc moriturus eram.
—Once it vas svet to me to leive, not that I leived, bvt I leived
to die."

James Stewart, who had been a soldier in his youth, is thus
commemorated :—

" In foreign lands where men with war engage,
He was sarvising at many a bloody saige ;
And was preserved wnhurt, yet gathered to his rest
In good old age—who trusts in God is blest."

PARISH OF BARRY.

On the floor of the parish church a gravestone commemorates Martha Forrester, "spouse to Umqvhile Thomas Mavle." The date is partially defaced, but the stóne seems to belong to the early part of the seventeenth century. Forrester as a family name was formerly common in the district.

In the north wall of the church a monumental tablet bears the following inscription :—

"✠ Griselis . Dirhamia . sponsa . Davidis . Alexander . de . Pits kellie . obiit . 6 . mensis . Ivnii . 1664 . ætatis . svæ . 34.

anagr .

Griselis . Dirhamia . ardeo . regiam . elisi . elisivm . vere . mea delectatio : qvando . in . vivis . eivs . svmmvs . et . ardor . erat elisivm . qvoniam . mea . delectatio : sola . nvnc . frvor . elisio perpetvoqve . frvar . vivet :

post . fvnera . virtvs."

David Alexander was served heir to his father James, in the lands of Balskellie, now Pitskellie, in December, 1676. This family had long previously possessed the adjoining property of Ravensby.

Several tombstones commemorate members of the family of Sim of Greenlawhill, including the Rev. David Sim, minister of the parish, who died on the 1st October, 1823, in his seventieth year and the forty-seventh of his ministry.

A mortuary enclosure has on the gate the following inscription :—

Major Thomas Hunter, of the 104th Regt., died 19th March, 1840, aged 59 years."

The following inscription is from the gravestone of Robert Crawfurd, who died in 1707 :—

" Mors tuo, mors Christi, fraus mundi, gloria Cœli,
Et dolor Inferni, sunt meditanda tibi.
Thy death the death of Christ,
The world's vexation ;
Heaven's glory, Hell's horror,
Make thy meditation."

From different tombstones we have these metrical epitaphs :—

> " As we be, so shall ye.
> To speak the truth let this suffice,
> She was a woman virtuous and wise,
> Not in the least to any vice inclin'd,
> Such was her prudent, civilized mind;
> Her rest from worldly cares doth pleasant prove,
> While her immortal soul triumphs above."

> " Here lies the dust that once enshrin'd
> A sober, honest, friendly mind;
> The heavenly part hath wing'd its flight
> To regions of eternal light.
> The body too which breathless lies,
> Redeem'd from death shall shortly rise,
> And join its kindred soul again,
> Fit to adorn its Maker's train."

> " Decreed by God in mercy to mankind,
> Our troubles are to this short life confined ;
> Want, weakness, pain, disease, and sorrow have
> Their general quietus in the grave.
> The living never should the dead lament ;
> Death's our reward, and not our punishment ;
> Keep death and judgment always in your eye—
> None's fit to live, but who is fit to die.
> Make use of present time because you must
> Take up your lodging shortly in the dust ;
> 'Tis dreadful to behold the setting sun,
> And night approaching ere your work is done."

> " How frail is man ! in how short a time
> He fades like roses which have pass'd their prime !
> So wrinkled age the fairest face will plow,
> And cast deep furrows on the smoothest brow.
> Then where's that lovely, tempting face ? alas !
> Yourselves would blush to view it in a glass.
> I stand to mark this good man's place ;
> Upon this earth he lived in peace ;
> He with his wife and family
> Still had the praise for honesty.

> While on this earth he did remain,
> There was no mortal could him stain ;
> When things sublimer did him tire,
> He long'd to meet the heaven's empire.
> Then Jesus came and bade him rise,
> His soul with Him to pierce the skies ;
> Ever to court the King of kings
> With those that hallelujah sings."

PARISH OF BRECHIN.

The cathedral of Brechin was founded by David I. about the year 1150. The chancel was destroyed at the Reformation : the western portion of the nave has long been used as the parish church. Within the cathedral rest the remains of the Rev. William Guthrie, minister of Fenwick, an eminent sufferer in the cause of Presbyterianism. Eldest son of the Laird of Pitforthie in this parish, he was born in 1620, and prosecuted his studies at the University of St. Andrews. Licensed to preach in 1642, he was, after being sometime employed as a tutor, ordained minister of Mauchline, in November, 1644. Refusing to submit to Episcopacy he was deprived by Archbishop Burnet, of Glasgow, in 1664. He died at Brechin on the 10th October, 1665, in the forty-fifth year of his age and twenty-first of his ministry. A powerful and eloquent divine, multitudes flocked to his ministrations. His work " The Christian's Great Interest," has obtained wide acceptance, and has been translated into French, German, and other languages.

In the churchyard a tombstone commemorates six hundred persons who died of the pestilence in 1647. It is inscribed thus :—

> " Luna quater crescens
>   Sexcentos peste peremptos,
>   Disce mori ! vidit,
>   Pulvis et umbra sumus."

The burial-place of William Ramsay Maule, Baron Panmure, is

denoted by a lofty granite obelisk. At the base of the column is the following inscription. Erected by the people to the memory of the Right Honourable William, Baron Panmure, of Brechin and Navar,—born 27th October, 1771, died 13th April, 1852, whose motto and action was " Live and let live."

The Honourable William Ramsay Maule, afterwards Baron Panmure, was second son of George, eighth Earl of Dalhousie. Consequent on the settlement of his grand-uncle, he obtained possession of the Panmure estates on the demise of his father, which took place in 1787. He entered the House of Commons in 1796, and continued to represent the county of Forfar, till 1831, when he was called to the Upper House as Baron Panmure. Succeeding to a princely inheritance when he was young, and at a period when social festivities were conducted in a manner now happily unknown, Mr. Maule was at the outset of his career chiefly known for his strange escapades and extravagant drollery. Latterly he was a pattern of benevolence, and a munificent benefactor and patron of county institutions.

A small tombstone commemorates Alexander Laing, author of "Wayside Flowers," a volume of interesting poetry. Laing died at Brechin, on the 14th October, 1857, in his seventieth year. Several of his songs have obtained an honoured place in the national minstrelsy.

PARISH OF CARESTON.

In the churchyard a tombstone commemorates the Rev. John Gillies, who died minister of the parish, on the 1st March, 1853, aged seventy-two. He was grandfather of Adam Gillies, a Senator of the College of Justice, and of Dr. John Gillies, author of " The History of Greece."

Within a mortuary enclosure, a memorial stone denotes the resting-place of the Rev. David Lyell, minister of the parish, who died 15th July, 1854, aged eighty-six, and of that of his wife, the Hon. Catherine, daughter of John, seventh Viscount Arbuthnot, who died 16th December, 1853, aged sixty-five.

From tombstones in the churchyard we have these rhymes :—

> "As our shorter day of light,
>   Our day of life posts on ;
> Both show a long course to the night,
>   But both are quickly run.
> Both have their night, and when that spreads
>   Its black wing o'er the day,
> There's no more work, all take their beds,
>   Of feathers or of clay.
> Chuse then before it be too late,
>   For choice with life will end ;
> Remember on thy choice thy fate,
>   Thy good or ill depends."

> "This stone doth hold these corps of mine,
>   While I ly buried here ;
> None shall molest nor wrong this stone,
>   Except my friends that's near.
> My flesh and bones lyes in Earth's womb,
>   Until Judgment do appear ;
> And then I shall be raised again,
>   To meet my Saviour dear."

PARISH OF CARMYLLIE.

On the south wall of the parish church a marble tablet in memory of the Rev. Patrick Bryce and his wife is thus inscribed :—

"In memory of the Revd. Patrick Bryce, 45 years minister of this parish, a sincere Christian, a faithful pastor, devout, charitable, and upright. He recommended that religion which he taught, by a peculiar mildness and simplicity of manner. Conscientious in the discharge of every relative duty, beloved, honoured, and universally respected, he died in the humble hope of a far nobler inheritance beyond the grave, 21 June 1816, in his eighty-fourth year. Also Mary Aitken, his wife, who closed a well-spent life in the same hopes of a blessed immortality, 19 Sep. 1801, aged seventy-two. A tribute of filial love and respect from their only child and affectionate daughter."

These metrical inscriptions are from different tombstones :—

> " When death's darts did approach so near,
> We parted with our children dear;
> And for them we had this respect—
> This monument we did erect."

> " Now cruel death hath us all three
> Right soon his captives made ;
> And by his mighty arm you see,
> Down in the grave hath laid."

> " He who was sober, just, and good,
> And fam'd for piety,
> No panygeric now doth need,
> His praise to amplify.
> His memory on earth is blest,
> His soul with glory crown'd ;
> His body here shall rest in peace
> Till the last trumpet sound."

> " Let marble monuments record
> Their fame, who distant lands explore,
> This humble stone points out the place
> Where sleeps a virtuous, ancient race.
> Their sire possess'd ye neighbouring plain,
> Before Columbus cross'd the main;
> And tho' ye world may deem it strange,
> His son, contented, seeks no change,
> Convinc'd wherever man may roam,
> He travels only to the Tomb."

> " Here, gentle reader, o'er this dust
> We crave a tear, for here doth rest
> A Father, Husband, and a Friend,
> In him those three did finely blend.

Worn by disease, and rack'd with pain,
Physicians' aid was all in vain,
Till God, in his great love, saw meet
To free him from his sorrows great.
How wonderful, how vast his love,
Who left the shining realms above;
How much for lost mankind he bore,
Their peace and safety to restore."

PARISH OF CORTACHY.

In the parish churchyard is the burial aisle of the noble House
of Airlie. Several marble tablets are thus inscribed :—

" Erected by David, Seventh Earl of Airlie, in kind and dutiful
remembrance of his Parents, Brother, and Uncle:—

" In memory of David, Fifth Earl of Airlie, who died at Cortachy
Castle 3d March, 1803, aged seventy-eight. His Lordship, in the
generous enthusiasm of youth, joined the Chevalier at Edinburgh in
October, 1745, with a regiment of six hundred men, and continued
loyal and true to his cause. He afterwards entered the French
service, in which he obtained the rank of Lieutenant-General. In
1778 His Majesty, George the Third, was pleased to restore him to
his country and estates, where his true nobleness and kinduess of
disposition will long be held in respectful and affectionate
remembrance."

" In memory of Walter, Sixth Earl of Airlie, a most respected
and venerable nobleman, who died at Cortachy Castle on the 10th
of April, 1819, in the eighty-sixth year of his age. And of Jane,
his Countess, a worthy and beneficent lady, who died on the 11th
of June, 1818, aged fifty-six."

" In memory of Captain John Ogilvy, of the First Regiment of
Foot, a brave and promising officer, who died at Berbice on the
24th August, 1809, in the twenty-sixth year of his age, greatly
beloved and lamented."

" In memory of Clementina, Countess of Airlie, who died in London on the 1st of September, 1835, in the forty-first year of her age, and whose mortal remains are here interred. As a most dutiful and affectionate wife, and a mother, she was a pattern to her sex, in all duty and affection ; to the poor and needy a bountiful, considerate, and unwearied friend ; and, after giving an edifying example of devout resignation to the Divine will under many and long protracted sufferings, she departed this life in the faith of a crucified and risen Redeemer, universally beloved, honoured, and lamented. Erected by her bereaved, sorrowful, and devoted husband, David, Earl of Airlie."

" Sacred to the memory of Margaret Bruce, Countess of Airlie, who departed this life at Brighton, Sussex, on the 18th of June, 1845, aged thirty-nine, having given birth to twin sons on the 16th of the same month. The Countess left four sons to her attached husband, David, Earl of Airlie, by whom this tablet is erected in grateful memory of an affectionate wife. Interred here 9th of July, 1845."

" By David Graham Drummond, Eighth Earl of Airlie, this tablet is erected, in grateful and dutiful remembrance of his father, David, Seventh Earl of Airlie. His kindness of heart and consideration for others won for him the love and esteem of those among whom he lived, and a place in the hearts of his people, whose welfare was his chief object. He died 20th August, 1849, in the sixty-fifth year of his age, after a long and painful illness, which he bore with Christian patience and fortitude."

" Sacred to the memory of Maria, wife of the Hon. Donald Ogilvy of Clova, who departed this life, at Leamington Priors, on the 9th of April, 1843, aged fifty-two years."

" In memoriam David Ogilvy, nat. 10th April A.D. 1826; ob. 20th July A.D. 1857."

PARISH OF CRAIG.

Within the parish church, a handsome mural cenotaph comme-morates David Scott, Esq., of Dunninald. It is thus inscribed :—

" In memory of David Scott, Esquire, of Dunninald, in this county, who closed a valuable and well-spent life on the 4th day of October, 1805, aged fifty-nine. His ardent desire to enlarge the sphere of his benevolence led him to forego the ease of indepen-dence, and those social enjoyments for which the sensibility of his heart was peculiarly formed, and to embrace the more arduous cares of public life. His native county experienced the full benefit of his unwearied services as one of her representatives in successive Parliaments, and the records of the *East India Company* amply attest the zeal, talent, and integrity with which, for many years, he directed the affairs of that great commercial body. After a severe and lingering illness, borne with manly fortitude and Christian resignation, though greatly aggravated in its progress by the loss of the best of wives and worthiest of women, he sunk depressed to the same grave with her who had most endeared life, and soothed its suffering.

" In pious memory of their parental affection, their mutual attach-ment and congenial virtues, this monument is erected by their afflicted son.'"

David Scott was succeeded in his estates by his only son David, who as heir to his uncle Sir James Sibbald, Bart., became a baronet, and assumed the name of Sibbald. The son of this gentle-man, Sir James Sibbald David Scott, Bart. is the present owner of the estate.

In the interior of the church a memorial tablet commemorates Peter Arkley, Esq., of Dunninald, born September, 16th, 1786, and died 31st December, 1825. Mr. Arkley was a zealous promoter of agriculture, and was held in high esteem for his patriotic enterprise.

Near the pulpit a monument commemorates Hercules Ross, Esq, of Rossie, who died 24th December, 1816, aged seventy-two, and Henrietta Parish, his wife, who died 14th June, 1811, aged forty-three; also several members of their family. The Ross family burial-place is on the north side of the church.

Memorial slabs commemorate Lieutenant-General Daniel Colquhoun, who died 17th November, 1848; also other members of the House of Luss.

By a plain tablet is commemorated John Turnbull, of Stracathro and Smithiehill, who died 10th October, 1693, aged sixty-three; he made a bequest for behoof of the poor.

In the picturesque churchyard of St. Skeoch rest the remains of James Brewster, Rector of the Grammar School of Jedburgh; father of Sir David Brewster, the distinguished philosopher (Vol. I., 246).

PARISH OF DUN.

The old parish church constitutes the burial-place of the family of Erskine, of Dun. Sir John Erskine, of Dun, Superintendent of Angus, and a zealous promoter of the Reformation, died at Dun, but his place of sepulture is unmarked. The estate of Dun came into the noble family of Kennedy by the marriage in 1793 of Archibald, first Marquis of Ailsa, with Margaret, second daughter of John Erskine, of Dun. The Marquis is buried in the family aisle; he died 8th September, 1846, aged seventy-six. The Marchioness, who died in 1848, rests in the same vault.

From tombstones in Dun parish churchyard we have the following rhymes:—

> "Within this grave I do both lie and rest,
> Because the Lord perfumed yᵉ grave at first;
> May when I rise unto me Christ grant this,
> To be with him in his eternal bliss."

> "Under this stone do sweetly rest
> A woman pious, virtuous, and chaste;
> Who in her life performed two duties great,
> A careful Mother and a Loving Mate."

"This woman here in hope doth rest,
　　Again to rise and be for ever blest ;
After this life we purpose here to lie,
　　And rise and reign with her eternally."

"Under this stone three mortals do remain,
　　Till Christ shall come and raise them up again ;
Altho' by death they be in Prison cast,
　　The Prince of Life will raise them up at last,
And give them life, which no more will decay,
　　And habitation which wasteth not away."

"Whoever him bethought
　　Seriously and oft,
What it were to flit
　　From his death-bed to the pit ;
There to suffer pain
　　Never to cease again ;
Would not commit one sin,
　　The whole world to win."

"When silver bands of nature burst,
　　And let the building fall,
The blest goes down to mix with dust,
　　Its first original.
The tyrant death he triumphs here,
　　His trophies spread around ;
And heaps of dust and bones appear
　　Through all the hollow ground."

PARISH OF DUNDEE.

The burying-ground, styled the Howff, is situated in the centre
of the town. Anciently the garden of the Franciscan Monastery, it
was in 1564 granted to the burgh by Queen Mary. Substantially
enclosed in 1601, the tombs of the more opulent were thereafter
raised against the walls.

Among the gravestone inscriptions in the Howff, many of which are no longer traceable, were the following :—

"Heir restis ane honorabile Baronne, Jhone Kynneir of yat ilk, quha departit out of this mortal lyf at Dundee, the 21st day of June, 1584, and of his age the 63 year."

"Monumentum sepulturæ, viri amplissimo honore, præclara eruditione, et multis in vita eximiis virtutibus ornati, D. Davidis Kinloch ab Aberbrothie, regum Magnæ Britanniæ et Franciæ medici peritissimi; quorum diplomatis et sigillis gentis suæ et familiæ. Nobilitas luculenter testata et comprobata est. Obitt decimo Septembris, anno salutis humanæ 1617. Ætatis suæ 58."

"Kinnalochi proavos et avitæ stemmata gentis
Clara inter proceres, hæc monumenta probant
Magnus ab his cui surgit honos: sed major ab arte
Major ab ingenio gloria parta venit."

Across one of the central walls a gravestone is inscribed as follows :—

"Heir lys ane godlie and honest man, Johne Roche, Brabener and Bvrges of Dvndie, qvha departit this lyfe the 10 of Febrvar, 1616 yeirs, being of age 43 yeiris. Vith his spovs Evfiane Pye, qva hes cavsit this to be made in rememberance of him. And thair 14 bearnes."

On the gravestone of Thomas Simson, dated 1579, are these lines:—

"Man tak hed to me hov thov sal be
Qvhan thov art dead
Drye as a trie, verms sal eat ye;
Thy great booti sal be lik lead.
Y^e time hath bene in my zoot grene,
That I ves clene of bodie as ye are,
Byt for my eyen, nov tvo holes bene,
Of me is sene, but benes bare."

A monument is thus inscribed:—

" HIC · DORMIENTI · PIETATE · ET · VIRTVTE · INSIGNI · VIRO ·
GEORGIO · ROGER · NAVCLERO · ET · CIVI · HVIVS · OPPIDI · QVI · OBIIT ·

ANNO · 1611 · DIE · PRIMO · OCTOBRIS · ÆTATIS · VERO · SVÆ · ANNO ·
33 · HOC · FACIENDVM · PROCVRAVIT · EIVS · CONIVNX · ELIZABETHA ·
LOCHMALOVNIE.   MIHI · HODIE · CRAS · TIBI."

George Roger was father of Bailie William Roger, merchant, who
bequeathed, in 1659, one-half of his real and personal estate for the
education and training of " seven poor male children " within the
burgh. His widow, Euphan Man, established a Merchants' Widows
Fund at Dundee.*

Walter Coupar, tailor, who died 25th December, 1628, aged fifty-
two, is thus commemorated :—

> " Kynd comorades heir Coupar's corps is layd,
> Waltir by name, a tailzour to his trayde,
> Both kynd and trew, and stvt and honest-heartit
> Condole vith me that he so soon depairtit,
> For I avow he never weyld a sheir
> Had better pairts nor he that's bvriet heir."

Mr. Andrew Scheppert, minister of Benvie, has thus celebrated
his father, who died 13th November, 1641 :—

> " Nathaniel's heart, Bezaleel's hand,
>   If ever any had ;
> Then boldly may ye say, had he
>   Who lieth in this bed."

Captain Alexander Baxter has in the following stanzas commemorated his daughter Katharine, who died 20th March, 1632, aged
seventeen :—

> " Stay, passenger—no more for marvels seek,
>   Among their many monuments of death,
> For here a demi-Scot, a demi-Greek
>   Doth lie, to whom the Cretan Isle gave breath ;
> And is not (this) a wonder, is it not ?
> Her birth and burial to be so remote.

> " So falls by winter blasts a virgin rose ;
>   For blotless, spotless, blameless did she die ;
> As many virtues nature did disclose
>   In her, as oft in greatest age we see.

* See " Scottish Branch of the House of Roger," p. 23.

Ne'er Jason glori'd more in the golden fleece
Than her brave sire in bringing her from Greece."

A tombstone without date in memory of Thomas Maule was inscribed thus :—

"Desideratissimo suo per annos 26 in matrimonio compari, magistro Thomæ Maule, doctori medico, insigniter felice; de summis juxta ac infirmis in hac urbe et tota ejus vicina, etiam de compluribus vitæ nobilitatis viris, optime merito; latine, græce, gallice sciente, astronomiæ preceptis haud leviter imbuto; pietatis in Deum, justitiæ in proximum eximio cultori."

The monument of James Fraser bears the following epitaph :—

"Jacobus Fraserius, vir domi forisque clarus, et de popularibus optime meritus, parentibus et affinibus, pro reconditorio suo, hoc erigendum curavit.

> "Jacobi Fraserii, viri clarissimi, elogium
> Annosam matrem cura qui perpete fovit;
> Defuncto hunc patri constituit tumulum;
> Germanos opibus juvit, charasque sorores;
> Anchora cognatis, portus et aura suis
> Qui captivorum sortem miseratus iniquam
> Eripuit duro languida colla jugo.
> Christicolas inter Turcasque interpres amicus
> Quem pietas coluit, barbaries timuit
> Usu multiplici rerum, virtute et honore,
> Divitiis, priscos nobilitavit avos."

Bailie George Brown, mortally wounded at the siege of the town by General Monk in 1651, is commemorated thus :—

"Monumentum Georgii Brouni, Deidonani prætoris meritissimi ; qui hoc præturæ munere per decennium feliciter defunctus, undique pugnando lethaliter ab hostibus vulneratus : quibus vulneribus per martem languidus, mortem naturæ debitum, pro civitate et patria, reddidit 2do nona Octobris, anno Dom. 1651. Ætatis sexagesimo."

The merits of Alexandro Milne, magistrate, are thus described by his son :—

"Patri optimo Alexandro Milne, sæpius in hac urbe prætura cum laude defuncto, tandem anno ætatis suæ 68, Dom. 1651. Vita functo, monumentum hoc magister Alexander Milne filius erigendum curavit.

> " Relligio, nivei mores, prudentia, candor
> In Milno radiis enituere suis :
> Consule quo, felix republica ; judice, felix
> Curia, et ædili res sacra semper erat."

The monument of Alexander Wedderburn of Easter-Powrie, Provost and member of Parliament, was thus inscribed :—

" Conditur hoc tumulo Alexander Wedderburn, dominus de Easter Pourie, familiæ suæ princeps ; nuperrime huic urbi præfectus ; ejusdem, ad Parliamentum primum supremi Domini nostri regis Caroli 2di delegatus. Obiit 9 die Aprilis, anno Dom. 1683, ætatis 68. Hic etiam conquiescunt ossa Elisabethæ Ramsay, illius primi amoris uxoris, filiæ unicæ Joannis Ramsay, fratris domini de Murie, hujusque urbis olim prætoris quæ obiit 2 die mensis Aprilis, 1643. Ætatis 22.

The following epitaph adorns the monument of Andrew Archbald, a noted surgeon :—

" Monumentum Andreæ Archbald, lithotomi insignis qui obiit pridie Septembris, anno salutis humanæ 1662, ætatis suæ 67. Ejusdem itidem conjugis Catherinæ Poureæ amantissimæ.

> " Hic situs Andreas Archbaldus, candidus, arte
> Lithotomus, gratis qui tulit almus opem
> Pauperibus ; sacri verbi memor usque tonantis
> Qui panem gelidis mittere mandat aquis.
> Lithotomi multi, tentantes tollere morbum
> Huic pro uno incolumi, mille dedere neci.
> Dum vixi, studui morbum quam calculi acerbum
> Tollere ; sic summus sensit et imus opem.
> Hic jacet Archbaldus, cautus qui et usque peritus
> Sanavit multos ; nullaque causa necis
> Hæc conjunx, cui liquit opes, monumenta marito
> Erigit hic, scriptis quæ super ossa notis
> Nomina forte rogas, lector ; Catherina Puræa
> Dicitur ; hæc vere pura quod usque fuit.
> M Mors solet, innumeris, Morbis, corrumpere vitam M
> O Omnia mors rostro O devorat usque suo :   O
> R Rex, princeps, sapiens seRvus, stultus, miser, æger R
> S Sis quicunque veliS, pulvis et umbra sumus. S."

David Yeman, merchant, and his wife, Margaret Pourie, had their monument thus inscribed :—

"Parentibus delectissimis, Davidi Yeman mercatori, notæ integritatis viro; necnon Margaretæ Puræ, uxori amantissimæ; Patricius Yeman mercator, filius, hoc monumentum cadendum curavit parentavitque. Pater decessit die 4 mensis Maii, anno 1654 Ætatis suæ 48, mater vero 31 Decembris 1669.

"Davidus est tumulus Yemani ; ubi sede quiescit
Hac placide, et charæ conjugis ossa jacent;
Sobrius ut prudens, dictis jucundus amænis,
Innocuus, nota est intaminata fides.
Vita Deoque placens ; uxoris maxima cura,
Usque viri cupiens stringere signa pedum ;
Nunc cœlo gaudent; animos ubi nulla fatigat
Cura, sed est lux, pax, gloria, plena, quies."

Patrick Gourlay, Town Clerk, was commemorated thus :—

"Monumentum probi ac spectatæ integritatis viri, magistri Patricii Gourlay, scribæ publici curiæ Taoduni; hac in arte a negotiis fidelissimi; qui laxato vinculo corporeo humanitus naturæ cessit 17 cal. Januarii, anno domini 1667. Ætatis suæ 47. Ejusdem itidem Marjoriæ Anderson, conjugis amantissimæ.

"Hic animo tranquillus erat librarius omni
Notus ut ingenuus, sic probitatis amans ;
In vita, hoc semper signis testatus apertis
Ulterius calamum dum manus ægra negat;
Sedulus arte sua, prudens, mitisque fidelis ;
Sic fragilis vitæ munere functus obit
Conjunx cui et natus, cupiens insistere patris
Vestigiis, curant hæc monumenta strui."

By his widow Marjory Watson, Bailie Andrew Forrester is celebrated as follows :—

"Monumentum hoc sepulchrale marmoreum mauceolum Andreæ Forresteri Taoduni prætoris præclari, que in officio præturæ Diem obiit July 8, 1671. Ætatis 34. In amoris testimonium, unica et selecta conjunx Marjoria Watson superstes cædendum curavit.

"Transmisi ad superos animam ; sed putre cadaver,
Quod vides inglorium ;
Tale Christus reddet vindex, quale extulit orco
Ad cœlites denuo redux."

These lines commemorate George Forrester, Dean of Guild, who died 3rd January, 1673 :—

> " Forresterus consul Taoduni, flore juventæ
> Surreptus subito, conditur hoc tumulo ;
> Integer, exornans Spartam, pietatis amator,
> Præluxit cunctis et decus urbis erat :
> Exemplar vitæ nobis insigne reliquit
> Exemplar, lector, nobile disce sequi."

The monument of Provost Scrymgeour was inscribed thus :—

" Memoriæ spectatissimi patris Joannis Scrymsouri, mercatoris ac consulis Taodunensis ; qui vitam cum morte commutavit mensis Augusti, anno Dom. 1657. Ætatis suæ 46. Et dilectissimi fratris magistri Gulielmi Scrymsouri, verbi divini præconis ; qui obiit 14 Septembris, anno æræ Christianæ 1666. Ætatis suæ 25. Necnon charisissimi matris Katherinæ Wrighteæ, adhuc superstitis, universæque nostræ prosapiæ, hoc mausoleum exsculpi curavit, parentavitque filius, Joannes Scrymsourus, junior.

> " Hic situs est consul Scrymsourus, lux Taoduni,
> Consule quo poterat Roma vetusta regi ;
> Filius hic primus, Gulielmus, præco fidelis
> Divini verbi, contumulatur humi.
> Consors chara tori vivens, natusque superstes
> Corpora post mortem sic tumulanda rogant.

" Obiit pientissima ac charissima mater Catharina Wright, Maii 30, 1675. Ætatis suæ 62."

Henry Craufurd of Seatoun, merchant and magistrate, is thus commemorated :—

" Sub hoc cippo, contumulantur ossa et cineres spectatissimi viri, D. Henrici Crauford a Seatoun, mercatoris peritissimi, prætoriaque dignitate inclytæ civitatis Taodunensis merito condecorati ; qui curriculi vitæ 32 annos, cum conjuge dilectissima Margareta Dunmuire, feliciter transegit : tandemque magno omnium bonorum mærori 9 die mensis Julii, anno æræ Christianæ 1684. Ætatisque suæ 56. Fatis concessit.

> " Optimus ille patrum, jacet hac sub mole sepultus ;
> Secula cui similem vix peperere virum.
> Singula si penses, nil non mirabile cernes
> Nam blando charites huc aluere sinu ;
> Huic Deus attribuit quæcunque dat omnibus uni :
> Et tandem meritis præmia digna tulit

Nempe adamavit, habet, crompressit, protulit, intrat,
Virtutem, pacem, murmura, vera, polum."

The monument of James Balfour, bailie, was inscribed as
follows :—

" Jacobum Balfurium, prætorem Deidonanum æquissimum, prudentia, vitæ integritate illustrem, sub hoc cippo, sepeliri nosces.
Ad annum 73 vixit, mense Decembris decessit 1686. Jonetam
Kinneries dilectam conjugem, virtute summa et probitate insignem
hic contumulari cernes ; quæ obiit mense Octob. 1685. Anno
ætatis suæ 74.

" Prætorem insignem tumulari hoc marmore nosces
Æquum ac ingenuum, judicioque gravem,
Conjuge cum chara ; gravitasque modestia cujus
Vitam condecorat, sobrietasque decor.
Spe, meritis Christi, clauserunt lumina morte
In cœlis, queis sunt gaudia, vera quies."

The epitaph of Alexander Wedderburn of Blackness, Town
Clerk, is brief and pointed :—

" Hic jacet D. Alexander Wedderburn, dominus de Blackness ;
civitatis Taodunanæ secretarius dignissimus ; qui obiit 18 Novembris, 1676, ætatis suæ 66."

Robert Davidson, merchant and bailie, who fell at the siege of
the town in 1651, is, with his wife, Grizel Man, commemorated
thus :—

" Monumentum Roberti Davidson, prætoris vigilantissimi ; qui
dum fortitier et magnanimiter, urbis oppugnatione, dimicabat,
lethaliter ab hostibus vulneratus, pro civitate et suis vitam reddidit.
Cal. Septembris, anno salutis humanæ M D C L I. Ejusdem itidem
conjugis amantissimæ Grissellæ Mannæ, quæ obiit MDCLXIIII.
Ætatis sexagesimo secundo.

" Prætor Davidides, hac qui requiescit in urna
Tum virtute potens, tum fuit urbis honos ;
Pro qua non timuit cum sanguine fundere vitam :
Urbe etenim capta nil nisi dulce mori.
Urbis honos, genitor ; sic filius urbis et orbis
Gloria, marmoreum qui dedit hunc tumulum.

Aliud in eundem.

> Pro patria Codrus qui se dedit, anni beatus
> Dicitur ? et merito nemo negare queat.
> Prætor Davidides igitur num juré beatus ?
> Pro urbe etenim moriens, fama perennis erit."

The monument of Robert Davidson, younger, of Balgay, has this epitaph :—

" Roberto Davidsono, juniori, Balgaiæ comarcho et mercatore; viro integritate vitæ, prudentia industriaque inter Deidonanos concives, admodum conspicuo: qui sæpe præturam, summo cum amore et laude gessit. Obiit calendas Augusti 1665. Ætatis suæ 50. Cui dilecta uxor Grisselis Broun superstes adhuc, hic contumulanda, hoc cædendum curavit, anno 1672.

> "Davididem cernes celebrem recubrare comarchum
> Marmoreo hoc tumulo ; munia celsa tulit
> Prætoris clari qui summa laude suorum
> Decessit, prudens, sobrius, innocuus ;
> Mente sagax, alacer vultu, venerabile morum
> Exemplar dormit, jussa timore colens ;
> Cui conjunx dilecta sibi vult carmina cœdi
> Hac fossa ut secum contumuletur humi."

These lines celebrate Margaret Ramsay, spouse of Andrew Mureson, who died 26th May, 1666 :—

> " Stay trav'ller ; notice, who entomb'd here lyes,
> One that was virt'ous, chaste, and very wise.
> Good to the poor ; still liv'd a godly life,
> Both first and last since she became a wife.
> To quarrel death, for her change, were but vain,
> For death spares neither godly nor profane ;
> To say she's chang'd were but a foolish story,
> If not to live eternally in glory."

On tombstones in the Howff are the following rhymes:—

> " Farewell, dear babe, thy little sun
> Has soon indeed its circle run ;
> Serene and bright it fled away,
> A short but yet a cloudless day."

> " The child of youth, the man of age,
> Here undistinguished lie,
> We plainly see by Heaven's decree
> That every age must die."

" From earth we'll turn our longing eyes,
    To regions far beyond the skies ;
    Oh fit us for that blest abode,
    Where dwells our Father and our God."

" Free from this dream of life, this maze of care,
    The tender mother rests and friend sincere ;
    She followed virtue as her truest guide,
    Liv'd like a Christian—like a Christian died."

" Faith without works is dead, the Scripture saith ;
    Show me thy works, and thou wilt show thy faith ;
    Both faith and works in this blest saint did tryst,
    And show unto the world his right in Christ."

" When death doth come in its full rage,
    It spares not young nor old,
  But cuts them down at every age ;
    It will not bribe with gold.
Take warning then all ye
    Who read this passing by,
And learn to live so that ye
    Be not afraid to die."

Within the fabric of the four churches a tablet formerly commemorated James Halyburton, of the family of Pitcur, Provost of the burgh. It was inscribed as follows :—

" Hic situs est Jacobus Halyburtonus, patruus nobilis viri, Georgii Halyburton de Pitcur, militis, qui præfecturam Deidoni urbanam fauciter annos 33 gessit. Obiit anno Dom. 1588. Ætatis suæ 70.

| { Alecti | Patriæ | Pupilli | Ecclesiæ Iesu } |
| { Præfectus | Vindex | Tutor | Alumnus Fuit. } |

Provost Halyburton was a zealous upholder of the Reformation. His father, who was also chief magistrate of Dundee, was one of the first to join the Protestant Assembly held at St. Andrews in June, 1559. In attempting, along with the Earl of Arran and Lord James Stewart, afterwards the Regent Moray, to rout a party of

Frenchmen at Leith, he fell mortally wounded. Provost Haly-burton's monument was effaced in 1841, when the churches were destroyed by fire.

In the cemetery a suitable memorial stone denotes the resting-place of William Thom, the Inverury poet. This ingenious but unfortunate person was born at Aberdeen in 1789. Bred as a handloom weaver he often suffered from stagnation in trade, but more frequently from his own unsteadiness. For a period he carried a pack; he at other times derived a precarious subsistence as an itinerant flute-player. His poetical abilities at length found him a patron; he was brought to London, and introduced to important literary circles. Pecuniary tributes to his genius came from all quarters. But the poet's habits were unsuited to his new sphere. He returned to Scotland and settled at Dundee, in a condition of penury. He died on the 29th February, 1848; his tombstone was reared by the admirers of his genius.

In the cemetery rest the remains of Thomas Dick, LL.D., author of "The Christian Philosopher." This estimable gentleman was born in Dundee on the 24th November, 1774. Studying at the University of Edinburgh, he became a probationer of the Secession Church, and for some time ministered at Stirling. He afterwards conducted an educational establishment in the city of Perth. In his 63rd year he retired from his scholastic duties, and erected a villa and observatory at Broughty Ferry. There he continued to reside till his death, which took place on the 29th July, 1857, in his 83rd year. Dr. Dick's philosophical works, eminently adapted for general circulation, obtained wide acceptance, both in Britain and America; yet, from his arrangements with his publishers, he failed to realize a corresponding profit. Latterly he enjoyed a pension on the Civil List.

Tombstones in the cemetery exhibit the following rhymes :—

> "They arras-like came forth in bloom,
> But soon they did decay;
> For God in his appointed time
> Did take them all away.'

" The grave, whatever thy degree,
Thy final resting-place must be,
What matters it, if few or more,
The years which our frail nature bore."

" I pass with melancholy state,
By all these solemn heaps of fate;
And think as soft and sad I tread
Above the venerable dead,
Time was, like me they life possessed,
And time will be, when I shall rest."

In St. Peter's churchyard a monument denotes the resting-place of the Rev. Robert Murray McCheyne, minister of St. Peter's church. This earnest evangelist was born at Edinburgh, on the 21st May, 1813. Licensed to preach in 1835, he was in November of the following year ordained to the pastorate of St. Peter's church. Through the fervour of his public services crowds were attracted to his ministry. In 1839 he proceeded to Palestine, on a deputation from the General Assembly. He died, after a short illness, on the 25th March, 1843. His memoirs and literary remains have obtained wide acceptance.

In Baxter Park, an elegant statue of Sir David Baxter, Bart., has been reared by the contributions of 17,000 persons. Sir David is represented in a standing posture, with a plan of the Park in his hands, as if in the act of presenting it to the town.

PARISH OF EASSIE AND NEVAY.

A sculptured cross near Eassie old church was recovered from the channel of a neighbouring stream. The cross is covered with circles, and on one side is a procession of figures in priestly vestments, with animals wreathed and consecrated as if for sacrifice.

Within the walls of the old church a mutilated tombstone, bearing the arms of L'Amy and Forbes, is inscribed thus :—

.... IOANNIS . . AMMEE, qvondam de Dvnkennie, qvi obiit 26 die mensis Septembar . . . . . D.L : 1603 : C. F.

The estate of Dunkenny has belonged to the family of L'Amy for three centuries.

In the area of Nevay old church a mutilated tombstone commemorates the Tyries, of Nevay, an ancient House, which possessed the estate of Drumkilbo.

Lieutenant David Barron, R.N., has in Nevay churchyard thus celebrated his wife and sons :—

> " Oft shall sorrow heave my breast,
> Whilst my dear Margaret lies at rest ;
> Oft shall reflection bring to view,
> The happy days I've spent with you."

> " Here are repos'd two goodly youths,
> Which loving brothers were ;
> Endued with grace beyond their years,
> And virtues very rare.
> Such was their life that we may hope,
> They're gone beyond the sky,
> To sing and spend, without an end,
> A sweet Eternity."

In Eassie churchyard the tombstone of Thomas White, who died in 1665, bears this couplet.

> " We are bvt earth, and earth is bvt fvme;
> We are bvt novght, as novght we do consvme."

A couplet not more classical in its construction is engraven on the tombstone of the Rev. Adam Davidson, minister of the parish, who died in 1720 :—

> " His soul still breathed upward, and at last,
> Arrived above—the mantle's here downcast."

These rhymes are from different tombstones in Eassie church-yard :—

> "Remember man, that against Death
> There is not an antidote ;
> Be rich or poor, or what you may,
> You'll die and be forgot."

> "This man and his wife were diligent,
> And in their dealings just ;
> Whose every way was excellent,
> But now they ly in dust.
> Waiting till Christ come in the skies,
> With angels all around,
> Commanding them straight to rise
> And be with glory crown'd."

> "She honoured as she bore the Christian name,
> Her closet nourish'd her celestial flame;
> Her social hours with love and pleasure flew,
> The love no art, no guile the pleasure knew.
> Unclouded virtue shone thro' all her life—
> The blameless virgin, and the faithful wife ;
> Long she endur'd affliction's sharpest pain,
> But turn'd her crosses into heavenly gain.
> All this her husband, and her son who witnessed this
> express'd,—
> Go, live like her, and die for ever blest."

PARISH OF EDZELL.

An aisle attached to the parish church is the ancient burial-place of the Lindsays, of Edzell, members of the noble house of Crawford. The fragments of a tombstone bear the Lindsay arms, and are the only traceable memorials of the family.

An altar tombstone commemorates James Duncan, and his wife Jean Michie, the parents of Jonathan Duncan, Esq., Governor of Bombay. The former died in 1792, and the latter in 1795.

These rhymes are from tombstones in Edzell churchyard :—

"Remember, man, as you pass by,
That grave stone under which I ly,
Read, and remember what I tell,
That in the cold grave thou must dwell,
The worms to be your company,
Till the last trumpet set you free."

"Reader, cease thy pace and stay,
Hearken unto what we say;
As you are such once were we;
As we are such shall you be.
Then provide whilst time you have,
To come godly unto your grave."

PARISH OF FARNELL.

A short distance to the south of Kinnaird Castle is the burial vault of the noble House of Southesk. It contains a marble monument to the memory of Sir James Carnegie, father of the present Earl of Southesk, who died 30th January, 1849, and several inscriptions commemorative of members of the family.

In the churchyard a marble tablet celebrates " Dame Christian Doig, relict of Sir James Carnegie, Bart., of Southesk, who died 4th November, 1820, aged 91 years." This gentlewoman was daughter of David Doig, of Cookston, near Brechin, by his wife the heiress of Symers of Balzeordie.

In the old Parish Church a monument commemorates David Carnegy of Craigo, Dean of Brechin, with his wife and children ; it is thus inscribed :

" Sepulchrum Mstri DAVIDIS CARNEGY de Craigo decani Brichinen, rectoris hujus ecclesiæ qui primo fuit ecclesiastes Brechinen annos 2, postea hujus ecclesiæ pastor fidelisimus annos 36, qui placide ac pie in Domino obdormivit anno Dom. 1672, ætatis suæ 77.

In hac urna simul cum eo recubant prior ejus uxor HELENA LINDE-SAY, ac decem eorum liberi. Placuit hic inscribere anagramma a seipso compositum.

> "Magistro DAVIDI CARNEGY
> anagramma.
> Grandis Iesu, duc me Gratia
> distichon
> Dum digo in terris expectans Gaudia cœli,
> Me ducat semper tua Gratia, Grandis Iesu."

The lineal representative of Dean Carnegy, of Craigo, was in 1856 succeeded in the family estate by his cousin, a son of Sir George McPherson Grant of Ballindalloch.

By a granite monument is celebrated Robert Lyall, factor on the Southesk estates from 1817 to 1850 ; he was born 27th November, 1778, and died 13th January, 1863. From an ancestor of this gentleman, who rented the farm of Carcary, in Farnell Parish, is descended Sir Charles Lyell, Bart., of Kinnordy, the celebrated geologist. The grandfather of Sir Charles was originally a trader in Montrose, and afterwards a purser in the navy; he purchased Kinnordy about the year 1780.

From tombstones in Farnell church we have the following rhymes :—

> "'Tis here the fool, the wise, the low, the high,
> In mixed disorder, and in silence lie ;
> No more beneath life's weighty load he goes,
> But in this chamber finds a quiet repose.
> O humbling thought, Pride must be thus disgrac'd,
> And all distinctions here at last effac'd."

> "When death doth come in his full rage,
> He spares not young nor old ;
> But cuts men down of any age—
> He'll not be brib'd by Gold.
> Take warning then ye that may see,
> And read this passing by ;
> And learn so to live as ye
> May not be fear'd to die."

" My bones in grave lie here below,
A resting place have found, yet know,
God hath a time when he'll me raise
Eternally to sing his praise.
Espoused I was to a husband dear,
Liv'd with him five and twenty year;
Now children four I left him have,
I rest in hope God will them save."

" Death is the passage through which we go,
It's just to all, spares neither rich nor low ;
If all the virtues could have made it stand,
Then here lies he who never one could brand
With any vice or yet perjury :
But it's ordained that all men once must die.
As he lived Godly so he died in peace ;
His fame survives an honour to his race."

" Here rest in hope of a most glorious life,
A frugal husband and a faithful wife,
Whose hearts were so united with divine love
That death could not those sacred bonds remove.
As rich perfumes broke up, as blown by wind,
Do leave a lasting fragrant smell behind,
So these blest souls now purg'd of earthly dross,
Who on eternal love themselves repose,
Have left on earth an obelisk of fame,
A dear remembrance of their precious name."

" Under this monument of stone,
Lie both the father and the son ;
Our nature's frail, we are made of dust,
And to the earth return we must ;
One part of man in ground doth ly,
The other mounts above the sky.
     The immortal soul to God resigned,
A happy union the rest to be,
Even to all eternity.
Remember man thou'rt made of nought ;
Thou sold thyself, Christ hath thee bought,
And ransom'd thee from death, the grave,
Which to obtain his life He gave.

PARISH OF FORFAR.

Within the parish church marble cenotaphs celebrate several deceased persons of local eminence. Two tablets commemorate members of the family of Carnegie of Lower. The inscriptions are as follow :

" H. M. H. S.—Sacrum memoriæ PATRICII CARNEGY, armigeri de Lower, pronepotis Davidis, secundi Comitis de Northesk, qui iii. Id. Novem. MDCCXX. natus, Prid. Id. Novem. MDCCXCIX. obiit; et qui bonis et honestis rationibus rem familiarem, profusione majorum pene perditam, suis posteris restituit."

" H. M. H. S.—Sacrum memoriæ PATRICII CARNEGY, armigeri de Lower, qui vi. Kal. Mart. MDCCLVII. natus est, et morte patris Prid. Id. Novem. MDCCXCIX. paternam hæreditatem adiit. MARGARETAM, filiam Alexandri Bower, armigeri de Kincaldrum, duxit, quam cum octo filiis et quatuor filiabus ad mortem deplorandam reliquit.
" Positum a Patricio Carnegy, armigero de Lower, xiii. Kal. Sept. MDCCCXX."

The wife of Patrick Carnegy, younger, was descended from a family of opulent merchants in Dundee. Patrick Carnegy of Lower, on succeeding in 1828 to the estates of Turin and Drimmie, assumed the name of Watson. In the churchyard he and his wife and son are thus commemorated :—

" Sacred to the memory of PATRICK WATSON CARNEGY, Esq., of Lower and Turin, who died at Lower, 3 Sept. 1838, aged 46 ; of Mrs. RACHEL ANNE FORBES, or CARNEGY his widow, who died at Edinburgh, 16 Nov. 1852, aged 50, whose remains are interred here. And of JAMES-FORBES CARNEGY, who died at Hertsmonceaux, 1 May, 1855, aged 17 years, whose remains are also interred here."

By a marble tablet in the south-west of the church is commemorated Elizabeth Ross, only child of Francis Ross, of Auchlossan, and his wife Anne Carnegy. It is inscribed thus :—

" D. O. M. S., et memoriæ ELIZABETHÆ ROSS, virginis forma

venustæ, at pietate et prudentia venustioris, Franc: Ross ab Auchlossan et Annæ Carnegy ex Alex. Carnegy et Ann Blair de Kinfauns projenitæ, gratæ, unicæ, quæ 2 Octob., an. 1705, vitam morta-
lem ingressa 7 Decemb., 1732, ad immortalem recepta est. Marmor
hoc mater et vitricus, Gul: Lyon 'a Carse, mærentes posuere."

The following rhymes are from different tombstones in Forfar
churchyard :—

> " There is a time for all things:
> 'Twill be yours.
> To weep, to tremble, to turn pale—
> To die!"

> " Here lies my wife, when that she died,
> She left her husband most aggriev'd ;
> Her children sore do her lament,
> Grant that all mankind may repent."

> " The sting of death hath cut the breath,
> And rid the soul from pain,
> In heaven with Christ that we may rest,
> But not on earth again."

> " To wain the heart from unsubstantial gain,
> How long shall sage experience preach in vain ?
> How false, how frail, how fleeting all below !
> Shall thoughtless man learn wisdom but in woe ? "

> " She left us young—she died in early life !
> The loving daughter, the endearing wife—
> With all a mother's cherish'd hope she gave
> Birth to her child ; but found herself a grave ;
> Yet trusting the power of Sovereign grace,
> To sanctify and save—'she died in peace."

> " Here lies a true and honest man,
> Through labouring gained his bread,
> And in beneath this monument
> His friends they laid his head.

> Besides some of his children died,
> And all the rest shall come
> Unto their true and quiet rest
> Till Christ shall call them home."

In St. John's Episcopal Church a monumental brass commemorates the Rev. John Skinner, Dean of Dunkeld, and minister of the church for forty-four years; he was born 20th August, 1767, and died 2nd September, 1841. Dean Skinner was grandson of the Rev. John Skinner author of "Tullochgorum." His first wife, Elizabeth Ure, daughter of Provost Ure, died 12th May, 1820, aged forty-four; her remains were interred in the parish churchyard, where she is commemorated by a tombstone, erected by her husband and children.

An elegant monument of white marble on the east wall of St. John's church celebrates Colonel Sir William Douglas, a descendant of the family of Douglas, of Glenbervie. It is thus inscribed:—

"In memory of Col. Sir WILLIAM DOUGLAS, K.C.B., this monument is erected by his brother officers of the 91st, or Argyllshire Regiment, as a tribute of their respect and esteem for his distinguished services in the field, and amiable qualities in private life. He fell an early victim to the duties of his profession at Valenciennes in France, on the 23rd of Aug. 1818, aged forty-two years, universally regretted by the Army and all who knew him."

The following epitaph is inscribed on the tombstone of Colonel Balfour-Ogilvie.

"Sacred to the memory of Colonel BALFOUR-OGILVY, who died at Balaclava, 12th July, 1855, aged 44. He earned well-merited distinction by his gallant conduct on the Danube and in the Crimea. A monument erected in the Valley of the Tchernaya, bears witness to the respect and affection felt towards him by his brother officers.

"Deus tuorum militum sors, et corona praemium."

Colonel Ogilvy was a cadet of the House of Balfour in Orkney; he married the heiress of Ogilvy of Tannadice.

In the ruins of the Priory of Restennet were deposited the remains of John, son of King Robert the Bruce. The chancel, which remains entire, is used as a burial-place by the families of Dempster of Dunnichen and Hunter of Burnside. In the west of the chancel rest the remains of George Dempster, of Dunnichen, M.P., the celebrated patriot and statesman. He was born about 1735. Having studied philosophy and law at the universities of St. Andrews and Edinburgh, he became a member of the Scottish bar. By the expenditure of £10,000 he succeeded in being returned member for the Fife and Forfar burghs. He retained his Parliamentary honours from 1762 to 1790. In the House of Commons he opposed the conflict with the American colonies, and as a director of the East India Company advocated a renunciation of all Sovereign rights in Hindostan. He obtained a special act for the protection and encouragement of the Scottish Fisheries. On his retirement from Parliament he largely devoted himself to the improvement of husbandry. He associated with the more distinguished of his literary contemporaries. He died at Dunnichen, on the 13th February, 1818, aged 86. In the estate of Dunnichen he is now represented by the descendant of his only sister.

A cemetery at Forfar was opened in 1849; it occupies a portion of rising ground, on the highest point of which stands an elegant monument in honour of the late Sir Robert Peel. Reared in Greek architecture, it contains a bust of the great statesman. On a panel at the western base is the following inscription:—

" Erected by the inhabitants of Forfar in memory of Sir Robert Peel, Baronet, Prime Minister of Great Britain, and in testimony of their gratitude for his exertions in obtaining the repeal of the Corn Laws.—MDCCCLI."

In the cemetery a monument reared " by an attached and mourning flock " commemorates the Rev. William Clugston, A.M., minister of the parish, and subsequently of the Free Church, Forfar. This excellent clergyman was born 2nd July, 1793, and died 3rd March, 1857.

PARISH OF FOWLIS-EASTER.

At the east end of the church is the burial aisle of the ennobled House of Gray. A window of stained glass commemorates John, 16th Lord Gray, who died 31st January, 1867, aged sixty-nine. Robert Begg, parochial schoolmaster, thus celebrates his departed wife; she died in 1766, aged sixty-three.

> " When nature first my slender body fram'd,
> Within a living grave of dust enchain'd,
> She destin'd me that I at last should have,
> And change this mortal for a living grave.
> But tho' my body in this urn doth rest,
> In small and scatter'd particles disperst ;
> My soul, that heavenly substance and divine,
> Hath soar'd aloft into its native clime.
> Which afterwards shall with me reunite,
> And make our union lasting and complete.
> For ever then employed in singing glore
> To the eternal three in one for ever more."

PARISH OF GLAMMIS.

In front of the parish manse stands a sculptured stone, tradition-ally regarded as the monument of Malcolm II. On one side are figures of two men, a lion and a centaur, on the other are figures of fishes of different sorts.

Within the plantation at Thornton, stands an obelisk sur-rounded by a cairn; it is believed to denote the spot where Malcolm was mortally wounded by the adherents of Kenneth V. The obelisk is sculptured with emblems resembling those on the monument. Malcolm II. was slain in the year 1034, and his as-sassins, endeavouring to effect their escape during a snowstorm, fled across the Loch of Forfar, in which they perished.

About a mile north-east of Glammis castle stands an ancient erection, known as St. Orland's Stone. On one side it bears the representation of a cross rudely flowered and chequered, while on the other are figures of four men on horseback, one of whom is trampling a wild boar under his horses' hoofs. The stone probably represents the vengeance which overtook King Malcolm's murderers.

The burial aisle of the Earl of Strathmore was originally the south transept of the parish church. In the pavement are some ancient monumental fragments, and by a plain altar-shaped tomb are commemorated Sir Patrick Lyon, Lord of Glammis, who died 21st March, 1459, and his wife Isabel Ogilvy, who died 12th January, 1484.

In the parish church a marble tablet commemorates the Rev. James Lyon, D.D., minister of the parish, who died 3rd April, 1838, in the eightieth year of his age and fifty-eighth of his ministry; also his wife, Agnes L'Amy, who died 14th September, 1840, aged seventy-eight. Mrs. Lyon composed the words of Neil Gow's "Farewell to Whisky," and other poems and songs.

In the churchyard the widow of Professor Andrew Alexander of St. Andrews, has on a granite slab, commemorated the members of her family. The inscription proceeds thus :—

"Erected by Esther Proctor Alexander, in memory of her father Patrick Proctor, who died here in July, 1819, aged 75 years, during 50 of which he was Factor on the Glammis Estate. And of her brothers, John, farmer, Mains of Glammis ; Robert W.S. Edinburgh ; George, Bengal Medical Staff ; Thomas, Bombay Army ; William-David, who died here, 3rd December, 1860, aged 74 years, during 40 of which he also was Factor on the Glammis Estate. David, H.E.I.C. Home Service ; Patrick, Royal Navy ; and of her sister, Jane, who died at St. Andrews, 18th April, 1865."

A retainer of the House of Strathmore, James Bruce, who died in 1680, is on his tombstone celebrated by the following acrostic :—

"I am now inter'd beneath this stone
Ah, Death's propitious to none ;
My name was James, my surname Bruce,
Exasperate against each abuse ;
Sure sanctity my life decor'd,
Bent to obey my Noble Lord.

> Rest, O my soul, in sacred peace,
> Whereas from sin I find releace.
> C . . . . read and praise,
> Each providential act thou sees."

Also by an acrostic is commemorated David Kid, an elder of the parish :—

> "Dear pilgrims, read this elegy,
> And spiritualize mortality ;
> Vice I declin'd, my life was just,
> In tillage I betrayed not trust.
> David by name, surnamed Kid ;
> Kind to the poor, now dignified
> In blissed state, triumphant high,
> Death's sting pluckt out, sin's source is dry.
> Eternal praise to Christ my king,
> Lord of all lords, who makes me sing,
> Delightful songs with angels bright,
> Enjoying day that's void of night ;
> Read gravely, pilgrim, mind thy doom—
> God wraps me up from ill to come."

On the tombstone of James Chalmers, musician to the House of Strathmore, who died 3rd March, 1770, are engraved these lines :—

> "When minstrels from each place around,
>   To meetings did repair ;
> This man was still distinguished
>   By a refined air.
> His powerful and his charming notes
>   So sweetly did constrain,
> That to resist, and not to dance
>   Was labour all in vain.
> He played with such dexterity,
>   By all it is confest,
> That in this grave interred is
>   Of Violinists the best."

William Cruikshank, a tailor, who died in 1718, is thus commemorated :—

> "Rare William, who will not thy name
> And memory still love ;

Since you the Trade did all around,
 So wond'rously improve?
Our Tradesmen justly did to thee
 Pre-eminence allow.
Being taught the rudiments of Art,
 Or else refin'd by you,
That skill of yours did on them all
 An ornament reflect;
And as you liv'd so did you die,
 In honour and respect."

A brass and iron worker, John Dalgety, has on his gravestone
these lines, engraved under the representation of a crown.

" O, dear John Dalgety ! who can
 Thy praises all express?
A most expert artificer
 In iron and in brass.
Discreet was't thou to ev'ry one,
 Obliging, just, and kind ;
And still thy tongue ingenuous spoke
 The language of thy mind.
Such was thy life, that now we hope
 Thy soul above doth shine ;
For thy skill, we dedicate,
 This Crown as justly thine."

From other tombstones in Glammis churchyard we have the
following :—

" This stone is set to celebrate
 This worthy woman's praise ;
Whose equal you will hardly find
 For candour now-a-days.
She sober, grave, and virtuous was,
 Belov'd by all around ;
She lived in the fear of God,
 Now is with glory crown'd."

" Lo, here lies one who never did
 An injury to man ;

Of whom we cannot say enough,
 Let us say what we can :—
Her actions all were genuine,
 Her words without disguise ;
Kind was her heart, her generous hands
 Could not the poor despise,
She liv'd at home, and walk'd abroad,
 Still like a harmless dove."

" Here lies a sweet and loving child,
 Ah, cover'd o'er with mud ;
Resembling well the lily fair,
 Cropt in the very bud.
But blessed is that happy babe,
 That doth thus early die ;
Not pleas'd to dwell with sinners here,
 But with the saints on high.
This charming child but just did peep
 Into this world, and then,
Not liking it, he fell asleep,
 And hasten'd out again."

" Below this monument, a jewel
 Of womankind doth lie
Who night and day was exercis'd
 In acts of piety.
No neighbour, mother, nor a spouse,
 More worthy was : Her aim
Was to speak truth, and that her word
 Should always be the same.
She long'd to leave this sinful earth,
 And this poor frail abode ;
Her home was heaven, where now she sings
 The praises of her God."

PARISH OF GLENISLA.

From tombstones in the churchyard we have these rhymes :—

" Death is a debt to nature due
 We've paid that debt and so must you."

" Short is the space allowed to man below,
Replete with care and crowded thick with woe
Death is the horizon when our sun is set,
Which will thro' Christ a resurrection get."

" Life is a journey and the silent Tomb,
To *every traveller* is the appointed Home."

" Live well and fear no sudden fate ;
When God calls virtue to the grave,
Alike 'tis justice soon or late,   .
Mercy alike to kill or save.
Virtue unmoved can hear the call,
And meet the flash that melts the ball."

" Reader, you see by heaven's decree
Since time at first began,
That man he must return to dust,
And who reverse it can ?
Should we not, then, while we remain,
Here in this mortal state,
Be on our guard for death prepared,
In case it prove too late ? "

PARISH OF GUTHRIE.

In 1774, Robert Spence, a parishioner, reared in the churchyard a monument to his family, with the following quaint inscription :—

" Beside this stone lye many Spences,
Who in their life did no offences,
And where they liv'd, of that ye speir
In Guthrie's ground four hundred year."

PARISH OF INVERKEILLOR.

At the east end of the parish church is the burial-vault of the noble family of Northesk. Within the church a marble tablet thus commemorates the sixth Earl of Northesk and his countess :—

Sacred to the memory of George, Sixth Earl of Northesk, Admiral of the White Squadron of His Majesty's Fleet : born 2nd Aug. 1716, o.s., and died 22nd January 1792. And Ann Leslie, Countess of Northesk : born 22nd Feb. 1730, o.s., and died 11th Nov. 1779.

In the front wall of the church a slab presents the armorial escutcheon of the Stewarts of Lorne, denoting that the family had anciently buried in the fabric. The Stewarts of Lorne and Redcastle are represented by the Ducal House of Argyll.

Within the church a marble tablet bears the following inscription :—

"Sacred to the memory of John Mudie of Arbikie, Esq., who died June, 1728, aged — years. And of his wife, Magdalen Carnegy, daughter of James Carnegy of Craigo, who died 27th December, 1771, aged eighty-nine years ; and of their family and descendants. Of their family, which consisted of six sons and eight daughters, three daughters only came to maturity, viz. 1st, Elizabeth, married to Robert Smith, of Forret, Esq., who left an only son, William Smith, of Forret, Esq., married to his cousin-german, 29th April 1784, the after mentioned Magdalen Hay : He died 2nd February 1785, leaving no issue. 2nd Agnes, married to James Hay, of Cocklaw, Esq., who left two sons and a daughter. Their eldest son, Charles Hay, Esq., advocate, afterwards Lord Newton, one of the Senators of the College of Justice, a man of distinguished talents, and inflexible integrity, died October 1811, aged sixty-four years. Their youngest son, James Hay, Esq., died at Edinburgh, 6th June, 1787, and was interred there. 3rd, Anne, married to Robert Stephen of Letham, Esq., left an only daughter Anne, who died November 1806. Magdalen Hay, only daughter of James Hay, Esq., and Agnes Mudie, and relict of William Smith of Forret, Esq., the last survivor of the family, has erected this monument as a tribute of respect to the memory of her relations who lie buried here. And it is her desire to be interred in the spot which contains the ashes of her husband and of her grandmother, and mother, Magdalen Carnegy, and Agnes Mudie, parents, with whom she was long united in the closest bonds of love and affection, whose virtues she reveres and whose example she most earnestly wishes to follow. 1818.

Mrs. Hay Mudie, who erected the monument, died in 1823.

A mortuary enclosure in the churchyard denotes the burial place of the family of Gardyne, of Middleton. From its several tablets we select the following inscriptions :—

" David Gardyne of Lawton, marrd Janet Lindsay of Edzell, 1603. Their only issue, John, marrd Elizh., daughr. of Sir John Arbuthnott of that ilk, 1643, who had issue 4 sons and 20 daughters. Robert, their heir marrd Grizel daughr. of Alexr. Watson, of Barry, 1676, their issue, David, William, Eliza., who marrd 1st Scott, of Hedderwick, 2nd Barclay, of Johnstone ; Grizel, who marrd 1st Wedderburn of that ilk, and 2nd David Graham of Duntrune. David, heir to Robert of Lawton, marrd Ann Graham of Fintray, 1706. Their issue, Eliza., who marrd James Guthrie, of Craigie, 1733.

Amelia, who married Alexr. Hunter of Balskelly, 1741 ; David fought under Prince Charles at Culloden, and died at Newport, in Flanders, 1749. James, who married Mary Wallace, 1741 ; Clementina, who marrd Alex. Graham of Duntrune, 1751."

" Sacred to the memory of Alexander and James Greenhill, sons of Charles Greenhill, Esquire of Fearn, and Clementina Gardyne. Alexander died 22nd May, 1832, aged forty-four years ; James died 25th June, 1817, aged twenty-six years.

" William Bruce-Gardyn, Esq, of Middleton, Major 37th Regiment, born 1777, died 15th June, 1846. Also their children, Anne, born 1826, died 15th May 1831 ; James Macpherson, born 1828, died 23rd April, 1828; Agnes-Mary, born 1835, died 25th March 1847."

PARISH OF KINGOLDRUM.

In the front of the parish church, a handsome mausoleum denotes the burial-place of the Farquharsons, formerly of Baldovie. On a marble tablet is this inscription :—

"The sepulchre of John Farquharson and Elizabeth Ramsay, of Baldovie; and of their children.   Elizabeth, born 4th January, 1768; died 18th June, 1855.   Agnes, born 26 March, 1769, died in infancy.   Thomas, a magistrate and deputy-lieutenant of Forfarshire, born 3rd October, 1770 ; died 21st November, 1860. He was last male representative of the Farquharsons of Brockdearg, in lineal descent from the Chieftain Findla More, the Royal Standard Bearer, who fell in defence of his country, on the field of Pinkey, 10th September, 1547, and was interred in the neighbouring cemetery of Inveresk. R. B. I. P.

Captain Mitchell, cousin and heir of Thomas Farquharson of Baldovie, bequeathed £50,000 for the support of aged priests of the Catholic church.   On his death in 1865 the estate of Baldovie was purchased by Sir Thomas Munro, Bart., of Lindertis.

These rhymes are from tombstones in Kingoldrum churchyard :—

> "Reader, repent ere time is spent,
>   Think on a future state ;
> Do not delay another day,
>   In case it prove too late."

> "Below this stone are here reposed
>   The ruins of a Tent,
> Where divine virtue deign'd to dwell,
>   But, ah ! how soon were spent
> Her mortal years ; the tyrant, Death,
>   Resistless gives the thrust ;
> The virtuous wife and virtuous Tent,
>   Strikes down into the dust."

> "What havoc makes impartial death
>   On all the human kind ;
> Gainst him a virtuous life's no guard,
>   Nor yet the purest mind.

> And most all clay—yes, it is destin'd
> For every sack and age,
> The old and bow'd, and young robust,
> And infants quit the stage."

PARISH OF KINNETTLES.

In the churchyard a monument commemorates Colonel William Patterson, a native of the parish, who became Governor of New South Wales, and attained distinction as a naturalist. Colonel Patterson died 21st June, 1810, aged fifty-five.

PARISH OF KIRKDEN.

In the parish churchyard a marble tablet within an enclosure commemorates Alexander Lyell, Esq., of Gardyne, who died in 1852, aged sixty-eight, and among other members of his family "Dr. Robert who unfortunately lost his life on the night of the 3rd July, 1857, in the thirty-second year of his age, while quelling the insurrection at Patna during the rebellion in India, and whose remains lie there."

From tombstones in Kirkden churchyard we have the following legends :—

> " Let none suppose the Relics of the Just,
> Are here wrapt up to perish in the Dust !
> No.   Like last fruits her time she fully stood,
> Till being grown in Faith, and ripe in good—
> With steadfast Hope that she another day
> Should rise with Christ—with Death here down she lay.
> The Poor her alms ; the World her praise ;
> The Heavens her soul ; and the Grave her body has.

" Here lyes a child, of sons the last,
    Wherewith this family was blest ;
    He like a morning flower appear'd,
    By him his parents' hearts were cheer'd.
    But what are children but a loan—
    When God calls back, are we to groan ?
    He's gone to heav'n and got the start :
    Long to be there, you'll no more part."

" The penetrating art of man
    Unfold this secret never can,
    How long men shall live on the earth,
    And how, or where give up their breath.
    The person of whom this I write,
    Ah ! dy'd by a mournful fate ;
    An old clay chimney that downfell
    Kill'd both his servant and himsel,
    Which should alarm men everywhere
    For their last hour well to prepare,
    That death may never them surprise ;
    For as the tree falls, so it lies."

PARISH OF LETHNOT AND NAVAR.

On the tombstone of two young men who perished while
crossing the West Water in 1753 is the following inscription,
composed by Dr. Beattie .—

" O thou whose reverential footsteps tread
    These low dominions of the silent dead,
    On this sad stone a pious look bestow,
    Nor uninstructed read this tale of woe ;
    And while the sigh of sorrow heaves thy breast,
    Let each rebellious murmur be suppressed.
    Heaven's hidden ways to trace for thee how vain !
    Heaven's just decrees how impious to arraign !
    Pure from the stains of a polluted age,
    In early bloom of life they left this stage ;

> Not doomed in ling'ring war to waste their breath,
> One moment snatched them from the power of death;
> They lived united and united died,
> Happy the friends whom death cannot divide."

On the gravestone of his wife, erected in 1741, James Black moralizes thus :—

> " Ah sin, hence momentary life, hence breath,
> Sighs for ye silent grave and pànts for death,
> What means ye warning of ye passing bell?
> A soul just gone to paradise or hell ;
> To darkness tends ye broad but slippery way—
> O frightful gloom, deny'd each cheering ray ;
> While such as walk in paths divinely bright
> Shall shine within ye courts of endless light."

In Navar churchyard, Margaret Fyfe, spouse to James Molison, is thus commemorated ; she died in 1712 :—

> " A pearl precious here doth lie,
>   As signifies her name ;
> Still shining to posterity
>   By her deservèd fame.
> Death battered down those walls of clay
>   To let her soul go free,
> And soar aloft to praise for aye
>   The Triune Deity."

> " Sleep, thou frail dust, within thy closest urn
> Till the morning of the resurrection dawn,
> When thou shalt wake, the heaven and earth shall burn,
> And be rejoined to thy immortal pawn."

PARISH OF LIFF AND BENVIE.

In the church of Liff, monumental tablets commemorate Major Alexander Watt, K.H. of the 27th Regiment, Bengal Native Infantry, who died at Edinburgh, 18th April, 1851, aged forty-six ;

Isaac Watt, Esq., of Logie, who died 11th July, 1823, aged fifty-one; and other members of the family.

A monument in Liff churchyard celebrates James Webster, Esq. of Balruddery, who died 17th May, 1827, aged sixty-two; also, the members of his family.

On a flat tombstone Mrs. Agnes Gray, who died in 1707, is thus commemorated :—

> "With husbands two I children
> had eleven,
> With two of odds I Lived
> Sixty-even ;
> My Body sleeps in hope,
> My soul I gave,
> To Him Who suffered
> death, the same to save."

William Waddell, who died in 1765, aged fifty-eight, has the following epitaph :—

> "Here lys beneath these sordid stones,
> A father to the poor ;
> To orphans and distressèd ones
> He kept an open door.
> Fair honesty and virtue pure
> Did strive in him for place ;
> Of charity a public store
> Was lost at his decease.
> Now though his body here doth ly
> To moulder in the dust ;
> His generous soul, the nobler part,
> In Christ alone doth rest."

A monument of Aberdeen granite denotes the resting-place and records the worth of the Rev. George Addison, D.D., for thirty-four years minister of the parish, who died 4th January, 1852, aged seventy-four.

The churchyard of Benvie contains an old sculptured stone, and a stone bearing the arms of Scrimgeour, second Viscount of Dundee, impaled with those of his wife, Isobel Ker, daughter of the first Earl of Roxburgh, with the date 1643. The Scrimgeours of Dudhope held the lands of Benvie till 1654, when they were alienated.

In the churchyard of Logie is the burial-place of Edward Baxter, Esq., of Kincaldrum, father of William Edward Baxter, Esq., M.P. for the Montrose burghs. On a freestone monument are recorded the names of Euphemia Watson, first wife of Edward Baxter, who died 22nd August, 1833; and of his second wife, Elizabeth Jobson, who died 2nd July, 1842.

Invergowrie church is described by chroniclers as the first built place of Christian worship north of the Tay. Two large globular stones in front of the church, and within the flood-mark of the Tay, are associated with a prediction of Thomas the Rhymer contained in the following couplet :—

> " When the Goors o' Gowrie come to land,
> The day of judgment is at hand."

PARISH OF LINTRATHEN.

In the parish churchyard a tombstone reared in 1857 by Mr. John Fenton, of Scrushloch, bears the names of his children and other relatives. To account for several blanks in connection with their births and deaths, Mr. Fenton has added the following rhymes :—

> The above will show to all that pass
> How thoughtless I have been ;
> In younger dais and aged years
> How careless I have been.
>
> " When friends departed to the dust,
> Their age by me not known,
> And infants' births by me not kept
> In registration.
>
> " My friends and relatives will learn,
> By these few lines of mine,
> To keep a date of registers
> When they are in their prime."

From tombstones in Lintrathen churchyard we have these rhymes :—

> " A deep and rapid stream divides—
> Death is the name it bears ;
> But o'er it Christ has laid a bridge,
> For heavenly passengers."

> " All Time relations here below,
> Tho' knit with strongest bands,
> Death soon dissolves ; when Time is spent,
> No bond his power withstands.
> He snatchèd off the virtuous wife,
> The husband fond doth mourn ;
> But death his days it soon did cut—
> Here he's beside her urn."

> " Below this tomb are laid the bones
> Of a good virtuous pair ;
> Both scholars pious and discreet,
> Accomplishments most rare,
> Whose knowledge served not to puff up,
> But for a nobler end ;
> That lowliness might them prepare
> A glorious life to spend."

PARISH OF LOCHLEE.

A gravestone denotes the resting-place of Alexander Ross, author of " The Fortunate Shepherdess," a pastoral poem, formerly popular. Ross was schoolmaster of the parish. He was a native of Kincardine O'Neil, and died at Lochlee on the 20th May, 1784, aged eighty-five. " The Rock and the Wee pickle Tow," " To the begging we will go," " Woo'd and Married and a'," " The Bride's Breast Knot," and other favourite songs, proceeded from his pen.

PARISH OF LOGIE PERT.

On the north of the parish church a burial aisle contains a marble tablet, celebrating James Macdonald, Esq., sheriff-substitute of the county, who died 23rd August, 1809, aged eighty-three ; also his wife Mary, daughter of James Allardice, Esq., of that ilk ; she died 4th January, 1801, aged seventy-five. Mrs. Macdonald was aunt of Sarah Anne Allardice, who in December, 1776, married Robert Barclay of Ury, and who in 1785 was served heir portioner of William, last Earl of Airth and Menteith, brother of her great-great-grandmother. On Mrs. Barclay's death, her eldest son, Mr. Robert Barclay Allardice, took certain steps to establish his right to the Airth and Menteith peerages. He died in 1854, and the claim has been renewed by his only child, Mrs. Margaret Barclay Allardice, who is seventeenth in lineal descent from David, Earl of Strathearn, eldest son of the second marriage of Robert II.

The old church of Logie is now the burial-place of the Carnegys of Craigo. Marble tablets commemorate Thomas Carnegy of Craigo, who died 9th June, 1793, aged sixty-four, and his wife, Mary Carnegy, who died 20th November, 1815 ; David Carnegy of Craigo, born 9th March, 1776, died 10th November, 1845 ; and Thomas Carnegy of Craigo, born 9th March, 1804, died 12th June, 1856.

These metrical legends are from tombstones in Logie church-yard :—

" My friends in Christ that are above,
    Them will I go and see ;
And thou my friends in Christ below
    Will soon come after me."

" Faith makes us sons and heirs to the Most High,
    Faith leads to glorious immortality ;
By faith the power of Satan we defy,
    If on Christ's merits we by faith rely ;
And if true faith unto the end endure,
    Your evidence for heaven is good and sure."

" All who pass by, behold, survey,
    Think on this awful shrine;
  Here musty bones and broken skulls,
    And graves all over green.
  But where the souls, those deathless things,
    That left these bodies here?
  Is not give answer, but refer
    Till Christ our Lord appear."

PARISH OF LUNAN.

Within the parish church a monument celebrates Walter Mill, the last martyr who suffered at St. Andrews before the Reformation. He was parish priest of Lunan. Reported to Archbishop Hamilton, of St. Andrews, as a favourer of Protestant doctrines, he was subjected to trial and condemned. Upwards of eighty years old, he was unable to walk to the place of execution. His martyrdom roused the populace to frenzy, and the fall of the Romish Church became certain. Mill was martyred in 1558, and the doctrines of the Reformation were publicly sanctioned in 1560.

PARISH OF LUNDIE AND FOWLIS.

In Lundie churchyard, within a sepulchral enclosure, rest the remains of Adam Viscount Duncan. Second son of Alexander Duncan, Esq., of Lundie, this distinguished commander was born at Dundee on the 14th July, 1731. His mother was lineally descended from Duncan, Earl of Lennox, and was heiress of Gleneagles in Perthshire. With an ordinary education in his native town, he was placed on board the *Shoreham* frigate to prosecute naval studies under his relative, Captain Robert Haldane. Three years afterwards he joined the Mediterranean fleet as midshipman in the *Centurion*.

Removed to the ship of Captain, afterwards Lord Keppel, he was promoted as post-captain in 1763. Having distinguished himself at the Havannah and at Cape St. Vincent, and under Lord Howe in 1782, in the *Blenheim*, he was in 1787 promoted as Rear-Admiral of the Blue. Appointed to the command of the North Sea fleet in 1795, he displayed extraordinary tact and intrepidity during the mutiny at the Nore. He maintained a strict blockade of the Dutch ports, watching the movements of the hostile fleet in the harbour of Texel, and on the 11th October, 1797, he brought them to close action off Camperdown, when De Winter, the Dutch Admiral, suffered total defeat. For this eminent service he was created a viscount, and received a pension of £2,000. In 1800 he retired into private life. He died suddenly on the 4th August, 1804. His grave is denoted by a plain marble slab, with this inscription, partly prepared by himself:—"Adam, first Viscount Duncan, Admiral of the White Squadron of his Majesty King George the Third's fleet, born 14th July, 1731, and died 4th August, 1804." His widow, Viscountess Duncan, died in 1822, and was interred in the Canongate'churchyard, Edinburgh (Vol. I., p. 90). Their son Robert second Viscount Duncan, was at the coronation of William IV, created Earl of Camperdown.

In a handsome mausoleum in Lundie churchyard are interred Sir William Duncan, Bart., M.D., and his wife, Lady Mary Tufton, daughter of Sackville, Earl of Thanet. Sir William realized a large fortune in India, and afterwards became Honorary Physician to the King. He died in 1769, and was survived by his lady, who caused this mausoleum to be reared in honour of his memory.

PARISH OF MAINS AND STRATHMARTIN.

Within the parish church of Mains a monumental tablet is thus inscribed:—

"Sacred to the memory of Charlotte, Lady Ogilvie, sole proprietor of the estate of Bank, in the parish of Strathmartin, eldest daughter of Walter Tullideph, Esq., of the island of Antigua, and relict of Sir John Ogilvy, Bart., of Inverquharity, late of the Scots Grays, &c., who died at the age of seventy-two."

Charlotte, Lady Ogilvy, was descended from the family which produced the celebrated Principal Tullideph of St. Andrews. The estate of Tullideph, now called Baldovan, of which she was owner, is the principal inheritance of her grandson, Sir John Ogilvy, Bart., M.P. The ancient burial-place of this branch of the House of Ogilvy was in the parish church of Kirriemuir, but the family ordinarily inter in the old church of Strathmartin. Therein a tablet commemorates Lady Jane, second wife of Sir John Ogilvy, Bart., and daughter of Thomas, Earl of Suffolk. This excellent gentlewoman founded the Asylum for Imbecile Children at Baldovan, and "The Home" at Dundee. She died 28th July, 1861.

In Strathmartin churchyard a mortuary enclosure protects the remains of Admiral Laird of Strathmartin, who died in 1811.

In Mains old churchyard a gravestone commemorates Charles Peebles, parish schoolmaster, and his wife Anne Crabb, who both died in 1801; it bears these lines:—

> "How useful they in training youth,
> When thoughtless of the paths of truth
> They need the guiding reins ;
> The east and west, the south and north,
> Doth testify from provèd worth
> Of youth spent at the Mains."

A miller, who died in 1655, is thus commemorated in Mains churchyard :—

> "Wnder this stone interrd lies he
> Who 40 two years living was,
> At miln and kiln right honestlie,
> And with his neighbours dealt he thvs ;
> Bvt death, in Apryl 55,
> From off the stage did him remove."

From other tombstones in Mains churchyard we have these epitaphs :—

> "He who with abundance did me bless,
> With riches, life, and breath,
> Me from these three did take away
> By sickness and by death."

> "This charming child most comely was,
> And pleasant once a day ;
> But now, alas ! he lowly lies
> Here in this bed of clay."

> "Among the rest of Adam's race,
> That in this world liv'd ;
> There's one confin'd within this tomb
> Who upright was and pious.
> He while in life was very just,
> Gave every man his due ;
> But now he is exalted high,
> In Heaven we hope he's now."

In Strathmartin churchyard, Thomas Low, who died in 1752, is thus commemorated :—

> "Thy name aye,
> Thy fame aye,
> Shall never be cut off ;
> Thy grave aye
> Shall have aye
> Thy honest epitaph."

On other gravestones in Strathmartin churchyard are these rhymes :—

> "From dust I came, and thither do return,
> Who here abide till tribes of earth shall mourn ;
> Till heaven and earth wrapt in a scroll shall be,
> And Christ with saints coming in clouds I'll see,
> When soul and body united shall again
> Be lifted up to Christ for to remain."

" Heir lies a godly honest man,
    All men that knew him said—
He was an elder of the church,
    And a weaver to his trade.
These words gave comfort unto him
    When God's word he did read—
If that the Son did make him free,
    He should be free indeed."

" Both in one grave until the time accord
That they shall hear the archangel of the Lord :
Our soul doth bend our bodies straight and even,
As with itself it would them raise to Heaven;
But all in vain it undergoes such toil,
The body will not leave its native soil.
Age pulls it down, and makes it stoop full low,
Till Death doth give his fatal overthrow;
Then through the bodies breach the soul doth rise,
And like a conqueror mount the skies,
To its eternal rest from whence it came,
As is their bodies in tomb here lies."

" I lived almost eighty years,
    Within this vale of tears ;
At last cold death on me laid hands,
    Whom every mortal fears,
And hath my body here enclosed
    Within this grave of earth;
When Christ's last trumpet gives the call
    I shall come forth in mirth.
When to his heaven He shall me bring,
    With songs of melody,
I shall His praises ever sing,
    To all eternity."

At Kirktown and Ballutheron, in Strathmartin parish, several sculptured stones present figures of serpents and nondescript animals. They belong to the pre-historic period.

PARISH OF MARYTON.

Within the parish church a handsome monument, adorned with the Lindsay arms, presents the following inscription :—

" Sub hoc marmore reconditus jacet Reverendus vir, David Lyndesius (ex prisca Lyndesiorum familia de Dowhill), oriundus ecclesiæ de Marytown, per 33 annos pastor vigilantissimus, vir singulari literarum, cognitione et summa rerum peritia ornatus pietati in Deum, fide in Regem, reverentia in Episcopos, et humanitate erga omnes insignis, obiit 16 Septembris 1706, ætatis suæ 62. Hic etiam siti sunt duo filii impuberes Gulielmus, et Alexander, et Katharina filia, cujus eximiam formæ venustatem omnes virgine dignæ virtutes facile æquabant."

Mr. Lindsay was son of Mr. David Lindsay, minister of Rescobie. His ancestors, the Lindsays of Dowhill, were descended from Sir William Lindsay, of Rossy, Fifeshire, son of Sir Alexander Lindsay, of Glenesk, by his second wife, a niece of Robert II.

On the tombstone of Alexander Greig, farmer, bearing date 1755, are these Latin lines :—

" Primo Deus ferro morales vetere terram instituit.
Agricola incuruo terram dimouit aratro ;
Hinc anni labor, hinc patriam paruos' nepotes sustinet."

A child of three years, drowned in a well, is thus commemorated :—

" Doth Infant's pain and death proclaim
That Adam did Rebel ?
His destiny declares the same,
Being drownèd in a Well.
Let all who mourn his early death,
Hate sin the fatal cause,
And flee to Jesus Christ by faith
Who saves from Satan's jaws."

PARISH OF MENMUIR.

Attached to the parish church, a mortuary enclosure forms the family burial-place of the old family of Carnegy, of Balnamoon.

On a tablet commemorating a person named Guthrie, and bearing date 1793, are the following lines :—

> " All passengers, as you go by,
>   And chance to near this stone,
> To mind you of Mortality,
>   Behold the skull and bone :
> Likewise the dart that wounds the heart,
>   And scythe that cuts the thread
> Of life, and coffin for to hold
>   The body when it's dead."

In Menmuir churchyard are two Roman crosses, which were formerly built in the churchyard wall ; one displays an equestrian figure, the other is sculptured with two mounted warriors and other emblems.

PARISH OF MONIFIETH.

Within the old parish church a monument commemorated a member of the house of Durham of Grange, now represented by Dundas-Durham of Largo. The monument was taken down on the removal of the church.

In the churchyard a monumental tablet, within an enclosure, celebrates David Hunter, fourth son of General Hunter, of Burnside, born 20th April, 1801, died 16th August, 1854.

Within another enclosure a marble tablet bears the following legend :—

" Here lyes interred the body of James Erskine, of Linlathen, who departed this life on the 26th of Aug., 1816, at Broadstairs, Isle of Thanet, county of Kent, aged twenty-eight."

David Erskine, advocate, father of James Erskine, purchased the estate of Linlathen from Graham of Fintray, about 1805; he married Anne, daughter of Graham of Airth. His younger son, Thomas Erskine, LL.D., who succeeded his brother as proprietor of Linlathen, is author of various theological works.

A handsome monument in Monifieth churchyard commemorates Thomas Kerr of Grange, of Monifieth, who died 22nd December, 1811; David Kerr of Grange, who died 5th October, 1843; and other members of the family.

A plain tombstone denotes the grave of David Rennie, farmer, Mill of Omachie, who died 3rd March, 1857, aged 102.

From the gravestone of Alexander Scott, who died in 1841, we have the following couplet :—

> " Life is uncertain—death is sure,
> Sin made the wound, and Christ the cure."

The tomb of Sylvester Steven, who died in 1734, is inscribed thus :—

> " Life's everlasting gates
> For ever had been shut
> Had not the death of Christ
> Them pulled up."

Alexander Paterson, who died in 1786, is by his widow thus celebrated :—

> " All men live in the same death power
> Who seized my beloved in an hour,
> One word to me he could not speak,
> Though floods of tears ran down my cheek."

These rhymes are from the tombstone of Henry Gordon, who died in 1815:—

> " Since our good friends are gone to rest
> Within the silent grave,
> I hope their souls among the blest
> O'er fruitless sorrows wave;

> Our loss is now their greatest gain,
>   Let no rude hand annoy;
> Their dust now sleeps exempt from pain,
>   In hopes of future joy."

These hortatory lines form the epitaph of John Barrie, in 1738 :—

> "In this cold bed Christ's dearest friends must ly
> Till they be wakened by the Angel's cry.
> The bed is cold, this dust lys here consumed,
> But Christ in grave did ly, and He the bed perfumed.
> Their souls dislodg'd to mansions bright do soar,
> Where Christ is gone to keep an open door.
> The dog of earth must stay awhile behind,
> No guest of Christ till thus it be refined.
> All who behold this monument,
> On Christ your trust repose,
> And of your sins pray now repent,
> Lest heaven and earth you lose."

From other rhymes in Monifieth churchyard we select the following :—

> "Beside this mournful monument
>   There lies my mother's dust.
> A loving wife's also there is,
>   And daughter young doth rest.
> Bemoan us not, surviving friends,
>   For this is God's decree,
> But seek for everlasting rest
>   Where God's enthroned on high."

> "A woman wise and diligent,
>   And in her dealings just,
> Tho' every way most excellent,
>   Lies in this bed of dust,
> Waiting till Christ come through the skies,
>   With angels all around.
> And then she shall triumphant rise,
>   With glory to be crown'd."

> "I in my young and tender years
>   By death am call'd away
> To rest from sin in bed of earth,
>   Where thousands more do lie;

> Yet on the Resurrection Day,
>   When waken'd from my sleep,
> Expect to join the blessed band,
>   Whom Christ doth call His sheep."

> " Here lies the dust that once inshrin'd
> A sober, honest, friendly mind.
> The heavenly part hath wing'd its flight
> To regions of eternal light.
> The body too which breathless lies,
> Redeem'd from death shall shortly rise
> And join its kindred soul again,
> Fit to adorn its Maker's train."

At Broughty Ferry, an obelisk of Peterhead granite commemorates Thomas Dick, LL.D., author of " The Christian Philosopher " (see *supra*, p. 220).

In Broughty Ferry old churchyard, Margaret Ross, wife of John Kid, shipmaster, is commended thus :—

> " Now she for whom this gravestone's placed
>   Was in virtue ever steady ;
> When asked a reason of her hope,
>   Had aye an answer ready.
> Though silent and forgotten here
>   She moulders with the clod,
> The day will dawn, a voice she'll hear
>   Say, Come and meet your God."

John Kid is personally celebrated in these lines :—

> " This life he steer'd by land and sea
>   With honesty and skill,
> And calmly suffer'd blast and storm
>   Unconscious of ill.
> This voyage now finish'd, he's unrigg'd,
>   And laid in dry-dock Urn ;
> Preparing for the grand fleet-trip,
>   And Commodore's return."

The following verses commemorate Janet Webster, wife of D. Liddell, shipmaster, who died in 1801 :—

> " Justice and truth, even from youth,
>   Adorn'd her deportment;
> Never revenging, nor exchanging
>   Evil for evil treatment.
> Tender dealing, without failing,
>   Was everly her aim;
> Even to those, who were her foes,
>   Beneficent and plain.
> She had to give, while she did live,
>   The sample of a mind ;
> Ever rejecting, but never respecting,
>   Resentment of any kind."

PARISH OF MONIKIE.

On Camustane Hill stands a Runic Cross, which is believed to mark the spot where Camus, a Danish General perished in battle. According to the narrative, the Scots had defeated an important section of the Danish forces, and slain the generals Eneck and Olave. Sueno, the Danish leader, sought revenge, and so despatched his puissant general, Camus, to make a terrible reparation. Camus landed an army at the Redhead, near Arbroath, and marched eastward. At Camustane Hill his troops were engaged by the Scottish army under Malcolm II. After a protracted and fierce conflict the invaders were routed and their general wounded mortally. The engagement took place in the year 1020 ; it terminated the last Danish incursion on the eastern coast.

On the highest point of the Downie hills stands a large and handsome monument in honour of the late William Ramsay Maule, Baron Panmure, (see *supra*, p. 202). The monument was reared in 1839, at the expense of the tenants on his Lordship's estate. It is a cylindrical column, resting on a double basement, and surmounted by a memorial vase. The lower basement is of rustic

S

work; it is surmounted by a quadrangular basement, flanked with open buttresses. The total height is 105 feet. A winding staircase conducts to the top of the structure. A finely sculptured bust of Lord Panmure is placed in the interior of the monument.

From gravestones in the parish churchyard we have these rhymes:—

> " Seeds die and rot and then most fresh appear
> Sancts bodies rise more orient than they were."

> " To lifeless dust and mouldering bones
>   In vain we pour our tears and groans,
>   In vain we raise our cries;
> Till a divine immortal breath
> Descending on the vale of death
>   Shall make the ruins rise."

> "The hours of my day are past,
>   My night of death is come,
> My toiling hands forget the task,
>   My feet no more shall run,
> The grave now holds my sweating brow,
> With sweat I gained my bread,
> To dust I am returned now."

PARISH OF MONTROSE.

In the principal street of this royal burgh stands a monumental statue of Joseph Hume, elegantly sculptured by William Calder Marshall, R.A., and erected in 1859. Hume was born at Montrose in January, 1777. His father was master of a coasting vessel, and on his early death his mother was necessitated to support the family by disposing of earthenware in the market place. Joseph was educated as a surgeon; in 1797 he proceeded to India in the marine service of the East India Company. Obtaining a succession of lucrative appointments he returned to Britain in 1807 with a fortune of £40,000. In 1812 he entered the House of Com-

mons as member for Weymouth.   He was in 1818 elected M.P.
for the Aberdeen burghs, which included Montrose, his native town.
He afterwards sat for Middlesex and Kilkenny.   In 1842 he was
elected for Montrose, and he continued to represent that constit-
uency till the period of his death.   He died on the 20th February,
1855, aged 78.   As a reformer of public abuses, and a zealous
advocate of financial retrenchment in all departments of the state,
Joseph Hume is entitled to honourable remembrance.

In the parish churchyard Robert Keith, of Polburn, a magistrate of the burgh, is on his tombstone thus commemorated :—

Sacrum memoriæ perillustris viri Roberti Keith, domini terrarum de Polburne, etc.   Prætoris hujus urbis dignissimi, ejusque
conjujis ac liberorum, extructum anno Dom. 1641.   R.K. L.G.

" Hic situs est præclarus vir Robertus Keith, dominus de Polburne, etc. prætor hujus urbis dignissimus, qui summo omnium
mærore, obiit anno salutis humanæ, 1640.   Ætatis vero suæ 56.

" Nobilis hæc Kethi prætoris saxea moles
Ossa tegit famam non teget ulla dies.
Prætorem civemve alium Ketho mage dignum
Urbs habuit nunquam, vix habitura parem.
Lex hæc firma manent moriendum esse omnibus ; ergo
Mors metuenda minus, morsque dolenda minus.
Principium vitæ mors est, sic itur ad astra,
Felix qui vivit, qui moriturque Deo.
Conditus hoc tumulo sic vixit mortuus et sic,
Quare O felicem terque quarterque virum."

James Scott of Logie, Bailie of Montrose, and his wife, Jean
Taylor, are celebrated thus :—

" Sacrum memoriæ illustrissimi viri, Jacobi Scoti terrarum de
Logie, de Domini, civitatis Montisroseæ prætoris dignissimi, qui
obiit cal. Novembris anno Dom. 1658.   Ætatis suæ 65.   Ejusque
pientisssimæ Joannæ Tailzor, quæ obiit. . . . . anno ætatis
suæ. . . . . .

" Hoc tegitur corpus prætoris marmore Scoti
Sed tegitur nullo vivida fama loco ;
Nempe reformandas, vitæ melioris in usum
Hic veteres posuit Loggius exuvias ;

Fortunatus erat, dum vixit; sed mage felix,
Post mortem, Domini certus amore frui.

"Hunc lapidem sepulchralem, novissimum pietatis officium,
erigendum curarunt ejus filii, qui hic quoque siti sunt. Anno
1659."

In the following epitaph Bailie Robert Arbuthnot commemorates
his wife and children :—

"Saxeum hoc monumentum egregium Robertus Arbuthnetus
urbis Montisrosanæ civis et subinde prætor in memoriam piæ juxta
ac dilectæ conjugis Joannæ Beatie, erigendum curavit; quæ postquam felix ac placidum cum marito conjugium per aliquot coluisset
annos, ex hac vita migravit, idibus circiter Novemb. anno Dom.
1682. Ætatis vero suæ 41. Quæque una cum liberis 5 in hoc
dormitorio sepulta jam quiescit.

"Corporis exuviæ tumulo conduntur et ossa,
Spiritus in Christi vivit at estque sinu.
Est ita; nam supera, quamvis moriantur, in arce,
Cum Christo vivunt, qui coluere Deum.

"Sub hoc etiam cippo, si Deus annuerit, sepulti jacebunt, ubi
suo quisque fato concesserit, maritus ipse ejusque liberi adhuc
superstites."

Professor James Wishart (Wise-heart) is thus commemorated by
his widow :—

"Lapidem hunc sepulchralem, conjugalis sui amoris indicium,
extrui curavit Helena Beatie, in memoriam pii ac dilectissimi sui
mariti, Jacobi Sophocardii, urbis Montisrosanæ civis philologiæ
professoris, qui obiit pridie idus Octobris, 1683. Ætatis suæ 60.

"Disce mori, quicunque legi mea scripta, viator,
Omnes æqua manent funera, disce mori.
Disce mori, frater; discat cum præsule clerus
Cum juniore senex, cum sapiente rudis."

Three persons named Duncan have on their common gravestone
these lines :—

"As everything a centre hath to which it doth incline,
So all men being made of earth, to earth return in time;

Those who do here from labours rest more lines stretch from a
 centre,
Some short, some long, as he thought best who is the divine
 painter ;
To write elogies of those dead, I find it's not my strain
If men be honest and fear God, they're free from future pain."

On the gravestone of Anna Ochterlony, spouse of Thomas
Cloudslie, merchant, who died in 1695, are these verses :—

> " A pious, prudent, modest wife
> And loving, frugal, without strife
> Hath left this momentary life
> And made choice of a better.

> " Friends, neighbours, children mourn their loss,
> Her husband bears it as his cross,
> But death who came on his pale horse,
> Would not away without her.

> " She's now above the reach of fate,
> Of change or chance whatever,
> As being in that happy state
> Of bliss which changeth never."

A husband thus laments his affectionate partner :—

> " Enclos'd within this coffin here doth lie,
> Exeem'd from cares and from all troubles free,
> A woman, whose great virtues were such that
> None can them well express, less imitate.
> Lo, here's a proof that death doth oft arrest,
> In this sad instance not the worst, but best ;
> Not much unlike those worms that almost still
> Do mar the fairest flow'rs, but spare the ill.
> Now cease, dull muse, and silently deplore
> A matchless loss, and if I could say more."

A deceased wife is on her tombstone thus emphatically commended :—

> " She was, but words are wanting to say what ;
> Think what a wife should be, and she was that."

A widow bemoans her husband and child in these lines :—

> "Traveller, attend, beneath the dust lies here
> A loving husband and a child held dear.
> A childless widowed wife bemoans their early fate,
> And sad laments her hard, untoward state ;
> Bow'd down with grief, although in years but young,
> Silent the husband, and child's lisping tongue.
> Death cross'd the child, the father nought could save,
> One day, one hour, consign'd both to one grave."

Parents thus lament their departed children :—

> "Beneath this turf our children ly
> And wait Christ's advent in the sky,
> When every grave shall open wide
> They'll climb to Heaven, and there reside.
> Death's lost his sting ; Christ, rising from the dead,
> Draws all the members to attend the head."

Robert Adam has, on a tombstone bearing date 1670, thus commemorated his four children :—

> "Oh cruel Death ! Oh furious Death ! what fury makes thee rage,
> Thus to cut down young, pleasant plants, and pass by crooked age?
> But yet these plants, in spite of this, shall yet revive and bloom,
> When thou, oh Death, with thine old scythe, art withering in the tomb."

PARISH OF MURROES.

Adjoining the parish church is the burial vault of Fotheringham of Powrie.

In the churchyard tombstones commemorate David Millar of Ballumby, who died 19th July, 1825, aged seventy-one; David Arkley of Clepington, who died 2nd August, 1822, aged seventy-four; and the Rev. Alexander Imlach, minister of the parish, who died 6th November, 1808, in the eighty-first year of his age and the forty-seventh of his ministry.

PARISH OF NEWTYLE.

In the parish churchyard a mural monument is thus inscribed :—

" Hic requiescit vir prudens ac gravis generosa de Balgillo familia
ortus, Magister GULIELMUS BLAIRUS, qui placide ac pie, obiit 16
Novem. an. Dom. 1656, ætat. suæ 58. In cujus memoriam conjunx
ejus amantissima Euphana Pattullo, hunc tumulum extruxit juxta
eum, ex quo filiam habet octennem sepelienda.

"Vivit post funera virtus.
Cujus hic tumulum cernis nunc incola cœli est,
Corporis exubias quam premis abdit humus."

The families of Blair and Pattullo have for several centuries been
connected with the district.

In the south wall of the church the following Latin inscription
on a monumental tablet commemorates James Alison, a progenitor
of the late Sir Archibald Alison, Bart. :—

"Post mortem vita. Infra conditur quod reliquum est JACOBI
ALISON, hujus parochiæ quondam incolæ et decoris : nisi quod viri
præstantissimi supersunt et vigent virtutes hoc marmore peren-
niores : rara sci prudentia intaminata fides, et pietas nescia fraudis.
Paterfuit facillimus, conjux charissimus, et certus amicus; omnibus æquus, benevolus, et charus, et ut cætera complectar, eximi
probus. Itaq. cum honesto, humili, forti, sanctoq. animo, hominibus,
maritis, sociis omnibus exemplum consecrasset integerrimum, terris
animo major, ad similes evolavit superos. Natus erat . . . .
denatus 4 Feb. 1737.

"Mors certa est, incerta dies, incertior hora ;
Consulat ergo animo qui sapit, usq suo."

Mr. Alison was factor on the estate of Belmont ; he was succeeded
in his office by his son, Patrick, who became proprietor of Newhall
in Kettins.

A tombstone celebrates George Watson, Esq., Bannatyne House,
a county magistrate, who died in 1813. His representative, Hugh
Watson, who rented the farms of Keillor and Auchterless, was
famed as an agriculturist; he died in 1865, aged seventy-seven.

Several old tombstones commemorate members of the family of Jobson, described as "indwellers in the Haltown of Newtyle." Of these the first named, James, son of James Jobson and Barbara Scott, died in July, 1660, aged nine years. The family became merchants in Dundee, and attained considerable opulence. A member of the house, Jane Jobson, heiress of Lochore, married the eldest son of Sir Walter Scott, Bart., and is now Lady Scott of Abbotsford (Vol. I. p. 61).

Robert Small, farmer Boghead, (died 1771) is on his tombstone thus quaintly commemorated :—

> "Here lies the dust of Robert Small,
> Who, when in life, was thick, not tall ;
> But what's of greater consequence,
> He was endowed with good sense,
> O how joyful the day in which
> Death's pris'ner shall be free,
> And in triumph o'er all his foes
> His God in mercy see."

A tombstone bearing date 1675, celebrates Gilbert Mille, whose name is made to form an acrostic. Mille attained his hundredth year. His epitaph proceeds thus :—

> "G reat are the Wonders God hath Worked
> I n Heaven, and Earth, and Sea ;
> L ykways he many mercies hath,
> B estowèd upon Me.
> E uen in this World, an Hundred Years,
> R emain'd I honestly ;
> T uo Wedded Wives the tyme I had ;
> M uch Comfort were to Me.
> I n Wedlock's Band we Procreat
> L awfully Ws Betwix ;
> L oues Pledges, Whos Right number were
> E uen tuo tymes ten and six.
>   My Spritt to God, I do committ,
>   My Body to the Grave ;
>   When Christ shall come and judge shall sitt,
>   Shall them both Recave.

From other tombstones in Newtyle churchyard we have the following rhymes :—

> " This honest man is from us gone,
>   Whose body lyes Within this Tomb ;
> His honest Reputation Shall
>   Remain To Generations all ;
> His Blessed Soul for Ever more,
> Doth magnify the King of Glore."

> " O that men in this world would live, said I,
> As not to be ashamed to live, nor afraid to die ;
> For all our friends and neighbours to us dear,
> Unto our lives can't add a single year.
> The righteous need not fear the sting,
> For Christ will them to heaven bring."

> " Vnder this stone interred doth ly
>   This man of honest fame ;
> And of his virtues while he liv'd
>   His name doth fresh remain.
> Who to his wife and parents both
>   A help and comfort was ;
> But now the Lord hath crownèd him
>   With joy in heavenly bliss."

PARISH OF OATHLAW.

In Oathlaw churchyard a tombstone commemorates the Rev. Thomas Raiker, minister of the parish, who died 20th June, 1803, in his ninety-second year and the sixty-third of his ministry. On his tombstone are engraved these lines :—

> " Rests before this stone, the mortal clay
> Of Thomas Raiker, till that awful day,
> When Christ will send his angel thro' the skies
> And to the dead proclaim—ye sleepers rise.
> Then may the Saviour to this servant say—
> Enjoy a Crown thro' an eternal day."

In the old chapel of Finhaven were deposited the remains of several Earls of Crawford and of other notable persons. The monuments have disappeared.

PARISH OF PANBRIDE.

A burial aisle belonging to the noble family of Dalhousie was constructed in 1672, by George, Earl of Panmure; it is attached to the parish church. To the aisle were committed the remains of Colonel the Honourable Lauderdale Maule, second son of William, Lord Panmure, who died at Varna, on the 1st August, 1854. A monumental tablet has been erected to his memory in the parish church. (Vol. I. p. 139).

Gravestones in Panbride churchyard present these rhymes :—

"In memory of Jacob's love,
Unto his Rachel, now above;
A pillar of stone we read he gave,
And set it up upon her grave;
The first and ancient to be seen,
In Genesis the 35 and 19."

"Though Boreas' Blasts and Neptune's waves,
Have toss'd me to and fro,
Yet from them all I was preserv'd,
And anchor'd here below.
Though fast aground I now remain,
Along with all the Fleet,
Yet once again I shall set sail
Our Admiral CHRIST to meet."

PARISH OF RESCOBIE.

Two upright stones at Pitscandly are supposed to denote the spot where, about the year 831, Feredeth, king of the Picts, fell while contending in battle with Alpin, king of the Scots.

In the burial-ground at Chapelyard, have interred for many generations the Piersons of Balmadies, now of The Guynd. Many of the tombstones remain entire. The tombstone of Mary, daughter of Robert Pierson, of Balmadies, who died 10th November, 1771, presents the following lines :—

> " Mildness of temper, innocence of mind,
> And softest manners were in her combin'd ;
> Sincere and open, undisguis'd by art,
> She form'd no wish but what she might impart.
> Easy and social, cheerful and resigned,
> Harmless thro' life, the sister and the friend.
> In early age, call'd to resign her breath,
> Patient in sickness, undismay'd at death,
> A sister's grief ('tis friendship's sacred claim),
> Pays this small tribute to a sister's name."

A monument, enclosed by a railing, is thus inscribed :—

" Sacred to the memory of Margaret Ouchterlony, second daughter of John Ouchterlony, Esq. of The Guynd, and widow of James Pierson, Esq. She died at The Guynd, 21st March, 1849, in her seventy-eighth year :—

> " Dear as thou wert, and justly dear,
>   We will not weep for thee ;
> One thought shall check the starting tear,
>   It is—that thou art free !
> And thus shall Faith's consoling power
>   The tears of Love restrain—
> Oh ! who that saw thy parting hour
>   Could wish thee here again ?"

On tombstones in Rescobie churchyard are these metrical inscriptions :—

> " My husband's here, and daughter dear,
>   Also a son of mine ;
> In dust do lie ; but yet on high
>   I hope their souls do shine.
> I've other five this date survive,
>   Two daughters, and three sons ;
> May they with grace, pursue their race
>   Till once their glass is run."

" Inconstant earth, why do not mortals cease
  To build their hopes upon so short a lease?
  Uncertain lease, whose term's but once begun,
  Tells never when it ends till it be done,
  We doat upon thy smiles, not knowing why,
  And while we but prepare to live, we die;
  We spring like flowers for a day's delight,
  At noon we flourish, and we fade at night."

" Like to the seed in earthy womb,
  Or like dead Lazarus in the tomb,
  Or like Tabitha in a sleep,
  Or Jonas like within the deep,
  Or like the moon or stars in day,
  Lie hid and languish quite away;
  Even as the grave the dead receives,
  Man being dead he death deceives.
  The seed springs, and Lazarus stands,
  Tabitha wakes, and Jonas lands;
  The moon appears, and stars remain,
  So man being dead shall live again."

PARISH OF ST. VIGEANS.

A Roman cross in St. Vigeans churchyard presents the usual emblems. A portion of another ancient cross is built in the wall of
the church.

A vault under the church contains the remains of Sir Peter Young
one of the preceptors of James VI. A mural tablet with a Latin
inscription celebrates his virtues. Son of a respectable burgess in
Dundee he was there born on the 15th August, 1544. He studied
under Theodore Beza. In January 1569 he was appointed assistant preceptor to King James. When the King attained the
government he appointed Young his royal almoner. Acquiring the
lands of Easter Seaton in St. Vigeans parish he there established
his residence. He died at Easter Seaton on the 7th January,
1628.

On tombstones in St. Vigeans churchyard are the following rhymes :—

> " Death rides on every passing breeze,
> He lurks in every flower,
> Each season has its own disease
> Its peril every hour."

> " Ye who with careless footsteps tread
> The hallowed mansions of the dead,
> Let every grave that meets your eye
> Remind you man was born to die !
> But know he has not liv'd in vain,
> Who dies prepar'd to live again."

> " Short was our life but long our rest may be
> Cut off in youth, as you may plainly see ;
> Nursed up with care for parents dear had we,
> Which loved us well but grieve to see us die.
> Dear parents weep no more but be content,
> For unto you alas we were but lent."

> " Think, vain fond heart, when on the day
> Of that tremendous awful deep
> Eternity in sad suspense I stood ;
> How all my trifling hopes and fears
> My senseless joys and idle tears
> Vanish'd at prospect of the frightful flood."

> " That tear I pay, with my last breath,
> In death I heard thee sing,
> Short was thy song but how sublime,
> Oh death, where is thy sting !

> " Our sun was nipt in early bloom,
> He left this scene of idle care,
> He's reached his Father's house in peace,
> We mourn, but there's no mourning there."

> " Ah, who of to-morrow can boast ?
> What mortal on earth is secure ?

To-morrow may vanquish a host;
  To-morrow a monarch be poor!
A day and our joys they are fled,
  An hour and we're laid with the dead,
A moment and we are no more."

" How frail, how short's the life of man!
Less than a hand breadth or a span,
Death's arrows thick about us fly,
The slain on every hand doth lye,
Some young, some old go off the stage,
Death spares not them of smallest age,
God plucks his flowers at any time,
He knows what's best, let none repine."

" Here lies a wife, a wife most dear,
A tender mother's dust lies here;
She liv'd belov'd and mourn'd she died.
Her life was asked, but God the gift denied;
Under the stroke of death's unsparing rod
She calmly yielded up her fleeting breath,
But with a hope that firmly cleav'd to God,
She felt not what is terrible in death."

"Frail mortal who dost read these lines,
  This truth fix in thy breast,
That in the course of rapid time
  Thou too shalt be at rest.
Death's shafts fly thick and unperceived,
  They pierce the young and old,
The good, the bad, the weak, and strong,
  The cowardly and the bold.
Uncertain of another day
  Make up thy peace with God,
And in the vale of death he will
  Support thee with his rod."

KINCARDINESHIRE.

PARISH OF ARBUTHNOT.

Attached to the parish church is the burial aisle of the noble house of Arbuthnot. This elegant gothic structure was reared by Alexander Arbuthnot, afterwards Principal of King's College, Aberdeen, a zealous promoter of the Reformation. Within the aisle is the recumbent effigy of Hugo de Arbuthnot, an early member of the House, who flourished in the thirteenth century. He married a daughter of the House of Moreville, and his wife's arms and his own are sculptured on his monument.

PARISH OF BANCHORY-DEVENICK.

In the parish churchyard a monument to the memory of the Rev. Dr. Morrison and his wife is thus inscribed :

"Erected by George Morrison, D.D., minister of this parish, as a tribute to the many virtues of his deceased wife Margaret Jaffray, who died 11th June, 1837, in her 80th year. In the same grave are deposited the remains of her husband, Dr. Morrison of Elsick and Disblair, the revered pastor and munificent benefactor of this parish during sixty years, who, on the 11th July, 1845, died Father of the Church of Scotland, in the 88th year of his age, and 63rd of his ministry."

Within the church a marble tablet celebrates Agnes Fordyce of the family of Fordyce of Ardo; she died 20th of November, 1834, aged 76.

Tombstones commemorate members of the family of Corbet of Beildside.

On Cotcraig Rock a granite obelisk commemorates the late Prince Consort ; it was reared by Alexander Thomson, Esq., of Banchory, and is thus inscribed :

" In remembrance of the visit of H.R.H. Albert, Prince Consort, to this spot, 15th September, 1859."

PARISH OF BANCHORY-TERNAN.

On Scultie-hill a monument erected by his tenantry and neighbours commemorates the late General William Burnett of Banchory Lodge. He was born 19th February, 1762, and died 7th February, 1839.

In the parish churchyard a mortuary enclosure contains three tablets thus inscribed :—

" In memory of Thomas Ramsay, second son of Sir Alexr. Ramsay of Balmain, Bart., and of his wife Dame Elizabeth, daughter of Sir Alexr. Bannerman, Bart. He was a Captain in H.B.M.'s Army, served in the Peninsula and at Waterloo : born 24th Feb., 1786, died 18th Decr. 1857, aged 71. And also of Thomas Ramsay, R.N., second son of the above Capt. T. Ramsay, and of Margaret, daughter of Sir Robert Burnett of Leys, Bart., his second wife, born 13th of Jany. 1828, died 17th of Jany. 1856, aged 28."

" Catherine Ramsay, second daughter of Capt. T. Ramsay, and Jane Cruikshank, born April 16th, 1822, died Aug. 21, 1843, aged 21.

" William Burnett-Ramsay of Banchory Lodge, late Captain in H.M's. Rifle Brigade, and Lieutenant-Colonel of the Forfar and Kincardineshire Militia Artillery, born 11th April, 1821, died 6th Nov. 1865.

In honour of Captain T. Ramsay a memorial fountain has been raised in the village of Banchory.

In the Tilwhilly aisle of the old church monuments celebrate John Douglas of Tilwhilly, who died 6th March, 1773, aged thirty-six; Mrs. Hannah Douglas, widow of John Douglas, of Tilwhilly, and daughter of Sir G. L. A. Colquhoun, of Tillyquharn, Bart., who died 16th April, 1835, aged eighty-three; John Douglas, of Tilwhilly, who died 6th July, 1812, aged forty; George Lewis Augustus Douglas, sheriff of Kincardineshire, died 30th October, 1847, aged seventy-six; and John Douglas of Tilquhillie and Talkenhorst, Austria, died 11th October, 1870. The learned John Douglas, D.D., Bishop of Salisbury, was son of the youngest brother of the proprietor of Tilwhilly.

A marble tablet is thus inscribed :—

"Hic jacent Reverendi Magistri Jacobus Reid, a familia de Pitfodels oriundus, Banchoriensis Ecclesiæ Pastor, a Reformatione primus; Robertus Reid dicti Jacobi filius, et Robertus Reid, Roberti dicti nepos, uterque Ecclesiæ ejusdem Pastores. Hic jacent Magister Thomas Reid, qui obijt in Eslie, anno ætatis 76; et Joanna Burnet, ejus conjux, quæ obiit anno ætatis 90. Necnon Thomas Reid, quondam in Pitenkirie, qui monumentum hoc erigi curavit, et obiit 31 Januarii 1733, ætatis suæ 76, et Agnes Ferguson, ejus conjux, quæ obiit 21 die Decembris, 1728, ætatis 70. Petrus Reid et Catherina Reid, eorum liberi."

Thomas Reid, first-named in the inscription, was classical secretary to James VI.; he composed latin verses, and made valuable additions to the library of Marischal College. Robert Reid (grandson of Robert) was great-grandfather of Professor Thomas Reid, the eminent metaphysician.

Tombstones commemorate George Read, M.D., physician in London, who died in 1754, aged eighty-seven; Rev. Robert Burnet of Sauchine, minister of the parish, who died 18th June, 1701, aged fifty-three; Duncan Davidson of Tilliechetly, and Inchmarlo, who died 8th December, 1849, aged 76; Rev. Francis Dauney, minister of the parish who died 2nd April, 1800, aged 82; and the Rev. James Gregory, minister of the parish, who died 8th September, 1829, aged eighty-three.

A granite obelisk at Bellfield thus commemorates the learned and ingenious Dr. Francis Adams :—

"In memoriam Francisci Adams, M.D., LL.D., medicorum omnium quotquot Scotia tolit, literarum thesauris necnon scientiarum opibus eruditissimi. Diu in hac valle reducta, ab aula et academia procul, medicinæ simul et musis, vir vere Appollinaris, fideliter inserviit. Natus Lumphanani III. Id. Mart. MDCCXCVI. Mortuus Banchoriæ IV. Kal. Mart. MDCCCLXI. Carissimi capitis desiderio amici posuere.

PARISH OF BENHOLME.

A monument, built in the wall of the church, being recovered from the aisle of the older structure, is inscribed as follows :—

"Hic . jacet . Domina . Maria . Keyth . charissima . filia . nobilissimi . commitis . illustrissimique . Domini . Georgii . comitis . Marescalli . Domini . Keyth . et . Altrie . &c. . et . nobilissimæ . clarissimæque . Dominæ . Dnæ . Margar . Ogilvy . Marescalli . comitissæ . quæ . fælix . in . Domino . obiit . 14 . Octob . Anno Domini . 1620 . Ætatis . suæ . 5o."

> "Vix lustrum vixit . mirabere plurima vixit
> Longæva illa mihi . quæ bene vixit . erit
> Fælix vita obitus fælicior . ultima vox hæc
> Cum Christo ut vivam . nunc mihi dulce mori
> Vera igitur Maria es. Marthæ mundana relinquis
> Cum Maria semper vive . fruare Deo."

Lady Margaret Ogilvy, daughter of James, Lord Ogilvy, ancestor of the Earls of Airlie, was second wife of George, fifth Earl Marischal, the munificent founder of Marischal College, Aberdeen. The Scotts of Benholm, interred in the churchyard. Their burial-place is denoted by a tombstone thus inscribed :—

"Piæ memoriæ justisque meritis patris et mariti optimi, Roberti Scott a Benholm qui mortalitatis cæno relicto, in immortalitatis sedem sublatus est, ætatis suæ anno LXIV. Salutis vero humanæ MDCXC. X. kal. Feb mausoleum hoc quale quale sacrum voluit superstes sua soboles et vidua Dna Catharina Ellis."

> "Tumulus seu defunctus
> Ne gemitu somnum, ne turbes gaudia luctu

Ne laurum lachrymis pollue quisquis ades.
Certavi hanc vitæ pugnam, victoria parta est
Et membris fessis obtigit alma quies
Explevi numerum vitæ ; terraque relicta
Carpo cœlestis gaudia Jerusalem."

PARISH OF BERVIE.

In the parish churchyard a tombstone commemorates George Small, a respected philanthropist. Born at Edinburgh, on the 26th May, 1782, he served some years as an officer in a regiment of fencibles. He subsequently became a partner in the firm of Muir, Wood & Co., music-sellers, Edinburgh. When a magistrate of Edinburgh, in 1832, he established the House of Refuge in that city ; he subsequently originated the Lock Hospital, and other benevolent institutions. In 1848 he retired from business. He latterly resided in Bervie, where he died, 11th July, 1861.

A monument denotes the resting-place of Alexander Aberdein, late Deputy Commissary of Ordnance, Bengal; he died in December, 1810, aged fifty-three.

PARISH OF DUNNOTTAR.

In the parish churchyard the burial-aisle of the Earls Marischal forms a conspicuous object; according to a date above the doorway it was built in 1582, by George, fifth Earl Marischal, the founder of Marischal College. His lordship died in 1623, and was buried in the aisle. Within the railing beside the aisle, a tombstone commemorates the parents of Sir George Ogilvy, Governor of Dunnottar Castle. It is inscribed thus:—

" Here lyes a famovs and worthy gentillman, William Ogilvy, of Lumger, and Catharin Straqvhan, his spovs, he being seventy-six years of age, departed this lyef the 28 of Feb. 1651."

Mr. Ogilvy was a cadet of the House of Inverquharity, and his wife was a niece of the Baronet of Thornton.

According to Wodrow, 167 persons were, in 1635, brought from the west of Scotland and imprisoned in Dunnottar Castle for supporting the covenant. Of these nine died at Dunnottar, and to their memory some of the survivors, after the Revolution, erected a tombstone, thus inscribed:—

"Here lyes John Stot, James Atchison, James Russell, and William Broun, and one whose name wee have not gotten, and two women whose names also wee know not, and two who perished comeing doune the Rock, one whose name was James Watson, the other not known, who all died prisoners at Dunnottar Castle, anno 1685, for their adherence to the Word of God and Scotland's Covenanted work of Reformation. Rev. 11 ch. 12 verse."

On the gravestone of David Rannie, who died in 1802, are these lines:—

"The grave has eloquence, its lectures teach
In silence, louder than divines can preach;
Hear what it says—ye sons of folly hear!
It speaks to you, lend an attentive ear;
It bids you lay all vanity aside,
A humbling lecture this for human pride."

PARISH OF FETTERCAIRN.

In the parish churchyard are mortuary enclosures belonging to the proprietors of Fasque, Fettercairn, and Arnhall. Fasque estate formerly belonged to the Ramsays, Baronets of Balmain; it is now in the possession of Sir Thomas Gladstone, Bart.

A monument of white marble, in the interior of St. Andrew's Episcopal Church, commemorates the late Sir John Gladstone, Bart., and his lady. It is inscribed thus:—

" Sacred to the memory of Sir John Gladstone, of Fasque and Balfour, Baronet; born 11th December, 1764, died 7th December,

1851. And of his wife, Ann Robertson, born 4 Aug., 1772 ; died 23 Sept., 1835." ·

Son of Thomas Gladstone, shopkeeper in Leith, Sir John Gladstone was there born in 1764. In his twenty-second year he proceeded to Liverpool, as clerk to a firm of corn-merchants ; he subsequently became a partner in the concern. Possessed of remarkable forethought and great commercial enterprise, he amassed a large fortune and entered Parliament. On retiring from business he purchased the estate of Fasque. He was created a baronet in 1846. Ann Robertson, his second wife, was daughter of the Sheriff of Dingwall.

In the same church a monumental cross celebrates Captain Gladstone, R.N. ; it is engraved thus :—

"In gloriam honoremque Dei et in memoriam dilectissimam Johannis-Neilson Gladstone, in Classe Regali Navarchi, qui obiit A.D. 1863, hunc cancellum ecclesiæ Sti. Andreæ adstrui curavit frater mærens, T. G., A.D. 1867.

Captain Gladstone was third son of the late Sir John Gladstone, Bart. ; he was sometime M.P. for Walsall.

Memorial windows in St. Andrew's Church celebrate Ann M'Kenzie Gladstone, born 1802, died 1829 ; and Robert Gladstone, who died in 1835 ; sister and brother of the present baronet.

A stained window in St. Andrew's Church, and a memorial fountain in Fettercairn village, commemorate Sir John Hepburn Stuart-Forbes, Bart., born September 25, 1804, died 28th May, 1866. Sir John was much esteemed as a social reformer and a promoter of agriculture. .

In Fettercairn churchyard a tombstone is thus inscribed :—

"Sacred to the memory of George Kinloch, Esq., Deputy Judge Advocate and Master in Chancery, in the island of Jamaica, who died at Stonehaven, 22 April, 1802, aged 60, and of Mrs. Susannah Wigglesworth, his spouse, who died at Edinburgh, 7 May, 1841, aged 81. Their surviving children, Alexander, George Ritchie, Lydia, and Maria Kinloch, have erected this stone as a mark of their filial affection."

George Ritchie Kinloch, named in the inscription, edited, in 1827, a volume of " Ancient Scottish Ballads."

These rhymes are from tombstones in Fettercairn churchyard :—

" The tyrant death spares neither age nor sex,
  The gayest mark he haughtily affects ;
  Parents from children, husbands from their wives,
  He often tears when most they wish their lives ;
  Learn then to fix on nothing here below,
  But on thy God,—he'll Heaven on thee bestow."

" He as a rock among vast billows stood ;
  Scorning loud winds and raging of the flood ;
  And fix'd remaining all the force defies,
  Muster'd from threat'ning seas, and thundering skies,
  To keep amen his end still to observe,
  And from the laws of nature neèr to swerve."

" Under this stone the man and wife do lie,
  What was one flesh, we but one dust now spy ;
  Their daughter also lodgeth in this grave,
  So for three bodies, we one ashes have.
  The great Eternal Three and One with ease,
  Will from one dust all the three bodies rise,
  Which, winged to the celestial joys above,
  Shall never cease to sing their praise and love."

PARISH OF FETTERESSO.

The interior of the old church is used as a place of interment.
At the east end is the burial place of Duff, of Fetteresso ; it contains an elegant marble monument in memory of Colonel Robert
W. Duff, and his wife, Mary Morrison, grand-daughter of General
Abercrombie of Glassaugh, M.P. The aisle is used by the
families of Hepburn of Rickarton and Gordon of Newhall. On
the north side, beside the aisle a stone, dated 1610, commemorates
Francis Hay, " son to the Laird of Wry."

A tombstone celebrates, in a latin inscription, the Rev. Andrew
Milne, minister of the parish, who died 12th October, 1640. His

father, who bore the same christian name, was originally master of the grammar school of Montrose, where he taught the celebrated James Melville, who has commemorated him in his Diary.

A monument, erected by the members of his congregation, commemorates the Rev. John Ballantyne, of the United Presbyterian church, Stonehaven, who died 5th December, 1830, in the fifty-first year of his age, and the twenty-fourth of his ministry. Mr. Ballantyne composed a philosophical work, entitled "An Examination of the Human Mind."

In the church a monument commemorates John Fullarton, who died 10th July, 1620, aged seventy-nine; he is supposed to have been one of the Fullartons of Cowie.

A plain stone denotes the grave of Robert Duthie, an ingenious poet. Born at Stonehaven on the 2nd of February, 1826, he was in his 14th year apprenticed to his father in the baking trade. He afterwards taught a school, but on the death of his father in 1847, he resumed his trade, with the view of supporting his mother and her young family. During his hours of leisure he composed verses. His "Song of the Old Rover" and "Boatman's Song" have obtained considerable popularity. After a period of declining health Mr. Duthie died, on the 4th January, 1865. His poems and songs, accompanied with a memoir, were published posthumously.

Within the ruin of the old chapel at Cowie, is the burial vault of Innes of Cowie. Tombstones commemorate John Innes "formerly of Leuchars, and for many years sheriff substitute of the county, who died 10th July, 1827, in his eightieth year;" also "Jean Innes, who died 26th June, 1831, aged eighty-two." Mr. Innes was a cadet of the ancient "House of Cowie;" his son is Professor Cosmo Innes, the eminent antiquary.

In the Howff Park at Ury is situated the burial-aisle of the Barclays and Bairds, the past and present owners of the estate. Over the entrance is a tablet, thus inscribed:—

"Anno 1741 conditum auspicio Roberti Barclay de Ury, sumptibus autem fratris sui Davidis Barclay, mercatoris Londonensis, ad majorum cineres tegendos, nempe Avi Colonelli Davidis Barclay de Ury, filii et hæredis Davidis Barclay de Matheris; Patris Roberti Barclay de Ury, Apologiæ Auctoris; nec non Matris, lectissimæ ob vitæ sanctimoniam et raram beneficentiam qua miseris et ægris, quotidie opitulabatur exemplum lucidum posteris indicatum est moribus ingenio candore, et sanguine clari cultores veræ religionis erant."

David Barclay, at whose cost the aisle was constructed, was an opulent merchant in London; he had the honour of entertaining Queen Anne and the first three Georges during their state visits to the city.

A monument in the aisle presents the following pedigree of the Barclay family :—

"1. Theobald de Berkeley, born A.D. 1110, lived in the time of Alexander the First and David the First, Kings of Scotland. 2. Humphrey his son, cousin of Walter de Berkeley, Great Chamberlain of the kingdom, became owner of a large domain in this county and from the lands of Balfeith, Monboddo, Glenfarquhar, and other portions of it granted to the monks of Aberbrothwick, donations that were confirmed by William the Lion. 3. Richenda, his only child, renewed and made additions to these donations, and her grants were confirmed by K. Alexander the Second. 4. Dying without issue, she was succeeded by John de Berkeley, brother of Humphrey, who dispossessed the monks of all these donations, but was obliged to compromise and give them instead a portion of his lands of Conveth, and that transaction was confirmed by K. Alexander the Second. 5. Robert de Berkeley, son of John, had concurred in his father's compromise with the monks. 6. Hugh de Berkeley, son of Robert, obtained from King Robert Bruce a charter over the lands of Westerton and Conveth. 7. Alexander de Berkeley, son and successor of Hugh, married Catherine, sister of William de Keith, Marischal of Scotland, A.D. 1351, and by that marriage added to the paternal estates the then extensive domain of Mathers, conveyed by charter from the Marischal confirmed by King David Bruce. 8. David de Berkeley, 2nd of Mathers, married the daughter of John de Seton. 9. His son Alexander de Berkeley, 3rd of Mathers, married Helen, daughter of Grahame of Morphie. 10. Their son David de Berkeley, 4th of Mathers, who built an impregnable castle called the Kaim of Mathers, and according to tradition, there took refuge on account of his concern in the murder of Melville, the sheriff; married the daughter of Strachan of Thornton. 11. His son Alexander, 5th of Mathers, married the daughter of Wishart of Pitarrow; he changed the spelling of the family name to *Barclay*. 12. His son David Barclay, 6th of Mathers married Janet, daughter of Irvine of Drum. 13. Alexander Barclay, 7th of Mathers, son of David, married the daughter of Auchinlech of Glenbervie, and anno 1497, sold the lands of Slains and Falside to Moncur of Knapp. 14. George Barclay, 8th of Mathers, his son, married the daughter of Sir James Auchterlony, of Auchterlony and Kelly. 15. His son David Barclay, 9th of Mathers, married, first the daughter of Rait of Hallgreen, by whom he had a son George; and second, Catherine Home, and to John, his son by her he gave the lands of Johnston. 16. George Barclay, 10th of Mathers, elder son of David, married first, the daughter of Sir Thomas Erskine of Brechin, Secretary to James V. of Scotland; second the daughter of Wood of Bonnington, to his son by her he gave the lands of Bridgeton and Jackston. 17. Thomas Barclay, 11th of Mathers. elder son of George, married the daughter of Straiton of Lauriston. 18. David Barclay, 12th of Mathers, son of Thomas, was born anno 1580 : polite and accomplished, he lived much at Court, incurring extravagant expenses, to the great impairment of his fortune, whereby he was obliged to sell five valuable estates ; he married first, Elizabeth, daughter of Livingston of Dunnipace, by whom he had five sons and a daughter ; second, Margaret Keith, granddaughter of Earl Marischal. To his daughter he gave a handsome fortune, to his sons a liberal education ; the two eldest died young. David, the third, became eminently conspicuous ; Robert, the fourth, was rector of the Scots College at Paris ; James, the youngest, a Captain of Horse, fell gloriously at the Battle of Philiphaugh. 19. Colonel David Barclay, the first of Ury, third son of David, 12th of Mathers, was born anno 1610, at Kirktonhill, the ancient seat of the family. Instructed in every accomplishment of the age, he entered as a volunteer the service of Gustavus Adolphus of Sweden, in which he so distinguished himself as to gain the favour of that Monarch ; but called home by the Civil Wars which distracted Scotland, he was, anno 1646, placed in the Colonelcy of a Royal Regiment of Horse, and was repeatedly entrusted with the command of an army, and the military government of considerable portions of the kingdom, in all which positions he acquitted himself with skill and bravery, and rendered important service to his country. In 1647, he married Catherine, daughter of Sir Robert Gordon of Gordonston, who was second son of the Earl of Sutherland by Jane, daughter of the Marquis of Huntly, and was also cousin to King James the Sixth of Scotland. The estates of the Barclays of Mathers having been nearly all disposed of by his father, the Colonel acquired, by purchase from Earl Marischal, the barony of Ury, and there fixed the residence of his

KINCARDINESHIRE.

family. He sat in the Scots Parliament as representative successively for Sutherlandshire and the counties of Angus and Mearns.
See his gravestone adjacent hereto.

Tablets and monuments containing the following inscriptions
are also to be found in the Barclay aisle:—

"The grave of Colonel David Barclay, of Urie, son and heir of
David Barclay, of Mathers, and Elizabeth, daughter of Livingston,
of Dunipace. He was born anno 1610; bought the barony of
Urie, 1648 ; having religiously abdicated the world in 1666, he
joined the Quakers, and died 12 of October 1686."

"The grave of Robert Barclay, of Urie, Author of the "Apologie
for the Quakers," son and heir of Colonel David Barclay, of Urie,
and Katherine, daughter of the first Sir Robert Gordon, of Gordonston.   He was born Decr. 23, 1648, and died Octr. 3, 1690.
Also of his wife, Christian, daughter of Gilbert Mollison, Merchant
in Aberdeen. She was born Anno 1647, and died Febry. 14,
1723."

"The grave of Robert Barclay, of Ury, son and heir of Robert
Barclay, of Ury, and of Christian, daughter of Gilbert Mollison,
merchant in Aberdeen, and eldest son of Thomas Mollison, of
Lauchintully.   He was born March the 25th, 1672, and died
March the 27th, 1747."

"The grave of Robert Barclay, of Ury, and Elizabeth O'Brian,
daughter of James O'Brian, Esq., of London, and son of Colonel
O'Brian, of the Kingdom of Ireland. He was grandson to Robert
Barclay, of Ury, Author of the " Apology for the Quakers;" was
born 20th July, 1699, and died 10th October, 1760."

"The grave of Une Cameron, wife of Robert Barclay, of Ury,
and daughter of Sir Evan Cameron, of Lochiel. She was born
March, 1701, and died March, 1762. Also of Jane Barclay, her
daughter, who was born in 1726, and died in August, 1750."

"The grave of Anne Barclay, the eldest daughter of Robert
Barclay, of Ury, great-grandson of Robert Barclay, of Ury, Author

of the " Apology for the Quakers ; " and Sarah Anne Allardice, of Allardice, daughter and heiress of James Allardice of Allardice. She was born 13 September, 1777, and died 29th October, 1782."

"To the memory of Robert Barclay, of Allardice, Esquire, 5th of Ury, great-grandson of the Apologist, who was born at Ury in 1731 ; and having acquired by marriage the estate of Allardice, thereupon assumed that additional surname. Inheriting from his father, Robert the Strong, symmetry of form and great muscular power, he excelled in all the athletic exercises. Succeeding to Ury on his father's death, in 1760, while it was yet in the rudest condition, he zealously devoted towards its improvement the energies of a vigorous mind, stored with a thorough knowledge of agriculture, attained by assiduous study of its theory and practice, in the best districts of England. Accordingly, he brought into high cultivation about 2000 arable acres, planted 1500 acres of wood, and executed the manifold operations connected with such works in a manner so unexampled and successful, that his practice became the conventional standard over an extensive district, and placed him in the foremost rank among Scottish agriculturists. By the grant of feu-rights on his estate of Arduthie, he laid the foundation of the New Town of Stonehaven, and lived to see it become a populous and thriving community. By unanimous election, he represented his native county in three successive Parliaments. Distinguished by his loyalty and patriotism, and honoured with the intimate friendship of the great William Pitt, and other eminent statesmen of the time, he died at Ury, the 7th of April, 1797."

"To the memory of Une Cameron, wife of John Innes, Esquire, of Cowie, who was born in 1778, and died at Cowie, in September, 1809. Mary, born in 1780, who died in 1799. James Allardice, born in 1784, who died, in the island of Ceylon, in 1803. David, Major of the 28th Regiment of Foot, who was born in 1786, and died at Otranto, in Italy, in 1826. Rodney, born in 1782, who died in 1853, all children of Robert Barclay Allardice, Esquire, of Ury, and Sarah Anne Allardice, of Allardice, heiress of line of the Earls of Airth and Menteith."

"In memory of Robert Barclay Allardice, Esquire, of Ury and Allardice, heir of line of the Earls of Airth and Menteith, born

August 25th, 1779, died on the 1st of May, 1854, in the 75th year of his age."

"Robert Barclay Allardice, of Ury, born 25th August 1779, died 1st May, 1854."

Robert Barclay, of Allardice and Ury, who died in 1797, contributed to "Archæologica Scotica" a paper on the site of the battle of *Mons Grampius*. Robert Barclay Allardice, who died in 1854, was renowned for his pedestrian feats. He exercised a profuse hospitality, and was a zealous agriculturist. With reference to the claims of the House on the earldom of Airth and Menteith, see *supra*, p. 246.

In the Barclay aisle are deposited the remains of Alexander Baird, of Ury, who died in 1862. By this gentleman, a member of the Gartsherrie family, the aisle was repaired and renovated.

The following rhymes are from gravestones in Fetteresso churchyard :—

> "Our lyefe is short, and 'tis
>   Fulle of sorrowe,
> We're here to-day, and straight
>   Are gone to-morrow."

> "Pain was my portion ;
>   Physic was my food ;
> Sighs were my devotion ;
>   Drugs did me no good ;
> Till Christ my Redeemer,
>   Who knows what is best,
> To ease me of my pain
>   Has taken me to rest."

PARISH OF FORDOUN.

A sculptured stone at St. Palladius' Chapel is supposed to commemorate the death of Kenneth III., in 994. According to the narrative, he was slain by two assassins employed by Finella, a royal princess, in revenge for his having caused her son to be put to death. The stone presents three figures on horseback, each provided with a spear—the first and third being evidently of inferior rank. At the feet of the central horseman lies a sceptre or decorated weapon. The stone was discovered under the pulpit of the old church. Kenneth III. occupied the castle of Kincardine, a royal structure in which John Baliol resigned the crown to the haughty Edward. It is now a ruin.

A vault of the old church was the burial-place of the Falconers, of Glenfarquhar, now represented by the Earl of Kintore. A tombstone in the vault is thus inscribed:—

" 1668.—In spem beatæ resvrrectionis hic velutí svffitvs thalamo svaviter in Domino obdormit dux Robertvs Irvin, a Monboddo, Dominvs, qui pie fatis cessit 6 Ivlii, anno salvtis hvmanæ 1652, et ætatis svæ anno 80:—

" Conjvge progenie felix ; virtvtis, honesti
Cvltor, et antiqvis exorivndvs avis,
Hoc cvbat Irvinvs monvmento. Cætera norvnt
Musa et vitiferis Seqvana clarvs aqvis."

Captain Robert Irvine was ancestor of the celebrated James Burnett, Lord Monboddo.

In the vestibule of the new parish church a marble tablet commemorates Alexander Crombie, of Phesdo, who died 21st November, 1832, aged sixty-six. He was in his estate succeeded by his first cousin, Alexander Crombie, LL.D., author of various works on philosophy and grammar.

A granite pillar, reared in 1850, commemorates George Wishart, the celebrated Martyr; it is thus inscribed:—

" This monument is erected to the memory of one of Scotland's first and most illustrious martyrs, George Wishart, of Pitarrow, in this parish ; and as a testimony of gratitude to the great Head of the Church, for the work of the Reformation, on behalf of which his servant suffered. He was born in 1513, and was burned at St. Andrews, 1st March, 1546. 'The righteous shall be in everlasting remembrance.' "

The estate of Pitarrow remained in the family of Wishart from the beginning of the thirteenth till the commencement of the seventeenth century.

The three following inscriptions are from tombstones belonging to the families of Leith and Arnott :—

" Under the flat stone, 5 feet south from this wall, lies the body of James Leith, of Whiteriggs, who died 20th Feb., 1788, aged 63. And on the south side of that stone lies the body of Margaret Young, his wife, who died 6 April, 1783, aged 58. The virtue of their lives made their deaths lamented, and this stone is in gratitude erected to their memories by their children. Here are also interred the body of Margaret Hacket, his mother, who died in April, 1765, aged 56. And Doctor Charles Leith, his brother, who died 6 of May, 1731, aged 56. And also of two of his children, Ramsay Leith, and —— Leith, who died in infancy."

" Sacred to the memory of James Arnott, Esq., who died at Arbikie, in Forfarshire, 3 Dec., 1799 ; and of his wife, Janet Leith, who died at Edinburgh, 29 Aug., 1827 ; and of their two younger sons, Charles Arnott, Esq., formerly solicitor in London, who died at Leithfield Cottage, in this parish, 21 Sept., 1841, and whose body is here interred. And David Leith Arnott, Esq., a Major in the East India Company's service, who died in India, 19th Oct., 1840. And of their youngest daughter, Helen Arnott, who died in Montrose, 21 Feb., 1807. James Leith Arnott, grandson of said James Arnott and Janet Leith, died at Edinburgh, 10 Novr., 1818, aged 2 years."

" James Leith, of Whiteriggs or Leithfield, and Margaret Young, spouses, whose names are mentioned on a tablet erected near this stone, left six children, viz. Alexander Leith, died at sea in Jan., 1805, aged 53. John Leith, died at Surinam in 1805, surgeon of the 16th regiment of Foot, aged 49. James Leith, died at Madras, 12th Nov., 1829, a Major-General in the service of the East India Company, aged 65. Janet Leith, or Arnott, wife of James Arnott, mentioned on the other side, died at Edinburgh, aged 73, leaving a family—Margaret Leith, died at Edinburgh, March 13, 1835, aged 77. Elizabeth Leith, died at Edinburgh, 29 April, 1841, aged 81. Erected by the three surviving children of the said James Arnott and Janet Leith."

An altar-stone denotes the resting-place of Dr. James Badenoch, of Whiteriggs, who died 21st December, 1797, aged fifty-four; he was grandfather of the late J. Badenoch-Nicholson, Esq., of Glenbervie.

Within a mortuary enclosure, a tombstone commemorates James Gammell, Esq., of Drumtochty, who died 15th September, 1825, aged eighty-nine. His son, Lieutenant-General Andrew Gammell, is interred in Westminster Abbey.

On tombstones in the parish churchyard are these rhymes :—

> " This dust which now obscurely lies,
> Once animated was by one
> Whose amiable qualities
> Seldom, if ever, were outshone."

> " This dust which here doth rest in sacred peace,
> Once lodg'd a soul enrich'd with every grace ;
> A safe companion, and a friend approv'd
> In death regretted and in life belov'd.
> Well pleased, Heaven crown'd his virtues with success,
> And soon receiv'd him to the seats of bliss ;
> At Life's mid age he gained that happy shore,
> Where friends unite, and death can part no more."

> " Love conjvgal in this lyfe keeps amity,
> Bvt death doth come and break society ;
> Yet here is love come to behold and see,
> That with death strove and got the victory.
> Together they did live, together dy,
> Together wer both bvried in one day ;
> Together they within this grave do ly,
> Together they shall reign with Christ for aye."

PARISH OF GARVOCK.

A gravestone in Garvock churchyard presents these lines :—

> " Each letter'd stone some lesson reads,
>   And bids you stop your pace ;
> Each warning you in solemn tone,
>   Where ends your mortal race.
> Soon will your own a lecture read,
>   In every cavil'ler's ear ;
> And bid the passing stranger halt,
>   And shed a pitying tear.
> Let thy mortality be grav'd,
>   Deep on thy faithful mind ;
> Before the journeyer o'er thy tomb,
>   Memento mori find."

PARISH OF GLENBERVIE.

In the Douglas aisle a monument commemorates Sir William Douglas, of Glenbervie, ninth Earl of Angus, and his wife, Egedia, daughter of Sir Robert Graham, of Morphie. From James V. his Lordship obtained a charter in 1591, confirming him in the ancient privileges of his house, viz., to vote first in council and in Parliament, to lead the van of the royal army, and to carry the crown at coronations. He died in 1591.

On a mural tablet are set forth the valiant exploits and distinguished alliances of the Barons of Glenbervie, from the supposed origin of that house in the eighth century.

The Stuarts of Inchbreck, formerly interred in the churchyard. On the ruin of the old church a brass plate presents a list of the lairds of Inchbreck, from 1550 downwards.

A tombstone commemorates James Burnes, farmer, Brawlinmuir, who died in 1743, and his wife Margaret Falconer. They were great-grand parents of the poet Burns.

PARISH OF KINNEFF.

In Kinneff churchyard are commemorated four persons, whose enterprise and patriotism form an interesting episode in the national history. When Scotland was overrun by an English army under Cromwell, the Estates determined (June, 1651) that for greater safety the Scottish Regalia should be removed to Dunnottar Castle, a fortress belonging to the Earl Marischal, and which was then garrisoned by George Ogilvie, of Barras, the Lieutenant-Governor. Ogilvie received the precious insignia, and resolved at all hazards to preserve them from the enemy. To Dunnottar Castle was laid a close siege, and an early surrender became inevitable. In March, 1652, Mrs. Grainger, wife of the minister of Kinneff, attended by her maid, both on horseback, requested permission from the English commander to enter the castle to visit her friend Mrs. Ogilvie, who, with the governor, belonged to Kinneff parish. Leave was granted, and after a short visit, Mrs. Grainger and her maid returned from the castle. The latter carried in a bag of lint, the sword and sceptre, while Mrs. Grainger bore the crown in a small bundle on her arm. The English general, unsuspecting a plot, helped Mrs. Grainger to her horse. That night Mr. Grainger made a hole under a pavement stone in front of his pulpit, and therein placed the crown and sceptre wrapped in linen. The sword of state he deposited in the soil under a pew in another portion of the edifice. Subsequently the regal symbols were kept in the manse in a double-bottomed bed.

Dunnottar Castle surrendered, and the governor was called on to deliver up the royal insignia. He protested that they were not in his keeping, and was in consequence subjected to some severity. At the Restoration, Mrs. Grainger restored to him the precious symbols, and on his delivering them up to the proper custodier he was rewarded with a baronetcy. His monument, which rests upon the south wall of the church, is thus inscribed :—

" Æternæ memoriæ sacrum D. Georgii Ogilvie de Barras, Equitis

Baroneti, qui Arci Dunotriensi præfectus strenue eam per aliquod tempus adversus paricidarum Anglorum copias tutatus, eam tandem dedere est coactus. Non ante tamen quam ipsius conjugisque suæ D. Elizabethæ Douglassiæ opera Imperii Scotici Insignia, Corona, sciz: Sceptrum et Gladius, ibi reposita, clam inde avecta atque in hac Kinneffi æde sacra in tuto essent collocata. Ob egregia hæc viri in Patriam merita constantemque et illibatam in Regiam Familiam fidem Equitis Baroneti honorem per literas patentes III. Non: Mart: anno MDCLX. a Rege datas, est consecutus: auctis ejus Paternis Insignibus gentilibus quibus in hunc usque diem familia sua utitur. Regio porro diplomate Magno Scotiæ Sigillo munito ei concessum est terrarum suarum possidendarum jus a tenura quam vulgo Wardam Simplicem appellant, in Albam quæ dicitur tenuram commutaretur. In utroque hoc instrumento Regio summa ejus in principes suos fidelitas atque egregia merita maximo cum delogia commemorabantur. David Ogilvie, Eques Baronetus supra dicti pronepos obiit Non: Decem: MDCCXCIX. annos natus LXX. Domina Ogilvie hujus conjux obiit XIV. Kal: Ian: anno MDCCC. annos nata LIII. Ambo in hac æde sepulti."

To Mrs. Grainger Parliament voted 2,000 merks. For her husband was reserved a gravestone, with these commendatory lines of Latin verse —

> " Scotia Grangeri cui Insignia Regia debet
> Servata hic cineres reliquiæq' jacent.
> Abstulit obsesso pæne hæc captiva Dunotro,
> Condidit et sacra qva tvmvlator hvmo.
> Proemia dant superi; patrii servator honoris
> Sceptra rotat superos inter athleta chor . ."

Mr. Grainger died in 1663, aged about fifty-seven. His widow, whose maiden name was Christian Fletcher, married a landowner in the district, named Abercrombie. In the parochial charge Mr. Grainger was succeeded by the Rev. James Honyman, son of David Honyman, baker in St. Andrews, and who was sometime assistant to Mr. James Sharp, minister of Crail, the future archbishop. A tombstone commemorates Mr. Honyman and his descendants, three of whom were in succession ministers of the parish. It is inscribed thus :—

" In memory of Mr. James Honyman, brother of Andrew, Bishop

of Orkney, and Robert, Archdean of St. Andrews, who was settled
minister of this parish of Kinneff, 30th Sept. 1663, and died 2nd
May, 1693, and is here interred. And of Mr. Andrew Honyman,
his eldest son, who succeeded in the charge, and died 30th Dec.
1732; and, together with his wife, Helen Rait, of the family of
Finlawston, is here interred. And of Mr James Honyman, his
eldest son, and successor in this charge, who died 16th Jan. 1780,
aged seventy-seven years, and is interred here, with his wife
Katherine Allardyce, daughter of Provost Allardyce in Aberdeen.
And of Mr. James Honyman, his eldest son, who succeeded him
in this charge, and died 5th Aug. 1781, aged thirty-six years, and
is here interred. This monument is erected by Mr. John, a dis-
senting clergyman in England, Dr. Robert, a physician in Virginia,
and Helen, the wife of Robert Edward, in Harvieston, brothers and
sister of the last deceased."

Mr. James Honyman, minister of Kinneff, grandson of the successor of Mr. Grainger, composed the popular song, "Hie, bonnie
lassie, blink over the burn," and other verses.

A member of the family of Graham, of Morphie, is on an
ancient gravestone thus commemorated:—

"Hoc . tvmvlo . conditvs . est . vir . pivs . et gerosvs . Robert .
Grahame . de . largie . Domini a . Morfe . fl' . terti' . qvi. et .
sancte . in . doio obdormiit . Anno . Christi . 1597 . anno . ætatis
svæ . 37."

An altar tombstone celebrates by the following inscription,
several yeomen descendants of the noble house of Lindsay:—

"Andreas Lindsay, teneno de Whisleberry filius Joannis et
nepos alij Joannis Lindsays, dict. prædij tenen., pronepos Jacobi
Lindsay, tenen. de Brigend, et abnepos Rogeri Lindsay, tenen. de
Barras, ab illustri et antiqua familia Lindseorum, primo de
Glenesque, et postea de Edzel designat., orti, diversarum nobilium
familiarum ancestorum, tribus ult. ment. apud Caterline sepultis,
hoc posuit memoriæ dict. sui Patris, qui obijt 20 De. 1724, ætatis
57 ; Joannæ Napier, ejus Matris, quæ fatis concessit 30 No. 1743,
ætatis 56 ; (sepultæ apud Bervy) ; Catharinæ Christy, ejus uxoris,
quæ decessit 25 Ap. 1743, ætatis 38 ; et Catharinæ Lindsay, suæ
filiæ, quæ obijt in pueritia. Obijt ille Andreas Lindsay 2do Julii
1761, ætatis vero 57, hic q sepultus. Ejus liberi superstites fuere,

Joannis (patris successor in Whisleberry), Hugo (scriba in Aberdeen) Joanna (uxor Gulielmi Cruickshank, civis Aberdonensis), Helena et Anna (adhuc innupta); Jacobo, filio primogenito (apud Cork, in Hibernia, in Classa Regia), mortuo mense Februarii 1759, ætatis 30. Joannes Lindsay, qui patri successit in Whistleberry, obijt 14 Jul. 1809, an. æt. 74, et hujus uxor, Christian Walker, decessit 14 Aug. 1830, an. æt. 94. Ambo hic sepulti. Alexander Lindsay, horum filius teneno de Whistleberry, obiit 6 Nov. 1831, an. æt. 68; cujus filia natu maxima, Margaret, innupta decessit 7 Nov. 1831, an. æt. 22. In hoc sepulchro una contumulati."

A tombstone inscribed as follows, celebrates John Young, of Stank, sheriff of the county, and his son William Young, M.D., of Fawsyde, with the members of his family:—

"Memoriæ Joannis Young de Stank, vicecomitis de Kincardine, qui obijt quarto die Martij, anno 1750, aetatis 52. Gulielmus Young, M.D., filius hoc marmor posuit."

"In memory of William Young, M.D., of Fawsyde, who died 9 March 1850; and of his wife, Mary Logie, who died 18 Nov. 1838. Also of their only child Jane Young, who died 2 March 1834."

PARISH OF LAURENCEKIRK.

In the churchyard a memorial slab is thus inscribed:—

"HER . LYIS . MASTER . PATRICK . BELLIE . SCHOLLE . MASTER . WHO DEPARTED . THIS . LYFE . FEBRUARY . THE . 10 . 1695. OF . AGE . 20 . YEIRS . 5 MONETHS . AND . 16 . DAYES."

As parochial schoolmaster Mr. Belbie was succeeded by the celebrated Thomas Ruddiman, who held the office four years.

On an altar stone, Bishop Watson, of the Episcopal Church, is celebrated thus:—

"Viro admodum Reverendo Jonathan Watson, in Ecclesia Scotiæ Episcopo, pietatis aliarumque virtutum vere evangelicarum emulo; in bonis literis inque theologia exercitato; animo firmo;

filio, patri, conjugi amantissimo. Sui omnibus officii sacri muneribus per 17 annos apud Laurencekirk fideliter functus, multum
defletus obiit 28 die Janu., 1808, annum 46 agens.   Vidua et mater
marentes H.M.P."

In 1792 Mr. Watson was consecrated Bishop of Dunkeld, but he
continued to minister at Laurencekirk till the period of his death.
By his marriage with Miss Edgar, of Keithock, he left a daughter,
who resides in Edinburgh, unmarried.

Tombstones commemorate the Rev. William Milne of the Episcopal church, Laurencekirk, who died in 1817, aged 42, and the
Rev. Robert Spark, also Episcopal clergyman at Laurencekirk, who
died 3rd May, 1839, in the eighty-first year of his age, and the
fifty-ninth of his ministry.

Alexander Beattie, who died in 1778, aged twenty-six, has on his
tombstone these lines, composed by his relative, Dr. Beattie, author
of "The Minstrel" :—

> " Ah ! early lost ! ah ! life ! thou empty name,
> A noontide shadow, and a midnight dream ;
> Death might have satisfi'd his craving rage,
> And mow'd down all the vices of the age,
> But Heav'n who saw, offended with our crimes,
> Begrudg'd thy virtues to the abandoned times ;
> By his cold hand transplanted thee on high,
> To live and flourish thro' eternity."

On the gravestone of Alexander Forbes, blacksmith, Dr. Beattie
has also inscribed a poetical epitaph.   Forbes was father of the
Rev. David Forbes, minister of the parish ; he died 7th August
1768 :—

> " Shall venal flattery prostitute the muse,
> To senseless titles spurious honours pay,
> And yet to rural worth such lays refuse,
> Which Truth may banish with her brightest ray.
> Forbid it Equity !   The task be mine
> To yield his memory all the praise I can ;
> The whole's compris'd in this conclusive line,
> God's noblest work (here lyes) an Honest man."

A tombstone is thus inscribed :—

" Sacred to the memory of Alexander Shank of Castlerig, sometime minister of the Gospel at St. Cyrus, who died at Laurencekirk
on the 5th Jany. 1814, aged 75 years :—Also, Diana, his wife,
daughter of the late Robert Scott of Dunninald, parish of Craig,
who died here on the 24th Feby. 1825, aged 84 years :—and
Jane, their youngest daughter, who died at her house in Laurencekirk, on the 23d of Nov. 1840 :—Also, in memory of Henry
Shank, of Castlerig and Gleniston, Esq., last surviving son of the
above Alexander and Diana Shank, who died January 4, 1860,
aged 81.

The Rev. Alexander Shank, son of the minister of Arbuthnot, was
admitted to the pastoral charge of St. Cyrus in 1759. He resigned
the living in 1781, on succeeding to the estate of Castlerig, Fifeshire,
and thereafter established his residence at Laurencekirk. His son
mentioned in the epitaph became a Director of the East India
Company, and his daughter, Diana, married the Rev. George
Cook, D.D., minister of Laurencekirk, and subsequently Professor
of Moral Philosophy at St. Andrews.

In the church a marble tablet thus commemorates Dr. Duirs, an
eminent army surgeon, born in the parish.

" In memory of William Duirs, M.A., M.D., Deputy Inspector-
General of Hospital and Fleets, a native of this parish, who fell a
victim to yellow fever, contracted in the execution of his duty at
the Royal Naval Hospital, Jamaica, 8 June 1867, aged 47 years.
This tablet is erected by sixty-two of his brother medical officers
as a testimony of their high appreciation of his sterling worth, kindness of heart, and professional abilities."

A plain tombstone celebrates Charles Stevens, the original manufacturer of the Laurencekirk snuff boxes; he died 6th August
1821, aged sixty-eight.

PARISH OF MARYCULTER.

Among the ruins of the old church are two recumbent figures believed to represent Menzies, of Maryculter, and his lady, who flourished in the fifteenth century. The family obtained by marriage the estate of Pitfoddles. John Menzies, of Pitfoddles, who died in 1849, bequeathed his lands and mansion-house for a Catholic College. The mansion, much enlarged, is now known as Blair's College; it contains an excellent library and some valuable portraits.

A granite monument on the hill of Auchlec celebrates John Irvine-Boswell, of Balmuto and Kingcausie, son of Claude Boswell, Lord Balmuto. The monument is inscribed thus :—

"In memory of John Irvine-Boswell, of Balmuto and Kingcausie. born 28th December, 1785; died 23rd December, 1860. A man who loved his Saviour, walked steadfastly with his God, and whose rule of life was—"Whatsoever ye do in word or deed, do all in the name of the Lord Jesus Christ." In early life he joined the Coldstream Guards, and carried their Colours in the battle of Talavera. Retiring from the army he settled at Kingcausie, and lived to transform the natural barrenness of the Estate into luxuriant fertility. He will long be remembered in the district for the enlightened zeal he displayed in the introduction of all the improvements of modern agriculture ; and he did not confine his attention to his own Estates, his knowledge and experience being ever at the service of his neighbours, rich and poor alike. In every position and relation of life he maintained, with rare fidelity, the character of a Christian Gentleman ; and he died in peace, trusting simply in the merits of his Saviour for acceptance with his God. His sorrowing widow, Margaret Irvine-Boswell, erected this monument as a solace in her bitter bereavement, A.D. M.DCCCLXII."

Members of the family of Gordon, of Ellon, are interred in the churchyard.

A tombstone with an inscription commemorates Dr. John Glennie, minister of the parish, who died in 1801, aged eighty-one. Dr. Glennie's youngest son, George, was minister of the West Church, Aberdeen, and Professor of Moral Philosophy in Marischal College.

PARISH OF MARYKIRK.

In the churchyard an aisle, which formed the transept of the old church, is the burial place of Strachan, of Thornton. The ceiling is adorned with heraldic devices. A marble tablet bears the following inscription:—

"Epicedium thrœnodicum . . memoriam fæminæ lectissimæ, Dominæ Elizabethæ Forbesæ, Dominæ a Thornton, æternitatis candidatæ, . . . meritorum . . . nissima, puerpera, immaturo fato . . . repta est, dum annum ætatis vigesimum . . . . quintum agebat, die decimo Ianuarij . . 61 : Cujus fragrantissimæ memoriæ, licet . . . . de monumentis omni ære perennioribus abunde satis litatum sit, hoc tam . . magnifico mausoleo, parentau' dum curavit conjunx ipsius pullatus, D. Iacobus Strahanus a Thorntonæ, eques auratus.

"Siste, viator, habes summi monumenta . . . .
Virtutis tumulum, pieridumq' vid . .
Omnis una fuit brevis hæc quam con . . . .
Lux nuper patriæ . . levis umb . . .
Aurea si tantas fudere crepuscula . . .
Luxisset, quanto sidere . . . .
Quanta fuit pietas quam stemmatis . . . .
Enthea mens roseus quam sine sente sinus.
Quantus et oris honos ; Phœnix vixitq' caditq',
Qualem non poterant reddere . . . decem,
At mutura polio cecidit Christoq' ; quid . . .
Ignavi sæcla numerant, facta boni.
Mors ipsa non separadit."

Lady Strachan was third daughter of Forbes, of Waterton, Aberdeenshire ; about the close of the seventeenth century the estate of Thornton became the possession of this house. It now belongs to Mr. Crombie, of Pitarrow. The baronetcy is dormant.

A mortuary enclosure belongs to the family of Taylor, of Kirkton Hill, cadets of the old house of Taylor, of Borrowfield.

A plain tombstone commemorates Margaret Low, wife of John Herd, tenant in Muirton, and mother of David Herd, the eminent collector of Scottish ballads ; she died 14th December, 1751, in her sixtieth year. (Vol. I., p. 83.)

On a tombstone, sculptured with his instruments of trade, is commemorated Adam Glyge, blacksmith, who died 4th March, 1698, aged eighty-six. His near relative, a blacksmith in Arbuthnot parish, was father of the Right Reverend Bishop Gleig, of Stirling, and grandfather of the Rev. George Robert Gleig, Chaplain-General.

Within the parish church a marble tablet is thus inscribed:—

"The Rev. James Shand, A.M., minister of this parish from 1805 to 1837, and previously of the College Church, Aberdeen, son of James Shand, Esq., merchant there, born 18th Aug. 1757, died 5th January, 1837. Margaret Farquhar, his wife, born 11th Aug., 1767, died 11th January, 1840, daughter of Alexander Farquhar, Esq., of Kintore, by his wife Elizabeth Harvey, great grand-daughter of James Harvey, of Kilmundy. and his wife, Margaret Baird, of Auchmedden. He was an accomplished scholar, a kind husband and father, and a devoted pastor. In all the relations of life she was equally examplary—both were united in that faith and hope which vanquish death, and realise the rest which remaineth to the people of God. This tablet is affectionately dedicated by their surviving sons to the memory of the best of parents."

The third son of Mr. and Mrs. Shand, Sir Charles Farquhar Shand, is Chief Justice of the Mauritius.

On gravestones in Marykirk burying-ground are these rhymes:—

"Thou hast the promise of eternal truth,
    Those who live well, and pious paths pursue,
    To man and to their Maker true,
Let 'em expire in age or youth,
            Can never miss
Their way to everlasting bliss."

"Death's shade is made the hiding-place,
    When worldly troubles do increase;
    When converts young are called home,
    Before these troublous days do come,
    It warning gives to older sort
    To fly to Christ their chief support,
    Though ye be young as well as I,
    Yet faith will learn you how to dy."

"Oh, that it were with me,
　As in the days of old,
With children about me,
　In number manifold!
But here mine only son,
　In this dark grave is laid,
And hindered not his father
　To sleep into his bed;
Because that the oppressor,
　Upon his side had power,
And none to comfort me,
　Altho' I mourned sore."

"He'll order Death, that porter rude,
　To open the gates of brass;
For, lo, with characters of blood
　Thy husband wrote thy pass.
At Jordan deep then be not feared,
　Tho' dismal-like and broad;
Thy sun will guide, thy shield will guard—
　Thy husband paved the road.
He'll lead thee safe, and bring thee Home,
　So still let blessings fall
Of grace while here till glory come—
　Thy husband's bound for all."

PARISH OF ST. CYRUS.

A massive monument is thus inscribed :—

"Sacred to the memory of Sir Joseph Straton, of Kirkside, Companion of the Bath; Knight of the Guelphic Order of Hanover, and of the Order of St. Waldemar of Russia; Lieut.-General of the British Army; youngest son of William Muter, Esq., of Annfield, Fifeshire, and Mrs. Janet Straton, of Kirkside, Kincardineshire.— This brave and accomplished officer entered the army in early life, and served with distinguished honor in the Peninsular War and at Waterloo, under Field Marshal the Duke of Wellington. He commanded his own regiment of the 6th Dragoons until the fall of the gallant Ponsonby, to whose brigade he belonged, when the command of the brigade devolved upon him. Towards the close of the action Sir Joseph Straton was wounded, and upon the termination of the war, as a reward for his services, he had various military honours conferred upon him. He died Colonel of the Enniskillen Dragoons, at London, 23d Oct., 1840, in the 63d year of his age, and is interred here by his own desire."

Sir Joseph Straton succeeded Joseph Straton, his maternal uncle, in the lands of Kirkside, a family representing the older and distinguished House of Straton, of Lauriston. Alexander de Straton fell, with several of his sons, at the Battle of Harlaw, in 1411. George Straton, of Lauriston, was one of the first persons of rank who supported the Reformed doctrines. His son, Sir Alexander Straton, was in 1603 Lord High Commissioner to the General Assembly.

A burial-aisle belonging to the Grahams of Morphie, has lately been restored by Barron Graham, Esq., of Morphie, the present representative of that House.

Within a mortuary enclosure, a monument celebrates George Beattie, an ingenious and short-lived poet; it is thus inscribed:—

"To the memory of George Beattie, writer in Montrose, who died 29th Sept., 1823, in the 38th year of his age, this monument was erected by the friends who loved him in life and lamented him in death. In his disposition, he was just, charitable and benevolent; in his principles, firm and independent; in his genius, forcible and pathetic; and in his manners, plain and social. His virtues are deeply engraved in the hearts of those who knew him, and his literary productions will be admired while taste for original humour and vigorous expression remain."

Beattie was a native of the parish. A writer of verses from his youth, he is best known as the author of "John o' Arnha," a poem in the manner of Burns's "Tam o' Shanter." Possessed of a morbid sensitiveness, he was led, through disappointed affection, to take his own life. He perished in his 38th year.

On tombstones in the churchyard are these rhymes:—

"If honour wait on pedigree,
    And ancient blood we boast;
  I claim descent from Adam,
    Who of mankind was first.

From Noah next my line I have,
  Through Cambria's hardy sons,
To Scotia's bleak, but friendly clime,
  In earth to lay my bones."

"When first I drew the breath of life
  I nothing knew at all;
Yet long before my death I knew
  That I with Adam fell.
My body lays near to this stone,
  Waiting the morning call;
When Christ will take me by the hand.
  He is my all and all."

"Low here his mouldering body's laid,
  Now wrapt in death's oblivious shade;
I trust his soul dwells with the blest,
  In mansions of eternal rest.
Let every one who reads his fate,
  Reflect on life's uncertain date;
And learn to run their worldly race
  That they through Christ may die in peace.
His parents hope to meet again
  Their son, beyond the reach of pain,
And sin, and death, when saints shall rise,
  To reign immortal in the skies."

An obelisk on the estate of Morphie, thirteen feet in height, is supposed to commemorate a son of Camus and some other Danish chief, who fell in battle at the spot. According to tradition, the Danes, after their defeat at Panbride, retreated northwards, and here were again attacked by the Scots, and again signally routed.

PARISH OF STRACHAN.

In the parish churchyard a marble monument commemorates Colin Campbell, Esq., of Kilmartin and Blackhall, who died 27th April, 1861, aged thirty-three.

A tombstone celebrates Joseph Grant, an ingenious writer; it is thus inscribed:—

" In memory of Joseph Grant, author of " Tales of the Glens," and other pieces in prose and verse, who died April 14, 1835, aged 30 years. Erected by his father and mother, Robert and Isobel Grant, Affrosk, Banchory-Ternan.

" Though young in years, and not unknown to fame;
Though worth and genius both had told his name;
Though hope was high and certain honour near,
He left the world without a sigh or tear;—
Yes! trusting in the Saviour's power to save,
No sting had death, no terror had the grave;
His parting words, in prospect of the tomb,
Were, 'Dearest Mother, I am going home!'"

Grant was born in the parish of Banchory-Ternan on the 26th May, 1805. He received an ordinary education at the parish school, and was thereafter employed in desultory work about his father's farm. After some changes he became clerk in the office of a solicitor. In 1828 he published his " Juvenile Lays," and in 1830 "Kincardineshire Traditions," a small volume of ballads. To *Chambers's Edinburgh Journal* he furnished a series of tales and sketches, and in 1834 committed to the press his best work, " Tales of the Glens," which was published posthumously. Of a fine genius and amiable disposition, Grant afforded promise of attaining literary eminence. He was cut off by a pulmonary ailment.

ABERDEENSHIRE.

PARISH OF ABERDEEN.

In the chapel of King's College (founded by Bishop Elphinston in 1494) a monument celebrates Henry Scougal, Professor, first of Philosophy and afterwards of Theology in that institution. The inscription is as follows :—

" Memoriæ sacrum Henricus Scougal reverendi in Christo patris, Patricii episcopi Abredonensis filius ; philosophiæ, in hoc academia regia per quadrennium totidemque annis ibidem theologiæ professor, ecclesiæ in Auchterless uno anno interstite pastor; multa in tam brevis vitæ curriculo, didicit, præstitit, docuit : cœli avidus et cœlo, maturus obiit anno Dom. 1678. Ætatis suæ 28 et hic exuvias mortalitatis posuit."

Second son of Bishop Patrick Scougal, the subject of the preceding epitaph was born in June, 1650. Educated at King's College, he there so greatly distinguished himself that in his nineteenth year he was appointed regent of philosophy. He was one of the first Scottish professors who taught the philosophy of Bacon. After ministering for a year in the parish of Auchterless, he was promoted to the Professorship of Theology in King's College. He died on the 27th June, 1678, at the early age of twenty-eight. He composed an able work, entitled " The Life of God in the Soul of Man," and left several treatises in MS. To the library of King's College he bequeathed his collection of books, with 5000 marks to increase the salary of the Professor of Theology.

St. Nicholas Church, an imposing ecclesiastical structure, was removed in 1732, when the present fabric of the West Church was raised upon its site. On a pillar of St. Nicholas church was inscribed the following epitaph :—

" Robert Davidson, provost of Aberdeen, was killed at the battle of Harlaw in the year 1411.

In St. Nicholas church was commemorated Sir Paul Menzies of Kilmundy, and his wife Barbara Gordon. Menzies, was on twelve occasions elected chief magistrate. His monument was thus inscribed :—

D. O. M. S.

" Et memoriæ Pauli Minesii a Kinmundy, equestris ordinis viri, qui nobili familia editus hic vitam egit, duodecies concord. civium suffrag. electus præfectus urbis. tot ann. tenuit; miti ingenio. comitate morum omnibus charus; unico eoque concordi conjugio felix jam octuagenarius in spem beatæ resurrectionis, mortalit exuv. deposuit mense Decembris M. D. C. L. I. Alexander filius et hæres optimo parenti F. C. Sub hoc etiam saxo quiescunt ossa Barbaræ Gordonæ ejusdem Alexandris conjugis, quæ vita abiit 4 Cal. Novembris anno MDCLVII."

A monumental brass in St. Nicholas church bore this legend :—

" Sub spe beatæ resurrectionis, hic quiescit D. Duncanus Liddelus, doctor medicus, Joannis Liddeli, civis Abredonensis filius. Obiit xvii. Decembris Anno Dom MDCXIII. Ætatis suæ LII."

" Æternæ memoriæ D. Duncani Liddeli doct. medici, quem virtus nascentem excepit; recondita in medicina ac omnibus philosophiæ et matheseos partibus peritia natum excoluit; liberalitas supra œquales extulit; cui annum stipendium debet publicus matheseos in academiæ Abredonensi professor, victumque ejusdem academiæ sex alumni, fama posthuma meritorum perpetua testis M. H. D. C. Q."

Dr. Liddel was born at Aberdeen in 1561, and was educated first, at King's College, and afterwards in Germany. He was appointed first physician at the Court of Brunswick, and professor of mathematics in the university of Helmstadt. He subsequently settled in his native city, and at his death, which took place in 1613, established a mathematical chair in Marischal College. Of his several works, the best known is that entitled "The Art of Preserving Health."

In St. Nicholas church Gilbert Menzies of Pitfoddels, and his spouse Marjory Liddel, are thus celebrated :—

" Tumulus honorabilis viri Gilberti Mengzeis de Pitfoddels

quondam præpositi burgi de Aberdeen et Marjoriæ Liddel, ejus conjugis qui Gilbertus obiit 1439."

In St. Nicholas church, a burial aisle belonged to the old family of Irvine of Drum. On a copperplate in the aisle was the following legend :—

"Hic sub esta sepultura jacet honorabilis et famosus miles Dominus Alexander de Irvyne secundus, quondam Dominus de Droum, Dachynder et Foreglen qui obit . . . die mensis . . . anno Domini MCCCC."

"Hic etiam jacet nobilis domina, Domina Elizabeth de Kyth, filia quondam domini Roberti de Kyth militis, Marescalli Scotiæ, uxor quondam dicti domini Alexandri de Irvyne, quæ obiit . . . die mensis . . . . anno Dom. MCCCC."

Sir Alexander Irvine was son of Sir William de Irwin, who received from Robert the Bruce a grant of the forest of Drum. Sir Alexander's son, who bore the same Christian name, held a command in the Lowland army at the battle of Harlaw. He fought hand to hand with Maclean of Dowart, and fell along with his combatant. In the ballad entitled "The Battle of Harlaw," he is celebrated thus :—

> " Gude Sir Alexander Irving
> The much renownit Laird of Drum,
> Nane in his days was bettir sene
> Quhen they war 'semblit all and sum ;
> To prais him we sould not be dumm,
> For valour, wit, and worthyness
> To end his Days he ther did cum
> Quhois ransom is remeidyless."

The " Drum aisle " contained the remains of Sir Alexander Irvine of Drum, an attached supporter of Charles I. He was excommunicated by the Covenanters, and falling into their hands, was sentenced to death. The defeat of his opponents at Kilsyth in 1645 led to his preservation. On the Restoration he was offered the

* " Scottish Ballads," edited by James Maidment. Edin. 1868. Vol. I. p. 208.

earldom of Aberdeen, but he preferred to retain his original designation. He died in 1687.

In St. Nicholas churchyard, Principal Guild of Marischal College, and his wife Katharine Rolland, are thus celebrated:—

"Sanctiss. et individ. Trinitati S. et piæ memoriæ Gulielmi Guild, qui in hac urbe natus et institutus sacrisque studiis a teneris innutritus primum curæ ecclesiæ de Kinedwar admotus, eaque per XXIII. annos administrata, a municibus suis in hanc urbem vocatus, jam S. S., theologiæ doctor et Carolo regi a sacris, per decennium hic ecclesiastis munere functus; inde translatus ad collegium regale ubi primarii onus ad decennium sustinuit donec rebus apud nos turbatis integritas ejus livorem temporum non effugit: inde igitur digressus, hic, ubi canabula, nidum senectutis posuit. Non tamen inerti otio deditus, sed voce, calamo et inculpata vita aliis exemplum fuit. Amplum et innocenter partum patrimonium multo maximam partem piis usibus legavit. Conjunx quoque quæ sua erant iisdem usibus addixit. Vixit annos lxxi. et ad vii. cal. Augusti anni, MDCLVII. in spem optassimæ resurrectionis, mortalitatem explevit.

"Catharina Rowen superstes vidua, dilectissimo marito, cumquo concorditer xlvii. plenos annos vixit H . M . L . M . F . C . hoc monumentum lugens mœstusque fieri curavit. Nec cœpisse, nec fecisse, virtutis est, sed perfecisse."

Dr. William Guild was son of a prosperous armourer in the city. Born in 1586, he was educated at Marischal College, and in 1609 was admitted minister of King Edward, in the Presbytery of Turriff. From King Edward he was, in 1631, translated to the second charge of St. Nicholas' church, and in 1640 was promoted to the principalship of King's College. Of this office he was deprived in 1651 by a military commission under General Monk. He died in 1657. Abounding in benevolence, he endowed an hospital for decayed workmen, and otherwise devoted an ample fortune to charitable uses. His ecclesiastical opinions were unfixed; he at first inclined towards Episcopacy, latterly he subscribed the Covenant, and upheld Presbytery. He composed numerous theological works, some of which have been reprinted. His portrait is preserved in Trinity Hall, Aberdeen. His widow left endowments for six bursars in philosophy and two bursars in theology, and made some other important bequests.

As a minister of Aberdeen Dr. Guild was succeeded by the celebrated Andrew Cant, whose monument in St. Nicholas churchyard is thus inscribed :—

" Sub hoc marmore, quiescit Dei servus, D. Andræas Cantæus, vir suo seculo summus, qui orbi huic et urbi ecclesiastes voce et vita inclinatam religionem sustinuit, degeneres mundi mores refinxit, ardens et amans Boanerges et Barnabas, magnes et adamas, academiæ rector labantem rem literariam levavit intemeratæ pietatis, illibatæ constantiæ, invicti animi ; quem tot annos cum Deo purum probasset hoc ævo virtutum effœto atque summam hujus vitreæ felicitatis videns in vanitati sistentem, veram eam, quæ nec temporum metis, neque voluptatis modis circumscribitur, propiore spe et augurio præcepisset, animam Christo suo placide reddidit XLIX. annis sui ministerii prius emensis, nec paucioribus auspiciatissimi fœderis cum Margareta Irvina, muliere lectissima, anno nat. Dom. CIↃIↃCLXIII., pridie calendas Maii. Ætatis suæ LXXIX. qui mortuus adhuc loquitur, vale."

Mr. Cant was a native of Haddingtonshire. From the office of Regent of Humanity, in King's College, he was admitted to the ministry at Alford about the year 1616, and in 1633 was preferred to the newly erected parish of Pitsligo. He was known as one of the apostles of the Covenant, from his zeal in procuring signatures to that document. In 1638 he was translated to Newbattle, and from thence to the first charge of Aberdeen in 1641. He was chosen Moderator of the General Assembly in 1650 ; he joined the Protesters in 1651, and being accused of publishing the sentiments set forth in Rutherford's " Lex Rex," he, in 1660, demitted his charge. He died on the 30th April, 1663, aged seventy-nine. An unbending advocate for the clerical prerogative, he for a time compelled both his congregation and the magistracy to submit to his ministerial authority. In temper somewhat uneven, he was actuated by sincere piety and abundant conscientiousness.

Resting on the wall of St. Nicholas churchyard a monument

thus commemorated Dr. Patrick Sibbald, a native of the city, and latterly Professor of Theology in Marischal College:—

"Patricius Sibbald, S.S.T.D. a primis annis, Deo, religioni et literis consecratus, ad animarum curam, hac in urbe natali, anno 1666 et ad SS.T. professionem in academia Mariscalle, anno 1685 vocatus; vir solidæ eruditionis, sinceræ pietatis, illibati candoris, in prædi- cando et docendo facundus, felix, veritatis et pacis cultor assiduus; in vita munificus; pietatem in dictam academiam templa egentes testatus, obiit 14 Novembris anno Dom 1697, ætatis suæ 57. Et hic, cum parentibus ac pia conjuge Joanna Scougal, reverendi patris episcopi Abredonensis filia, mortalitatis exuvias deposuit."

In St. Nicholas churchyard a monument thus celebrates three members of the old family of Mowat.

"Jacobi Mowat de Airdo, viri privatim publiceque egregii, quic- quid fuit, hic jacet; quod est si requiras, cælum specta.
"Hic beatam præstolatur resurrectionem, magister Jacobus Mowat de Logie, Antiquissimæ Mowatorum gentis secundus; pietate vero et omnigena virtute, paucis aut nemini secundus, qui obiit 5 Maii 1662. Necnon Margareta Mowat conjunx ejus dilectissima, eadem familia oriunda, quæ monumentum hoc a majoribus con- ditum, denuo instaurandum, et pecunia civitati huic legata per- petuo conservandum curavit, et fatis concessit septimo martii die anno 1700.

"Debita naturæ solvis, lætare triumpha
Corporis O tandem carcere liber abis."

In St. Nicholas churchyard John Jaffray, of Dilspro, Provost of Aberdeen, with his wife, Janeta Forrest, and Thomas Jaffray, of Dilspro, with his wife, Margaret Gordon of Aberzeldie, are thus commemorated:—

"Hic jacet vir nobilissimus, Joannes Jaffray, de Dilspro, Abre- doniæ, qui obiit 10 Junii, 1684. Necnon magister Thomas Jaffray, de Dilspro, ejus filius, qui obiit 19 Septembris, 1695. Hic in Christo requiescit Joneta Forrest, illustrissimi D. Joannis Jaffray, quondam Abredoniarum, Præfecti, conjunx pientissima; quæ divinis animi, virtutis et gratiæ dobitus, supra ætatis sortem et seculi genium evecta, molestæ exuviis mortalitatis libera, cœlum ac immortalitatem induit 4 March, Anno Dom. 1656. Necnon et Margareta Gordon ab Aberzeldie, excultissima ejusdem conjunx quæ fato cessit Octob. 11, Anno Dom. 1678."

The following Latin epitaph adorns the monument of Professor John Menzies :—

"Hic situs est D. Joannes Menesius, Presbyter et S. S. theologiæ professor in academia Abredonensi, 34, annis ; illustri familia ortus sublimis ingenio et eloquentia æque clarus ; in scholis disputator, subtilis acer et eruditus ; in verbo divino prædicando præpotens facundus et frequens ; orthodoxæ religionis propugnator invictus ; vera pietate, vitæ innocentia, morum suavitati omnibus charus ; tandem laboribus officii fractus : in spem beatæ resurrectionis, mortalis exuvias deposuit, February 1, 1684, ætatis 60.

"Hic etiam requiescunt cineres filii ejusdem magistri Joannis Menesii, A.M. optimæ spei juvenis, qui obiit 20 Augusti, 1682, ætatis 18. Poni curavit mæstissima conjunx et mater Margareta Forbes."

In 1649, Mr. Menzies was promoted from the second charge of St. Nicholas parish to Greyfriars' church. He joined the Protesters in 1651, and at the call of Cromwell proceeded to London in 1654 to deliberate respecting ecclesiastical affairs. After the Restoration he inclined towards episcopacy, and was supposed to desire the office of a bishop. In 1679 he obtained his professorship in King's College. Before his death he expressed his firm adherence to the cause of Presbytery. His wife, who is named on his tombstone, was eldest daughter of Sir William Forbes, of Craigievar.

George Davidson, of Pettens, a builder and endower of churches, has the following epitaph :—

"Æternæ memoriæ Georgii Davidsone, de Pettens, viri vitæ integritate, ac profusæ in egenos largitate et in Deum pietate, vere insignis, de ecclesia universaque republica et hac civitate Abredonensi quam optime meriti. Hic præter plurimas donationes in perpetuum pauperum subsidium ac usus publicos, pontem de Inche reparandum, pontemque haud inelegante structura de Bruxburne construendum curavit. Terras de Pettens et Bogfairlie, cum quibusdam pecuniarum summis, ecclesiæ Abredonensi donavit, in perpetuum usum divini ibidem verbi præconis ; templum etiam de Newhills ædificari fecit, ac pro majore regni Dei incremento, in sustentationem prædicatorum evangelii ibidem, dictas etiam terras de Newhills, raro exemplo dicavit. Denatus est anno M. D. C. LXIII."

In St. Nicholas churchyard the following classical inscription, composed by Dr. James Gregory, of Edinburgh, adorns the tombstone of Dr. Beattie, author of " The Minstrel " :—

" Memoriæ Sacrum Jacobi Beattie, LL.D., ethices in academia Marescallana hujus urbis per XLIII. annos Professoris meretissimi viri, pietate, probitate, ingenio atque doctrina præstantis, scriptoris, elegantissimi poetæ suavissimi Philosophi vere Christiani. Natus est V. Nov. anno MDCCXXXV. Obiit XVIII. Aug., MDCCCIII. Omnibus liberis orbus quorum natu maximus Jacobus Hay Beattie, vel a puerilibus annis, patrio, vigens ingenio. Novumque decus jam addens paterno suis carissimus patriæ flebilis, lenta tabe consumptus periit, anno ætatis XXIII., Geo. et Mar. Glennie, N. M. P."

Dr. Beattie was born at Laurencekirk, where his father kept a small shop. Educated at Marischal College, he was in his eighteenth year appointed parish schoolmaster of Fordoun. In 1753 he was elected usher in the grammar school of Aberdeen ; and, his abilities becoming known, he was in 1760 preferred to the chair of Moral Philosophy in Marischal College. Ten years afterwards appeared his "Essay on Truth," an answer to the sceptical tenets of David Hume. This work obtained unprecedented favour, and the author was introduced to George III. and had conferred on him a Civil List pension of £200 a year. In 1771 Dr. Beattie produced the first part of the " Minstrel ; " the second part was added in 1774. This delightful poem entirely justifies its author's fame ; it retains its place as a British classic. Dr. Beattie suffered a severe trial in the death of his son, James Hay Beattie, a young man of remarkable attainments, and who had been appointed his assistant and successor in his professorial chair. The mental aberration of his amiable wife was another trial which bore heavily on his sensitive nature. He died in 1803, in his sixty-eighth year.

In St. Nicholas churchyard, monuments commemorate Principals Blackwell, Osborne, Campbell, and Brown, and Professors Stuart and Kidd, all of Marischal College.

Monumental tablets in the West Church celebrate Mrs. Allardyce of Dunnottar, Captain Cushnie, a public benefactor, and Dr. Copland, Professor of Natural Philosophy in Marischal College. In the East Church are commemorated the Rev. Adam Heriot, first Protestant minister of St. Nicholas Church, and his wife "Effemie Schevis," a native of Fifeshire. Mr. Heriot died on the 28th August, 1574.

In Drum's aisle a monumental statue commemorates James Blaikie, Provost of Aberdeen. Executed by Mr. Steell, it was. erected in 1844.

A statue of the Prince Consort, executed by Baron Marochetti, was erected at Aberdeen in October, 1863. The Prince is seated, dressed as a field-marshal.

In September, 1866, a statue of Her Majesty the Queen was placed at the corner of St. Nicholas Street, opposite the top of Market Street. Raised at the cost of £1,000, subscribed by working men, it was sculptured by Alexander Brodie, a local artist. The figure, composed of Sicilian marble, is eight feet six inches in height, and rests on a richly polished pedestal of Aberdeen granite. The Queen is represented standing, bearing a sceptre in her right hand, and clasping in her left the folds of a Scottish plaid.

PARISH OF ABERDOUR.

Within the nave of the old church is the burial-place of the Bairds, of Auchmedden. The first of the House commemorated is George Baird, of Auchmedden, who died 29th May, 1593. The estate was acquired by Andrew Baird, in 1534; it was sold to Lord Haddo in 1750. The Bairds of Newbyth and Saughtonhall, baronets, are descended from this House.

The family of Leslie of Coburty inter in the old church.

A burial-aisle to the south of the church is used by the Gordons of Aberdour.

Tombstones commemorate several incumbents of the cure, and their families.

PARISH OF ABOYNE.

In the parish churchyard a tombstone thus commemorates the wife of the Rev. James Gordon, for some years minister of the parish :—

"Within this isle, interred behind these stones,
Are pious, wise, good Mary Forbes' bones,
To Balfling daughter, and of blameless life,
To Mr. Gordon, pastor here, the wife."

Mrs. Gordon was daughter of Mr. Forbes, of Balfling; she died 27th April, 1738, aged 46. Her husband was translated to Alloa in 1736. He was moderator of the General Assembly in 1734, and died 6th August, 1749.

A gravestone is inscribed thus :—

"Here lys below these stones
Pious, virtuous Jean Wishart's bones,
Wife to John Bain;
Sometimes in Bridgend, of Knockandock.
All that was decent and discreet
Did in her parts and in her person meet;
She made appear in her unblemished life
The tender mother and the loving wife."

PARISH OF AUCHTERLESS.

The family mausoleum of Duff of Hatton, contains several monumental tablets. These commemorate Alexander Duff, Esq., of Hatton, who died 7th December, 1753; Gordon William Duff, of Hatton, who died 17th September, 1866, and other members of the House.

An altar-stone is thus inscribed :—

"James Cruikshank, in Toukshill, died 13 Jan., 1814, aged 71. His mother, Margaret Topp, died 1769, aged 64. He endowed a

bursary at King's College, another at Marischal College, each of
£20 a year, and astricted to the names of Cruikshank and Tapp or
Topp, or otherwise to accumulate; and left handsome charities in
legacies to his friends. Inscribed in testimony of respect to the
said James Cruikshank in Toukskill, New Deer, by Alex. Cruikshank, in Middlehill, his nephew, 1818."

A monument celebrates several members of the family of
Chalmers, "in Kirktown." Three of those commemorated are James
Chalmers, died 1846; Alexander Chalmers, died 1848; and George
Chalmers, died 1852. The last founded and endowed an Infant
School at Turriff.

PARISH OF BELHELVIE.

A funeral vault, now disused, belonged to the Earls of Panmure.
Gilbert Innes, of Rora, progenitor of Innes of Stow, is interred
in the churchyard.

From different tombstones we have these rhymes:—

> " We're here to-day, to-morrow yield our breath;
> O reader, tremble and prepare for death."

> " All you that have a soul to save,
> Extend your views beyond the grave;
> And whilst salvation is brought nigh,
> To Christ the Friend of sinners fly."

> " O trifle not your time away,
> Though youth be in its bloom;
> Prepare now to follow me
> And mind the world to come."

> " Some lonely friend will drop a tear,
> On these dry bones, and say,
> These once were strong, but now lies here,
> And mine must be as they."

PARISH OF BOURTIE.

At the east end of the church the stone effigies of a knight in armour and his lady are supposed to belong to the House of Meldrum, formerly potent in the district.

Within a mortuary enclosure an altar tomb is thus inscribed:—

"Here lie the remains of John Leith, of Kingudie, Esq., who died in 1764; and of his spouse Helen Simpson, who died in 1753; and of John Grant, of Rothmaise, Esq., who died in January, 1800, aged 86; and of Ann Leith, his spouse, liferentrix of Kingudie, who died 3 April, 1807, aged 84; and of Lieut. P. Grant, their son, who died in Sept., 1810; and also of Miss Jean Grant, their daughter, who died in April, 1815, aged 57.

PARISH OF CHAPEL OF GARIOCH.

About half a mile north-west of the parish church an upright stone commemorates a daughter of the *laird* of Balquharn, who was killed in a scuffle consequent on her attempt to elope with the son of a neighbouring landowner, who was obnoxious to his family.

In this parish was fought the battle of Harlaw, on the 24th July,. 1411, the combatants being the Earl of Mar, with the Scottish army, and Donald, Lord of the Isles, and his followers. In the field stone coffins and human remains are frequently found. Two mounds are known as Dennis' Cairn and Maclean's Grave; the former denotes the burial-place of Irvine, of Drum, the latter that of the chief of Maclean, both of whom perished in battle.

PARISH OF CRATHIE AND BRAEMAR.

On the south bank of the Dee, half a mile east of Balmoral, a monumental statue commemorates H.R.H. the Prince Consort. The Prince is represented in bronze as a Highland chief in full costume. The pedestal, a rough natural cairn of huge granite boulders, is ten and a half feet high ; it is surmounted by the figure, which is in height thirteen and a half feet. The left leg is slightly advanced. A favoured staghound leans against the Prince's right knee, and his right hand rests on the dog's head. The left hand grasps a rifle.

In the Free Church of Crathie, a tablet commemorative of the Prince, is thus inscribed :—

"To the noble and illustrious Prince Albert, K.G., Consort to Her Majesty Queen Victoria, and Lord of the Castle and lands of Balmoral, this tablet is dedicated, in deep sorrow for his early death, and in pious remembrance of his beneficent gift of the site whereon this church is erected, by those who worship under its roof."

In the churchyard a burial-aisle belongs to the old family of Farquharson, of Monaltrie and Balnabodach. It presents the following inscriptions :—

"1699. Within these walls lie the remains of Alexander Farquharson, of Monaltrie; John and Francis, both of Monaltrie, his sons ; Robert, his youngest son, and several other children, who died in infancy. Here also are interred Anne Farquharson, the wife of Alexander, Anne Ogilvie, the wife of John ; and Isobel Keith and Helen Baird, the wives of Robert. As also Amelia, Francis, and James, the children of Robert and Helen Baird. For their memory this stone is erected, with the warmest filial and fraternal affection, by William Farquharson, of Monaltrie. 1808."

"Erected A.D. 1824, by James Farquharson, Esq., Balnabodach. Sacred to the memory of James Farquharson, of Tullochcoy, who died in 1760; and his spouse May Farquharson, died 1729 ; Peter Farquharson, of Tullochcoy, born 1733, died 1801 ; Isabella Forbes, his spouse, born 1733, died 1780. George, Francis, and Donald, their sons, the former died 1787, the two latter in their infancy, James and Katherine, son and daughter of James Farquharson, Balnabodach, and Tullochcoy. The son died in 1805, the daughter in 1807. Ann, daughter of James Farquharson, of Balnabodach, and wife of Dr. Robertson, who died at Indego, 31 August, 1842, aged 34."

"In memory of James Farquharson, of Balnabodach, who died at Ballater, 10th October, 1843, aged 85 years; and Isabella McHardy, his wife, who died at Balnabodach, 9th September, 1827, aged 64 years. This tablet is erected as a mark of filial respect and affection by their three sons, Peter, John, and Alexander Farquharson, 1844. Also of their younger brother, George Farquharson, who died at Balnabodach, 26th December, 1841, aged 38 years."

In Braemar churchyard a burial-aisle belonging to the Farquharsons, of Invercauld, occupies the site of the old church. On marble tablets are these epitaphs :—

"Sacred to the memory of John Farquharson, of Invercauld, who was born in 1750. Sacred also to the memory of James Farquharson, of Invercauld, his son, who died 24 June, 1805, aged 83 ; and Amelia, Lady Sinclair, his spouse (daughter of Lord George Murray), who died in 1779. They had eleven children, all of whom, with the exception of the youngest, Catherine, died before them. Mary, Matilda, Jane, John, and George, lie interred with their parents in the ground adjoining; Charlotte, at Arnhill; Fanny, at Lisbon ; and Amelia, Margaret, and Ann, in the burying ground of North Leith."

"To the memory of Catherine, youngest daughter and heiress of James Farquharson, of Invercauld, born 4 May, 1774, died 27 Feb., 1845. To the memory of James Ross-Farquharson, her husband, Capt. R.N., (2d son of Sir John Lockhart-Ross, of Balnagowan, baronet), who died at Edinburgh, 5 Feb., 1809, aged 38 years. This tablet was erected after his mother's death, by her affectionate son, Aug., 1845."

"Sacred to the memory of James Farquharson, Esq. of Invercauld. Born April 25, 1808 ; died Nov. 20, 1862. This tablet is erected in affectionate remembrance, by his eldest son, Lieut.-Col. Farquharson, of the Scots Fusilier Guards."

On the north bank of the Dee, opposite Braemar Castle, a granite obelisk has been reared to the memory of the late Mr. Farquharson. It is thus inscribed :—

"In memory of James Farquharson, Esq., of Invercauld, by his tenantry and servants, to whom he was greatly attached. Born 25th April, 1808; died 20th Nov., 1862. 'The righteous shall be in everlasting remembrance,'—Psalm cxii. 6.

In Braemar churchyard a plain gravestone commemorates Peter Grant, farmer, who died at Auchendryne, 11th February, 1824, aged one hundred and ten years. Grant was a sergeant-major in the army of Prince Charles Edward, at Culloden, and, being taken prisoner, was carried to Carlisle; he escaped by scaling the wall of the castle. In 1820 he presented a petition to George IV., in which he described himself as "His Majesty's oldest enemy;" it was graciously received, and brought to the petitioner a pension of a guinea a week during the remainder of his life.

PARISH OF CRIMOND.

Near the mill of Haddo a spot called " Battle fauld" denotes the grave of Sir James the Rose, who was slain in a combat by Sir John the Graeme, as they contended for the hand of Lord Buchan's daughter. On the event is founded the ballad of " Sir James the Rose."

PARISH OF CRUDEN.

A burial-aisle in the old church belonged to the noble family of Errol. Herein was interred Dr. James Drummond, Bishop of Brechin, who died in 1695, aged seventy-six. In a mortuary enclosure a granite monument is thus inscribed :—

"In memory of Lady Florence-Alice Hay, infant daughter of

the Earl and Countess of Errol; born May 28th, 1858, died May
15th, 1859.   (Jer. 31. 3 ; Mal. 3. 17.)

Within an enclosure, a flat gravestone celebrates Charles Gordon
of Auchlenchries, who died 9th June, 1777, aged seventy-three.

An altar-stone commemorates Peter Smith, of Aldie, physician,
who died 22nd November, 1813, aged seventy-two ; also his wife
and two of their children.

A gravestone commemorates the Rev. J. Duncan, minister of
Dunrossness, who was lost in the schooner ' Doris ' opposite Slains
Castle, during a gale on the 22nd February, 1813.

On a flat tombstone, the Rev. Alexander Keith is celebrated
thus :—

" S. M. of the Rev. Mr. Alexander Keith, whose probity of heart,
sanctity of manners, earnestness of conversation, and unwearied
attention to all the duties of his office as a minister of the Church
of Scotland, under the many trying events of 8 and 40 years,
rendered his life valuable, his death lamentable, and his memory
precious.   Ob. Oct. 27, 1763, æt. 68 :—

> Ultime Scotorum in Crudenanis, Kethe, Sacerdos,
> Fratribus et plebi diu memorande, vale,
> Posuit unici nati pietas."

Son of the Rev. George Keith, minister of Deer, the subject of
the preceding epitaph was born on the 22nd May, 1695.   He
became Episcopal clergyman at Cruden, where he officiated till the
period of his death.   His epitaph was composed by the Rev. John
Skinner, author of "Tullochgorum."   Mr. Keith was author of " A
View of the Diocese of Aberdeen," which, under the editorial care
of the late Dr. Joseph Robertson, has been printed for the Spalding
Club.

The following rhymes are from tombstones in Cruden churchyard :—

> " After the cares of former life,
>   And many labours past ;
> Here is the harbour of old age—
>   Its safeguard now at last."

"When mortal man resigns this transient breath,
The body only I give o'er to death;
The part dissolv'd and broken frame I mourn,
What came from earth, I see to earth return."

"Here lys intomb'd under this mould'ring dust,
A man whose soul was truly virtuous:
A woman, too, who baseness did despise,
And they both rest, in hopes again to rise
To happiness ; thou, reader, drop a tear,
And virtue's path to follow, learn here."

"Here in one grave two lovely virgins ly,
Two sisters dear, destined in youth to dy ;.
Their persons beauty, grace their souls adorn'd,
No wonder then their death is deeply mourn'd.
In glory they shall rise and bless their doom,
Then shall they have an everlasting bloom—
Learn hence, fair virgins, in your early days,
Your great Redeemer by your lives to praise."

PARISH OF DRUMBLADE.

In the parish churchyard a mortuary enclosure belongs to the old family of Bisset, of Lessendrum. It contains the following inscriptions :—

"Hic iacet honorabilis vir, Georgivs Bisset de Lessendrvm, qvi obiit 25 Ianvarii 16 . ., et ætatis svæ anno 73 : Aetatem ornavit primam mihi vivida virtvs et prisca at lapsu sovs redi.viva domvs famam terra sol . . . perennem indigetvm regviem posthvma vita dedit."

"Sacred to the memory of Maurice-George Bisset, Esq., of Lessendrum, who died at Lessendrum, on the 16 of I)ec., 1821, in the 64th year of his age. This tablet is jointly inscrib ed by Harriet his affectionate and mournful widow, and his broth er and imme- diate successor, William, Lord Bishop of Raphoe, in honour of his name, and in grateful recollection of the many virtues that adorned his endearing character."

" Sacred to the memory of William Bisset, D.D., late Lord Bishop of Raphoe, and proprietor of Lessendrum, who died on the 4th Sept., A.D. 1834, aged 75 years."

Tombstones commemorate the Rev. George Abel, minister of the parish, died 14th September, 1794; Rev. Robert Gordon, minister of the parish, died 27th November, 1820, aged seventy; Major-General John Gordon, R.A., died 1861; and George Macpherson, factor on the Huntly estates, died 1864.

These rhymes are from tombstones in Drumblade churchyard:—

> " Mourn not, my friends, for me in vain ;
> This silent tomb cures all my pain—
> For death ere long will visit thee,
> Therefore prepare to follow me."

> " Beneath a sleeping infant lyes,
>   To earth whose body's lent,
> More glorious shall hereafter rise,
>   Tho' not more innocent.
> When the archangel's trump shall blow,
>   And souls to bodies join,
> Millions shall wish their days below
>   Had been as short as thine."

PARISH OF ECHT.

In the churchyard a tombstone commemorates John Elphinston, of Bellabeg, died 10th October, 1742, aged seventy ; Rev. Alexander Henderson, minister of the parish, died 30th May, 1813, aged fifty-seven ; and the Rev. William Ingram, minister of the parish, died 16th May, 1848, aged seventy-nine.

PARISH OF ELLON.

Within the parish church a marble tablet is thus inscribed :—

" John Leith-Ross of Arnage, died 15 May 1839, aged 63 : Elizabeth Young, his spouse, co-heiress of Bourtie, died 9 June, 1852, aged 70 : their third son William Ross, M.D., died 28 Sep. 1834, aged 22 ; George, their fourth son, and Frederick, their grandson, died in childhood."

Mr. Ross, merchant in Aberdeen, acquired the estate of Arnage about the close of the seventeenth century.

The two following inscriptions commemorate members of the old family of Annand :—

" Monumentum marmoreum honorabilis Alexandri Annand, baronis quondam de Ochterellon, qui obiit ix. Julii, A.D. 1601 ; ejusque piæ conjugis, Margaretæ Fraser, filiæ quondam Do de Philorth quæ obiit Aug., A.D. 1602.—Salus per Christum."

" Sub hoc quoque tumulo resurrectionem expectant corpora Alexandri Annand de Ochterellon, filii dicti Alexandri, qui obiit——, et caræ suæ conjugis, Margaretae Cheyne, filiæ Dō de Esselmont, quæ obiit——

A burial aisle belongs to the family of Forbes, of Waterton.

Within an enclosure a monumental tablet is thus inscribed :—

" To the memory of Keith Turner of Turnerhall, this stone is erected by his sorrowing widow.   He was born January 20, 1768 ; departed this life Oct. 20, 1808, and was, by his own desire, laid into the grave of his beloved mother, Elizabeth Urquhart of Meldrum, born July 10, 1735 ; died Feb. 28, 1786.   Also to the memory of his widow, Mrs. Anna Margaret Turner of Turnerhall, ob . . Oct. 1823 ; Æ. 50 years."

In St. Mary's episcopal chapel a marble tablet celebrates Charles Napier Gordon, of Erlemont, and three of his sisters, children of George Gordon, of Hallhead, nephew of George, Earl of Aberdeen.

PARISH OF FOVERAN.

An ancient burying-ground belongs to the family of Udny, of Udny.

These monumental inscriptions are from the parish church-yard :—

> "Some kindly friend will drop his Tear
> On our dry bones and say
> These once were strong as mine appear
> And mine must be as they."

> "My flesh which all consumed is
> The very same shall rise
> Yea I shall see Christ's lovely face
> With these my very eyes."

"We have their names here but themselves are gone, they have the crown indeed but we have the cross, they find the gain but we the loss. Death broke the cage, he let the sparrows flee, who now have found a nest on high, even God's own altar to Eternity."

PARISH OF FYVIE.

In the parish churchyard is the old burial-place of the Gordons of Gight, maternal ancestors of Lord Byron. A gravestone denotes the grave of Agnes Smyth, the heroine of "Tiftie's Bonnie Annie," a pathetic Scottish ballad.

PARISH OF GLENMUICK, TULLICH AND GLENGAIRN.

In Glenmuick churchyard is the burying-place of the Gordons of Abergeldie, cadets of the noble house of Huntly. Monuments belonging to the family are thus inscribed :—

"James Gordon, 1754. Alexander Gordon his son, and Agnes Mawer Gordon, 1766, died Dec. 1798, aged 48.

"To the memory of Charles Gordon, Esq., of Abergeldie, who died March 1796, and of Alison Hunter, his spouse, of the family of Burnside, who died March 1800. They lived together nearly half a century on this part of Deeside; the best of parents, giving good example in every way, and serving to the utmost of their power all who stood in need."

"Here lies interred the remains of the late Peter Gordon, Esq., of Abergeldie, eldest son of Charles Gordon, Esq. He succeeded his father in 1769, and died the 6th of Dec., 1819, aged 68."

Within the ruin of the old church of Tullich is a burial-place of the Farquharsons of Whitehouse, a branch of the Invercauld family. Two of the monuments present these legends :—

"These walls inclose the burial-ground of the family of Farquharson of Whitehouse and Shiels; where are interred the remains of James Farquharson of Whitehouse, brother of Colonel Donald Farquharson of Monaltrie (called Donald Og), who died in 1666, and Harry his son, who died in 1716, and Margaret his granddaughter. Also the remains of Francis Farquharson of Shiels, the eldest son of Harry, who died in 1733; and Harry, the son of Francis, and his wife Jean Rose, who both died in 1760, and their sons Hugh and Donald, who died in early youth. This memorial has been erected by their surviving descendants, 1826.— Requiescant in pace."

"Margaret Garden, wife of William Farquharson of Monaltrie, died at Aberdeen, January 25, 1857, aged 83."

At a short distance from Tullich churchyard an obelisk on the top of a knoll is inscribed thus :—

" In memory of William Farquharson of Monaltrie, who died at Vevay, in Switzerland, 20 Nov. 1828, aged 75 years. Erected by his affectionate widow, Margaret Garden, in 1836. She died Jan. 1857, and was buried at Tullich.

PARISH OF INSCH.

Two flat stones commemorate James Jopp, farmer, who died in 1672, and Andrew Jopp, merchant, progenitors of Provost Jopp of Aberdeen, who conveyed to Dr. Samuel Johnson the freedom of that city.

Tombstones denote the graves of the Rev. Alexander Mearns, minister of the parish, who died 4th October, 1789, aged eighty-nine, and the Rev. George Daun, minister of the parish, who died 21st May, 1821, aged seventy.

From tombstones in Insch churchyard we have these rhymes :—

> " Here with the aged lies a lovely boy,
>   His father's darling and his mother's joy ;
>   Yet Death, regardless of the parents' tears,
>   Snatch'd him away while in the bloom of years."

> " Nipt by the wind's untimely blast,
>   Scorch'd by the sun's directer ray ;
>   The momentary glories waste,
>   The short-liv'd beauties die away.
>   Yet these, new rising from the tomb,
>   With lustre brighter far shall shine ;
>   Reviv'd thro' Christ with 'during bloom,
>   Safe from diseases and decline."

PARISH OF INVERURY.

A tombstone, adorned with the Innes and Elphinstone arms, is thus inscribed :—

" Heir lyis Valter Innes in Artones, vha depairtit the 27 day of Ivnii 1616 zeiris ; and Meriorie Elphinstovne, his spovs, vha depairtit the 15 day of November 1622 zeiris."

A monument enclosed by a railing bears the following legend :—

" Sacred to the memory of James Anderson, depute-clerk of Justiciary, who died at Edinburgh, 2 Jan. 1833, aged 66. By his own unaided merit he raised himself to a situation of great trust and responsibility, which for the long period of 45 years he filled with the greatest credit, and concluded a life spent in the public service regretted by all who knew him. Also Margaret Anderson, his sister, who died at Edinburgh, 2 June, 1850, aged 80."

PARISH OF KEITH-HALL AND KINKELL.

In Keith-hall churchyard a mortuary enclosure belongs to the noble house of Kintore. It contains memorial tablets bearing the following inscriptions :—

" In memory of Anthony-Adrian, eighth Earl of Kintore, who was born 20th April, 1794, and died at Keith-hall, 11th July, 1844, in the 51st year of his age. ✠ And also of his son William-Adrian, Lord Inverury, who was born 2d Sept, 1822, and died Dec. 17th, 1843, aged 21 years."

" Erected by Lord Kintore to the memory of his beloved Aunt the Lady Mary Keith, daughter of William, 7th Earl of Kintore, who died at Bath, July 5, 1864, aged 69 years."

The Rev. George Skene Keith, D.D., is on his monument celebrated thus :—

" Near this wall are interred the mortal remains of the Rev. Dr. George-Skene Keith, minister of the parish of Keithhall for 44 years, and of Tulliallan in Perthshire for 8 months. Born at Auquhorsh, Nov. 6, 1752, he died at Tulliallan House, March 7, 1823. Distinguished and beloved as the clergyman of a parish, remarkable in a wide sphere for his learning and science, of great mental and bodily activity, he preserved in age the same vivacity and cheerfulness, the same love of knowledge, warmth of feeling, and untiring Christian benevolence which characterised his youth and manhood. Some gentlemen of this county, who had intended to present him with a memorial of their high respect for his character, but were prevented by his death, have erected this monument to his memory."

Dr. Keith represented the family of Keith of Auquhorsk. Indefatigable in the discharge of parochial duty, and an eloquent preacher, he composed a "Life of Principal George Campbell," "A View of Great Britain," and other works. His eldest son, Dr. Alexander Keith, minister of St. Cyrus, is author of a valuable work on Scripture Prophecy, and other esteemed publications.

Within the old church of Kinkell a pavement slab bears on one side the incised effigy of a warrior in mail armour, with the following marginal inscription:—

"Hic . iacet . nobilis . armiger . Gilbertus . de . Grie . . .
. . . . anno . . om . m . cccc . xi."

A shield on each side of the helmet indicates that the person commemorated belonged to the House of Greenlaw of that Ilk, Berwickshire. On the reverse of the stone, is the Forbes arms with the following legend:—

"Hic iacet honore illustris et sancta morum pietate ornat' Joannes Forbes d' Ardmurd' ej' cognois haeres 4 qui anno ætatis suæ : 66 : 8 iulii A.D. 1592 obiit."

John Forbes, of Ardmurdo, thus commemorated, was father of Alexander Forbes, Bishop of Aberdeen.

In the Balbithan aisle at Kinkell, a tablet is inscribed—

"Sacred to the memory of Benjamin Abernethie-Gordon, Esquire, the last Heir of Entail of Balbithan. Born 22nd May, 1782, died at Strand Villa, Ryde, Isle of Wight, 4th February, 1864."

Balbithan estate now belongs to the Earl of Kintore.

PARISH OF KILDRUMMY.

A portion of the old church forms the burial-aisle of the noble family of Elphinstone.

In the aisle are the following fragmentary inscriptions:—

. . . . VILLIAM . PATRICK . AND . DAVID . ELPHINSTOVN .
. . . . . ALEXANDER . LORD . ELPHINSTOVN . . . . TIT .
YIS . LYF."

"✠ HEIR . LYIS . ANE . . . . . MAN . MASTER . LO . . . ELPHYN-
STOVN . ALEXANDER . LORD . ELPHINSTOVN . QVHA . DEPARTIT
. FRA . YIS . LYF . YE . F . RST . OF . MAII . 1616 . BEING . OF
. . YE . AGE . OF . XXX . ZEIRIS."

" . . . . R . OF . THIS . COVE
. . . . . MEMBRIT . EVER . ON . DEATH
. . . . THE . MOST . GLORISLY . MAY . RINGE
. . . . AND . WITH . HIS . SAVLS . REDIMER
. . . . IN . . . NE . OF . BARNS."

Within a recess tomb in the old church, which represents an
armed knight and his lady, is the following fragmentary inscription:—

" Hic . iacet . alexr . de . forbes . quondam . dns . de
burchus . et . marjora. . . . . 155 . . ."

Alexander Forbes was great grandson of Alister Cam; his wife
was Marjory, third daughter of the sixth Lord Forbes.

Several tombstones commemorate members of the House of Reid
of Newmills, a family now extinct.

A mortuary enclosure forms the burial-place of the Lumsdens,
of Auchendor and Clova. It contains these legends :—

" Before this ston lyes Robert Lumsden, of Cushnay, and John
Lumsden of Auchendor, his second son, and Agnes Gordon, his
spous; and also Charles and Marjorie Lumsdens, laufvll son and
daughter to John Lumsden and Agnes Gordon. John Lumsden
dyed Janure 8, 1716, and of age 71 years, 1724 :
" Hoc, lector, tumulo tres contumulantur in uno,
" Cognati, Mater, Filius, atque Pater.
" Mors Janua vitæ."

" D.O.M. H.L. : K.G. Befor this stone lyes Kathrin Gordon,
daughter to the Laird of Buckie, and spouse to Hary Lumsden of
Cushnie, and five of her children ; and she depr. this life August
the 22nd, 1733, aged 31. Also the said Hary Lumsden of Cushnie
died the 8 day of June 1754, in the 69th year of his age.

" Befor this stone lyes James Lumsden, eldest lawfull son to
William Lumsden in Titaboutie, who depr. this life in Nov. 1730,
aged 40 years."

"In this ground are deposited the remains of John Lumsden of Cushnie, who died 12th June, 1795, aged 68; and Mrs. Anne Forbes, his spouse, daughter of John Forbes of New, who died 11 Nov. 1811, aged 76. In testimony of warm affection for their memory, this tablet is erected by their son John Lumsden, now of Cushnie, 1814."

"The grave of William Lumsden of Harlaw, who died at Mid Clova, Feb. 1758. Rachel Lumsden, his spouse, daughter of Chas. Lumsden, 2d son of John Lumsden of Auchindoir : she died at East Clova, Feb. 11, 1788, aged 77. Katharine, his daughter, spouse to John Leith, died at West Hills, Feb. 2, 1792; and of Harry Lumsden of Auchindoir, who died in April 1796. Margaret Rannie, widow of Dr. Jas. Young, R.N., died at Mid Clova, 6 June 1841, aged 76. Also Harry Leith-Lumsden of Auchindoir, youngest son of John Leith and Katherine Lumsden, who died at Aberdeen, 27 March 1844, in the 68th year of his age, and was interred here, 4 April following. Janet Young, or Duncan, wife of Harry Leith-Lumsden of Auchindoir, died at Edinburgh, 7 Jan. 1861, aged 73, and was interred here, 16th of same month."

An altar stone on the grave of the Rev. James Mc.William, minister of the parish, who died 6th April, 1771, aged seventy-one, bears these lines :—

> "Revd. and grave, he preached heaven's King,
> Because he knew it was a weighty thing ;
> And at his hearers, as he aim'd the dart,
> You'd well perceive it from his heart.
> Now called Home, a Faithful servt., lov'd
> Of his Great Master, and by him approv'd,
> Posest. of joys eternal, and above,
> He Sings, he Shines, he Reigns, where all is love.
> No pain is yr., no tears flow from his eyes,
> His Master purchas'd, he enjoys the prize."

PARISH OF KINCARDINE O' NEIL.

Within the chancel of the old church is a burial place belonging to the Frasers of Findrack. It presents these legends :—

"HERE . LYES . FRANCIS . FRAZER . OF . PITMVRCHIE . VHO .

D ... RTED . THIS . LIFE ... RIL . 29 . 1718 . IN . THE . 69TH .
YEAR . OF .. HIS . AGE."

"Near this stone, with the remains of many of his ancestors, is
interred the body of Francis Fraser, Esquire of Findrack, a Commander in the British, and Post Captain in the Portuguese Navy,
eldest son of Francis Fraser of Findrack, and Henrietta, daughter
of William Baird of Auchmedden. He served his country with
distinction for a long series of years, and was present at many
remarkable engagements. Born 22d August 1762, died 24th April
1824."

At Tornaveen an obelisk, reared by William N. Fraser, Esq., of
Tornaveen, brother of the proprietor of Findrack, is thus inscribed :—

"Colonel Robert Winchester, K.H., Born A.D. 1783 : Died A.D.
1846. During 37 years of active service with a spirit which shunned
no danger, he accompanied in sieges and in many marches and
battles the 92nd Regt., Gordon Highlanders. Lieut.-General the
Honourable Sir William Stewart, G.C.B., thus records his merits :—
'Many memorable services were rendered to the division of the
Army under my command during the arduous campaigns of the
years 1813-14, in the Peninsula and South of France by him, and
the gallant Light Infantry under his orders. I should be truly
ungrateful if I were ever to forget the valuable aid that I received
from him on that 25th of July, when we so nearly lost the Rock
and Pass of Maya. But his and his noble corps' conduct on that
and on every occasion where valour and self-devotion were eminently
called for during these campaigns, and in the decisive conflict of
Waterloo, are on record, and ever will be so, in the military annals
of those days.' To whom this memorial is erected by his nephew,
William N. Fraser, Esquire, 1865."

PARISH OF KING EDWARD.

In Craigston's aisle of the parish church a monument commemorates John Urquhart, tutor of Cromarty, and other members of
the family.

A mural monument is thus inscribed :—

"Joannes Urquhart, hoc in honorem Dei, et matris suæ Beatricis
Innes, dominæ a Cromertie memoriam erexit opus, anno 1599."

PARISH OF LEOCHEL.

In Leochel churchyard a burial aisle belongs to the family of Forbes, of Craigievar. Here was interred, in 1668, John Forbes, son of the Bishop of Caithness. Dr. John Forbes, Professor of Divinity in King's College, Aberdeen, son of Bishop Patrick Forbes, was buried at Leochel in 1648.

A plain tombstone celebrates the parents of the late Dr. Joseph Robertson, the eminent antiquary (vol. i., p. 141); it is thus inscribed :—

"In memory of Joseph Robertson, late merchant in Aberdeen, who departed this life 18th Feb. 1817, aged 42 years; and of Christian Leslie, his spouse, who died 11th March, 1859, aged 83 years."

A plain slab bears the following lines :—

"Here lyes Peter Milner, a sober man,
Who neither used to curse nor ban ;
Elizabeth Smith, she was his wife,
He had no other all his life.
He died in July 1784,
Aged 77, or little more,
And she in July 1779,
Years 55, was her lifetime.
With Robert and Jean, their children dear,
Elizabeth Milner, and Janet Fraser,
Their grand-children.
In Rumlie they lived just near by
And in this place their dust doth ly."

PARISH OF LOGIE-BUCHAN.

The Buchans of Auchmacoy formerly interred in the parish church. At their burial place two marble tablets bear the following inscriptions :—

"As a mark of affection and regard for the memory of Robert Buchan, third son of Thomas Buchan, Esq., of Auchmacoy, assistant-surgeon, H.E.I.C.S., who died at Cawnpore, 4 Sep. 1825, in the 24th year of his age. His brother John died in London, 4 Feb. 1829, aged 22 years, and is interred in the burying-ground belonging to the Church of St. John, Waterloo Road, London. Also, in memory of Euphemia Turner, widow of the late Thomas Buchan, Esq., of Auchmacoy, who died at Edinburgh, 22 Dec., 1832, and whose remains are interred here."

"Sacred to the memory of Thomas Buchan, Esq., of Auchmacoy, who died on the 12 Aug. 1819, and was interred in the family burying-ground within this church. Also, in remembrance of his eldest son Thomas, who died at Marseilles, in France, 3 Dec. 1818, aged 21 years, and was interred in the Protestant burying-ground of that city."

PARISH OF LOGIE-COLDSTONE.

In the churchyard of Coldstone a granite block presents the figure of an elegantly incised cross. It denotes the grave of an unknown churchman.

A tombstone commemorates the Rev. Andrew Tawse, minister of Greyfriars Church, Aberdeen, who died while in the act of performing Divine service on the 15th December, 1833, in his forty-seventh year.

On the altar stone is the following legend :—

"To the memory of Mr. George Forbes, Master in the R.N., who served many years in that rank, and gained high praise for his courage and conduct in many engagements, particularly in the memorable battle of Trafalgar, where Lord Nelson fell. On retiring from the Service, he became tacksman of Kinord, where he died 11 July 1821, aged 62. His wife Margaret Forbes, died 7 Oct. 1847, aged 74."

In the Logie churchyard a mortuary enclosure constituted the burying-place of the Gordons of Blelack, of whom the last male representative was an adherent of Prince Charles Edward.

Tombstones at Logie bears these rhymes :—

" Unmark'd by trophies of the great and vain
Here sleeps in silent tombs an honest train;
No folly wasted their paternal store,
No guilt, no sordid avarice, made it more ;
With honest fame, and sober plenty crown'd
They liv'd and spread their cheering influence round."

" Altho' this tomb no boasted titles keep
Yet silent here the private virtues sleep ;
Truth, candour, justice, altogether ran
And form'd a plain upright, honest man.
No courts he saw, nor mixt in publick rage,
Stranger to all the vices of the age ;
No lie, nor slander did his tongue defile—
A plain old Briton free from pride and guile.
Near five-score years he numbered ere he died,
And every year he number'd he enjoy'd.
This modest stone which few proud Marbles can,
May truly say Here lies an honest man ;
Ye great whose heads are laid as low,
Rise higher if you can."

PARISH OF LONGSIDE.

Within a mortuary enclosure monuments commemorate the Rev.
John Skinner, author of " Tullochgorum," and his wife, Grizel
Hunter. The inscriptions follow :—

"Glory to God above. Sacred to the memory of the Rev[d] John
Skinner, for 64 years and upwards Episcopal clergyman in this
parish, whose attainments as a Scholar, and Scriptural research as
a Divine, of which many written documents remain, acquired him
a name, never to be forgotten in the church in which he exercised
his ministry, while his Pastoral Labours in the charge committed
to him endeared him almost beyond example to the sorrowing flock,
by whom, in testimony of their heartfelt regard, this monument is
erected. "On the 16th day of June 1807, aged 86 years, he slept

the sleep of death in the arms of the Right Rev. John Skinner, Bishop of the diocese of Aberdeen, his only surviving son, who, with his family, and other numerous descendants, shall never cease to feel the most devout and lively veneration for the talents, the acquirements, and character of a progenitor, who lived so justly respected, and died so sincerely lamented."

" In the same grave over which the adjoining monument is placed to the memory of her venerable husband, lie the remains of his beloved wife Grizel Hunter, who died on the 21st day of Sept. 1799, in the 80th year of her age, having shewn herself through life the humble Christian, and, for nearly 58 years, a partner of every conjugal virtue.

" When such friends part—'tis the survivor dies."

Mr. Skinner was born on the 3rd October, 1721, at Balfour, parish of Birse, Aberdeenshire. His father, who was parochial schoolmaster, had as his first wife Jean Gillanders, widow of Donald Farquharson, of Balfour. The future poet was the only issue of this marriage. Having studied four sessions at Marischal College, he became assistant in the schools of Kenmay and Monymusk. By the persuasion of the non-juring clergyman at Monymusk, he was induced to join the episcopal church. Obtaining the appointment of private tutor, he proceeded to Zetland, where he formed the intimacy of the Rev. Mr. Hunter, a non-juring clergyman, whose eldest daughter he married. Returning to Aberdeenshire, he was in 1742 ordained as episcopal clergyman at Longside. In 1746 his chapel was destroyed by the soldiers of the Duke of Cumberland, and in 1753 he suffered six months' imprisonment at Aberdeen for preaching to more than four persons without accepting the oath of allegiance. He lived in a small thatched cottage, and satisfied with his lot declined all offers of preferment. He composed poetry in his youth; his songs were written at different periods for the amusement of his children. With the poet Burns, whose genius he early recognised, he maintained a friendly correspondence. A powerful theologian and general scholar, he published commentaries on different portions of Scripture, a Church History of Scotland, and other works. After the long incumbency of nearly sixty-five years at Longside, he removed to Aberdeen, at the invitation of his son, Bishop Skinner; he survived the change only a few days. Besides "Tullochgorum," Mr. Skinner composed the songs " John o' Badenyon," " The Ewie wi' the Crookit Horn," and " Lizzy Liberty."

On a plain tombstone a latin epitaph, composed by the Rev. John Skinner, celebrates William Tait, joiner, and his wife, Agnes Clerk, and the members of their family. It proceeds thus :—

" Sub hoc lapide cineres Gulielmi Tait, carpentarii in Ludquharn, et' Agnetis Clerk, ejus conjugis ; ille, humanæ salutis, 1725, ætatis suæ 57 ; illa, 1739, ætatis 70 annos, obierunt; necnon Joannis, Gulielmi, alterus Gulielmi, et Agnetis Tait, sobolis eorum qui prædecesserunt, sepulti sunt. Hic quoque conduntur exuviæ Thomæ Tait in Thunderton, filii S. D. Gulielmi et Agnetis natu maximi qui in arte lapidaria dum potuit, gnavis, in alenda familia fælix, morbus probus, animo æquus, vicimis amicus, tandem, annoram satur, fideque et spe fultus, ad patres migravit anno 1770, æt. 79. R. I. P.

Thomas Tait, mason at Thunderton, eldest son of William Tait, joiner, both named in the preceding epitaph, was father of John Tait, who settled in Edinburgh. A son of this person, Crawfurd Tait, acquired the estate of Harviestoun, Clackmannanshire (see *supra*, p. 62), and in 1797 married Susan, daughter of Sir Islay Campbell, Bart., Lord President of the Court of Session. Their youngest son, the Most Reverend Archibald Campbell Tait, D.C.L. is at present Archbishop of Canterbury and Primate.

On a plain tombstone a grand-uncle of Archbishop Tait is, with his wife, commemorated thus :—

"To the memory of George Tait in Redbog, who, after having liv'd 48 years in the fear of God, and love of all good men, was, upon the 30th of May, 1758, killed by the fall of a stack of timber at Peterhead, justly lamented by his friends, and sincerely regretted by all who knew him :—

"Stay, reader, and let fall a tear,
On looking at this stone ;
But call not anything severe
That Providence has done.

> " Expecting death, the good man lives
>   Prepared from day to day ;
>   And when God's will the summons gives
>   He's ready to obey.
> " This good man lived by all beloved
>   And dy'd by all deplor'd ;
>   Dwelt here awhile, and then removed
>   To dwell with Christ the Lord."

" Ann Mundie, spouse of George Tait, died 14 Sep. 1772, aged 59,"

George, eldest son of George Tait in Redbog, held office as stipendiary magistrate at Edinburgh. His treatise on the " Law of Evidence," and on the " Powers and Duties of a Justice of the Peace," are much valued.

Within the area of the old church a monument thus commemorates the late Mr. Bruce of Longside, who left £40,000 for charitable purposes.

" Erected in memory of James Bruce, Esquire, of Innerquhomery and Longside, second son of James Bruce, late farmer, Middleton of Innerquhomery, and Barbara Gray, his spouse : Born at Middleton 3d June 1787, he died there 16 May 1862."

These rhymes are from different tombstones :—

> " Happy the man whose God, who reigns on high,
>   Hath taught to live, and hath prepared to die ;
>   His warfare o'er, and run his Christian race,
>   Ev'n Death becomes the Messenger of peace—
>   Dispells his woes, then wafts his soul away
>   To endless glory in eternal day."

> " Here lies, consigned a while to promis'd rest,
>   In hope to rise again among the blest,
>   The precious dust of one whose course of life
>   Knew neither fraud, hypocrisy, nor strife.
>   A Husband loving, and of gentle mind,
>   A Father careful, provident, and kind,
>   A Farmer active, with no greedy view,
>   A Christian pious, regular, and true.
>   One who, in quiet, trod the private stage
>   Of rural labour, to a ripe old age.

Belov'd by neighbours, honour'd by his own;
Liv'd without spot, and dy'd without a groan.
Long may his humble virtues be rever'd;
Long be his name remembered with regard;
And long may Agriculture's school produce
Such honest men as Alexander Bruce."

"And, is she gone, the once so lovely maid?
Gone hence, ... dear departed shade!
Call'd from this world in early dawn of life,
When but beginning to be called a wife?
Ye virgin tribe, whom chance may lead this way,
When brightest beauty moulders in the clay,
Behold this stone, nor be asham'd to mourn
A while o'er Margaret Alexander's urn—
Then pause a little, while these lines you read,
And learn to draw instruction from the dead.
  "She who lies here was once like one of you,
Youthful and gay, and fair, as you are now:
One week beheld her a young blooming bride,
In marriage pomp, laid by her husband's side;
The next we saw her in death's livery drest,
And brought her breathless body here to rest.
Not all the world's gay hopes, nor present charms
Nor parents' tears, nor a lov'd husband's arms,
Could stamp the least impression on her mind,
Or fix to earth the soul for heaven design'd;
Calmly she left the scene so lately try'd,
Heav'n call'd her home, with pleasure she comply'd,
Embrac'd her sorrowing friends, then smil'd, and dy'd."

PARISH OF LUMPHANAN.

The usurper Macbeth was slain at Lumphanan; a heap of stones
denotes his grave.

PARISH OF MIDMAR.

Six tombstones on the south side of the church commemorate
members of the family of Tytler, who for three centuries have

farmed land at Corsindae in this parish. From this family descended the Tytlers of Woodhouselee (Vol. I. p. 43).

PARISH OF MONQUHITTER.

Within ,the old parish church a tomb commemorates William Coming of Achry, who, among other benevolent works, reared the fabric of the church at his own expense. His epitaph is as follows :—

"Memoriæ viri optimi, Gulielmi Coming ab Achry et Pittuly, Elgin quondam consolis, qui ptochotrophium quatuor inopum mercatorum ibidem mortificavit, ac postea templum hoc impensis suis hic condidit, ac 29 Octob. A.D. 1707, ætat. an. 74, pie obiit, monumentum hoc posuit uxor ejus dilectissima, Christiana Guthry. Observa integrum, et aspice rectum ; finem illius viri esse pacem. Ps. 37, v. 37. Vive memor lethi ; fugit hora."

William Coming was related to the house of Cumming of Altyre. From his descendant, Archibald Cumming, the principal portion of the estate of Auchry was in 1830 purchased by James Lumsden, Esq.

In the churchyard an altar-stone is thus inscribed :—

"Erected by Francis Garden-Campbell, Esq. of Troup and Glenlyon, to the memory of Alexander Garden, natural son of Col. Garden of Johnston ; and Robert Gordon, son of James Gordon in Newbyth. Alexander Gordon was drowned in the Canal of Auchry, 2 July 1806, by adventuring out of his depth : Robert Gordon gallantly strove to save his life, and shared the same fate. Reader, take warning from the awful fate of these two youths ! Shun unavailing danger ; Be ever prepared for Death.

From a tombstone in this churchyard we have the following quaint epitaph :—

"To keep in memory the burying-place of the family of James Faith, part of whom lies under, and on each side of this stone :—

"Reader, where I am you will soon be: Are you young, healthy, and prosperous ? So was I ; but Death seized me, and I am gone to my place. If I have lived in the fear of God, and goodwill to man, think of my happiness ; but if I have done evil—Beware."

PARISH OF OLD MACHAR.

The cathedral of St. Machar, the nave of which forms the parish church, was founded in 1357, and completed in 1522. At the Reformation it was stripped of its leaden roof and considerably dilapidated; the chancel was in 1654 demolished by Cromwell's soldiers. The nave was remodelled in 1832.

The south transept of the cathedral was constructed by Bishop Gavin Dunbar, and in its interior lies his effigies on an altar placed under a flowered arch, on which is engraved his escutcheon. Bishop Dunbar was son of Sir James Dunbar of Cumnock, by his wife, Jane, eldest daughter of the Earl of Sutherland. His nephew was Gavin Dunbar, Archbishop of Glasgow. After various preferments he was appointed Bishop of Aberdeen in 1518. He induced Hector Boece to prepare his "History," constructed a bridge across the Dee, and endowed an hospital. He died on the 9th March, 1532.

A handsome monument in St. Machar's cathedral commemorates Patrick Forbes of Corse, bishop of the diocese. It is inscribed thus:—

"Hic requiescit vir incomparabilis, fulgentissimum quondam Scotiæ sidus, Patricius Forbes, episcopus Abredonensis, prudentissimus pastor, fidelissimus prædicator, eximius scriptor, egregius consilarius regius, studii generalis Abredonensis instaurator et cancellarius, et novæ professionis theologicæ in eodem fundator, Baro de Oneil ac Dominus a Corse qui placide ac pie obiit, pridie Paschatis 28 Martii, anno Dom. 1635. Ætatis suæ 71."

"Apocalyps ✠ 6 Græce.

"Cætus stella sacri, pastorum gemma, regentum gloria, cura poli Deliciæ Corsæ.

"Salus per Christum. Nemo tollat qui Deum timet."

Eldest son of William Forbes, of Corse, the subject of the preceding epitaph, was born in 1564. Studying at the universities of Glasgow and St. Andrews, he became a licentiate of the church. He declined ordination till his forty-eighth year, when he was admitted minister of Keith. In 1617 he was elected one of the ministers of Edinburgh; and in the following year was consecrated Bishop of Aberdeen. In the discharge of his episcopal duties he exhibited a sound judgment and becoming zeal. He married a daughter of David Spence of Wormeston, Fifeshire; his eldest son, John, became Professor of Divinity in King's College. He composed a Commentary on the Book of Revelation, and other works.

In the cathedral a plain monument, with the following legend, celebrates Bishop Patrick Scougal:—

" Hic in Christo requiescit R. P. Patricius episcopus Abredonensis D. Joannis Scougalli de eodem filius; ivri omni elogio dignus: utpote pie pacificus, modeste prudens, eruditæ probitatis decus et exemplar. Nec morose gravis nec superbe doctus; egenis, dum viveret, prœsens asylum: basilicam Sancti Macharii bibliothecam Collegii regii, necnon hospitium publicum veteris Abredoniæ, propensæ munificentiæ indiciis haud spernendis ditavit. Ad episcopale munus consecratus, die Paschatis (Aprilis 10) anno Dom. 1664. Fatis cessit Feb. 16 anno salutis 1682. Episcopatus 18 ætatis vero suæ 75. Hoc monumentum qualequale piæ memoriæ charissimi parentis sacravit magister Jacobus Scougal, commissarius dioceseos Abredonensis.

Patrick Scougal was successively minister of Dairsie and Leuchars in Fife; he was in 1658 translated to Salton. From that charge he was in 1664 promoted to the bishopric of Aberdeen. He took active part in the conviction of persons accused of sorcery, and was in ecclesiastical affairs chiefly guided by Archbishop Sharp. In his personal aspects he was coarse and ungainly. His son James, who erected his monument, was latterly commissary of Edinburgh. His son Henry is commemorated in the chapel of King's College, Aberdeen (see *supra*, p. 302).

PARISH OF PETERCULTER.

A tablet in the church wall is thus inscribed:—

"Close to this wall, in front of this tablet, lie the remains of Sir Alexander Cuming of Culter, Baronet, and his lady, Elizabeth Dennis, co-heiress of Pucklechurch in Glostershire. Where they now lie was formerly under their own seat in the Old Church, where they were buried."

In the churchyard a tombstone in honour of Patrick Duff, of Culter, presents the following legend:—

"To the memory of Patrick Duff of Culter, Esq. He was born November the 16, 1692. He died October 20, 1763. He examined Christianity, and believed it firmly, and loved it warmly. From Christian principles he performed social virtues; in relieving distress and promoting useful arts he delightod. The affection of his Widow raises this monument."

From tombstones in the churchyard we have these rhymes:—

"While manly beauty in meridian bloom,
Untimely hastening to the ghastly tomb,
Calls from the eye the sympathetic tear;
Pause, Friend, and shed the mournful tribute here.
If social manners, with a taste refined;
If sterling worth, with unassuming mind;
If filial tenderness possess a charm;
If steady friendship can your bosom warm;
Then, reader, imitate, applaud, revere,
What triumph'd in the man that's buried here."

"Within this narrow house of clay,
The bones of William Martin ly;
He was an honest man and just,
All honest men might well him trust.
By sweat of brow his bread he won,
He liv'd and dy'd an honest man.
O Lord, said he, thy strength and grace
I ever will admire;
For by Thy sending me relief,
Thou'st taught me to aspire.

The heavens Thou hast open set,
And rent the vail that I
May upward look, and Thy dear Son,
With glory grand espy."

PARISH OF PITSLIGO.

Within the parish church a marble tablet commemorates the Rev.
James Robertson, D.D., Professor of Church History in the University of Edinburgh. This accomplished and eminent divine was
son of a farmer in this parish. He was born on the 2nd January,
1803, and in his twelfth year was enrolled as a student of Marischal College. In 1825 he was elected schoolmaster of this
parish, and in other three years was preferred to the head-master-
ship of Gordon's Hospital, Aberdeen. To the church of Ellon he
was appointed in 1832. From the first he preached without notes,
and with that power and energy which characterised his future
appearances. In the non-intrusion controversy he took part with
the Conservative section of the Church. At the Disruption in 1843
he was promoted to the Professorship of Church History at Edinburgh, and was appointed Secretary to the Bible Board. He undertook the Convenership of the Endowment Committee of the Church,
dedicating to the duties his chief energies and the whole of his
leisure. His success in raising money was unprecedented, and he
was privileged to secure the endowment of many important chapels.
But his labours proved entirely overwhelming. He was seized with
an illness, to which he succumbed on the 2nd December, 1860, in
his fifty-eighth year. At Edinburgh a " Memorial Church " has
been erected in celebration of his patriotism and Christian devotedness.

These metrical legends are presented on tombstones in the
parish churchyard :—

" Here lies in hope beneath this stone
A pious, wise, meek, upright one,

Who 'midst this daily toil and care
By saving truths his life did square."

"A wit is a feather,
  A chief is a rod,
    But an honest man
    Is the noblest work of God,
    His path is straight,
    His end is peace."

"One joy we joy'd, one grief we grieved,
One love we loved, one life we lived,
One was the hand, one was the word,
That did his death, her death afford,
As all they rest, so now the stone
That tombs them two, is justly one."

"John Renny ly's under this stone,
O'ercome by death, that spareth none,
Take heed and read and you shall see
As I am now so must you be,
Rotting in dark and silent dust,
Prepare for death, for die you must."

PARISH OF RATHEN.

Within a vault of the old church a monument celebrates
Christian Frazer, younger daughter of Sir Alexander Frazer, first
knight of Philorth. She was wife of William Hay, of Fedderat,
and grandmother of Alexander Crawfurd, of Rathen.

. A monument in the old church is thus inscribed —

"Erected by Miss Elizabeth Frazer to mark the Burial ground
of the family of Memsie, which extends 8 feet 10 inches from the
arch within the aisle. The remains of her Father, Mother, and
Aunt are deposited in the following order from the arch. 1st.,

Mrs. Sarah Frazer, of Memsie, died 3d April, 1807, aged 74 ; 2d, William Frazer, Esquire, of Memsie, died 13th Sept., 1813, aged 74; 3d, Mrs. Elizabeth Abernethy, died 23d January, 1816, aged 74."

An ornamental granite cross in the churchyard commemorates John Gordon, of Cairnbulg, who died 18th September, 1861, aged seventy-five.

PARISH OF RAYNE.

On the tombstone of the Rev. John Middleton, minister of the parish, are sculptured these lines :—

> " As late I stood in pulpit round,
> And now I ly alow the ground,
> When as you cross my corpse so cold,
> Remember the words that I you told."

Mr. Middleton died 4th August, 1653, aged forty-four. He was a zealous supporter of the Covenant, and joined the Protesters in 1651.

PARISH OF ST. FERGUS.

In the churchyard a tombstone commemorates Robert Arbuthnot, of Scotsmill, grandfather of the celebrated John Arbuthnot, M.D., physician to Queen Anne. On the tombstone the arms of the ancient families of Arbuthnot and Gordon are impaled. The stone was repaired by the late Sir William Arbuthnot, Bart., of Edinburgh (Vol. I. p. 79), a descendant of the House.

PARISH OF SKENE.

Within the church a marble tablet is thus inscribed:—

"Near the southern wall of this church are interred the mortal remains of George Skene, of Skene, descended from a long line of that name, who was born on the IX. day of May MDCCXLIX., and died on the XXIX. day of April MDCCCXXV."

The lands of Skene were conveyed to the family by King Robert the Bruce in 1317. The male line is extinct, the House being now represented by the Earl of Fife.

In the churchyard a tombstone commemorates James Davidson, Esq., of Kinmundy, who died 3rd November, 1827, aged seventy-two.

An altar stone is thus inscribed:—

"Within this enclosure are interred the remains of Katherine-Ann-Buchan Forbes, the wife of William McCombie of Easter Skene and Lynturk, and daughter of Major Alexander Forbes of Inverernan, who died on the 16th day of April 1835, in the 26th year of her age. And of their son, Thomas, who died on the 15th day of September 1841, in the 10th year of his age."

The mother of Mr. McCombie was daughter of Duncan Forbes-Mitchell, Esq., of Thanestone, second son of Sir Arthur Forbes, of Craigievar.

A tombstone commemorates Catherine Henderson, relict of the Rev. Dr. Walter Ireland, minister of North Leith, who died 22nd January, 1853, aged eighty. (Vol. I, p. 123.)

PARISH OF STRATHDON.

Separated by a railing from the nave of the church is the burial-place of Forbes of Newe. Here a freestone monument commemorates "William Forbes, of Newe," who died 10th January

1698, aged seventy-six. On a marble monument is the following inscription :—

"To the memory of John Forbes, Esquire, of Newe (formerly of Bombay), second son of John Forbes, Esquire, of Bellabeg. Born there the 19th September 1743, died in Fitzroy Square, London, 20th June, 1821, and buried in this church. A dutiful son, an affectionate brother, a warm and steady friend, his amiable manners and goodness of heart endeared him to all who knew him—his active benevolence was extended to all who stood in need of assistance. But, the 'widow and fatherless,' in India and in Britain, were the special objects of his protection. This monument was erected by his nephew, Sir Charles Forbes, Baronet of Newe and Edinglassie, 1837. Altius ibunt qui ad summa nituntur."

Sir Charles Forbes, Bart., was, like his uncle, long connected with Bombay, where a statue, executed by Chantrey, was erected in his honour. He sat in Parliament upwards of twenty years. In 1823 he was created a baronet, when his tenantry reared on Lonach hill a cairn celebrating the event. It is inscribed thus :—

"The tenantry of the lands of Newe, Edinglassie, Bellabeg, and Skellater, in testimony of their affection and gratitude, have erected this pile to their highly distinguished and beloved landlord, Sir Charles Forbes, Bart., M.P., on his elevation to the dignity of a Baronet of the United Kingdom by his Majesty George IV., in 1823."

Sir Charles Forbes died at London on the 20th September, 1849, aged seventy-six.

In the south wall of the church a monumental tablet commemorates Charles Forbes, Esq., of Auchernach, keeper of the castle of Corgarff, who died 5th May, 1794, aged sixty-four; Major-General David Forbes, C.B., of the 78th Regiment, son of the preceding, who died 29th March, 1849, aged seventy-seven, and Lieutenant-General Nathaniel Forbes, of Auchernach and Dunnottar, eldest son of Charles Forbes of Auchernach, who died 16th August, 1851, aged eighty-six.

Mural tablets celebrate Captain Alexander Forbes of Inverernan, who died 5th June, 1819, aged seventy-five, and Major Alexander Forbes of Inverernan, who died 20th July, 1830, aged fifty-five. The Rev. Dr. George Forbes of Blelach and Inverernan, is commemorated by an appropriate monument. ' Born on the 8th April 1778, he studied at Marischal College, and was ordained minister of Strathdon in 1804. He demitted his charge in 1829, and died suddenly on the 16th February, 1834. Dr. Forbes was a keen promoter of agriculture, and was highly esteemed for his beneficence.

Tombstones commemorate Alexander Anderson, of Candacraig, died 13th March, 1817, aged sixty-five ; Major John Anderson of Candacraig, died 24th December, 1845, aged forty-five ; Robert Farquharson of Allerg, died 31st January, 1771, aged seventy-seven ; Robert Farquharson of Allargue and Breda, died 14th February, 1863 ; Alexander Stuart, Esq., writer to the signet, died 19th September, 1787, aged eighty-seven, and Lieutenant Hugh Robert Meiklejôhn, son of the Rev. Robert Meiklejohn, minister of Strathdon, who was killed at Jhansi, in Central India, 3rd April, 1858, aged twenty-two.

These metrical inscriptions are from various gravestones,—

" Moulder'd we with our fathers lie,
    In earth and common dust ;
Bring down, O man thy lofty eye,
    As we died so thou must."

" A watchman faithful, honest, just
Who ne'er betrayed his sacred trust,
Whose love to Christ and to his flock,
Breath'd in all that e'er he spoke."

" Weep not for us ye parents dear,
Blest was the time that we came here,
For tho' we can't return to you
And you yourselves to death must bow,
Yet if ye fear and serve your God
You'll meet us in his blest abode."

PARISH OF STRICHEN.

In the churchyard a tombstone commemorates the Rev. William Anderson, minister of the parish, who died 17th July, 1806, aged forty-nine. His son Alexander Anderson became Lord Provost of Aberdeen, and was knighted by Her Majesty when a statue of the Prince Consort was inaugurated in that city in 1863.

Tombstones in the churchyard present these rhymes :—

> " In hope to sing without a sob
> The anthem ever new,
> I gladly bid the dusty globe
> And vain delights adieu."

> " John Baxter and M. Davidson his wife,
> Lived fifty years a conjugal life ;
> On one night they both died, and here are interr'd,
> By relations and neighbours rever'd."

PARISH OF TURRIFF.

Within the church a handsome monument thus commemorates one of the Barclays of Towie :—

Anno $\begin{matrix} P. & B. \\ A. & D. \end{matrix}$ 1636.

> " Barclaivs jacet hic tovaæ gloria gentis sæcvla cvi priscvm qvina dedere decvs calcvlvs hvnc jvvenem poster tria lvstra peremit nec medicæ qvidqvam profvit artis opvs ossa tegit tellvs animam cælestis origo fvit ætheriæ limina sedis habent."

BANFFSHIRE.

PARISH OF BOINDIE.

Near the ruin of the old church is a burial vault, formerly used by the Ogilvies of Boyne, cadets of the House of Ogilvy in Forfarshire.

Within the area of the church a tombstone is thus inscribed :—

"To the memory of the Stuarts, formerly of Ordens, this being the burial-place of that family for many ages this stone is placed by the Rev. James Stuart, one of their descendants, late Rector of George Town Parish, South Carolina, and Chaplain to the King's Rangers in North America, 1785."

A mortuary enclosure contains several gravestones commemorating descendants of Milne of Kirstare. A marble tablet, erected by his friends, celebrates John Milne, Esq., surgeon in Banff, who died by a fall from his horse, 20th May, 1833, aged twenty-six.

PARISH OF BOTRIPHNIE.

Within an enclosure a monument thus commemorates several members of the House of Cubin and Drumuir :—

"Near this spot lie interred the remains of Major Alexander Duff, younger of Cubin, who died at Davidston, in the year 1777. Also of his son, Admiral Archibald Duff, of Drumuir, who departed this life at Braemorriston, near Elgin, the 9th day of Feb., 1858, aged 84. Frances Jones, widow of Admiral Duff, died 21 Dec., 1861, aged 74."

The Ardbrach aisle has a monument thus inscribed :—

" Memoriæ sacrum. Hic subtus siti sunt cineres Annæ Gordon
et Katharinæ Leslie, Ioannis et Iacobi Andersonorum ab Ardbrake
conjugum dilectarum, una cum liberis exutraque susceptis, quarum
hæc, annos nata 39, 7 Id. Mart. A. Æ. C. 1667, fatis succubuit, illa
vero . . annorum matrona, 13 Kal. Decembr, A.D. 1670, lumina
clausit ; inquarum decus et perennem famam, quippe quæ fuerint
claris editæ natalibus, eximiis que excultæ virtutibus, pro summo
in demortuas affectu et observantia monumentum hoc superstruen-
dum curarunt Ioannes et Iacobus Andersoni, pater et filius.

A mural slab bears the following :—

" 1760 : This monument is erected by John Stuart in Rosarie,
in memory of his grandfather, William, and his father, Thomas,
who both lived and died at Bodinfinnich, and of his uncle Hendry,
who sometime lived and died in Rosarie. John, William, Alexander,
George, Hendry, Mary, and Beatrix, Hendry's children, also lie
here. It is to be observed that this has been the burial place of
the said Stuarts long before, and ever since the Reformation."

PARISH OF CABRACH.

A tombstone commemorates John Gordon, sometime farmer in
Drumferg, who died 21st July, 1759, aged fifty-one. His son,
Lieut.-Colonel John Gordon, of the 92nd Regiment, died at Coy-
nochie, 27th March, 1827, aged seventy-five.

On the tombstone of Patrick Gordon, are these lines :—

" Death of all men is the total sum,
The period unto which we all must come ;
He lives but a short life that lives the longest,
And he is weak in death that in life was strongest."

PARISH OF CULLEN.

The parish church was for several centuries the burial-place of the Houses of Findlater and Seafield. A monument, reared in 1554, to the memory of Alexander Ogilvie, Baron Findlater, and his wife, Elizabeth Gordon, is thus described by Mr. Cordiner, in his "Remarkable Ruins of North Britain":—"The splendid enrichments that crown the pyramidal columns have a very elegant and beautiful effect. The bas-reliefs are well raised and minutely finished. The figures of the entombed, in devotional attitudes, are well rounded and correctly drawn. The sculptures of the central and interior part, according to the ideas of early ages, have most learned and sublime allusion. Two angels guarding an altar-piece, on which the virtues of the deceased are inscribed, seem to call the dead, represented by a skeleton laid under the altar, to appear before the tribunal of the Most High, expressed by a hieroglyphic above. 'The Ancient of Days sat on the clouds of heaven, and they came near before him to judgment,' was the bold imagery by which the prophet Daniel pointed out the things that must be hereafter. The well known symbol here on the tomb of this one, upholding the globe in his arm, implies the intellectual power and wisdom which is the origin and support of creation. The attitude of Benediction and the Triple Crown, though seemingly of more modern allusion, yet, in the Egyptian wisdom, refer to the three great attributes of Deity, and the Supreme pronouncing a blessing on his works. The pillars of heaven, expressed by columns supporting an arch, rest on the cloud and a circumambient vine. From that arch diverging rays are spread, in which a dove is descending, and they beam on the cross that rises over the globe—the most ancient and venerable symbols of the universal benignity of the Uncreated Light of the World manifesting the Divine favour to man."

Another superb monument, formerly in the church, represented the figure of an armed warrior recumbent; it celebrated John Duff,

of Muldavat, a reputed ancestor of the Earl of Fife, who died in
1404. This monument was in 1790 placed in the mausoleum of
Duff House Park.

PARISH OF GAMRIE.

A decorated monument in the wall of the church is thus inscribed :—

"patricius . brlay . Z . hoc . me . fiere . fecit.
hic . iacet . honorabilis . vir . patricius . barclay . dns . de .
tolly . qui . obiit — die . mencs —— ano . Dni . m⁰ . q^{mo} .
et . ioneta . ogiuy . eius . sponca . qui . obiit . cexto . die .
mencs . ianuarii . ano . dm . m⁰ . qvi⁰ . quadrage⁰ . septimo."

Patrick Barclay of Tolly, thus commemorated, was descended
from a family which owned lands in Gamrie from the time of King
Robert the Bruce. The male line failed early in the seventeenth
century, when Isabella the heiress married Charles, second son of
the sixth Earl of Lauderdale. William Barclay, the eminent scholar
and father of the author of "Argenis," was a native of the parish,
and was nearly related to the proprietor of Tolly; he died in 1605,
aged about sixty.

A stone, engraved with the Keith arms and the motto "Victoriæ
Limes," is on the margin thus inscribed :—

"Heir lyis the rycht honorabil Alexander Keyth of Trvp, depairtit yis lyf the xxv of Marche 1605."

Sir Robert Keith the Marischal acquired the barony of Troup by
marrying the heiress; he granted it in 1413 to John, his second
son, a progenitor of the Keiths of Northfield, one of whom was
second heir to the barony in 1628.

On a flagstone are these words :—

"Bessy Strachan, and Mrs. Bathia Forbes, ladies of Troup, 1781."

Major Gordon, son of the proprietor of Banchory, served in the army of Gustavus Adolphus. Returning to Scotland in 1654, he purchased the estate of Troup, and marrying Betty, daughter of Strachan of Glenkindie, became ancestor of Francis Garden, Lord Gardenstone. His lordship died in 1793. In the old church a monumental frame has been erected to his memory.

An altar tombstone of white marble commemorates Alexander Chalmers, Esq., of Clunie, who died 11th August, 1835, aged seventy. This benevolent gentleman bequeathed £70,000 for the erection and endowment of an hospital and free dispensary at Banff. The institution is designated the "Chalmers' Hospital."

PARISH OF GRANGE.

In an aisle of the old church Alexander Duff of Braco, who died in 1705, was interred. A handsome monument reared over his remains has long disappeared.

A burial aisle belonging to the family of Innes of Edingight presents a mural tablet, with the following legend :—

"This monument is erected by John Innes of Mwiryfold to the memory of Thomas Innes, of Mwiryfold, his father, who lyes here interred. He died the 12 of Sept., 1754, aged 73 years."

Thomas Innes was son of the proprietor of Edingight, and was factor to the Earl of Fife. The family is represented by Sir James Milne Innes, Bart., of Balveny and Edingight.

A monument, with a latin inscription, commemorates George Wilson, father-in-law of James Ferguson, the self-educated astronomer; he died 22nd March, 1742, aged sixty-four.

Tombstones celebrate the Rev. Alexander Kerr, minister of the parish, who died in 1693; the Rev. Archibald Campbell, minister of the parish, who died 16th October, 1774; Rev. Andrew Young,

minister of the Associate church, died 21st May, 1788; Rev.
John Primrose, of the Associate church, died 28th February, 1832;
and the Rev. William Duff, minister of the parish, who died 23rd
September, 1844, in his fifty-third year and the twenty-third of his
ministry. A son of the last, who has assumed as a cognomen his
baptismal name, Andrew Halliday, has attained distinction as a
dramatic writer.

PARISH OF INVERAVEN.

From tombstones in the parish churchyard we have these quaint
legends:—

"This stone was erected here by John Hendrie, who died the
24th December, 1815, in the 63d year of his age, with the concur-
rence of Penuel Cameron, his spouse, who died 7 May, 1818, in the
57th year of her age."

" Adieu, dear friends, who laid me here,
Where I must lie till Christ appear;
When he appears I hope 'twill be
A joyful rising unto me."

PARISH OF KEITH.

Within the ruin of the old church a monument commemorates
the first wife of the Rev. James Strachan, minister of the parish,
who succeeded to the baronetcy of Thornton. It is thus inscribed:—

"Sub scamno D^d. Kinnminnitie cineres lectissimæ feminæ D.
Kath. Rossæ D. de Thorntone, cuius etiamsi fragrantissimæ memoriæ
monumentis omni ære perenniorib, abunde satis litatum sit hoc
tamen mauseoleo parentandum duxit coniunx ipsius pula . . . D.
Iac. Strachanus de Thornt. : huius ecclesiæ pastor. Obiit puerpera 6th Apr. anno 1689 . . . . quiescunt et hic Gul., Rob., et
Joshue Strachanus filii eorum."

Mr. Strachan was educated at King's College, Aberdeen, and was ordained minister of Keith in 1665. On his succeeding to the family honours he was locally celebrated in these lines:—

> " The beltit knicht o' Thornton,
> An' laird o' Pittendreich,
> An' Maister James Strachan,
> The Minister o' Keith."

He was deprived, 7th November, 1689, for having in prayer entreated the restoration of James VII. He continued to minister at Keith in an Episcopal meeting-house. He died at Inverness in 1715, about the age of seventy-four. As stated in the preceding inscription, he married Katharine Ross, who died in childbed, 6th April, 1689. His sons by this marriage,—William, Robert, and Joshua,—predeceased their father. It is believed that Mr. Strachan married secondly a daughter of Forbes of Waterton. To his eldest son James, he presented the family estate. He fell in the rebellion of 1715, and the succession devolved on his brother Francis, who became a Jesuit and resided abroad. Hugh a younger brother, also a Jesuit, afterwards succeeded to the baronetcy; he died at Douay in 1745.

Within a mortuary enclosure a monumental tablet celebrates " James Thurburn," of Smailholm, Berwickshire, only son of the Rev. John Thurburn, minister of Kirknewton, who died at Drum, near Keith, 9th May, 1798, aged fifty-nine.

A monument commemorates James Milne, of Kinstair, who died 9th May, 1771, aged eighty-three; it bears the names of his children and some of his progenitors.

A tombstone denotes the resting-place of the Rev. James McLean, sometime minister of the parish, who died 14th November, 1840, aged eighty-two. His son George, born in 1801, was husband of Letitia Elizabeth Landon, the celebrated authoress; he was governor of Cape Coast Castle, and died in 1847.

A plain tombstone marks the grave of James Jamieson, late Master in the Royal Navy, who died 18th July, 1817, aged eighty-two. He was master of the *Boreas* frigate, and is mentioned as *Jamie Jamieson* in Lord Nelson's dispatches.

A tombstone embellished with a floral cross commemorates the Rev. John Murdoch, Episcopal clergyman, who died 29th April 1850, aged eighty-three. His son-in-law, the Rev. J. F. S. Gordon, D.D., has published several works relating to Scottish antiquities.

A gravestone denotes the grave of Elizabeth Anderson, daughter of the Rev. James Anderson, sometime minister of Keith, and wife of James Glashan, writer; she died 10th July, 1773. aged twenty-two. Jean, his eldest daughter, married Robert Stuart of Aucharme; their son John Stuart, LL.D., is the distinguished antiquary.

On the tombstone of John Giles, whs died in 1787, are these lines :—

> " Beneath this stone, in hope again to rise,
> The relics of an honest man are laid ;
> So, Reader, learn superior worth to prize,
> That what is said of him, of thee be said.
> Such peaceful neighbour, and a friend so sure,
> Such tender parent, and such a husband kind ;
> Such modest pattern of Religion pure,
> In Keith's wide precincts we too seldom find.
> His hands industrious and his heart sincere,
> Of worldly wise men, he disdained the wiles ;
> Go, Passenger ! make haste thy God to know,
> And in thy actions imitate John Giles."

PARISH OF KIRKMICHAEL.

Within the church a freestone monument is thus inscribed :—

" Here lies the body of Ann Lindsay, spouse of John Gordon of Glenbucket, and daughter of the Right Hon. Sir Alexander Lindsay of Evelack, who departed this life on the 9th day of June, 1750, aged fifty years. Also Helen Reid, spouse of William Gordon, Esq. of Glenbucket, and daughter of the Right. Hon. Sir John Reid of Barra, who died on the 5th May, 1766, aged 52 years ; and Lilias

McHardy, spouse of John Gordon, Esq., of Glenbucket, and daughter of William McHardy, late in Delnilat, who died May 30th, 1829, aged 78 years. And of Elspet Stewart, spouse of Charles Gordon, Esq., St. Bridget, and daughter of William Stewart, Esq., Ballentrewan, who died 2nd February, 1856, aged 63 years."

The Gordons of Glenbucket sprung from the House of Rothiemay, and the Lindsays of Evelack descend from a younger son of Sir Walter Lindsay of Edzell.

A massive monument, appropriately dedicated, denotes the grave of Lieutenant General William Alexander Gordon, C.B., colonel of the 54th Regiment; he died at Nairn, 10th August, 1856, aged eighty-seven.

On an altar tombstone is the following legend :—

"To preserve this burying-ground, and in pious regard to the memory of Finlay Farquharson of Auchriachan, who possessed this place since 1569, son to Findlay Farquharson, Esq., of Invercauld ; likewise William Farquharson, who died anno 1719 aged 80 years, who was the ninth man of that family who possessed Auchriachan, and Janet Grant his spouse, who died anno 1720, aged 78. Also William Farquharson, son of Invercauld . . . . who died anno 1723, aged 30, and Elizabeth Farquharson his spouse who died anno 1720, aged 78. Also Sophia McGrigor, who died 15th May, 1769, aged 59, spouse to Robert Farquharson in Auchriachan, who erected this monument, 1789.

"The said Robert Farquharson died in 179—. William his son died in April, 1811, and Alexander the last in the male line, died 11th Nov. 1835, aged 78. Janet Farquharson, Robert's eldest daughter, married James Cameron, Ballenlish, and this tablet is renewed by their son Angus Cameron, of Firhall, 1851.

> "These bodies low lie here consign'd to rest,
> With hopes withal to rise among the blest:
> Sweet be their sleep, and blessed their wakening,
> Reader! pray for those that pray for thee."

The estate of Auchriachan, possessed by the Farquharsons for two hundred years, has for a century formed part of the Gordon estates, belonging to the Duke of Richmond.

In the south wall of the church, a marble tablet commemorates

Patrick Grant, Esq., of Glenlochy, formerly of Stocktown, who died 15th April, 1783, aged seventy-four, and his wife Beatrice, daughter of Donald Grant, of Inverlochy, who died 24th January, 1780, aged sixty-nine. Their elder son, John Grant, (Vol. I., p. 59) purchased Kilgraston, in Perthshire, and was succeeded in that estate by his brother Francis, who married, in 1795, Anne, eldest daughter of Robert Oliphant, Esq., of Rossie, and died in 1819. Sir Francis Grant, fourth son of Francis Grant of Kilgraston, is president of the Royal Academy. The fifth son, Sir James Hope Grant, G.C.B., Lieutenant-General, is highly distinguished for his military services.

PARISH OF MARNOCH.

Within a mortuary enclosure, monumental tablets celebrate John Innes, Esq., of Muryfold, died 3rd October, 1780; James Rose Innes, died 4th August, 1814, aged forty, and Mrs. Elizabeth Mary Rose Innes, of Netherdale, died 17th January, 1851, aged seventy-three; James Rose Innes, died 10th June, 1845, aged forty-four; also other members of the family.

In the churchyard tombstones commemorate the Rev. Dr. George Meldrum, proprietor of Crombie in this parish, who died in 1692, aged seventy-six; John Gordon, Esq., of Avochie and Mayne, who died 27th of November, 1857, aged sixty; and the Rev. Hugh Chalmers, minister of the parish, who died 5th June, 1707, in the fifty-ninth year of his age, and thirty-sixth of his ministry.

PARISH OF MORTLACH.

At the south west corner of the church a mural monument is thus inscribed:—

" Hoc conduntur tumulo, reliquiæ Alexandri Duff de Keithmore et Helenæ Grant, uxoris suæ charissimæ: Qui quadraginta annos et ultra, felici et fæcundo connubio juncti, vixerunt. Uterq. quidem

ingenue natus. Ille ex nobilissimis Fifæ Thanis per vetustam
familiam de Craighead, paulo abhinc superstitem, proxime et legi-
time oriundus: Illa ex splendida et potenti Grantæorum familia,
eodem quoq. modo originem trahens. Ortu non obscuri, suis tamen
virtutibus illustriores; opibus affluxerunt, et liberis ingenue educa-
tis, floruere pie, juste et sobrie vixerunt; et sic in Domino mortem
obiere; Illa anno Domini 1694, ætatis suæ sexagesimo."

Alexander Duff served under the Marquis of Montrose, and was
some time imprisoned by the Covenanters. He died in the year
1700, at the age of seventy-six. Along with four daughters he left
three sons, who were respectively designated of Braco, Dipple, and
Craigston. William Duff, eldest son of the proprietor of Dipple,
represented some years the county of Banff in Parliament, and
was in 1735 raised to the peerage as Baron Braco, of Kilbryde. In
1759 he was created Viscount Macduff, and Earl of Fife. The
present Earl of Fife is his lineal descendant.

In the north wall of the church a stone effigy in armour is supposed to represent Alexander Leslie, first baron of Kininvie; he
died about 1549. The grandson of his third son, George, who received
the lands of Drummine, was the celebrated General Alexander
Leslie, afterwards Lord Balgonie, and Earl of Leven. Isobel Leslie,
eldest daughter of the fifth baron of Kininvie, was mother of Archbishop Sharp. In the churchyard John Leslie of Kininvie (uncle of
the Archbishop) commemorates his wife Helen Grant, who lived
with her husband sixty years and departed 11th May, 1712, in the
eighty-second year of her age. The family of Kininvie is now represented by George A. Young Leslie, Esq., the present proprietor.
A marble tablet in the church is thus inscribed.

"M.O.V.S.: Mri. Hugonis Innes, filij honorabilis viri Joannis
Innes de Leichnet, qui, cum annos triginta quatuor, sacra in hoc
templo peregisset, obijt anno Christi MDCCXXXII., natus annos
LXVIII. Posuit hoc monumentum pia ac dilectissima conjux
Eliz. Abernethie filia domini de Mayen."

Mr. Innes was celebrated for his bodily strength. His family,

Innes of Lichnett sprung from Sir Robert Innes of that ilk. His wife was descended from Abernethy of that ilk in Perthshire.

Major Cameron, a distinguished Indian officer is by a memorial tablet celebrated thus :—

"To the memory of Major John Cameron, C.B., E.I.C. Native Infantry, on the establishment of St. George, who after serving his country in India for thirty-two years, both in civil and military capacity, and particularly in most of the principal events during that period, died on the 15th June, 1838 while officiating as Resident at the Court of Hyderabad, aged 47 years. This tablet has been erected to his memory, and placed in the church of his native parish, by a few of his friends in India, as a mark of esteem and affection for his public and private character."

In the churchyard a tombstone bearing the Farquharson arms has, with the date 1417, the following legend :—

" Hic iacet honorabilis vir Robertvs Farquharson de Lauchtitvany qui obiit mar de quinto meri anno dni. mo quo. xio sexto cum sua pro piqiet."

A tombstone commemorates Alexander Sturm, merchant, Dufftown, who died in April, 1848. His son James Sturm, who died at Hampstead, 7th May, 1869, bequeathed, among other legacies for charitable purposes, £3000 to Mortlach parish.

A sculptured stone in the haugh of the Dullan is believed to have been erected by King Malcolm, to celebrate the overthrow of an army of Danes.

On Mortlach hill a monument has lately been erected in honour of Charles, tenth Marquess of Huntly, who died 18th September, 1863. The monument is sixty feet in height; it consists of a plain obelisk resting on a pedestal of grey granite. An inscription bears that it was reared by the tenantry on the late Marquess's estates.

PARISH OF RATHVEN.

The aisle of the old church forms the burial place of the Hays of Rannes; on the entrance it is thus inscribed :—

"IN . DEI . HONOREM . ECCLESIÆ . VSM . ET . IA . HAYE . DE . RANNES KA . DVNBAR . EI' . CONIVGIS . EORV . POSTERIORV . GRATIAM . FIT . HÆC AVSTVALIOR . ÆDIOLA . AN . DNI 1612."

Within the aisle a marble monument presents the following pedigree:—

"To the memory of the Hays of Rannes and Lenplum. 1421, Sir William Hay of Locharat was ancestor of the noble family of Tweeddale; 1474, he married a second wife Alicia, daughter of Sir Wm. Hay of Errol, by whom he had Sir Edmund Hay of Lenplum, and Moram, who married Margaret Kerr, and had Dugald Hay of Lenplum, who married Helen Cockburn of Newhall. Their children were, 1520 (I.) Edmund Hay of Lenplum; (II.) George Hay of Rannes; (III.) William Hay of Edderston; (IV.) Andrew Hay of Ranfield. 1562, The above George Hay was Superintendent of Glasgow and Aberdeen, Secretary to the Privy Council in the year 1567, and Rector of Rathven. He added the lands of Faskin and Findachy to his patrimonial inheritance. He also acquired the lands of Edderston, which he bestowed on his brother William, and the lands of Ranfield, which he gave to his brother Andrew. 1567, The above George Hay married Marriot, daughter of Henderson of Fordel, of whom there were (I.) George, who died unmarried in the year 1586. 1603 (II.) James Hay of Rannes and Lenplum, who married Katherine, daughter of Dunbar of Grange. Their children were (I.) George Hay of Rannes; (II.) James Hay of Muldavit; (III.) John Hay of Langshed; (IV.) Andrew; (V.) William; (VI.) Katherine; (VII.) Anne. The above James Hay of Rannes succeeded to the estate of Lenplum in consequence of the failure of heirs-male of William Hay of Lenplum, as is instructed by a deed recorded in the books of Session, 28th of May 1599; but afterwards sold this property to Sir William Hay, a younger son of the family of Tweeddale. 1630, In the estate of Rannes he was succeeded by his eldest son George, who married Agnes, daughter of Guthrie of Guthrie, Bishop of Murray, and had, 1645, James Hay of Rannes, who married Margaret, daughter of Gordon of Park. Their children were (I.) James Hay of Rannes; (II.) Andrew Hay of Mountblairy, of whom the Hays of Cocklaw and Faichfield are descended. 1684, The above James Hay of Rannes married Margaret, daughter of

Gordon of Glengerrack. Their children were (I.) Charles Hay of Rannes, born 1688, and died in London in 1751; (II.) James Hay, who married Helen Lauder, dowager Lady Banff, of whom were James, Charles, and William Hay. 1710, The above Charles Hay of Rannes married Helen, only child of Dr. Andrew Fraser, Inverness. Their children were (I.) Andrew Hay of Rannes; (II.) Alexander Hay, died 1771, aged 47; (III.) Mary, married to Leith of Leithall; (IV.) Katherine, married to Gordon of Sheilagreen; (V.) Clementina, married to Duff, of Whitehill; (VI.) Margaret, married to Russell of Montcoffer; (VII.) Jane, unmarried.

"1789, The above Andrew Hay died, unmarried, the 29th of August 1789, aged 76, and his remains are deposited in this aisle. Mr. Hay was distinguished for those qualities which add grace and dignity to human nature. Possessed of true piety, he was an affectionate kinsman, a steady friend, a pleasant companion, and an honest man. The urbanity of his manners, and the kindness of his disposition, were universally felt and acknowledged. He made use of his fortune with that happy prudence which enabled him, while alive, to share enjoyment with his friends, and to leave to his successor an ample and independent inheritance. Rev. xiv. 13."

, The estate of Rannes now belongs to the Earl of Seafield.

Within a mortuary enclosure are the following inscriptions:—

"Memoriæ charissimæ suæ conjugis Elizabethæ Gordon, quæ decessit die decimo quinto Januarij calendas, 1725, ætatis suæ 31. Monumentum hoc extrui curavit maritus superstes Alexander Gordon de Cairnfield, Signeto Pagio Scriba."

"Sacred to the memory of James Gordon, second son of Alex. Gordon of Cairnfield, who died at Banff on the 1 January 1815, aged 77; and Janet Mercer, his spouse, who died at Nairn, on the 24 May 1842, aged 84. This tablet is placed by Adam-Garden Gordon, their youngest son, and Francis Gordon of Kincardine, 1844."

" 'Bydand'—To the memory of Adam Gordon of Cairnfield, who died 17th March 1847, aged 74. Elizabeth Cruickshank, his wife, eldest daughter of the late Patrick Cruickshank of Stracathro, Forfarshire, died 29th January 1847, aged 67, and their two sons and two daughters, who predeceased them. Erected as a tribute of respect and affection by their surviving sons—John Gordon of Cairnfield; Patrick, Major, H.E.I.S.; George, merchant, U.S., America; James C. Duff, and William, Lieutenant, H.E.I.C.S."

By the first inscription is commemorated Elizabeth Gordon, heiress of Cairnfield, and first wife of Alexander Gordon, writer to the signet, a cadet of the Gordons of Dykeside, Morayshire. James Gordon, commemorated in the second inscription, was son of Alexander Gordon by a second wife.

A marble slab thus commemorates the Stewarts of Tanochy:—

"Sacred to the memory of the late family of Stewart of Tanochy, all of whom, but two, lie interred here. Patrick Stewart of Tanochy, died 31 Dec. 1779, aged 50; Elizabeth, his wife, died 4 April 1804, aged 60. Their three sons, George Stewart of Tanochy, W.S., died Oct. 1814, aged 45; Alexander, Major 75th regt., killed in Calabria, April 1813, aged 40; Andrew died in the Island of Jamaica, ——. Their two daughters,—Harriet-Mary, died 19 July 1864, in the 93 year of her age; Elizabeth-Margaret, died 24 July 1858, aged 82.

Within the Catholic chapel at Buckie two mural tablets are thus inscribed:—

"Pray for the Soul of Sir William Gordon, Baronet, of Gordonstone and Letterfourie. Born 26th December 1804; deceased 5th Decr. 1861, whose remains are interred in this church. May he rest in peace."

"Pray for the Souls of Sir James Gordon, Baronet of Gordonstown and Letterfourie, born in the year 1779; deceased on the 24th December 1843. And of his spouse, Mary Glendonwin of Glendonwin, born in the year 1783; deceased on the 18th May 1845; whose remains are interred within this church. May they rest in peace. Amen."

The first Gordon of Letterfourie was James, fourth son of George, second Earl of Huntly; he was in 1513 appointed admiral of Scotland. The Hon. Robert Gordon of Gordonstone was created a baronet of Nova Scotia on the 28th May, 1625; he was the first who attained this honour. He held various public offices.

In Chapelford burial-ground an altar tombstone celebrates Thomas Nicolson, Bishop of Peristachium and Vicar Apostolic in Scotland. It is thus inscribed:—

"D.O.M. Reu^{enus} D. Thomas Nicolson, Epis. Peristach. Vic. Ap.

in Scotia, hic iacet. Vir fuit primæva pietate, insignis candore et simplicitate christiana, admirandus integritate, et morum innocentia eximius, ingenio acutus, doctrina et eruditione clarus, prudentia et sapientia singularis, zelo et charitate fidelibus charissimus, beneficentia comitate et liberalitate etiam iis qui foris sunt venerabilis. Abi, viator, et bene precare. Vixit annos circiter 76, obiit quarto Idus Octobris anno repate salutis 1718."

Bishop Nicolson was a younger son of Thomas Nicolson of Kemnay, by his wife, a daughter of Abercromby of Birkenbog. Born a Protestant, he adopted the Romish faith.

ELGINSHIRE.

PARISH OF ABERNETHY.

On gravestones in the churchyard are these rhymes:

> "Troubles sore we surely bore,
>   Physicians were in vain,
> Till God above by his just love
>   Relieved all our pain."

> "All in this lonesome house of rest
>   I lie but for a time,
> In hopes to rise as Jesus rose,
>   And spend a life divine."

> "The world's a city
>   Full of streets,
> And death's a market
>   That every one meets;
> But if life were a thing
>   That money could buy,
> The poor could not live
>   And the rich would ne'er die."

PARISH OF BELLIE OR FOCHABERS.

In the churchyard a tombstone commemorates John Ross, Professor of Oriental Languages in King's College, Aberdeen, who died 9th July, 1814, aged eighty-four.

A gravestone celebrates William Marshall, Factor to Alexander

Duke of Gordon, eminent as a composer of Scottish music, especially strathspeys. He died 29th May, 1833, in his eighty-fifth year. Four of his sons were officers in the army, and several of them acquired distinction.

An altar tombstone denotes the grave of the Rev. John Anderson, sometime minister of the parish, who died 22nd April, 1839, in his eightieth year and the fifty-seventh of his ministry. Skilled in the affairs of business, Mr. Anderson was employed as factor by the Duke of Gordon, and was nominated a Justice of the Peace. On account of his several offices he was thus rhymed upon by a local poet.

> " The Rev. John Anderson,
>   Factor to His Grace,
>   Minister of Fochabers,
>   And Justice of the Peace."

The General Assembly, by a deliverance in 1819 highly disapproved of ministers holding secular offices, and in consequence Mr. Anderson resigned his charge.

On tombstones in the churchyard are these verses:

> " Unknown to pomp, and bred to rural toil,
>   To him the Christian's faith and hope were given;
>   Unskilled in art, nor trained in courtly guile,
>   He lived to God, and died— to wake in heaven."

> " It was in the bloom of manhood's prime,
>   When death to me was sent;
>   All you that have a longer time,
>   Be careful and repent."

> " O, the grave, whilst it covers each fault, each defect—
>   Leaves untarnish'd the worth of the Just;
>   His memory we'll cherish with tender respect,
>   Whilst his body consumes in the dust."

PARISH OF DALLAS.

In the church a marble monument commemorates " Helen Cuming Campbell, daughter of Alexander Cuming of Craigmill, and Elizabeth Tulloh, died 14th November, 1800." The estate of Craigmill now belongs to Grant of Elchies.

PARISH OF DUFFUS.

On a tombstone in the parish churchyard is the following quaint epitaph :—

" Reader, would you wish to hear
Who took and placed me here ?
Well, as you seem to be at leisure,
I was placed here by Sandy Fraser.
'Tis here John Fraser's ashes ly,
As soon as born he began to die.
In figure and feature and powers of mind,
As perfect as most of his peers
As gratefully held, as serenely resigned
Life's lease, which was eighty-four years.
With low and with lofty frank candid and fair,
Soon bargained and counted and cleared ;
On folly and vice and imposture severe,
Yet neither was hated nor feared."

PARISH OF DUTHIL.

Adjoining the church is a mausoleum belonging to the Earl of Seafield. Here the Grants of Castle Grant, now represented by the Earl of Seafield, interred for three hundred years.

In the church a marble tablet is thus inscribed :—

" Captain William Grant, 27th Regt., Bengal N.I., Assistant-Adjutant-General of Affganistan, eldest son of the late Major Grant

Auchterblair, was killed in the action at Gundermuck, during the disastrous retreat of the British Army from Cabool, on the 13th of January, 1842, aged 38 years. Erected by his bereaved widow."

Within a mortuary enclosure are commemorated Colonel Sir Maxwell Grant, who died 22nd October, 1823, and other members of the families of Grant of Tullochgorm and Tullickgriban.

PARISH OF DYKE AND MOY.

In Dyke churchyard a mortuary enclosure bears the following inscription:

" Valter : Kinnaird : Elizabeth : Innes, : 1613.
" The : Bvildars : Of : This : Bed: Of : Stane :
    Ar : Laird : And : Ladie : Of : Covbine :.
Qvhilk : Tua : And : Thars : Qvhane : Braithe : Is : Gane :
    Pleis : God : Vil : Sleip : This : Bed : Vithin :"

PARISH OF ELGIN.

Elgin cathedral was founded in 1224 by Andrew de Moravia or Moray, bishop of the diocese. It was destroyed in 1390 by Alexander Stewart, third son of Robert II., known as the *Wolf of Badenoch* (see *supra*, p. 159), but was rebuilt soon afterwards. It presented the form of a Jerusalem cross, having five towers, two at each end and one in the centre. The interior consisted of a nave, choir, and two aisles. Reared in richly decorated Gothic architecture the fabric presented a gorgeous and most imposing aspect. At the Reformation it was stripped of its leaden covering and thereafter allowed to fall into decay. Even as a ruin it claims the attention of the admirers of architectural art.

In the choir a large block of blue marble denotes the resting-place of Bishop Andrew de Moravia, the munificent founder. The bishop died in 1242, after an episcopate of about twenty years.

In St. Mary's aisle a monument commemorates Alexander

Seton, who in 1449 was created Earl of Huntly; he died in 1470. St. Mary's aisle also contains a monument in memory of Henrietta, daughter of Charles, Earl of Peterborough and Monmouth, and wife of Alexander, second Duke of Gordon; she died in 1760.

In the south transept were interred the remains of Alexander Stewart, Duke of Albany, second son of James II.; he died in 1480 and his effigy is preserved in a mural recess.

As a burial place the old family of Innes, now represented by the Duke of Roxburghe, made use of the south transept. It contains a full length figure of Robert Innes, of Innesmarkie, who died in 1482. In the cathedral churchyard a monument commemorates Robert Innes of that Ilk and his wife Elizabeth Elphinstone. It is thus inscribed :—

"Requiescunt hic Robertus Innes ab eodem, et Elizabetha Elphinstone, ejus conjux, qui fatis concesserunt 25 Septemb. et 26 Febr. anno sal. hum. 1597 et 1610. Ideoque; in piam gratamque; memoriam charissimorum parentum, hoc monumentum extrùendum curavit Robertus filius."

In the aisle (styled of St. Peter and St. Paul) is the burial-ground of the Dunbars of Grange, an ancient house in Morayshire. A monument erected by Robert Dunbar of Grange Hall, chief of Clan Durris, in memory of his wife, is inscribed thus :—

"A holy virgin in her younger lyff,
And next a prudent and a faithful wyfe,
A pious mother, who with Christian care
Informed her children with the love and fear
Of God and virtuous acts. Who can express,
Alone reader by a volume from the press."

In the nave these lines formerly commemorated Robert Leslie, younger son of George, fourth Earl of Rothes, and his wife, a daughter of the House of Elphinstone."

"Robertus Lesly, comitis qui filius olim,
Rothusie fuerat, simul et suavissima conjux,

Elpstonii soboles herois, conduntur in antro
Hoc licet obscuro celebres pietate supersunt.
Hos quondam binos Hymenæus junxit in unum,
Corpus, et his vivis semper suis una voluntas,
Unus amor, domus una fuit; nunc lumine cassos
Una duos iterum condit libitina sepultos."

In the Apprentice aisle a monument commemorates the Rev. Robert Langlands, minister of the first charge, and formerly of the Barony Church, Glasgow. The monument bears the following legend :—

"Hic requiescit vir pius reverendus, dominus Robertus Langlands fulgentissimum quondam ecclesiæ sidus mellifluus verbi præco, fidelis mysteriorum Dei œconomus ecclesiæ Glascuensis per annos aliquot pastor vigilantissimus; et ad Elginum, paulo ante obitum generalis hujus ecclesiæ synodi decreto translatus, ubi pie ac placide obiit pridie idus Augusti, anno Dom. 1696. In cujus memoriam monumentum hoc extruendum curarunt amici et reverendus collega, dominus Jacobus Thomson.

"Hac situs est humili clarus Langlandius urna,
Flebilis heu cunctis occidit ille probis,
Præco pius reserans sacri mysteria verbi
Et docuit populum sedulus usque; suum
Doctrinæ laudes variæ, prudentia rerum,
Ornabant animum consiliumque; sagax;
Et licet Elginum teneat quem Glascua quondam,
Dilexit, proprium vendicat ipse polus."

In the Apprentice aisle the Rev. James Thomson, of Newton, Fifeshire, minister of the second charge, has thus celebrated Elizabeth Paterson, his first wife, who died 12th August, 1698, aged thirty-six :—

"Elizabeth here lyes, who led her life
Unstained while virgin and twice married wife.
She was her parents' image—her did grace
All the illustrious honours of the face;
With eminent piety and complaisance—
All the decorements of exalted sense.
David's swan song much in her mouth, she had
More in her heart on it established.

Departed hence, it being her desire,
All and delight, just when she did expire;
By all bewailed she in the flower of age,
As Jacob's Rachel, was turned off the stage;
One only child beside, death, by his sting,
Unto this urn within three days did bring."

By the subscriptions of opulent persons in the town and district a monument has recently been placed in the cathedral, on the site of the great altar, in honour of the Rev. Lachlan Shaw, one of the collegiate ministers of the parish, and author of the "History of the Province of Moray." Son of a respectable farmer at Rothiemurchus, Mr. Shaw studied at King's College and the University of Edinburgh, and in 1716 received licence as a probationer. During the same year he was admitted to the pastoral charge of Kingussie; he was in 1719 translated to Cawdor, and in 1734 was preferred to the second charge of Elgin. An accurate scholar and accomplished antiquary, his friendship was cultivated by his learned contemporaries. He demitted his charge in 1774, and died 23rd February, 1777, in his eighty-fifth year and the sixty-first of his ministry. Besides his valuable provincial history he composed a description of Elgin, continued Rose's "Genealogy of the Family of Kilravock," and edited the Rev. Dr. Macpherson's "Critical Dissertations." His great-granddaughter was second wife of the celebrated Francis Jeffrey.

From the area of the cathedral and the surrounding churchyard we have the following rhymes :—

" Stay, passenger, consider well
That thou ere long in dust
Must dwell. Endeavour then
While thou hast breath
Still to avoid the second death
For on tymes minute
Doth depend torments
And joy without an end.
Therefore consider what you read,
For the best advice is from the dead."

" This world is a city
Full of streets ;
Death is the mercat
That all men meets.
If lyfe were a thing
That monie could buy
The poor could not live
And the rich would not die."

" The Tyrant Death he triumphs here ;
His Trophies spread around !
And Heaps of Dust and Bones appear,
Thro' all the hollow Ground.
But where the souls, those deathless things,
That left this dying clay !
My Thoughts now stretch out all your Wings
And trace eternity.
There we shall swim in heavenly Bliss,
Or sink in flaming Waves ;
While the pale carcass thoughtless lies,
Amongst the silent Graves.
Some hearty Friend shall drop a Tear
On our dry Bones, and say
These once were strong as mine appear,
And mine must be as they.
Thus shall our mouldering Members teach,
What now our Senses learn,
For Dust and Ashes loudest preach
Men's infinite Concern."

PARISH OF FORRES.

In the churchyard Emilia Dunbar has commemorated her husband
thus —

" A Loving Husband & a Father dear
A Faithful trusty Friend lies buried here
He was the man that ne'er oppressed the poor
Nor sent the stranger hungry from his door.

Death can't disjoin whom Christian Love has joined
Nor raze his memry from his Widow's mind.
Esteem'd, revered, respected and beloved
He e'er shall be by her whom once he lov'd.
Not from a stranger comes this heartfelt verse
Emilia Dunbar's griefe shall never cease."

On the gravestone of the Rev. Joseph Brodie, minister of the parish, his nephew, Alexander Brodie of Brodie, inscribed these lines :—

"Why choosest, thou man, when fallen asleep,
   This place of rest ?   Even still my flock to keep,
As living dying preached I, so my grave,
   Tomb, dust, these bones, dead walls, and porch shall have
A voice to witness, teach, cry, call to mind
   The good word preached, which true ere long they'll find."

Fourth son of the David Brodie of Brodie, the subject of the preceding epitaph was admitted minister of Keith in 1631. He was translated to Forres in 1646, where he ministered till his death, which took place on the 27th October, 1656. He married a daughter of Bishop Guthrie of Moray.

PARISH OF KNOCKANDO.

In the parish churchyard is a slab stone adorned with Runes; its history is unknown.

Within a mortuary enclosure a tombstone celebrates James William Grant, Esq., of Elchies, who died 17th December, 1865, aged seventy-seven. Mr. Grant held a civil appointment in India, and was distinguished as an astronomer.

In the old churchyard of Elchies is a burial-vault which belonged to Grant of Easter Elchies, but which is now possessed by the Earl of Seafield. In the interior a monument, with a long inscription in Latin, celebrates John Grant of Elchies, a captain in the army and zealous patriot, who died 4th March, 1715, aged fifty-six. His son Patrick, who reared the monument to his memory, passed advocate in 1712, and was raised to the bench as Lord Elchies in 1732. A profound and industrious lawyer, he impaired his popularity both as an advocate and judge by an impatient manner. He collected the "Decisions of the Court of Session from 1733 to 1757," and prepared "Annotations on Lord Stair's Institutes," which were both published posthumously. Lord Elchies died on the 27th July, 1754.

These metrical epitaphs are from Knockando churchyard :—

> "Stay, passenger, consider well,
>   Whilst thou art on this stage,
> When Death with his commission comes,
>   He will not ask thine age.
> Here lies a blossom quickly pulled,
>   Ere it came to its prime ;
> Therefore, I say, improve it well
>   Whilst thou hast precious time."

> "To Death's despotic sceptre all must bend,
> He spares not parent, child, nor weeping friend ;
> Not manhood's bloom, nor youth's fair tender flower,
> Can move his pity or resist his power.
> Meagre consumption here a FATHER laid,
> And BURNING FEVER slew his LOVELY MAID.
> 'Twas sin that gave tyrannic pow'r to Death,
> And, at his summons, these resigned their breath,
> Until their Saviour calls them from the grave,
> Destroys grim Death, and shows his pow'r to save."

PARISH OF ROTHES.

In the churchyard a tombstone commemorates the Rev. James Leslie, first Presbyterian minister of the parish ; it is thus inscribed :—

"Here lies ane noble man, Mr. James Leslie, Parson of Rothes, Brother German of George, umquhile Earl of the same, who departed in the Lord 13th October, 1575."

PARISH OF ST. ANDREWS LHANBRYDE.

An enclosure attached to the parish church is known as the Leuchars aisle. Therein two tablets commemorate Alexander Innes Matthie Mill, who died 1st November, 1636, and Alexander Innes, who died 1688. The former was brother of John Innes, proprietor of Leuchars.

The family of Innes of Coxton interred in the choir of Lhanbryde church. Within the choir a recess tomb presents the effigies of an armed knight, with a freestone tablet at the side thus inscribed :—

"HIC . REQVIESCIT . IN . DNO . ALEX . INNES . COKSTOVNS . EX . ILLVSTRI . FAMILIA . INNERMARKIE . ORIVNDVS . QVI . FATIS . CONCESSIT . 6 . OCTOB . -612 . SVÆ . VERO . ÆTATIS . 80."

Another slab presents the following:—

"HIC . REQVIESCIT . MARIA . GORDON . FILIA . . . . EQVITIS . DE . GIGHT . QVÆ . FATIS . CONCESSIT . 20 . AVGVSTI . ANO . . . 1647 . . . . IN . PIAM . . . MEMORIAM . HOC . MONVMENTVM . CONSTRVENDVM . ALEXANDR . INNES . DE . COXTON . MARITVS . CVRAVIT."

NAIRNSHIRE.

PARISH OF CAWDOR.

In the old churchyard a plain tombstone thus commemorates a granduncle of the celebrated Lord Macaulay :—

"Under this are interred the Remains of the Revd. Kenneth Macaulay, Minister of Calder, who died 2nd March MDCCLXXIX. in the 56 year of his age and in the 32nd of his ministry. 'Notus in fratris animi paterni.'"

Mr. Macaulay published a "History of St. Kilda," which was carefully revised by Dr. John McPherson, minister of Sleat. He was visited by Dr. Samuel Johnson, who held a low estimate of his abilities.

PARISH OF NAIRN.

In the parish church two monuments, belonging to the House of Rose of Kilravock, have these inscriptions :—

"Mors Christi mors mortis. Sic itur ad astra. Positum Davidi Rose de Earlesmill, filio Gulielmo Rose et Liliæ Hay, Domini et Dominæ de Kilravock, qui obiit 30 Maii 1669. Ætatis 76. Necnon conjugi, Christinæ Cuthbert, filiæ Jacobi Cuthbert de Drakie, quæ obiit 8 Septemb 1658. In memoriam parentum et fratrum Jacobi, Gulielmi et Alexandri et Gulielmi Rose, adornandum curavit Magister Hugo Rose, divini verbi Minister apud Nairn, 1667."

"Joannes Rose de Broadley, filius Gulielmi Rose et Liliæ Hay, Domini et Dominæ de Kilravock, obiit 19 April, 1662. Ætatis 72. Anna Chisholme ipsius conjunx filia Domini de Cromlix, obiit 29 Maii, 1658. Filii et conjugis . . . Joannes primogenitus, 1, Joanna Kynnaird, filia Domini de Coulbine; 2, Christina Fraser, filia . . . ."

Fraser de Strouie. Jacobus secundo genitus, tribunus militum in Gallia, 1641. Gulielmus tertiogenitus Lilias Grant, soror Joannis Grant de Moynes. Hugo quartogenitus, Margareta McCulloch, filia Andreæ McCulloch de Glastalich. Alexander quintogenitus obiit 1661. Henricus sextogenitus, Joanna Ross, filia magistri Thomæ Ross de Morenge. Filiæ et conjugis Anna primogenita, Alexander Dunbar de Boath. Maria secundogenita, magister Joannes Dallas de Budzett decanus Rossen. Joanna tertiogenita, magister Jacobus McKenzie, divini verbi minister apud Nigg, 1670."

The family of Rose settled in Nairnshire in the reign of David I., they were first designated of Geddes. The House is now represented by Major James Rose, the twenty-third laird of Kilravock.

INVERNESS-SHIRE.

PARISH OF DUIRINISH.

In the churchyard of Duirinish, Isle of Skye, an obelisk about thirty feet in height presents on a marble tablet the following inscription :—

"This pyramid was erected by Simon, Lord Fraser of Lovat, in honour of Lord Thomas his father, a Peer of Scotland, and Chief of the great and ancient Clan of the Frasers. Being attacked for his birthright by the family of Atholl, then in power and favour with King William, yet by the valour and fidelity of his clan, and the assistance of the Campbells, the old friends and allies of his family, he defended his birthright with such greatness and firmety of soul, and such valour and activity, that he was an honour to his name, and a good pattern to all brave chiefs of clans. He died in the month of May, 1699, in the 63rd year of his age, in Dunvegan, the house of the Laird of MacLeod, whose sister he had married, by whom he had the above Simon, Lord Fraser, and several other children. And, for the great love he bore to the family of MacLeod he desired to be buried near his wife's relations, in the place where two of her uncles lay. And his son, Lord Simon, to show to posterity his great affection for his mother's kindred, the brave MacLeods, chooses rather to leave his father's bones with them than carry them to his own burial-place, near Lovat."

Thomas Fraser of Beaufort, commemorated in the above inscription, did not obtain legal recognition of his family honours. His claim to the title and estates of Lovat was disputed by Amelia Fraser, eldest daughter of Hugh, tenth Lord Lovat, and his wife Amelia Murray, daughter of John, Marquis of Athole. After a period the opposition was withdrawn, and Simon Fraser of Beaufort, son of Thomas, was served heir to the title and estates. His career forms a curious episode in the national history. He was beheaded on Tower Hill, London, 9th April, 1747.

In the churchyard at Trumpan, at Waternish, were secretly

entombed the remains of the ill-fated Lady Grange. Daughter of John Chiesley of Dalry, who murdered Sir George Lochhart, Lord President of the Court of Session, this unhappy gentlewoman was subject to fierce ebullitions of temper. Married to Mr. James Erskine, a judge in the Court of Session, by the title of Lord Grange, and younger brother of the Earl of Mar, who promoted the rebellion of 1715, she became cognizant of her husband's disaffection. She threatened him with exposure, which implied deprivation of office, and probably death upon the scaffold. With the approval of his children, Lord Grange negotiated her abduction. A report of her death was circulated, and a mock funeral enacted, while the unhappy woman was by devious routes carried to the isle of Skye ; she was afterwards sent to Uist, and subsequently to St. Kilda, where she remained seven years. Again she was removed to Uist, and from thence to Skye. By concealing a letter in a clue of yarn sent to Inverness market, she contrived to inform her relatives of her detention. These applied to the authorities on her behalf, and a ship-of-war was dispatched to her rescue. But a strict watch was maintained, and she was not discovered. Latterly she was kept at Waternish, where she died in May, 1745, after a captivity of thirteen years.

PARISH OF HARRIS.

Within the old church of Scarista, island of Lewis, are deposited the remains of the Rev. Aulay Macaulay, minister of Harris. This reverend gentleman was son of "The Man of Brenish," celebrated in song and legend, for his feats of strength. His grandfather Donald Macaulay of Lewis distinguished himself on the patriotic side in the troubles which arose first with the Fifeshire colonists at Stornoway, and afterwards with the Mackenzies. Born in 1773, Aulay Macaulay took his degree at the University of Edinburgh, in 1693, and afterwards studied theology in the college of Glasgow. In 1704 he was admitted minister of Tiree, where he endured many privations till his translation to Kilmalie in 1712. In the following year he was preferred to Harris, where he ministered till his death, which took place on the 20th April, 1758. In his Will he stipulated that his remains should be interred at the threshold of the Church, so that every Sunday his people might tread upon his grave. His desire was not fully complied with, for his remains were deposited within the church, and on the right side of the passage. The coffin, according to the practice of the island, was placed only a few inches under the surface. Many years after, as the church officer was scooping the earthen floor of the church, he partially exposed a human skull, which he dug up. It was that of Mr. Macaulay.

Mr. Macaulay married Margaret Morison, and left three sons, Æneas, John, and Kenneth. The last died minister of Cawdor (see *supra*, p. 374). John, the second son, was born in 1720, and studied at King's College, Aberdeen. Having obtained licence, he was, in 1745, admitted minister of South Uist. In 1755 he was translated to Lismore, and thence in 1765 to the second charge of Inverary. In 1774 he was preferred to the parish of Cardross, where he ministered till his death, which took place on the 31st March, 1789. By his marriage with Margaret, daughter of Colin Campbell, of Invergregan, he had seven sons and five daughters. His third son Zachary was some years a merchant at Sierra Leone. Returning to Britain he became a prominent member of the Anti-Slavery Society. He was father of Lord Macaulay, the distinguished historian.

PARISH OF INVERNESS.

In the old church, a monument reared by his son-in-law, John Cuthbert, of Castle-hill, Inverness, celebrates William Hay, D.D., Bishop of Moray, who died 19th March, 1707, aged sixty-one. It is inscribed thus :

P. M. S.

" Reverendi admodum in Christo patris Gulielmi Hay, S.T.P.

episcopi Moraviensis meritissimi, qui primævæ pietatis et summæ eloquentiæ præsul, constans ubique ecclesiæ et majestatis regiæ assertor, nec magis florentis utriusque quam afflictæ; episcopales infulas pietate ornavit vitæ integritate, morum suavitate decoravit ; tandem, studiis et paralysi vicennali exhausto, vitam integerrimam beatissima secuta est mors; Martii 19, 1707. Ætatis suæ 60. Hoc monumentum, qualequale est, qui ejus duxerat Joannes Cuthbert, A.R.M. posuit, ejus filiam duxerat Joannes Cuthbert, A.R.M. posuit."

Bishop Hay was a pious and exemplary prelate. On the abolition of episcopacy in 1690, he retired to Inverness. Of mild disposition he abhorred persecution, and exhorted his clergy to ministerial earnestness and brotherly love.

In the chapel burying-ground a monument celebrates the Hon. Sybella Mackay, daughter of John, second Lord Reay, and wife of Alexander Rose, bailie of Inverness. It is inscribed thus :—

" Hic jacet corpus mulieris non tantum natalium splendore, sed etiam propriis virtutibus illustris, Dominæ Sibyllæ M'Kay, filiæ legitimæ nobilis quondam et potentis Domini, Joannis reguli a Reay et Dom. Barbaræ M'Kay Alexandri Rose, prætoris Innernessensis sponsæ, quæ obiit 16 cal. Novemb. anno æræ Christi 1691. Ætatis autem suæ 27."

On the tombstone of John Cuthbert, of Drakies, Provost of Inverness, who died 21st November, 1711, is the following couplet :—

" In death no difference is made
Betwixt the sceptre and the spade."

On tombstones at Inverness are these rhymes :—

" The life of man's a rolling stone,
Mov'd to and fro and quickly gone."

" Here we lie asleep, till Christ the world surround,
This sepulchre will keep until the trumpet sound."

" Asks thou who lies within this place so narrow,
I'm here to-day, thou may'st be here to-morrow,
Dust must return to dust, our mother,
The soul returns to God our father."

" Here lies my friend, yet he'll no longer lie
Than death is swallow'd up in victory;
We parted were when he resigned his breath
He'll make us meet again who conquer'd death."

" Beholder,
Take time while time doth serve; 'tis time to-day,
But secret dangers still attend delay,
Do what thou canst, to-day hath eagle's wings,
And who can tell what change to-morrow brings."

PARISH OF KILMALIE.

The following inscription on an obelisk commemorates a hero :—

" Sacred to the memory of Colonel John Cameron, eldest son of Sir Ewen Cameron of Fassfern, Baronet, whose mortal remains, transported from the field of glory, where he died rest here with those of his forefathers. During twenty years of active military service, with a spirit that knew no fear, and shunned no danger, he accompanied or led, in marches, sieges, and battles, the gallant 92nd Regiment of Scottish Highlanders, always to honour, almost always to victory; and at length in the 42nd year of his age, upon the memorable 16th day of June, A.D. 1815, was slain in the command of that corps, while actively contributing to achieve the decisive victory of Waterloo, which gave peace to Europe. Thus closing his military career with the long and eventful struggle in which his services has been so often distinguished, he died lamented by that unrivalled general to whose long train of success he had so often contributed; by his country from whom he had repeatedly received marks of the highest consideration, and by his sovereign, who graced his surviving family with those marks of honour which could not follow to this place, him whose merits they were designed to commemorate. Reader, call not his fate untimely who thus honoured and lamented closed a life of fame by a death of glory."

PARISH OF KILMUIR.

In the churchyard of Kilmuir, Isle of Skye, a monument has lately been reared at the grave of Flora Macdonald. Composed of grey granite it presents the form of an Iona Cross, rising with the basement to the height of nearly thirty feet. The site is elevated, and the monument is conspicuous over a wide area.

As the dauntless protector of an unfortunate prince, Flora Mac-Donald possesses no uncertain claim to honourable commemoration. Daughter of a gentleman who occupied a farm in the isle of Uist, she lost her father in early childhood, and her upbringing not long after devolved on her kinsman, Macdonald of Armadale in Skye, whom her mother accepted as her second husband. Armadale commanded a company of Militia in the service of the government; but Flora was like the majority of highland gentlewomen, deeply interested in the cause of the Chevalier. Introduced to the Prince after the battle of Culloden, she conducted him in disguise as her waiting maid from the Long Island to Monkstadt. Discovered to have been privy to his escape she was seized, carried to London and committed to the Tower. Her heroic conduct made her an object of general concern. She was visited by the Prince of Wales, who graciously procured her liberation. At the residence of Lady Primrose, she received visits from many of the nobility, who warmly commended her generosity. Returning to Scotland, she married in November, 1750, Allan Mac-donald, younger of Kingsburgh. She accompanied her husband to North Carolina, where he took part in the War of Independence. Having endured many privations and hardships, Mr. and Mrs. Macdonald returned to Skye. Their children who attained maturity were five sons and two daughters. The sons joined the army and the daughters became officers' wives. One of the sons Lieutenant-Colonel John Macdonald, F.R.S., was a distinguished officer, and possessed some celebrity for his scientific attainments. He died in 1831. Mrs. Flora Macdonald died at Kingsburgh on the 5th March, 1790. Her funeral was attended by three thousand persons.

About two years afterwards the remains of her husband were laid by her side within the mortuary enclosure of the House of Kingsburgh.

In Kilmuir churchyard a gravestone denotes the resting-place of the Rev. Donald Macqueen, minister of the parish, who died 1st February, 1785. By Dr. Samuel Johnson he was commended for his learning.

PARISH OF PETTY.

Since the year 1606, when Lachlan, third of that name, and sixteenth Laird of Mackintosh was buried at Petty, it has been the family burial-ground of the Chiefs of clan Chattan. Four chiefs and two of their ladies are laid in the family vault; the other members of the house are sepulchred within a railed enclosure.

At the east end of the old church is the burial-place of Captain John Mackintosh of Kellachie, father of Sir James Mackintosh, the distinguished philosopher.

The chief of the Macgillivrays, who was killed at Culloden, was interred in the churchyard.

PARISH OF SLEAT.

In the churchyard an elegant monument, executed at Rome, commemorates Sir James Macdonald, Bart., the "Scottish Marcellus." This short-lived scholar, eighth baronet of Sleat, and male representative of the Lords of the Isles, was born in 1741. At Eton he greatly distinguished himself by his attainments, and high hopes were entertained of his career. In course of his travels he was seized with a complication of disorders, of which he died on the 26th July, 1766. His monument is thus inscribed:—

" To the memory of Sir James Macdonald, Bart., who in the flower of his youth had attained to so eminent a degree of knowledge in Mathematics, Philosophy, Languages, and in every other branch of useful and polite learning, as few have acquired in a long life wholly devoted to study; yet to this erudition he joined what can rarely be found with it, great talents for business, great propriety of behaviour, great politeness of manners! His eloquence was sweet, correct and flowing; his memory vast and exact; his judgment strong and acute; all which endowments, united with the most amiable temper and every private virtue, procured him, not only in his own country, but also from foreign nations, the highest marks of esteem. In the year of our Lord 1766, in the 25th of his life, after a long and extremely painful illness, which he supported with admirable patience and fortitude, he died at Rome, where notwithstanding the difference in religion, such extraordinary honours were paid to his memory as had never graced that of any other British subject, since the death of Sir Philip Sydney. The fame he left behind him is the best consolation to his afflicted family, and to his countrymen in this isle, for whose benefit he had planned many useful improvements, which his fruitful genius suggested, and his active spirit promoted under the sober direction of a clear and enlightened understanding. Reader, bewail our loss, and that of all Britain. In testimony of her love, and as the best return she can make to her departed son for the constant tenderness and affection which, even to his last moments, he showed for her, his much afflicted mother, the Lady Margaret Macdonald, daughter to the Earl of Eglintoune, erected this monument A.D. 1768."

Sir James Macdonald's younger brother, Alexander, was in 1776 created Baron Macdonald of Sleat; he died in 1795. The third brother, Archibald, studied for the English bar, and became Lord Chief Baron; he was created a baronet in 1813, and died in 1826.

PARISH OF URQUHART AND GLENMORISTON.

Within the churchyard of St. Columba is the burial enclosure of the Grants of Glenmoriston. Two tombstones belonging to the family are thus inscribed:—

"This stone is erected here in memory of the much honoured John Grant, laird of Glenmoriston, who died 1730, aged 79.

"A.D. 1840: Alexander Grant, son of John Grant, fifth laird of

Glenmoriston, and his spouse Janet Mackenzie, grand-daughter of Captain Alexander Mackenzie of Gairloch, ancestors of Captain George Grant of the Indian Army, has erected this monument as a token of affection, esteem, and regard, with which he cherishes their memory. They died at Bre, about the year 1730.—Deut. 32, 7; Prov. 10, 7.

"The tomb of James Grant of Burnhall, W.S., 2d son of Patrick Grant of Glenmoriston, by Henrietta, daughter of James Grant of Rothiemurchus, died 1834, aged 66 years. His family James, died at Barbadoes, 1829, aged 20; Simon-Fraser died at Edinburgh, 1829, aged 11; John Charles, E.I.C.S., Bengal, died at Singapore, 1836, aged 28, at whose desire this tomb of his father and family was erected. Helen, spouse of Alexander Macdonald of Berbice, died at Dawlish, Devonshire, 1840, aged 34."

ROSS AND CROMARTY.

PARISH OF ALNESS.

In the parish churchyard an obelisk reared by a widow in memory of her departed husband, has the following epitaph :—

> " Cold is that breast where every virtue glow'd,
> Still is that heart whence pure affection flow'd,
> Silent that tongue, whose mild and welcome sound
> Sooth'd all my cares and heal'd my every wound.
> Thy pure affections manly, gentle, kind,
> Rest deep engraved on thy dear partner's mind ;
> Nor could her fruitless tears, her heartfelt grief
> In worldly consolation find relief,
> But God in mercy to her woes hath given
> The cheering hope to meet again in heaven."

PARISH OF CONTIN.

In Contin churchyard, under the shadow of the elevated Tor-Achilty, a simple tombstone denotes the grave of William Laidlaw. This intimate friend and amanuensis of Sir Walter Scott was born in Ettrick Forest, in November, 1780. Unsuccessful in farming, he was invited by Scott, in his thirty-seventh year, to act as land-steward at Abbotsford. There he remained with a brief interval, till the death of his patron in 1832. He was now appointed steward on the Ross-shire property of Mrs. Stewart Mackenzie of Seaforth ; a situation which he subsequently exchanged for the factorship of Sir Charles Lockhart Ross, of Balnagowan. He

2 c

latterly resided at Contin, where he died on the 18th May, 1845. Laidlaw became known to Sir Walter Scott, from his love of Border ballad. He composed several songs, of which the most popular is "Lucy's Flittin."

PARISH OF CROMARTY.

Near the Gaelic Chapel, a monumental statue of Hugh Miller, executed by Handyside Ritchie, has been reared by public subscription. (Vol. I., p. 147.)

In front of the Free Church, a massive monument of Aberdeen granite commemorates the Rev. Alexander Stewart, an eminent minister of the parish, who died 5th November 1847, aged 54. In 1843 Mr. Stewart adhered to the Free Church.

PARISH OF DINGWALL.

On an artificial mound near the parish church an obelisk fifty-seven feet in height was erected by Sir George Mackenzie, first Earl of Cromarty, to denote the spot he had selected as a place of sepulture. Son of Sir John Mackenzie, who was created a baronet in 1628, this accomplished statesman supported Charles II. by military service, and on the Restoration was appointed a Lord of Session, with a seat in the Privy Council. By James VII. he was in 1685 created a peer with the title of Viscount Tarbet. At the Revolution, William III., who knew his abilities, accepted his services as Lord Clerk Register: in the beginning of Queen Anne's reign he held office as Secretary of State. In January, 1703, he was created Earl of Cromarty. He died in 1714; his present representative is the Countess of Cromarty, Duchess of Sutherland.

PARISH OF FEARN.

The Abbey of Fearn was founded by Ferquhard, Earl of Ross, about the year 1230. An aisle at the east end of the structure has for centuries been the burying-place of the ancient House of Ross. Here a handsome monument with a Latin inscription celebrates General the Honourable Charles Ross, a distinguished member of the sept. Second son of George, eleventh Lord Ross, he was born on the 8th February, 1667. As an officer in the army he countenanced the Revolution, but afterwards joined Sir James Montgomery in his plot for restoring the exiled House. In 1695 he was appointed colonel of the royal regiment of Irish dragoons, and took part in the continental war. Elected M.P. for Ross-shire in 1707, he gave an active support to the Tory administration. In 1712 he attained the rank of general. He was one of the Secret Committee to enquire into the conduct of the South Sea Directors, and in this capacity distinguished himself by his activity and candour. He died at Bath on the 5th August, 1732, and his remains were conveyed to the Abbey of Fearn, and there laid in a sarcophagus.

In the Ross aisle were interred the remains of Sir John Lockhart Ross, Bart., of Balnagowan. This gentleman was fifth son of the Honourable Grizel Ross, sister of General Ross, and her husband Sir James Lockhart, of Carstairs. Born on the 11th November, 1721, he entered the navy in his fourteenth year. In 1756 he obtained command of the *Tartar* frigate of twenty-four guns, with which in the course of fifteen months he captured in the channel nine of the enemy's ships. In 1787 he was promoted as Vice Admiral of the Blue. By the death of his brother George, in July, 1778, he succeeded to the family baronetcy. He died at Balnagowan on the 9th June, 1790, in his sixty-ninth year. He was eminently benevolent.

In Hiltoun burying-ground a gravestone now removed bore these lines:—

" HE . THAT . LIVES . WEIL . DYES . WEIL . SAYS . SOLOMON . THE . WISE.
HERE . LYES . ALEXANDER . DVFF . AND . HIS . THRIE . WIVES."

PARISH OF FODDERTY.

Near the parish church two upright stones are traditionally associated with the history of Fingal. A stone near Castle Leod bearing the figure of an eagle denotes the spot at which a number of the clan Munro were slain by the Mackenzies of Seaforth. Another engagement which took place between the Mackenzies and Macdonalds is commemorated by a group of monoliths.

PARISH OF GAIRLOCH.

In the churchyard a tombstone commemorates William Ross, the celebrated Gaelic bard. Born at Broadford, Isle of Skye, in 1762, he was educated at the school of Forres, and in his twenty-fourth year was appointed schoolmaster of this parish. He died at Gairloch in his twenty-eighth year. He is styled the Burns of the Gaelic Highlands.

PARISH OF KINCARDINE.

A portion of a sarcophagus in the churchyard is associated with a Prince of Loellin who died of his wounds, and was buried at the spot. The end of one of the sides bears some sculptures, including a man on horseback throwing a spear, and the figure of a crown.

PARISH OF NIGG.

Attached to the parish church is an ancient Runic cross; it represents two priestlike figures in the act of offering sacrifice, with other emblems.

A sculptured stone at Shadwick bears on one side the figure of a cross, wrought into an intricate species of fret-work, while intervening spaces present figures of different kinds of animals. On the reverse side are processions, hunting scenes, and other sculptures.

PARISH OF ROSEMARKIE.

The ancient church of Rosemarkie was founded in the seventh or eighth century, by Boniface, an Italian ecclesiastic. During repairs on the church in 1735, a vault was discovered, which contained several stone coffins of rude workmanship, one of which may have belonged to the venerable founder.

In the churchyard are deposited the remains of Andrew Murray, Regent of Scotland in the reign of David II. Having overcome the English in many battles, and restored peace to the country, he retired to his estate at Rosemarkie, where he died in 1338.

Near the town of Fortrose stood the cathedral church of Ross, now a ruin. It was reared in Middle Pointed Gothic, about the beginning of the fourteenth century, and was unroofed at the Reformation. Now only remain the south aisle to the chapter and nave, and the detached chapter house. Under the remaining arches are the fragments of several tombs; in one is a canopied tomb of a lady, said to have been the Countess of Ross. A canopied tomb in the most easterly arch was opened in 1854, and was found to contain the skeleton of a full grown man, enveloped in a tunic of reddish silk. A small piece of wood was found on the left side, probably the crosier of a bishop.

In the cathedral, at the burial place of the Earls of Seaforth a monument commemorates Dr. George Mackenzie, author of the "Lives of Scottish Writers." This laborious compiler was the son of the Honourable Colin Mackenzie, and grandson of the second Earl of Seaforth. Born on the 10th December, 1669, he studied medicine and sought practice as a physician at Edinburgh. His work is embraced in three folio volumes.

On the monument of Alexander Mackenzie of Coul, and his wife
Christian Munro, are these Latin verses:—

> " Hoc Mc'Kenzeus pius atque sponsa
> Pulchrum opus cæli domino dicarunt
> Cui suam vitam quoque semetipsos
>   Corde dederunt.
> Una mens illis, amor unus, unum
> Gaudium vitæ ; hic rogus unus, in quo
> Dormient donec veniet supremi
>   Judicis hora."

Alexander Mackenzie, of Coul, was brother of Kenneth, first
Lord Mackenzie of Kintail ; his son Kenneth was created a baronet
of Nova Scotia, 16th October, 1673.

A gravestone belonging to the Mackenzies of Coul, is thus inscribed :—

> " As man as soon as born begins to die,
> So death begins man's life of immortality.
> Death, nature, time adieu, all hail eternity ;
> Man's endless state must be or happiness or woe.
> Tremendous their cause who strive to show
> Annihilation as a safer creed.
> And mankind a *mutum pecus* breed,
> Were not a hereafter man's predestined lot.
> Man's destiny would be to revel and to rot
> Nature's shame and foulest blot."

The monument of Thomas Urquhart of Kinundie, who died in
1633, formerly bore these lines,

> " My hope shall never be confounded,
> Because on Christ my hope is grounded,
> My hope on Christ is rested sure,
> Who wounded was my wounds to cure ;
> Grieve not when friends and kinsfolk die,
> They gain by death eternity."

Bailie Thomas Forbes, who bequeathed £1200 Scots, for behoof
of the parochial incumbent, is by his widow celebrated thus :—

> " Unica virtus, fama superstes,
> Gratia Christi, causa salutis.

"Sub spe beatæ resurrectionis in Domino, hic conduntur cineres Thomæ Forbesii, quondam balivi Fortrosensis, mortui 21, sepulti 25, Maii 1699. Qui, in indicium grati erga Deum animi, et charitatis erga homines, 1200 lib. Scot, ad sustentandam evangelii prædicationem, hac in urbe, dicavit.

"Monumentum hoc, mariti impensis, extruendum curavit Helena Stuarta, relicta conjunx, hic etiam sepelienda sperans."

Jean Grant, daughter of Sir James Grant of Moynes, who died 18th August, 1688, aged twenty, has these lines upon her tomb :—

"Under this stone behold is laid,
A modest, pious, spotless maid ;
Whose life was short, but yet well spent,
Her soul was still heavenward bent,
Her virt'ous grace and innocence
Against all vice did prove a fence,
Although her body lies in dust,
Her better part lives with the just,
Enjoying the dread majesty
Of Trinity in Unity."

SUTHERLANDSHIRE.

PARISH OF ASSYNT.

Near the parish church an enclosure forms the burial-place of the Macleods of Assynt, a branch of the Macleods of Lewis. Here several members of the House have been interred. The lands of Assynt now belong to the Duke of Sutherland.

PARISH OF DORNOCH.

Within the church a handsome monument commemorates William seventeenth Earl of Sutherland and his countess, both of whom died in June, 1766, and were interred in the abbey church of Holyrood (Vol. I., p. 109). A monument celebrates George Granville Leveson Gower, first Duke of Sutherland, who died at Dunrobin Castle, 19th July, 1833.

PARISH OF GOLSPIE.

The old churchyard contains the remains of several Earls of Sutherland. Their only memorial is a stone in the church wall, inscribed as follows :—

"In hoc diruto cæmeterio Sutherlandiæ plurimorum comitum cineres conquiescunt."

Within the enclosures of Dunrobin castle a monumental statue celebrates George Granville, second Duke of Sutherland, who died

28th February, 1861, aged seventy-five. Reared at the cost of the tenantry the monument was inaugurated on the 25th September, 1866, in presence of the Prince and Princess of Wales. It consists of a bronze figure of the Duke supported on a massive pedestal of grey granite. The statue, ten feet in height, represents the Duke standing in an easy attitude, clad in modern costume, with the robe of the Garter thrown across his shoulder.

PARISH OF LAIRG.

In the churchyard a square monument, with tablets on its four sides, commemorates the Rev. John Mackay, his son and two grandsons, all connected with the parish. The Rev John Mackay ministered at Lairg, from 1714 to 1753. He found the people in a condition of ignorance and superstition, and addicted to disorderly practices, but by his wholesome teaching and salutary discipline he effected a thorough change. He died 23rd February, 1753, aged seventy-four. In his ministerial office he was succeeded by his son Thomas, who influenced by an earnest piety discharged the duties of the pastoral office for the period of fifty-four years. He died 28th August, 1803, aged eighty-seven. Of his three sons, Hugh and William are commemorated on the monument. Entering the service of the East India Company in 1784, Hugh Mackay served in the Madras Native Cavalry. Obtaining a staff appointment under General Wellesley he became exempted from regimental duty, but such was his military ardour that he sought and obtained permission to join his regiment at the battle of Assaye. In the brilliant charge of cavalry, which gained that battle, he was killed at the muzzle of the enemy's guns. At the spot where he fell a monument was consecrated to his memory.

William, youngest son of the Rev. Thomas Mackay went to sea in his sixteenth year, and early acquired distinction by his nautical abilities. In 1795, he was as second officer of the ship *Juno* of

Calcutta sent to the coast of Pegu for a cargo of teak-wood. On the coast of Arracan the vessel sprung a leak, and settled down leaving her masts only above water. The mainmast was cut off, and the crew, seventy-two in number, took refuge on the rigging of the two remaining masts. Without food or water, fourteen persons lived twenty-three days. Among the survivors was the gallant commander, who has published a thrilling account of his sufferings and those of his companions. His more striking details supplied materials to Lord Byron for his description of a shipwreck in "Don Juan." In 1801 he was by the Bengal government sent to the Red Sea with stores and provisions for the armies of General Baird and Sir Ralph Abercrombie. He died at Calcutta in 1804. In reference to the two brothers their monument bears :—

"Their bodies lie in the opposite quarter of the globe, but their monument is erected where their memory is dearest, near the remains of their pious fathers, and amidst many living, whose gratitude will attest that fraternal affection has not overcharged this record of their virtues."

PARISH OF TONGUE.

A monument, reared by the parishioners, celebrates the Rev. William Mackenzie, minister of the parish. This devoted clergyman was admitted to the charge in 1769. He found the people ignorant and careless, and his earlier efforts for their improvement proved inefficacious. But his incessant labours at last became fruitful. In the district he was styled "the great minister," on account of his ministerial fidelity and abundant success. He died on 5th January, 1834, in his ninety-sixth year and the sixty-seventh of his ministry.

CAITHNESS-SHIRE.

PARISH OF HALKIRK.

The ruin of the chapel at Spittal, founded in the twelfth century, by Ronald, Count of Orkney, was long the burial-place of the clan Gunn, a powerful and warlike race inhabiting the district. For interment in the chapel at Spittal members of this clan carried their dead, especially the remains of their chiefs, from long distances amidst the utmost inconveniences of travel.

PARISH OF LATHERON.

On tombstones in the parish churchyard these quaint epitaphs are engraved :—

> " If nature's charms with virtue joined
> Could stop death's fatal blow,
> She had not died whose body lyes
> Interred this stone below."

" Cormack . Cormack . and . Helen . Sotherland .
To . these . tuo . belongs . this . stone .
As . a . memorandum . of . them . when . gone .
Six . times . seven . years . they . lived .
A . happy . life . as . it . becomes . to . man . and . wife .
A . stage . for . strangers . they . were .
Anon . her . fame . and . virtue . to most . were . seen .
And . of . injury . none . could . her . blame .
To . death . all . are . free .
But . yours . I . wish . not . to . see .
Now . Passenger . if . thou . hast . a . tear .
I . pray . you . stay . and . drop . it . here ."

PARISH OF REAY.

In the wall of the old chapel at Crosskirk, a freestone tablet is thus inscribed :—

1778

"This motiue stone is put here by me Donald Gunn, son of the let decest Alexander Gunn—this Donald Gunn being a residenter in Forss, and his forfathers befor him of an old deat liued in the forsaid pleac whos dust lys here. He scned his name with Iohn Gunn and Alexr. Gunn, George Gunn and Imes Gunn."

PARISH OF THURSO.

Harold's Tower, situated about two miles east of the town of Thurso, was reared by the late Sir John Sinclair, Bart., to denote the burial-place of Earl Harold. The earl was owner of half of Orkney and Zetland and the half of Caithness ; he fell in battle in 1190, while endeavouring to recover his estates from the hands of a usurper.

In the parish churchyard a monument, reared by public subscription, commemorates Robert Dick, an eminent naturalist. Mr. Dick was born at Tullibody, Clackmannanshire ; he long resided at Thurso, where he died in 1866.

PARISH OF WICK.

At Ulbster a stone with some untraceable sculptures is said to have marked the grave of a Danish Princess, whom Gunn, the founder of the clan of this name, married in Denmark. The vessel in which the chief was bringing home his bride was wrecked on the shore of Caithness, and the Princess was drowned.

In the parish churchyard a tombstone is thus inscribed :—

"Here lies entombed ane noble and worthie man, John Master, of Caithness, who departed this life 15 March, 1576, aged 45 years."

John Master of Caithness, thus commemorated, was eldest son of George Sinclair, fourth Earl of Caithness. He married Jean Hepburn, daughter of Patrick, Earl of Bothwell, and left four sons and one daughter. The eldest son was fifth earl.

ORKNEY.

PARISH OF KIRKWALL.

Kirkwall Cathedral was founded in 1138, by Ronald, Count of Orkney, and dedicated to the memory of his uncle Magnus, Earl of Orkney, who was canonised for his piety.   It was spared at the Reformation, and the choir has long been used as the parish church.

Margaret, the Maiden of Norway, grand-daughter of Alexander III., and his recognised successor on the Scottish throne, died at Orkney in her progress from Norway to Scotland on the 7th October, 1290; her remains were deposited in St. Magnus cathedral.

In the cathedral rest the remains of Andrew Honyman, bishop of Orkney, who died in February, 1676.   While entering the carriage of Archbishop Sharp, at Edinburgh, in July, 1668, he received in his arm a poisoned bullet, shot at the primate by one Mitchell, a covenanter.   From the shock he did not wholly recover.

In the cathedral a memorial tablet celebrates Malcolm Laing, an ingenious historian, who died in 1818, aged 56.   His principal work, a "History of Scotland from the Union of the Crowns to the Union of the Kingdoms," appeared in 1800, in four volumes octavo.

PARISH OF STROMNESS.

In the parish churchyard the tombstone of a shipmaster is thus inscribed:—

" Death steers his course to every part of the terrestial globe,
    And where he lands, cuts quickly down all living on this orb,
    For I, who underneath this stone ly sleeping in the grave,
    While here on earth did stoutly scorn proud Neptune's raging
        wave,
    Great swelling seas I overpast, when stormy winds did boast,
    Yet death me seized when I was near unto my native coast;
    Kind reader, then, be warned, whether by Land or Sea,
    To learn to live well, then thou shalt prepared be to die."

The gravestone of a young woman bears these lines :—

        " Insulting death puts no
            Respect on mortals here below
        But mocks them all so,
            That they must to the shades down go.
        Now death's cut down a pleasant flower,
            Of young and tender age,
        Which plainly tells us none are free,
            From his prevailing rage;
        But God, whom she on earth adorned,
            Took her up to above,
        Where now, we hope, she sings sweet songs,
            Of soul-redeeming love."

PARISH OF WESTRAY.

These monumental rhymes are from Westray churchyard :—

        "Death's but a servant pale
            That leads the little flock
        Into the glorious vaile."

        " Death's trophies over our bodies stand,
        Our souls above at Christ's right hand,
        And Halelujas still doth sing.
        Unto the Lamb our Heavenly King."

APPENDIX.

EDINBURGHSHIRE.

———◆———

GREYFRIARS CHURCHYARD.

P. 52 l. 21. For Alexander Smellie, read William Smellie; his tombstone is thus inscribed:—

"Infra sepultæ sunt reliquiæ GULIELMI SMELLIE, S. S. Reg. et Antiq. Soc., qui doctrinæ gloria principatum inter sui sæculi Typographos tenebat. Librum illum eximium, cui titulus 'The Philosophy of Natural History,' conscripsit protulitque in lucem; et Gallico in Anglicum sermonem cel. Buffonii opera vertit. Annos natus LIV. e vita excessit, die xxiv. Junij M.DCC.XCV."

———

THE DEAN CEMETERY.

P. 135 l. 17. Thomas Thomson, commemorated in the Dean Cemetery, is erroneously described as the distinguished chemist of that name. (see Vol. I. 485 and *postea*.) Thomas Thomson was a principal clerk of session, and well known antiquary. Eldest son of the Rev. Thomas Thomson, minister of Dailly, he was born on the 10th November, 1768. Originally intended for the Church he was sometime a theological student; he afterwards attended the law classes at Edinburgh, and in 1793 passed advocate. Devoted to historical inquiries he edited the works of Lord Hailes, and proving himself efficient as an examiner of records was in 1806 appointed deputy clerk register. His valuable services in the Register House were acknowledged by his being appointed in 1828 to a principal clerkship in the Court of Session. For the Bannatyne club he edited many important antiquarian works, and he was latterly appointed its president. Many valuable works published under the authority of the Record Commissioners were prepared under his superintendence. He died on the 2nd October 1852, at the advanced age of eighty-four. His younger brother, the Rev. John Thomson of Duddingston, was a celebrated landscape painter.

PARISH OF BORTHWICK.

Lord Borthwick, whose effigy is preserved in the old church of Borthwick (Vol I. p. 156) was son of Sir William Borthwick, who sat on the assize of the Duke of Lennox, and constructed a castle on the lands of Lochwarret. His lordship was not raised to the peerage before the year 1430, as previously stated; he was created a peer by James II. in 1452. The family of Borthwick came from Hungary and entered Scotland in the train of Margaret the Saxon princess, afterwards queen of Malcolm Canmore. They first obtained lands in Aberdeenshire, and proceeding southwards became possessed of extensive territories in the counties of Dumfries, Selkirk, Roxburgh, and Haddington.

PARISH OF NEWBATTLE.

In the churchyard a tombstone, elaborately sculptured, presents the following inscription:—

"Here lys Walter Welsh of Lochquareat, who died the 29th of June, 1705, and Helen Parkinson his spouse, who died the 19th of March, 1696, and Josias Welsh, their son, who died the 15th of October, 1695, and Alexander Welsh, their son, who died the 11th of July, 1717."

> " Wisdom and virtue ly
>   Beneath this stone,
> Which rare accomplishments
>   Surpassing many one,
> Courageous bold with
>   Meekness mixt together ;
> A loving husband, parent,
>   And a brother,
> A courteous wife, sweet
>   Children here doth ly,
> Ane emblem clear that
>   We must surely dy."

The descendants of Walter Welsh claim descent from John Knox. The reformer's youngest daughter, Elizabeth, married the Rev. John Welsh, minister of Ayr; she became mother of four sons and two daughters. One of the sons, Josias, was Presbyterian minister at Temple Patrick, in Ireland. He was father of John Welsh, minister of Kirkpatrick Irongray, a sufferer in the cause of Presbytery, who died at London in 1681, aged about fifty-four. Walter Welsh, of Lochquareat, is described by his descendants as a younger brother of the minister of Irongray.

A tombstone, the oldest in the churchyard, is thus inscribed :—

> " Vive memor lethi.
>
> " Maria delectu pietatis Martha labore
>   Pervigil assiduo quam teget urna cava.
>
> " Heir godlines vith
>   Verteu in ane Vombe,
> Marie and Martha
>   Interrd in this tombe.
>
> " Hic jacet Isobella Purves
> Roberti Porteous insignis
> Pietate viri quondam conjux
> Quæ obiit anno ætatis
> Suæ 52, die 20 Octobris
> Anno Domini 1620. Tres liberos
> Reliquit Prædicto
> Roberto. Robertum Guli-
> elmum et Isobellam."

On the tombstone of a son of James Chirnsyde, bailie, who died in 1682, aged twelve, are these lines, intended to form an acrostic:—

" I n this frail life how soon cut off are we !
H e that on earth do breath must suerly die,
M ount up, O Soull, to that seraphick spheare,
E ternall life if thou wolds have a share;
S ure God doth for the blessed it prepare.
C ælestiall joy what can compare with thee !
H ere nothing is but grif and vanitee,
I nvieous death, thou could not hurt the soulle
R ipen'd for glory, though the grave did moulle,
N atour and strenth, yea, youth thou soon can kill;
S o here thou did accomplish divine will.
Y et where ar now thy fourious darts thy sting,
D eath cannot stop the soull from taking wing,
E ternity with God above to sing."

A tombstone bearing the Murray shield is inscribed thus :—

"Heere lyeth Frances Murray, daughter of Sir John Murray, one of the family of Black Barronie, who deceest the 4th of February, 1641, ætatis suæ 8."

Sir John Murray was uncle of Sir William Kerr, first Earl of Lothian, being his mother's brother.

ROXBURGHSHIRE.

PARISH OF CASTLETON.

A decorated obelisk, sculptured with the family arms, commemorates John Armstrong, M.D., physician and poet. It is inscribed thus :—

> " If yet thy shade delights to hover near
>   The holy ground where oft thy sire hast taught,
> And where our father fondly flocked to hear,
>   Accept the offering which their sons have brought,
> Proud of thy muse, which gave to classic fame
>   Our vale and stream, too long before unknown,
> We raise this stone to bear thy deathless name,
>   And tell the world that Armstrong was our own,
> To learning worth and genius such as thine."

Son of the Rev. Robert Armstrong, minister of the parish, the subject of the preceding epitaph was born in 1709. Having studied at Edinburgh University, and obtained a medical degree, he began practice as a physician in London. In 1744 he published his " Art of Preserving Health," a poem in blank verse, which has attained a well-deserved popularity. For some time he attended as physician the army in Germany. He associated with Dr. Smollett and the poet Thomson, and was at first the friend and afterwards the enemy of Wilkes. He composed a work on medicine, and other works chiefly in verse. He died on the 7th September, 1779.

Messrs. Robert and William Armstrong, both ministers of the parish, father and brother of Dr. John Armstrong, are commemorated by tombstones. The former died 16th April, 1732 ; the latter 10th April, 1749.

A gravestone denotes the resting-place of the Rev. Angus Barton,

D.D., minister of the parish, who died 19th April, 1861, in the seventy-sixth year of his age, and thirty-ninth of his ministry.

Tombstones commemorate John Elliot, of Thorlieshope, who died in February, 1698, aged seventy-seven, and John Elliot, of Binks, who died in August, 1751, aged seventy-seven.

The tombstone of Daniel Young (died April, 1774) bears these lines:—

> " Oh, reader, stay your car, and stay
> And read what I have here to say ;
> You walk on earth as once did I,
> Remember you and all must die.
>
> " For in my health I little thought
> My glass was run so near ;
> But now the hour for me is come
> No longer to be here."

At Milnholm, near the old churchyard of Ettleton, and on the right bank of the Liddel, a cross, about eight feet high, is fixed in a large stone resting on the surface. On the cross are engraved the letters I.H.S., M.A., and A.A. ; while beneath, on the shaft, is sculptured a two-handed sword with guard curving towards the blade. This erection is supposed to denote the spot where the body of Armstrong of Mangerton, who was murdered at Hermitage Castle by the Lord of Liddesdale, was placed before interment to await the inspection of the clan.

In Ettleton churchyard a large tombstone bears on the margin these words:—

> " Heir lyes ane worthie person, calit William Armstrang of Sark, who died the 18th day of June, 1658, ætatis suæ 56."

In the centre is the following legend :—

> " Jenet Johnstoun, Relek to the sed desised persn heth put up this monamente in anno Dom. 1660.
>
> " Man is grass, to grave he flies,
> Grass decays, and man he dies ;
> Grass returns and man does rise,
> Yet few . . . . the prise."

Below the inscription, on a panel, are shields displaying the arms of the Houses of Armstrong and Johnstone.

In Ettleton churchyard a massive obelisk is inscribed thus :—

" In this spot, near which rest the ashes of his forefathers, is interred William Armstrong, of Sorbytrees, who to the great grief of the neighbourhood was shot, without challenge or warning, by the Rev. Joseph Smith, Incumbent of Walton, Cumberland, on the night of Wednesday, the 16th April, 1851, in the 38th year of his age.

" In affectionate remembrance this monument was erected by a numerous body of friends on both sides of the border, as a tribute of their respect for one whose manly, straightforward, and generous disposition gained him the love and esteem of all who knew him. MDCCCLII."

For causing Mr. Armstrong's death, Mr. Smith was subjected to an assize, and was acquitted. It appeared that Mr. Armstrong had rode up to the reverend gentleman's residence late of a dark night, on his return from market. Suspecting danger, Mr. Smith opened his house door, and without uttering a word fired a pistol at the supposed intruder, who fell mortally wounded. Mr. Armstrong was deeply lamented by a wide and attached circle of friends and neighbours.

DUMFRIESSHIRE.

PARISH OF CUMMERTREES.

In the churchyard a tombstone commemorates the Johnstones of Back-Kerr, who have for several centuries been connected with the parish. It is thus inscribed :—

" In memory of John Johnstone, of Back-Kerr, who died on the 3rd day of June, 1804, aged 80 years.

" Also of Janet Pool (his spouse), who died at Bryde-Kirk, 3rd September, 1828, aged 83 years.

" Also of Jane Coulthart, spouse to Robert Johnstone, of Back-Kerr, who died 12th January, 1809, aged 29 years.

" Also of Robert Johnstone, of Back-Kerr, who died on the 15th December, 1847, aged 77 years."

An older tombstone, belonging to the Johnstones of Back-Kerr, is undecipherable.

PARISH OF DALTON.

In the parish churchyard a handsome altar tomb, supported by ornamental pillars, commemorates John Ross, a descendant of the Rosses of Halkhead, in the county of Renfrew, who resided at Dalton Park, and was much esteemed for his urbanity and public services. Born on the 25th January, 1732, he married, 15th July, 1763, Margaret, daughter of Alexander Glendinning, of the Isle of Dalton, by whom he had a large family. His present representative is John Ross Coulthart, of Ashton-under-Lyne, county of Lancaster. The following inscriptions are on the tomb :—

"In memory of Margaret Ross, wife of John Ross, of New House, in Butterthwaite, and daughter of the late Alexander Glendinning, and Agnes Johnstone of the Isle of Dalton, who died on the 17th day of January, 1867, in the 64th year of her age.

"Here also rest the remains of John Ross, husband of the above Margaret, who died on the 6th day of June, 1813, in the 81st year of his age.

"Erected to their memory by John Ross, their son, of Halifax, Yorkshire."

In the churchyard, tombstones commemorate Michael Ross, of Aldgirth and Smallholmbank, who died 5th April, 1807, aged seventy, and his wife Agnes Rae, who died 10th April, 1807, aged sixty-five; also James Ross, of Dormont, who died 27th November, 1815, aged eighty-two; and Joseph Ross, of Wellingborough, county of Northampton, who died 30th June, 1815, aged seventy-four. There are also tombstones and inscriptions to the memory of the Rosses of Bridekirk.

An altar tomb celebrates Alexander Glendinning of the Isle, and Agnes his wife, daughter of John Johnstone, of Graitney. The Glendinning family were long connected with the parish. Their present representative is Sidney Glendinning, late of Seedley, near Manchester, whose father, Alexander Glendinning, of Ashgrove, in the county of Kent, served the office of high sheriff of that county in 1854. The inscriptions on the Glendinning tomb are—

"To the memory of Alexander Glendinning, in Isle, of this parish, who departed this life February 12th, 1785, in the 77th year of his age.

"Also Agnes Johnstone, his spouse, who departed this life on the 23rd day of July, 1792, aged 74 years."

PARISH OF KEIR.

A descendant of the Rosses of Halkhead, in the county of Renfrew, is on his tombstone thus commemorated :—

"To the memory of John Ross, tenant of the farm of Barnden-noch, in this parish, who died on the 25th day of March, 1763, aged 63 years."

PARISH OF KIRKPATRICK-FLEMING.

In the parish churchyard members of the House of Coulthart are on an altar tomb celebrated thus :—

"Gulielmus Coulthart de Coulthart et Collyn arm. nominis gentisque suæ facile princeps nat. die Januar. vi. M.DCC.XXXIX. denat. die Feb. xv. M.DCCC.VII."

"In hoc tumulo sepultus est Gulielmus Coulthart armiger gentilium suorum et cognominum primarius Jacobi Coulthart de Coulthart in Comitatu Wigtoniæ et de Largmore in seneschalsia Kirkcudbright ex uxore Griselda Macturk filius idem atque heres qui apud Westdenbie in parochia Dalton Feb. xv. An. M.DCCC.VII. Ætat. LXVIII. diem obiit supremum.

"Una recondita est Jenetta ejusdem viri conjux et vidua Alexandri autem Macnaught de Milton Park in parochia Dalreensi filia nata est Janetta Jan. xxiv. An. M.DCC.XLI obiit apud Collynhouse in parochia Torthorwald Maii xviii. M.DCCC.XXXII.

"Intus etiam jacet Alexander Coulthart supra memorati Gulielmi Coulthart et Janettæ filius natus Alexander Junii xxi An. M.DCC.LXIX. vixdum annos viginti egressus morte immatura raptus est apud Turfrigg hujus ipsius parochiæ die Julii xix. Anno M.DCC.LXXXIX."

Of these inscriptions, the first surrounds the cornice of the tomb in raised letters, and the three others are cut into the horizontal tablet. The panels of the monument on the sides and ends are adorned with armorial shields of the Coulthart family.

PARISH OF MOUSWALD.

In the churchyard a tombstone commemorates the great-grand-father and great-grandmother of John Irving of Boreland, in the parish of Dunscore, a collateral descendant of the Irvings of Bonshaw. It is inscribed thus :—

"Margaret Charteris, spouse to George Irving, died 1746."

On an adjoining tombstone inscriptions commemorate the following members of the same family, viz. :—

"Christopher Irving, Butterthwaite, died 2nd March, 1798, aged 83 years.

"John Irving, his son, died 20th March, 1782, aged 21 years.

"Mary Irving, his daughter, died 20th April, 1782, aged 11 years.

"Mary Palmer, his spouse, died 20th December, 1807, aged 81 years."

KIRKCUDBRIGHTSHIRE.

PARISH OF BUITTLE.

In the churchyard a handsome obelisk, of Craignair granite, commemorates John Tait, master of the grammar school. Son of John Tait of Miltown Park, parish of Dalry, and his wife Jane McNaught, a descendant of the McNaughts of Kilquhanity, Mr. Tait was celebrated for his classical and mathematical acquirements. His monument is thus inscribed:—

" Erected to the memory of John Tait, 43 years parish schoolmaster of Buittle, by old pupils and friends, in testimony of his public usefulness and private worth.

" During a period of unexampled progress in the art of teaching, he steadily kept pace with improvement in that profession which to his last hour he adorned. He died 27th January, 1857, aged 66 years."

PARISH OF KELLS.

A tombstone is thus inscribed:—

" This stone is erected by James Coulthart, in memory of Grizel McTurk, his spouse, who died 14th July, 1767, aged 66 years.
" Also of James Coulthart, son of Andrew Coulthart, and grandson of the said James Coulthart, who died 10th February, 1771, aged 6 years."

On the tombstone is presented a curiously sculptured shield, bearing the arms of Coulthart and McTurk impaled thus:—On the dexter a fesse between two colts in chief, and one in base courant, for Coulthart; and on the sinister a hunting-horn stringed, for McTurk.

PARISH OF KIRKPATRICK-DURHAM.

In the churchyard a tombstone belonging to Robert Watson, who died 15th June, 1839, aged seventy-seven, has the following metrical inscription:—

> "Three years in trouble I endured the rod,
> But in affliction I was loved by God ;
> For God in mercy had decreed the cup,
> Therefore I willingly did drink it up."

Robert McMillan and his sister Mary have on their tombstone these lines:—

> "Dear is the spot where Christians sleep,
> And sweet the strains that angels pour ;
> Oh ! why should friends in anguish weep ?
> For they're not lost, but gone before."

On a vertical tombstone, having a skull and cross-bones carved on one side, and a nearly obliterated inscription on the other, Margaret Heron is thus commemorated :—

> "Here lies Margaret Heron, daughter of Patrick Heron, of Heron, who was married to George Gordon, of Troquhain, Sept. 21, 1726, and died Aug. 13, 1742, aged 44 years."

The Rev. Dr. Lamont, an eminent minister of the parish, is on a handsome monument thus commemorated :—

> "Sacred to the memory of David Lamont, D.D., minister of this parish, who having been always distinguished by talent of a very high order, a candid and charitable disposition, and a temper peculiarly amiable, died on the 7th January, 1837, in the 84th year of his age, and 63rd of his ministry."

WIGTONSHIRE.

PARISH OF WHITHORN.

In the parish churchyard a tombstone belonging to Provost Broadfoot, and bearing date 1783, presents these lines :—

> " The tender parent with the child here laid,
> Their sacred dust commingles with the dead ;
> Immortal souls have winged the shining way
> To the pure regions of eternal day."

On his wife's tombstone, Bailie McKelvie has inscribed the following :—

> " While dwelling here she led a virtuous life,
> By rich and poor esteemed a loving wife,
> Discreet and kind was ever to the poor,
> And sent no person hungry from her door."

John McGuffog, who died 12th April, 1780, aged twenty-one, is thus commemorated :—

> " Though born with genius, well improved by art,
> Blest with an honest uncorrupted heart,
> Bloom'd just to cheer us with a transient ray,
> And close at morn the short enduring day ;
> Surprise us for a moment with delight,
> And then for ever vanish from our sight."

By these rhymes James Bell commemorates his wife :—

> " I loved her for her virtues here,
> But God doth part the dearest ties,
> The loan from God, the dust, lies here ;
> The spirit's safe above the skies."

LANARKSHIRE.

PARISH OF BOTHWELL.

The collegiate church was founded in 1398 by Archibald the Grim, Earl of Douglas. Against the church wall, under the east window, rests a fragment of a large double incised slab. It is of Bothwell stone, about four feet long and three broad. Divided into two compartments, the upper presents a circle enclosing a cross with triangular headed limbs, between which are four small circles in low relief. Of the lower compartment the dexter half presents a plain surface; the sinister represents a rudely incised shield, bearing the Moray stars, and its lower extremity prolonged into a two-handed sword, pointing downward. It is conjectured that the stone celebrates William or Walter de Moravia, both of whom flourished in the thirteenth century.

Within the church two large monuments in floral architecture commemorate James, Marquess of Hamilton, and Archibald Douglas, Earl of Forfar. The latter died of wounds received at the battle of Sheriffmuir* in 1715.

PARISH OF GLASGOW.

P. 465, l. 2. John Orr, of Barrowfield, died 16th December, 1803.

---

* For these particulars in connexion with Bothwell parish, we are indebted to a Paper contributed by Mr. Joseph Bain to the Society of Antiquaries of Scotland. (Proceedings, vol. viii., pp. 395, 403.)

FIFESHIRE.

P. 465, l. 23. For *Bonner*, read Banner; and in following line for Brevet-Major John Anstruther read Major John Anstruther Mac-Gowan.

P. 477, l. 17. Michael Scott, author of " Tom Cringle's Log," was a native of Glasgow.

P. 485, l. 13. For life of Professor Thomas Thomson, M.D., the distinguished chemist, see vol. i., p. 135. The professor was interred in the Necropolis, Glasgow; he has no monument in the Dean Cemetery, Edinburgh, as has been stated inadvertently.

FIFESHIRE.

PARISH OF FORGAN.

At St. Fort in this parish is the ancient burial-vault of the old family of Nairne, of Sandford, owners of the estate from the fourteenth century till about the year 1717. The founder of the House was Alexander Nairne, of Sandford, Lyon King of Arms, and Comptroller of the Household of James II. At the entrance of the vault a freestone slab, dated 1647, with the family arms, and the initials A. N., has the following inscription :—

" Stvip . low . poore . sovle . and . mone . for . sinne . Cry . vp . to . Christ . to . bring . the . in That . vhen . the . bodie . is . lovdged . heir . Thov . may . inioy . his . preasence . deir . Vntil . the . day . of . the . gryte . cal . When . we . mvst . rys . to . Jdgmente . al . Then . rewvnytit . we . shal . be . To . prais . the . glorivs . Trinitie."

Alexander Nairne, thus commemorated, obtained a crown charter 27th July, 1633. His son, Sir Thomas Nairne of Sandford, was Lieutenant-Colonel of Horse and member of the Committee of War in 1649. On the Restoration he was fined £1,800. The estate of Sandford, or St. Fort, is now the property of John Berry, Esq., who in 1870 was served heir of line to Sir Thomas Nairne.

KINCARDINESHIRE.

PARISH OF LAURENCEKIRK.

In this churchyard was formerly interred the family of Wyse or Wise, of Mains of Thornton, Kincardineshire, and now of Hillbank, Forfarshire. On the tombstone of a member of the House who died in 1710 are inscribed these lines :—

> " Here lyes a person while alive
> His worth I cannot weall describe,
> He was reliever of the poor
> And needy called at his door;
> Therefor I hope he doth not miss
> For his reward, eternall bliss."

The individual commemorated was a near relative of David Wise, of Mains of Thornton, an opulent and benevolent gentleman, who at his death bequeathed funds for behoof of the poor in the parishes of Lunan, Montrose, St. Cyrus, and Laurencekirk. He married in November, 1681, Margaret, daughter of Alexander Nairne, of Pitbuddo, by whom he had two sons and three daughters.

David, the eldest son, predeceased his father; he died in November, 1712, aged twenty-two. A square stone at the west door of the church denotes his place of sepulture. The family of Wise is of Norman descent. A chief of the House commanded the force by which the Lord of Lorne was defeated at Brander-awe in Argyllshire, and afterwards fought in the patriotic army of Bruce at Bannockburn. Several branches of the family acquired lands in the counties of Aberdeen, Nairne, Kincardine, and Forfar. In the middle of the seventeenth century the repre-

sentative of the Kincardineshire branch was Alexander Wyse,
or Wise, of Mains of Thornton.   He was father of David Wise
formerly named, and grandfather of Alexander Wise, of Lunan,
whose second wife, Margaret Strachan, was descended from the
Strachans, Baronets, of Thornton.   Their grandson, Thomas
Alexander Wise, M.D., of Hillbank, is the present representative
of the family.

INDEX TO VOL. II.

LONDON:
PRINTED BY J. AND W. RIDER,
BARTHOLOMEW CLOSE.